CISTERCIAN STUDIES SERIES: NUMBER THIRTY-SIX

Revised Edition

THE MONASTIC RULE OF IOSIF VOLOTSKY

CISTERCIAN STUDIES SERIES: NUMBER THIRTY-SIX
Revised Edition

THE MONASTIC RULE OF IOSIF VOLOTSKY

Edited, translated, and introduced by
David M. Goldfrank

Cistercian Publications
Kalamazoo, Michigan — Spencer, Massachusetts

Iosif (né Ivan) Sanin of Volokolamsk, 1439/40–1515
Translated from *Iosif Volotskii. Monastyrskii Ustav. Poslaniia Iosifa Volotskogo* (eds. Ia.S. Lur'e and A.A. Zimin. Moscow-Leningrad: Nauka, 1959), pp. 296–319; and from *Iosif Volotskii. Dukhovnaia gramota prepodobnago igumena Iosifa o manastyrskom i inocheskom ustroenii. Velikie Minei-chetii, sobrannye vserossiiskim mitropolitom Makariem* (St Petersburg, 1868–1917), volume 1 (September), cols. 499–615.

On the history of the icon used on the cover, see Mikhail V. Alpatov, *Feofan Grek / Theophanes the Greek*. Moscow: Izobratel'noe iskusstvo 1990. Page 201.

Library of Congress Cataloging in Publication Data
Iosif Volotskii, Saint, 1439 or 1440-1515.
Monastic rule.

(Cistercian studies series; no. 36)
Translation of: Avvy Iosifa ot bozhestvenykh pisanii o zhitel'stve obshchezhitel'nym slovesa k svoim emu uchenikom;
and of: Dukhovnaia gramota prepodobnogo igumena Iosifa o manastyrskom i inocheskom ustroenii.
Cover title: The rule of Iosif of Volokolamsk.
Half title: Iosif Volotsky's monastic rule.
Bibliography: p. 211
Includes index.
Monasticism and religious order, Orthodox Eastern—Rules. 1. Title. II. Title: Rule of Joseph of Volokolamsk. III.Title: Iosif Volotsky's monastic rule. IV. Series.

BX386.I5513 255'.8 81-16647
ISBN 0-87907-836-7 AACR2

Contents

PART II: THE TEXTS OF THE RULE

Preface to the First Edition

MONASTICISM WAS a crucial component of medieval civilization, and the monks of the Christian East and West have common ancestors and a common source of inspiration.[1] Only after the rise of distinct orders in the West did the monastic traditions take somewhat different paths, and even then parallel, if not mutually influential, developments continued. The ideals remained the same. Similar debates raged over appropriate life styles, connections with the secular world, and accumulation of property. Reforming abbots faced similar problems.[2]

The conditions in which Russian monasticism developed and flourished were also quite like those of medieval Western and Central Europe before the proliferation of cities and the rise of universities. Ideologically and culturally, moreover, fourteenth- and fifteenth-century Muscovy had something in common with the more pluralistic Carolingian Germany and its successor states. Russian monks and bishops (all former monks) played analogous roles as colonizers, entrepreneurs, and administrators to those of their counterparts in Central and East-Central Europe.[3] The large, rural Russian monastery, like the European, was often the center of a seigneurial theocracy which attracted, subdued, organized, ruled, and protected its peasants.[4]

1. See Skaballanovich, *Tolkovyi tipikon* 1:1:372.
2. See, for example, *Bernard of Clairvaux: Treatises* 1, CF 1:3–69.
3. See Weber, *Economy and Society* 3:1167–70.
4. Budovnits, *Monastyri*, 77–256. Smolitsch, *Russisches Mönchtum*, 180–245.

A combination of physical labor, ascetic feats, choral chanting, and mystical spirituality gives Russian cœnobitic monasticism, in its highest achievements, a certain affinity to their Western counterparts. Structurally the Western monastery was close to that of the Benedictine and, to some extent, Cluniac, house in the West. Russian monasteries were administratively distinct from each other and linked by a common set of traditions and rules, which stemmed from Basil of Caesarea and other *typica*. Major Russian monasteries tended to be dominated by the upper class; and if they were not princely foundations, many nevertheless tended to become the equivalent of 'royal abbeys'. Just as the structure and practice of the large Russian monastery of the fourteenth and fifteenth century was akin to the Benedictine and Cluniac abbey, so the reformist ideals of some of the Russian monks resemble those the Cistercians originally advocated—equality of monks, the universal requirement for physical labor, and rejection of dependent villages and peasants.[5]

Muscovy, however, failed to have a Cistercian-like reform, even though this was advocated by some who referred back to genuine Byzantine traditions.[6] Rather, the colonizing and economically active monasteries retained their villages and ceremonial emphasis, while the genuine 'non-possessors' retreated to hesychasm and other reclusive practices. Overall, Muscovy's failure to produce a far-reaching monastic reform was symptomatic of the underdevelopment of high culture within the Russian Church as a whole and the weakness of civil society.[7] Muscovy's crude civilization and despotic political structure[7a] stifled both anti-clerical and genuinely

5. On the organization and social role of Byzantine monasticism, which was the model for its Russian counterparts, see Kazhdan, 'Vizantiiskii monastyr''. For the transmission of Byzantine monasticism to Russia, see Casey, 'Early Russian Monasticism'.

6. Ikonnikov, *Maksim Grek*, 361–425, PIV, 350–53. *Tüpikon*, 45.

7. Florovsky, 'Problem of Old Russian Culture'.

7a. [Added for the Revised Edition.] The disputable and somewhat disreputable notion of 'despotic political structure' does not preclude a weak chief, consensus rule at the top, a powerful ruling class, informal negotiations between superiors and inferiors, private property, and domains of meaningful individual and community autonomy, but implies a state or system of governance that can

ecclesiastical reform movements.[8] These factors also underlie the failure of Russian monasticism to play the social and educational role that characterized Western monasticism and its quasi-monastic offshoots.

Within this setting, Iosif Volotsky's life and work are worthy of examination and study, for they reveal many of the contradictory forces that operated within the Muscovite Church and its monasticism. Iosif himself was nothing if not a monastic hierocrat who spared no effort to buttress Church doctrines and practices against religious dissidents and to defend ecclesiastical land-holdings in the face of political and ideological pressure to secularize some of them. Something of a social reformer remarkable for his time and his class, he accepted the brutality and tyranny of his society and merely wanted them directed against genuine felons (among whom he numbered heretics) rather than innocent Orthodox Russians. At the same time he was a fanatically devout monk, generous, deeply grounded in ascetic traditions and not hostile to mysticism. Like many successful 'other-worldly' ascetics, he was a diligent and successful 'this-worldly' entrepreneur who both defended his material profits and placed them at the service of his religious ideals. Despite his strict adherence to Eastern Christian traditions and his own medieval Russian mentality he was so much a 'rationalizer' in his monastic rule and so good a lawyer and dialectician in defending 'cases' involving doctrinal or administrative disputes that he has been considered by some scholars to have been somewhat western in his mentality and perhaps inspiration.[9] Iosif's Rule, with its emphasis on structure and administration, is closer to Western monasticism in spirit than are late medieval Russia's other original rules, yet it is the only important rule not yet translated into a Western language. Original in conception, vivid, and in many places expertly written or compiled from available authorities, it reflects

---

mobilize property and labor, confiscate wealth, and imprison and execute without clear boundaries between the legal and illegal.

8. Outside of liturgical revisions, serious reform and restructuring of the Russian church and monasticism were instituted by the state during Peter the Great's regime in the early eighteenth century.

9. Treadgold, *West in Russia and China* 1:1–23.

a powerful individual struggling with the problems of organization, discipline, and worldly temptations within the framework of a physiologically based spiritual outlook and a semi-barbaric people who gave great prestige to outstanding monks.

The West experienced conditions similar to Iosif's Muscovy. Did the West produce a similar monasticism or a similar monastic ideologist? Was there any western influence on the monasticism of Russia's Church Militant? Perhaps the publication of Iosif's Rule in English will help students of Western monasticism to understand more fully the affinities and differences between the Medieval Eastern and Western ecclesiastical and monastic worlds. Students of Russian, Byzantine, and medieval history should welcome the availability of another important and little known document.

A work of this type has necessary limits. Unable to work extensively in the Soviet Union when I was studying Iosif's Rule, I was forced to rely chiefly upon published materials. Nevertheless, by utilizing published Old Russian and Greek patristic writings, as well as a few microfilms of Russian manuscripts and rare printed works, I have been able locate most of Iosif's sources, which are noted in the translation. Iosif's originality and his reliance on sources thus can be evaluated. Space requirements have also necessitated that I present Iosif's brief Rule only in the form of variants to his later Extended Rule. The interested reader is urged to try to follow the Brief Rule as whole, nevertheless., for it is an important and illuminating work in its own right. I have restricted myself to a short biography, and I make relatively few comments about the more renowned aspects of Iosif's life and work: his apologetics and inquisitorial activities, his political theories and his ideology as a whole. My introduction to the content of the Rule touches upon these subjects but is more concerned with what the Rule itself mentions, directly or indirectly. The connection between his monastic theology and his general ideology I have examined in an article published in the *Slavic Review*, 1975.

It was M. Basil Pennington OCSO who suggested that I publish Iosif's Rule, and he has supported me all along, as have Georgetown's Department of History and Russian Area Studies Program, which supplied encouragements and typists, Barbara

Saragovitz and Jane Wolf, as well as support for a bibliographic assistant editor, Nancy Yanoshak, and a typist-editor, Maureen McHugh. They were all more generous than they needed to be. I owe a considerable debt of gratitude as well to the works of Ia.S. Lur'e (Leningrad) and Joseph Scaronpîdlík, sj (Rome), A.A. Zimin (Moscow), and my former mentor, Professor Marc Szeftel of the University of Washington, Seattle, for their contributions toward my understanding of Iosif, and to the staff of The Dumbarton Oaks Center for Byzantine Studies, who gave me working space and access to its remarkable collection and the opportunity to consult with Professor Ihor Ševčenko (Harvard University) and Professor George Majeska (University of Maryland). Finally, the graduate students in my 1974 and 1975 Medieval Russian Documents seminars at Georgetown—Linda Katz, Wayne Lord, Barbara Smith, David Wiedeman, Ms. Yanoshak, and Elizabeth Zelensky—aided me in acquiring books, proofreading and following the labyrinthine Orthodox Order of services and rituals. The numerous shortcomings, it goes without saying, are my own.

D.G.

June 1980

Preface to the Second Edition

THE SECOND EDITION OF *The Monastic Rule of Iosif Volotsky* retains the basic structure of the first, but is also a thorough revision wherever content or style so warranted. The introduction covers a few more problems than before, including iconography. Iosif's Brief Rule is now a presented in a separate, full translation along with the Extended Rule. The recent work of literally dozens of specialists, especially Dumbarton Oaks's *Byzantine Monastic Foundation Documents*, already available in prepublication form on the web, have contributed to my revisions. This kind of scholarship, moreover, lends itself constantly to updating. Devotees of patristics, Muscovite literature, and Church history have continued to make new discoveries and publish sources, which allow for further specification and amplification. The full identification of Iosif's sources may be possible and accomplished some day—if not by me, then by some other scholar with more ready access to the manuscripts of *Slavia orthodoxa* and their numerous pseudepigrapha. At any rate, those who wished simply for a reissuing of the first edition ought to be pleased with the improvements of the second. And whatever the case, Iosif, deserves to be read, because he, or at least his type of religiosity, is still a force in the now revived Orthodox Church of Russia. He remains the unique combination of dedicated pastor, effective philanthropist, lively writer, and intolerant inquisitor of the Russian Church, and his self-taught rhetoric is still an effective—and perhaps unfortunate—antidote to open ecumenism.

As I complete the preparations of this edition, I would like to express my gratitude to the series editor Dr. E. Rozanne Elder for agreeing to the design for revisions and bearing with my delays; again to Georgetown University and Dumbarton Oaks (and the present Director of Studies, Professor Edward Keenan) for research support and facilities; to Professor Wladimir Vodoff of Paris for his meticulous review of the first edition; to my numerous colleagues, students and former students for their interests and ideas—among whom I must single out Argyrios Pisiotis for proofreading the Greek terms and bringing to life the Byzantine context; and to my immediate family, especially my wife Jane, for the requisite 'released time' and overall love and understanding.

D.G.

October 1999

Table of Abbreviations

ACTA SS	*Acta Sanctorum.*
AfED	Kazakova and Lur'e, *Anti-feodal'nyeereticheskie dvizheniia.*
AFZKH	*Akty feodal'nogo zemlevladeniia i khoziaistva.*
AI	*Akty istoricheskie.*
AN	*Arkhitekturnoe nasledstvo.*
ANF	Ante-Nicene Fathers
ANSSSR	Akademiia nauk SSSR
ASEI	*Akty sotsial'no-ekonomicheskoi istorii severo-vostochnoi Rusi.*
BMFD	*Byzantine Monastic Foundation Documents*
ChOIDR	*Chteniia v Imperatorskom* OIDR.
DDG	*Dukhovnye i dogovomye gramoty velikikh i udel'nykh kniazei XIV-XVI vv.*
FC	Fathers of the Church series.
HLEULET	Harvard Library of Early Ukrainian Literature. English Translations.
IAN	Imperial Academy of Sciences.
IIISSSR	*Issledovaniia po istochnikovedeniiu istorii SSSR dooktiabr'skogo perioda*
KTsDR	Likhachev et al., *Knizhnye tsentry Drevnei Rusi*
K:VPS	Kazakova, *Vassian Patrikeev i ego sochineniia.*
L:IB	Lur'e, *Ideologicheskaia bor'ba v russkoi publitsistike.*
MERSH	*Modern Encyclopedia of Russian and Soviet History*

MRKIS/CIM	*Moskovskaia Rus' (1359–1584): kul'tura i istoricheskoe samosoznanie*
NPF-I,-2	A Select Library of the Nicene and Post-Nicene Fathers. First Series, Second Series.
OC,OCA	*Orientalia Christiana [analecta].*
OLDRP	Obshchestvo liubitel'ei drevnerusskoi pis'mennosti
OIDR	*Obshchestvo istorii i drevnostei rossisskikh.*
ORT	Old Rus/Russian Translation.
PG	Migne, *Patrologiae . . . graeca.*
PIV	Lur'e and Zimin, *Poslaniia Iosifa Volotskogo.*
PL	Migne, *Patrologiae . . . latina.*
PSRL	*Polnoe sobranie russkikh letopisei.*
SPR	Slavistic Printings and Reprintings.
TODRL	*Trudy otdela drevnerusskoi literatury.*
VMCh	Makarii, Metropolitian, *Velikiia Minei-chetii*
VV	*Vizantiiskii vremennik.*
Z:KFV	Zimin, *Krupnaia feodal'naia votchina.*
ZhMNP	*Zhurnal Ministerstva narodnago prosveshcheniia.*
ZORGBL	*Zapiski Otdela rukopisi Gosudarstvennoi biblioteki imeni Lenina.*

For full references to other short and abbreviated citations in the notes, see the Bibliography.

Part I

Iosif Volotsky (1439/40–1515) and His Rule

I

An Hagiographic and Historic Portrait of Iosif

DATA FOR IOSIF'S BIOGRAPHY is rich for a Russian of his time; a living person, as well as a stereotypical monk-saint, emerges from his writings and *Lives*. Over twenty of his letters have survived, as have other writings, including two major tracts on theology and monasticism, each published in two editions.[1] His public and his monastic life can be followed with more detail than any other Russian monk of his time. His

1. Iosif's letters, exclusive of his missive-penances composed for laymen, have been critically published by Lur'e and Zimin in PIV, 139–228. Two more recently discovered letters have also been published: Kloss, 'Neiżvestnoe poslanie Iosifa Volotskogo', and Kobrin, 'Poslanie Iosifa Volotskogo Arkhimandritu Evfimiiu'. The five missive-penances are found in the appendix to Smirnov, *Drevnerusskii dukhovnik,* 224–34. The anti-heretical letters and the earliest versions of Iosif's apologetic discourses have been published by Lur'e in AfED, 305–9, 320–73, 414–510, 513–20. The complete version of the Brief (eleven-discourse) *Enlightener (Prosvetitel')* was the basis for the Kazan Seminary's publication of the first eleven discourses of Iosif's Extended (sixteen-discourse) *Enlightener.* See below, Part 1, Chapter 2, notes 1–2, for bibliographic information about the Rules and related writings. His presumed discourse on widower-priests is found in Kozhanchikov, *Stoglav* 79:237–8. His presumed treatise on monastic lands was published in the appendix of Malinin, *Filofei,* 128–44. His presumed defense of monastic lands, allegedy composed for the synod in 1503, is found in PIV, 322–26. Most recently Andrei Pliguzov has subjected Iosif's literary legacy to a new, rigorous analysis: 'O khronologii poslanii Iosifa Volotskogo'.

three hagiographers, who rarely contradict each other, worked from written sources as well as family and oral traditions.[2] This biographic sketch, therefore, can adhere to the strictest principles of scholarship and at the same time present the hagiographic portrait by which he has been known for almost half a millennium.

Iosif (originally Ivan) Sanin was born in 1439/1440 into a reputedly pious family of military servitors which held the village of Iazvishche near the small city of Volok or Volokolamsk, ca. 115 km. northwest of Moscow. His great-great grandfather, Aleksandre, called Sania, had migrated there from Belarus ('Lithuania').[3] Iosif's paternal grandfather Grigorii (as a monk, Gerasim) Sanin is quoted as having said: 'May God grant us the heavenly kingdom; for paradise is our fatherland which we destroyed and received again from the Lord by his incarnation'. Iosif's father Ioann (as a monk, Ioannikii) Sanin suffered, 'like Job', for twenty years from scabs, tremors and paralysis, and yet reportedly was grateful to God to the end of his life. Iosif's mother Marina (as a nun, Maria), is chracterized as having been a zealous ascetic and devoted philanthropist and having exclaimed continuously during her terminal illness: 'Mary, daughter of Jacob! Mary Magdalene! Mary of Egypt! Here I come, my ladies; here I come with you, my ladies'. Two of his brothers became monks: one, Vassian, was later Archimandrite of the Simonov Monastery in Moscow (1502–06)

2. Iosif's cousin or nephew, Dosifei Toporkov, an important iconographer in the monastery, composed the first *Life* of Iosif as a funeral oration, and also the portions of the *Volokolamsk Patericon* relevant to his biography. The second, official *Life*, found both in the *Patericon* and with the Extended Rule in the *Great Menaia,* was written by Savva Cherny, an important Iosifov monastery elder from as early as 1515, and successively Archimandrite of the Moscow Simonov Monastery (1543–44) and Bishop of Sarai-Krutitsa (residing in Moscow, 1544–54). The third, written in a grammatically complex and archaic style, was possibly composed by Lev the Philologist, a Balkan Slav active in Russia in the mid-sixteenth century. See Kliuchevsky, *Drevnerusskie zhitiia,* 291–94. Lur'e, *Istoki*, 410–18. *Volokolamskii Paterik.* Dosifei Toporkov, *Nadgrobnoe slovo.* Savva Cherny, *Zhitie*. Belokurov, *Zhitie*. Russian interest in Iosif's *Lives* was confined in the sixteenth century chiefly to his own monastery: See Dmitrieva, 'Volokolamskie cheti sborniki', 210–12.

3. For the exact location and agrarian status of Iazvishche in 1769–74, see Chernov, *Volok Lamskii*, 352, 360.

and Archbishop of Rostov (1506–1515). Two cousins, both skilled in iconography, also took the tonsure: the writer Dosifei Toporkov and his brother Vassian, Bishop of Kaluga (1525–42).[4]

The span of time from Iosif's great-grandfather through the Toporkovs corresponds roughly with the dynamic age of Muscovite monasticism. This started with the careers of Metropolitan Aleksii of Moscow (1354–1378) and Sergii of Radonezh (d. 1392) and continued into the mid-sixteenth century in the central regions and somewhat beyond in the northern peripheries. During this period Russians founded at least two hundred fifty new cloisters in the cities and wilderness, sometimes under very harsh conditions. In addition hermits, hermitages, and scetes proliferated in North Russia, and an intensification of spiritual interests set in, as evidenced by the spread of hesychasm (or 'neo-hesychasm') in Muscovy and some of the outstanding iconography.[5] By the time Iosif was a young man, however, the age of Sergii and his disciples had about passed, and a period characterized by consolidation of 'communities of venerators', growth of landholding, active involvement in the economic life of the country, and debate over lifestyles had begun.[6]

Iosif's youth has been painted in the traditional hagiographic manner. From the start, we are told, he shunned the usual activities of young men and from the age of seven devoted himself to a monk-like existence and to study at the local Volokolamsk Vozdvizhensky (Elevation) Monastery. He had an extraordinary memory, quickly

4. Dosifei Toporkov, *Nadgrobnoe slovo*, 128–29. Savva Cherny, *Zhitie*, 454–55. Z:KFV, 38. At this time Lithuania ruled what is now Belarus (Byelorussia), and Russian sources referred to the Belarus as well as the Lithuanian parts of that realm as *Litva*. In 1408, the Lithuanian prince Svidrigailo Olgerdovich came with a suite of followers to serve Moscow. For Iosif's family tree, see Chernov, *Volok Lamskii*, 194.

5. Smolitsch, *Mönchtum*, 79–100. Fedotov, *Mind* 2:246–64, 344–76. In a colorful play of language enshrining respect for Egyptian traditions, the Russians applied the term 'desert' (*pustyn'*) for small communities in their well-watered, forested north. The archaic term 'scete', either from the Greek *asket* . . . or the name of a huge early Egyptian cloister complex Sketis or Wadī Naţrūņ, was used for small, individualistic monastic communities.

6. Nikol'sky, 'Obshchestvennaia i keleinaia zhizn', 153–89. Smolitsch, *Mönchtum*, 116–18. Ivina, *Krupnaia votchina,* 49–75. Miller, 'Donors', 450–74.

mastered the Psalter and 'all the Divine Scriptures' and became a lector and a cantor. His decision to become a monk at the age of twenty, it is claimed, was prompted by a thorough grasp of the Fathers' contention that this earthly life is vain.[7]

The search for an appropriate mentor led Iosif first to the Savvin Monastery in Tver, ca. 150 km. northwest of Moscow, where, it is claimed, he refused to eat at table with the other guests because of their foul language. He was directed by the elder Varsonofii to Pafnutii of Borovsk, ca. 150 km. southwest of Moscow.[8] A disciple of an acolyte of the great Sergii of Radonezh, Pafnutii had founded his own cœnobitic monastery fifteen years earlier and become one of the dominant personalities of his time, displaying talents as an estate manager, monastic superior, and father confessor.[9] Pafnutii also commanded the respect of the royal family, even though he had stood against the central political and ecclesiastical authorities in commemorating his patron, the rebel prince Dmitrii Shemiaka (d. 1453).[10]

Pafnutii welcomed and tonsured Iosif on 13 February 1460 and summoned him to the *hegumen's* (abbot's) cell for personal instruction. Iosif then worked in the cook house and sang in the choir and for a while was also the *ustavshchik*, the official in charge of the service *typicon*. The *Lives* claim that he was of sharp and sound mind, very patient and disciplined (eating at most once a day), generous and sympathetic (especially toward the sick), diligent, exceptionally talented as a singer, and in all regards the

7. Dosifei Toporkov, *Nadgrobnoe slovo*, 130. Savva Cherny, *Zhitie,* 455–56. Belokurov, *Zhitie*, 14–51.

8. Savva Cherny, *Zhitie,* 456–57.

9. Kadlubovsky, *Ocherki*, 54–59. Lur'e, *Istoki*, 411–20.

10. PIV, 191, 365–66. Though not at all a central to Iosif's monasticism, it should be of interest to some readers that Pafnutii, in fact, was commemorating a prince who had sought the help of an objectively ecumenically inclined patron—for Prince Shemiaka's Novgorodian allies had the followed the beleaguered Constantinople authorities in accepting the abortive Union of Florence (1439), while Moscow had supported those centers of Byzantine traditionalism that rejected any ecclesiastical tie with Rome. Pafnutii's *Life*, however, states that he had no tolerance for the slightest heresy—which to the Russians included any peculiarly Latin dogmas and practices. See Vernadsky, *Mongols*, 298–329; Halecki, *Florence to Brest,* 33–82.

most able within Pafnutii's brotherhood. Accordingly, Pafnutii allegedly prophesied a career more illustrious than his own for Iosif and divulged to him the secret of psychic divination. During his stay at Pafnutiev Monastery, Iosif convinced his parents to join cloisters, and he personally attended and guided his enfeebled father for fifteen years.[11] As his brothers became monks too, Iosif to all extent and purposes became head of a family, which was officially 'dead to the world', but not at all inactive.

Perhaps the most impressive event at Pafnutiev during Iosif's early years there was the raising of the stone church in 1467/68, which was decorated by some of Russia's most eminent painters.[12] Previously Iosif's regular material surroundings had been wooden. Now he enjoyed the acoustical and iconographic advantages of masonry construction, which were not at all trivial in the largely oral and visual culture of his day. Probably just as important for him, if not more, was the greater availability of books (either owned or obtainable by an early form of inter-library loan) at Pafnutii's prestigious and hence well-funded abbey. Surely Iosif's conection to a place like Pafnutiev, as well as his abilities and drive, account for his being in a position, while a monk 'in the rank of disciple', to write with authority. Around 1476/77 he crafted a rhetorically masterful and theologically sound little tract in the form of a letter to an inquiring archimandrite with an explanation of the prefiguration of the Trinity in the Old Testament (and thus an implicit justification of the prevailing Trinity Icon).[13]

Upon Pafnutii's death in 1477, where, incidently, Iosif was not one of the three brothers in attendance,[14] he nevertheless succeeded as *hegumen*. The *Lives* differ as to how he was selected. Iosif's claimed that Pafnutii and/or the brothers requested permission for this from the Grand Prince, Ivan III (r. 1462–1505).[15] Pafnutii's

11. Dosifei Topokov, *Nadgrobnoe slovo*, 130–31. Savva Cherny, *Zhitie,* 458–59. Belokurov, *Zhitie*, 15–17. *Volokolamskii Paterik,* 216.

12. Pliguzov, 'Letopischik Iosifa Sanina', 178.

13. PIV, 141–44. See below, Ch. 2, HERESY AND AUTHORITY.

14. Kliuchevsky, *Drevnerusskie zhitiia,* 439–53.

15. Dosifei Toporkov, *Nadgrobnoe slovo*, 131; Savva Cherny, *Zhitie*, 459–61; Belokurov, *Zhitie*, 18.

Life, however, states that he refused to state his preference, and Iosif himself insisted that he was forced by Ivan III to take charge of the abbey.[16] The *Lives* also indicate that although Iosif was honored by the brothers as a worthy successor, many of them took issue with his desire strictly to enforce the rule of common property. Since we do not know to what degree Pafnutiev or other monasteries like it were cœnobitic, or how much power the major monk-donors had as quasi-share holders there or elsewhere, we cannot ascertain what Iosif was actually attempting to reform, what problems he had in asserting his authority. Perhaps Iosif was by nature unable to compromise his ideals and allow a gradual cœnobitic reform, just as several Byzantine monasteries had done.[17]

At any rate, Iosif's response to this discord was to arrange with seven eminent elders to leave Pafnutiev and found their own monastery, but at first he traveled incognito as a disciple of one of them, Gerasim Cherny, to inspect other monasteries' customs and to seek out a suitable place. One *Life* claims that on the way several of his hosts recognized him (as if he were a superstar of his profession, which he clearly was) and asked him to be *hegumen* of their cloister. The other *Lives* indicate that he was still disguised when, around 1478, he reached Kirillov Monastery, ca. 500 km. north of Moscow, the only major Muscovite abbey at the time, where the cœnobitic rule was reputed to be fully observed. It is also said that he worked in the Kirillov cook house and chanted the psalms surreptitiously. When he was discovered, the Kirillov elite were ready to make him one of their own, and offered him a 'favorite cell . . . among them', but he refused. He did, however, master the Kirillov Rule.[18]. On his return home, he stopped again at the Tver-Savvin Monastery. Although the secular authorities there

16. PIV, 144–45, 244–46.

17. Dosifei Toporkov, *Nadgrobnoe slovo*, 141, Savva Cherny, *Zhitie,* 461. Belokurov, *Zhitie*, 18. Zhmakin, *Daniil*, Appendix 19:57. The *Patericon* claims that Iosif and his close friend Kassian Bosoi conceived of cœnobitic reform as a special mission: *Volokolamskii paterik*, 216–17. The issue may well have been that of completely pooling resources to expand the monastery's collective activities. Iosif's subsequent career points in that direction. For a gradual cœnobitic reform, cf. Athanasius the Meteorite 1:1460.

18. Savva Cherny, *Zhitie*, 462–63. Belokurov, *Zhitie*, 18.

almost detained him, after he substituted as a lector and revealed his vocal talents, he escaped back to Pafnutiev. In the interim, the reigning Grand Prince Ivan III, fearing that he had afflicted Iosif and so caused his departure, forbade the selection of a new *hegumen* until Iosif's fate was ascertained. Upon his return, it is said, a monk who had reviled Iosif and had been stricken by some disease, fell at his feet, begged forgiveness and was cured.[19]

Iosif did not remain in Pafnutiev for long. He and his seven comrades left with at least fourteen books (and there, strictly speaking, violated strict cœnobitic principles) for his native Volokolamsk, where he was welcomed on 1 June 1479 by the local territorial prince, Boris Vasilevich. Immediately, the story goes, a hunter or fisherman was sent as a guide into a thick forest and either followed or was carried by a whirlwind to a place were lightning struck on a clear day and where, earlier, someone had mysteriously heard church bells. There, at the confluence of two little rivers, Iosif founded his monastery. Within a week of his arrival work commenced on a wooden church dedicated to the Dormition of the Mother of God. Prince Boris, his chief nobles, and his retainers are all said to have worked on the construction, and the church was completed within seven weeks.[20] After about twenty years, the son of a modest provincial warrior had returned home with his own small band of followers, all prepared to make a mark on local and national society that would have been beyond their reach as laymen. They were off to fine start.

The *Lives* give no hint of conflict between Iosif and Ivan III, but the chronicles relate that in 1479 Boris and the Grand Prince had strained relations. Boris almost committed treason the following year when he threatened to join Tatar and Lithuanian opponents of Moscow's momentous ascent, of Ivan's disturbing centralizing policies, and of his mode of annexation of the Republic of Novgorod with its vast domains.[21] Iosif himself claimed in a letter

19. Dosifei Toporkov, *Nadgrobnoe slovo*, 131–32. Savva Cherny, *Zhitie,* 463–64. Belokurov, *Zhitie,* 18–20.

20. Dosifei Toporkov, *Nadgrobnoe slovo*, 132. Savva Cherny, *Zhitie,* 464–65, 484–85. Belokurov, *Zhitie,* 20–21. Zhmakin, *Daniil*, Appendix 19:57.

21. Fennell, *Ivan III,* 66–88. L:IB, 50–66.

to the Pafnutiev monks that he had left because he could not get Ivan III to stop his agents from seizing the monastery's peasants.[22] Whatever the case, the fact remains that Iosif, like his mentor Pafnutii, founded a great cloister under the patronage of a political opponent of the reigning Sovereign.

Construction of the monastery proceeded rapidly. A wooden refectory with an attached bakery and kitchen followed the first church, as did a few hut-cells. Iosif personally took part in the erection of the stone Church of the Dormition in 1484–85, the leading iconographers of the day painting with frescoes *gratis*—apparently in appreciation of his passionate advocacy of their art and its spiritual value.[23] The stone refectory with attached heated church, the stone kitchens and bakery, and the artificial pond outside the cloister were all completed by about 1506.[24]

Donations facilitated all this construction. At the outset Prince Boris (d. 1494) granted a few neighboring hamlets and a village to the monastery. Subsequently, during Iosif's lifetime, Boris, his widow Uliana (d. 1499), his sons Fedor of Volokolamsk (d. 1513) and Ivan of Ruza (d. 1503), Archbishop Gennadii of Novgorod (1484–1504), and a number of less renowned benefactors bestowed to the monastery a total of more than ten villages, plus other properties and exploitation rights, as outright gifts or as payments for specified memorial services.[25] Iosif, on his part, fostered a diverse and productive monastic economy and actively promoted and defended the exchange of requiems and other commemorations for payments and donations necessary for monastic prosperity.[26] Despite Iosif's claims to be following Russian norms, he and monastery seem to have played an instrumental

22. PIV, 144–45.

23. See below, Ch. II, Aspects of Iconography.

24. Dosifei Toporkov, *Nadgrobnoe slovo*, 132–33; Savva Cherny, *Zhitie* 465–66; Belokurov, *Zhitie*, 20. Zimin, 'Kratkie letopistsi', 16. Z:KFV, 54–55.

25. Budovnits, *Monastyri*, 235–38. AFZKh 2.10–65. Titov, *Rukopisi* 5, Appendix. Chernov, *Volok Lamskii*, 316–18. Chernov argues that Iosif's monastery owed its peculiar corporate spirit and militancy to the traditions of the local, frontier region service gentry, which had developed since the 1340s.

26. PIV, 179–83. also see below, Appendix I.

role in the rationalizing of these profitable rites of remembrance in Russia.[27]

The *Lives* present an idyllic picture for the early years of the monastery—a picture taken in part from Iosif's own *Rule*. Accordingly, the brothers all labored intensely and diligently, not only physically, but also spiritually. They helped each other to observe and maintain continence, obedience, personal poverty, tearful and silent prayer, and mindfulness of death. The monastery itself was said to have followed the strictest principles of common property and equality, so that the monks, regardless of origin, received equal food, except for those voluntarily abstaining. The monks were said to have trusted each other enough to dispense with locks to cell doors (which, one might note, Byzantine rules often forbade). One *Life* states—as if to verify the sanctity of the cloister's early period—that a simple monk-visionary, Vissarion-Selifont, predicted the day of his own death, witnessed a dying brother's soul exit 'white as snow from his lips', and on an Easter eve saw a white dove above Iosif's head as he was helping to carry the processional shroud of Christ.[28] During that time Iosif gave each monk his personal cell rule and encouraged heroic asceticism. Some of the monks dressed in iron mail. Others wore heavy iron and made one-to-three thousand daily prostrations. Iosif's traveling companion Gerasim Cherny lived as a hermit and copied books. Kassian Bosoi, who as a layman had instructed Ivan III in archery and as a monk lived to be a hundred, is said never to have worn shoes, even in winter. Dionisii Zvenigorodsky reputedly performed two men's work at the ovens and recited seventy-seven psalms and made five hundred prostrations a day.[29]

Into the monastery came Prince Boris's court tutor, Iona Golova, who after 1494 fled the allegedly uncontrollable fury of his former pupil, Fedor of Volokolamsk. Iona became an important mentor

27. Steindorff, *Memoria*, 164–66, 172, 195–96. See below Ch. II, RELATIONS WITH THE TRANS-VOLGANS.

28. Savva Cherny, *Zhitie,* 468–69. Belokurov, *Zhitie*, 29.

29. Savva Cherny, *Zhitie,* 467. Belokurov, *Zhitie,* 30–31. The *Patericon* notes that Iosif's role in the life of Kassian Bosoi, however, was to limit the latter's ascetic excesses: *Volokolamskii paterik,* 217.

within the cloister and the brothers' choice to succeed Iosif. Iona's disciple Epifanii is said to be graced with incapability of anger and a body that remained whole in the grave for seven years, even though—as was pointed out—he died young and thus had a more readily corruptible body. Iona and Kassian sometimes served as Iosif's special emissaries. A later eminent elder and capital 'catch' for Iosif was Prince Andrei-Arsenii Golenin, of royal blood, who donated four villages, lived exceedingly humbly, and seems to have had a peculiar psychological dependence upon Iosif.[30]

Iosif himself, by all reports, worked hard by day, prayed through the night, dressed in the meanest garb, had no personal servant, did not often leave the monastery as other abbots did, and was extremely strict about segregation of the genders. He even refused to see his mother before her death and commanded her rather to pray that they might see each other 'where the saints repose'.[31] He is also said to have been forgiving to those who found his *Rule* too difficult and departed, and to have released a man caught pilfering grain.[32] He was too practical to be uniformly strict and claimed in his *Rule* that he was somewhat lax in the early period and 'condescended greatly to weakness' in order to build up a materially comfortable abbey.[33]

Iosif turned young monks over to supervisors and composed didactic sermons, but there is little evidence that he devised a formal rule during his first two decades back at Volokolamsk.[34] Nevertheless, explicit written regulations and instructions did occupy his attention, and this was consistent with the spirit of the time. Russia's first genuine *Rule*, resonating the strictest Eastern Christian cœnobitic principles and specifically banning individual deposit/donations, sprang from the pen of Evfrosin of Eliazarov Monastery (d. 1479) in the autonomous, western frontier

30. Savva Cherny, *Zhitie*, 493–94. Belokurov, *Zhitie*, 26–30. AFZKh 2.42–43.

31. Dosifei Toporkov, *Nadgrobnoe slovo*, 132–33. Savva Cherny, *Zhitie*, 466–70. Belokurov, *Zhitie*, 25–26.

32. These stories have parallels in the Life of Feodosii Pechersky: Nestor, Life of . . . Feodosii, 72–74.

33. Savva Cherny, *Zhitie*, 470. See also below, XIII.51–54.

34. PIV, 145–52, 246–47.

province of Pskov during the period of Iosif's apprenticeship under Pafnutii. The next *Rules*, the *Tradition* (*Predanie*) and *Typicon* (*Ustav*) of the gifted hesychast and semi-recluse Nil Sorsky (d. 1508)—modifications of Byzantine scete rules and Sinaite hesychastic theory—were probably composed after the time when Iosif founded his monastery.[35] None of these responded to the needs of monastic reform within the context of the large, economically active, 'possessing' monasteries that trained most of the prelates. Moreover, at the time of Iosif's abbacy, not only were the acquisition and possession of villages by monasteries coming into question among some of the Orthodox elite,[36] but the very institution of monasticism, apparently, was challenged by dissidents.[37] These problems may have provided an extra stimulus for Iosif to avoid the standard abuses and to produce a public statement of monastic principles, as well as to delineate a structure for enforcing discipline.[38] At at rate, as an adept speaker and writer, Iosif seems continuously to have been composing sermons and regulations for his monks[39]—certainly far more than any other of his several hundred fellow, pre-modern East Slavic cloister-founders.

The *Lives* note not only that Iosif was a pastor to his monks, but

35. Evfrosin's Rule was published by Serebriansky, *Ocherki*, and translated into German by von Lilienfeld, *Nil Sorskij,* 295–313. Nil's *Tradition (Predanie), Typicon (Ustav)* and (perhaps spurious) *Testament (Zaveshchanie)* were published by Borovkova-Maikova, *Nila Sorskogo,* 1–91, and translated, along with his letters, also by von Lilienfeld, *Nil Sorskij*, 193–283. A good English translation of the letters, and also some spurious ones, is found in Maloney, *Russian Hesychasm*, 245–62. However, Prokhorov, 'Poslaniia', should be consulted on the anthenticity of Nil's letters, as ought be Ostrowski, 'Toward establishing a Canon of Nil Sorsky's Works'. A rather unsatisfactory and incomplete translation of the *Typicon,* as well as the *Tradition* and *Testament*, by Helene Izwolsky, is found in Fedotov, *Treasury,* 90–133. A later, functioning rule from Nil's hermitage has been found: Beliakova, 'Ustav Pustyna Nila Sorskogo'.

36. We really do not know how and when monastic lands became an issue between state authorities and the large cloisters and between Iosif's faction and some of Nil's followers—and maybe, as has been traditionally seen, Nil himself: See Meyendorff, 'Partisans', 28–30. Ostrowski, 'Church Polemics and Monastic Land Acquisition'. And below, Ch. 2, RELATIONS WITH THE TRANS-VOLGANS.

37. AfED, 416–19, 470. *Prosvetitel'* 11:405–64.

38. Such is Lur'e's view: 'Kratkaia redaktsiia "Ustava" Iosifa Volotskogo'.

39. See below, Ch. II, first paragraph.

also that many laymen from the highest strata, including Prince Boris himself, selected Iosif as their confessor and spiritual director. Some of them became monks. His extant 'penances', written for laymen, reveal a strict, external approach to repentance, an effectual equating of charity (as a substitute) with abstinence, and a high esteem for monastic vows as a second baptism. Similarly, his general instructions to laymen, which emphasized their responsibilities for the physical care and moral upbringing and conduct of their servants, slaves, and other dependents, included a self-serving stricture that adolescents be permitted to enter cloisters rather than marry.[40]

Iosif's teachings and activities had a social side. He admonished landlords to be gentle with their peasants and subjects, and this is said to have increased the prosperity of his locality. He was reputed to have helped peasants by covering their unforeseen losses and always to have fed visitors and the hungry. During a famine that hit Russia early in 1512 he urged princes to fix grain prices, exhausted his monastery's reserves to feed the starving, and built an orphanage for children abandoned outside the cloister walls. Ultimately he was reimbursed by pious laymen for his philanthropy. He also established a daughter monastery to serve as an infirmary. His lofty principles, however, did not prevent him from tonsuring other peoples' runaways and pursuing those who left him, notwithstanding what the *Life* says about his kindly attitude toward those who departed.[41]

The *Lives* claim that Iosif's peaceful existence foundered aroud 1487 with the news of Jewish-inspired heresy having erupted in Novgorod[42]—the second city of the realm—which Moscow had recently subdued and reorganized.[43] This was the year when the

40. Dosifei Toporkov, *Nadgrobnoe slovo*, 134. Belokurov, *Zhitie*, 21–22. PIV, 148–54, 232–36. Smirmov, *Drevnerusskii dukhovnik,* Appendix, 224–34.

41. Dosifei Toporkov, *Nadgrobnoe slovo*, 134–35. Savva Cherny, *Zhitie*, 482–84. Belokurov, *Zhitie*, 32–33, 39–40. PIV, 182, 235–36. Pliguzov, 'O khronologii poslanii Iosifa Volotskogo', 1056.

42. Dosifei Toporkov, *Nadgrobnoe slovo*, 133. Savva Cherny, *Zhitie*, 472–75. Belokurov, *Zhitie*, 32, 34–36.

43. Skrynnikov, *Tragediia Novgoroda*, 8–37.

new, Moscow-appointed Novgorodian archbishop Gennadii, who named Iosif his vicar for Volokolamsk, began an inquisitorial and literary campaign against dissidents. Here one must tread very carefully, for Gennadii and Iosif are our chief sources and are extremely biased. The accusations that some heretics accepted Judaism must be taken *cum grano salis*, since the charges contain no references to the Talmud-oriented Ukrainian and Lithuanian-Belarusian Jews, who at that time were bearers of High Medieval Mediterranean civilization and important sources of astronomical and other scientific knowledge in Eastern Europe. What can be identified are two types of heresy: an anti-sacramental, anti-clerical, iconoclastic, and, perhaps, anti-Trinitarian movement, allegedly prevalent among the married secular clergy and some laymen of Novgorod, and a rationalist intellectualism, found both in Novgorod, where Jewish versions of a few scientific and philosophical works circulated in translation, and at the court of Moscow, where Italians were directing the reconstruction of the Kremlin palace and churches, and where all sorts of cultural currents crossed. The Russian Church thus faced the twin dangers of first a social movement opposing the Church's typically medieval, hierocratic structure and sacramental emphasis and secondly intellectual interests, which, while themselves not necessarily heretical, touched subjects which most native ecclesiastics, lacking higher education, were not prepared or willing to debate.[44]

Iosif's part in the first actions against the heretics (1487–90) is impossible to pin down. The prime mover appears to have been Gennadii, although Iosif may have begun at this time to write again in defense of icons and the Trinity.[45] The Moscow Synod of 1490 condemned several of the indicted to a humiliating

44. AfED, 318–20. L:IB, 75–203. Klibanov, *Reformatsionnye dvizheniia*, 187–255. Vernadksy, 'The Heresy of the Judiasers'. Wieczynski, 'Hermetism and Cabalism'. Goldfrank, 'Burn, Baby, Burn'. Recently Prokhorov revived the notion that the 'Jewish thinking' allegedly involved stemmed from the Karaites: 'Prenie Grigorii Palamy "s khiony i turki"'. The literature on this intriguing problem is vast and inconclusive. See Taube, 'Kievan Jew', and '"Poem on the Soul"'.

45. AfED, 320–73.

auto-da-fe in Novgorod and to harsh imprisonment, but left others free and active.[46] Iosif then began his own campaign with a barrage of missives, which were summons to action, even martyrdom, in defense of the faith. His chief individual target was Metropolitan Zosima (1490–1494), whose circle apparently included intellectuals and accused heretics, and whose alleged offenses included sodomy and denial of the resurrection of the body. Writing with the passion of apocalyptic foreboding, Iosif moved to topple Zosima, 'the forerunner of the Antichrist and the first apostate among our bishops'. In order completely to neutralize him, Iosif argued the inefficacy of the 'heretic' bishop's anathema and the propriety and necessity of condemning and punishing heretics.[47] Iosif also composed polemical discourses in defense of four general aspects of Orthodoxy: 1) the doctrines of the Trinity and Incarnation, the abrogation of the Old Law, and the Christian concept of the 'Divine Economy'; 2) ritual, especially veneration of icons, and specifically the *Old Testament Trinity* (*Hospitality of Abraham*) depicting three angels, sometimes in the form of men, visiting Abraham and Sarah;[48] 3) the validity of the Fathers, the Apostles, and the Gospel, given that the fact that the '7000th year' (1492) and hence the 'last age' was about to have passed or had arrived without the Second Coming or the world ending as predicted in some prestigious writings;[49] and the legitimacy of monasticism as a divine, not a human institution. No scholar has been able to prove that Russian dissidents of the period actually contested these doctrines. Whatever the case here, on behalf of a weighty faction of Russian clergy and aided, perhaps, by a team of collaborators, Iosif composed a very useful didactic tract—later known as the *Enlightener*—to instruct and fortify the faithful

46. AfED, 382–86, 472–73.

47. Dosifei Toporkov, *Nadgrobnoe slovo*, 133. PIV, 154–78, 248–57.

48. In the opinion of specialists, one of the greatest surviving Russian icons is Andrei Rublev's famous *Old Testament Trinity* from the late fourteenth or early fifteenth century, now housed in the Tretiakov Gallery in Moscow. A fine illustration of it is found in Alpatov, *Early Russian Icon Painting*, Pl. 82.

49. AfED, 318–20; 394–414.

and to separate them clearly, sharply, and unquestioningly from deviants.[50]

Iosif's crowning success came with the Moscow Synod of 1504 against the heretics, which sentenced the leading dissidents to death or life imprisonment. Capitalizing on his spiritual prestige and the religious notions of his society, Iosif made his 'forgiveness' of the aging Ivan III for having 'known the Novgorod heretics' conditional upon the latters's implementation of new inquisitional proceedings, and to this end put pressure on Ivan's father-confessor.[51] As a service to throne, Iosif facilitated the transfer of the small Ruza principality from its dying prince, the young Ivan Borisovich, to his uncle—Ivan III—and hence Moscow, rather than to the surviving brother Fedor, the territorial prince of Volokolamsk.[52] In fact, the synod was a political victory for the new heir presumptive, Vasilii III (r. 1505–33), the eldest son of Ivan III by his second, Greco-Italian wife, Sofiia (d. 1502), over his primogenitary grandson Dmitrii, whose Moldavian mother Iosif accused of 'Judaism'. It has also been suggested that Moscow's expansionist war against Lithuania during 1500–1503 under the slogan of defense of Orthodoxy in the Ruthenian (Belarusian and Ukrainian) territories of that realm helped create an atmosphere favorable to the purge of 'free-thinkers'.[53] The *Lives* of Iosif, without mentioning any of these dealings and circumstances, conflate the Synods of 1490 and 1504 and consider, as did Iosif's enemies, the final verdict to have resulted from his suasion and influence.[54]

50. AFED, 320–73, 391–419. *Prosvetitel',* Discourses 1–11. Recent Soviet scholarship has shown that Nil Sorsky was the copyist of part of the earliest surviving manuscript—which has fueled speculation concerning his possible collaboration with Iosif in the composition of this, Russia's first serious attempt to create a general theological treatise. See Lur'e. 'Unresolved Issues', 164–65. For a sympathetic, Roman Catholic critique of Iosif's theology, see Špidlík. *Joseph de Volokolamsk.*

51. PIV, 175–76.

52. Fennell, *Ivan III,* 333–53.

53. Szeftel, 'Joseph Volotsky's Political Ideas', 23–25. Iosif was present when Ivan of Ruza composed his will: *Dukhovnye i dogorvornye gramoty*, 350–53.

54. Savva Cherny, *Zhitie*, 472–75. Belokurov, *Zhitie*, 34–36.

The Synod of 1504 did not end Iosif's problems with dissidence. He was genuinely upset that some of the convicted 'heretics' were being confined in monasteries, including his own, as if their mere presence could 'destroy' a sacred place. Evidently his cloister was not prepared, as it would be later, to serve as a penitentiary for spiritual felons. Iosif rather wanted those spared execution to be sent to genuine prisons.[55] Moreover, many influential persons were ready to accept the prompt repentance of some of these new convicts and urged the Sovereign to free them. Iosif, on the other hand, following Gennadii and using logic that any trained Dominican could recognize, argued for a harsh sentence on the ground that such culprits were oath-breakers and hence could not be trusted.[56] Iosif thus opened himself to the charge that he refused merciful correction to penitents.[57] According to a later source, when the 'Novgorod Heretics contrived a feigned repentance', Iosif convinced the new ruler Vasilii III not to believe them.[58] One *Life* reports the timely, miraculous appearance of the Christ Child to a false penitent heretic-priest, who after a liturgy had emptied the chalice into a stove. The apparition exclaimed, 'You have delivered me to this fire; I shall deliver you to eternal fire'! It was this which convinced Iosif to insist that the 'heretics' remain confined for life.[59]

Iosif's own writings reveal that immediately after the 1504 Synod he had to defend inquisitorial proceedings, condemnation, execution, and the authority of the Synod against monks from Russia's 'Trans-Volgan' North (the Kirillov Monastery elders and *kelliotai*, including some of Nil Sorsky's disciples). Around 1510–1511 Iosif was especially worried that the heresy might revive. Going on the offensive, he clouded the issue by misrepresenting not only the indicted, but also their supporters, whose arguments

55. PIV, 178–79, 257–58. Cf. Thomas Aquinas, *Summa Theologica* 2.2.108: 1218–19.

56. AFED, 373–82, 506–09. *Prosvetitel'* 15:510–26. See also Goldfrank, 'Theocratic Imperatives', 34–36.

57. PIV, 227–28. K:VPS, 277.

58. PIV, 367.

59. Savva Cherny, *Zhitie*, 474–5.

he attributed as well to the 'Novgorod Heretics'. His final words on the subject were to remind the Sovereign of his majesty and responsibilities, and to warn him that other 'Orthodox empires' had fallen due to heresy. Iosif and/or his collective of literati combined these polemics, as well as his earlier apologies, in the final, 'extended' version of the *Enlightener*, his most famous work.[60]

Iosif was involved in two other public disputes, one of which, the issue of widower priests, came to a head in 1503. Here he represented the monastic party, which did not trust such secular priests to remain chaste, since the Orthodox canons prohibited deacons and priests from marrying after ordination. He thus wanted such widowers automatically to enter monasteries. Their defenders, most surely supported by communities of laymen wishing to retain their parish priests at a time when mortality rates were high and women frequently died from the burdens of pregnancy, were not silent. The parish view was that only a priest who committed a grave sin need relinquish his post, while the bishops were at fault for their extensive secular powers and administrative apparati. The higher clergy, claiming that widower priests who remained among laymen unfailingly acquired concubines and thereby defiled any liturgy they performed, backed (or sponsored) Iosif's position, which carried the day.[61]

Various sources discuss a second pressing concern of the Synod of 1503—that of ecclesiastical estates. Recent scholarship, however, has seriously questioned if this matter was actually deliberated there.[62] According to one tale favorable to Iosif, he had left Moscow after the decision on widower priests, when Nil Sorsky raised the issue of monastic villages, and Iosif had to hurry back to defend them.[63] This question bore on Ivan III's land policy. After incorporating Novgorod into his realm, he had confiscated

60. AfED, 486–510. *Prosvetitel',* especially Discourses 13–16. On the latest hyptheses concerning the dating of these events, see Pliguzov, ' "Kniga na eretikov Iosifa Volotskogo" ', 131–35; and O khronologii', 1046, 1055–56.

61. Belokurov, *Zhitie,* 36. Kozhanchikov, *Stoglav* 237–38. ChOIDR 1848, 6.4, 45–50.

62. Ostrowski, 'Church Polemics and Monastic Land Acquisition', 358–61.

63. PIV, 367. K:VPS, 279.

about half the very extensive church lands to be redistributed as retractable benefices (*pomestie*) for Muscovites sent there to help govern the territory and serve as the core of the local army. The most recent sequestration had occurred in 1499 and had evoked bitter protests from Archbishop Gennadii, who was aided by a Slavic (Croatian or Ruthenian) Dominican friar named Benjamin.[64] There is no record of Muscovite ecclesiastical support for Gennadii. Around 1502 or 1503, however, Ivan may have been pondering the seizure of lands from the major Muscovite episcopacies and monasteries, a policy that specialists have traditionally considered in line with the goals of secular magnates, lesser military servitors, and 'Non-Possessor' monks led by the 'Trans-Volgan Elders'. One source indicates that the hegumen (abbot) Serapion of Troitse-Sergiev Monastery (1495–1505, subsequently Archbishop of Novgorod, 1505–09) independently led the defense of monastic estates.[65] Other sources point to Iosif or both Iosif and Serapion. A purported synodal response of 1503 and a slightly later treatise in defense of monastic land, both tentatively attributed to Iosif by scholars, have survived. These works, which betray Iosif's influence if not his pen, argued from precedent, canon law, general strictures against taking another's property, and traditions of 'donations' starting with Emperor Constantine I and including Prince Vladimir I (d. 1015), who 'baptized the land of Rus'.[66] One *Life*, implicitly referencing the frequent lavish commemorations and accompanying charitable feasts, also claims that Iosif held that property was necessary to finance monastery church services under

64. L:IB, 63, 225–29, 403–04. Lur'e, 'Sobranie na likhoimtsev'. Skrynnikov, *Tragediia*, 37. Veniamin, apparently, introduced the two-sword theory into Muscovy, but soon after the 1503 synod Archbishop Gennadii was removed from office 'much against his will' on grounds of simony.

65. Begunov, 'Slovo inoc', 351–64.

66. PIV, 322–26; Malinin, *Filofei*, Appendix 20: 128–44. 50. The fact that the sources for the '1503' controversy over monastic lands stem from later debates has led to revisions of the traditioinal view: Ostrowski, 'Church Polemics and Monastic Land Acquisition', 360–61. Cf. Pliguzov, '"Prenie s Iosifom"'; 'Tekstologicheskaia istoriia "Sobraniia nekoego startsa"'; '"Traktat o neprikosnovennosti tserkovnykh i monastyrskikh imushchestv"'; and 'Vstuplenie Vassian Patrikeev v polemiku o monastyrskikh zemliakh i tvorcheskaia istoriia 'Sobraniia nekoego startsa'".

contract and that any monk who failed to live up to his obligations would be anathematized.[67] Another source friendly to Iosif has him asserting that villages were necessary to attract nobles to monastic life, and that without such well-born monks Russia would lack a source of prelates capable of keeping the faith firm and society in order.[68] Iosif's opponents disputed the validity of the alleged precedents, the canonicity of monastic villages, and the propriety of monks actively exercising control over laymen and living off their labors—but to no avail.[69]

A personal quarrel with Fedor Borisovich, the territorial Prince of Volok (r. 1494–1513) compounded Iosif's conflicts over widowed priests, church lands, and the inquisition. One of the *lives*, using a standard binary trope, states that Boris's younger son Ivan of Ruza (d. 1503), always honored Iosif,[70] but that the elder one, Fedor, 'forgot his father's command' and ordered the monastery to prepare banquets with meat and wine, although this violated a promise to respect the founder's strict *Rule*. Another *Life* emphasizes Fedor's irascibility. Always in debt to the monastery, Fedor had begun to extort his subjects' wealth and demand 'gifts' from the creditor-cloister.[71] In 1506 or 1507 he was supposed to have enticed away fourteen of Iosif's monks (who absconded with fifteen books) to help a rival, Aleksii Pil'mev, restore the fortunes of Volokolamsk's Vozmitsky Monastery.[72] Fedor's actual rights are not at all clear. European *de jure* notions do not apply very well to

67. Belokurov, *Zhitie*, 37–39. 51. See, below, Appendix I.

68. PIV, 367.

69. K:VPS, 223–49, 254–70. Ostrowski reminds us that none of the writings against monastic lands can be proven to have been written in Iosif's lifetime: 'Church Polemics', 362–63. Cf. Pliguzov, as above, note 66.

70. The will of this Prince Ivan indicates a tie to not only Iosifov, but also a host of monasteries connected to Iosif at this time: DDG, 352.

71. In fact Fedor in 1506 (when he wrote a will before setting out on a campgain to the East) was not that much more in debt than his brother Ivan had been in 1504, and both of them were more in hock to a certain Vepr Vasilevich than to any monastery. A difference was that only 9% of Ivan's 571-ruble debt was to monasteries, while 37% of Fedor's 847-ruble obligation was to cloisters: DDG, 351–2, 406–06.

72. Savva Cherny, *Zhitie,* 475–80. PIV, 185–86.

Muscovy, and *de facto* Vasilii III had more rights over his provincial cousin Fedor, than the latter did over Iosif's monastery.[73]

Iosif, by his own account, which appears to be the source here for the *Lives*, claims that he was ready to abandon the cloister, but that the brothers insisted that he stay and safeguard their property and the 'eternal commemorations' that the monastery was obliged to maintain. Deciding to ask the Sovereign for protection, but unable, because of plague in Novgorod, to reach his new spiritual superior, Archbishop Serapion, for approval, Iosif sent two elders to ask Metropolitan Simon (1494–1511) to petition Vasilii 'to take the monastery into his realm'. Vasilii himself, it is claimed, promised to smooth things over with Serapion but then 'forgot'. It seems, though, that Iosif was no passive participant in this matter, for he composed an official will, dated March 1507, handing over the monastery to the Grand Prince and demanding that he protect the *Rule* and expel unruly and disobedient monks.[74]

This action provoked the wrath of Serapion who allowed himself, according to Iosif, to be involved in a ridiculous plot to discredit and then excommunicate Iosif on shaky grounds and without any investigation. Serapion, however, insisted all along that Iosif's fundamental offense was his failure to supplicate his Archbishop to mediate the scrape with Fedor. Iosif contended that Fedor's ferocity, together with the plague and quarantine in Novgorod, had necessitated the prompt appeal to Moscow.[75] The immediate outcome was the exoneration of Iosif and the demotion and confinement of Serapion and Pil'mev. Upper-class Muscovite public opinion, however, questioned Iosif's actions toward Fedor and admired Serapion's uncompromising stance in the face of adversity. In turn Iosif (and his assistants) countered with a set

73. PIV, 193–94. Serapion and Fedor did have a point: the monastery, according to Iosif's own records, originally belonged in some sense to Fedor's father Prince Boris: *Sinodik*, 3.

74. AI I.288: 524. It is possible that this testament was a demonstrative act of loyalty, for Iosif's princely patron, Vasilii's brother Iurii, had received from King Sigismund of Poland that year a letter encouraging him to attempt a *coup d'état*: Zimin, *Rossiia,* 82–83.

75. PIV, 185–227, 262–80.

of canonical-legal and *ad hominem* tracts.[76] The *Lives* insist that Iosif's actions in no way damaged Serapion's legitimate income and that Fedor was eventually reconciled with Iosif. The latter is likely, for Fedor was buried at the monastery when he died in 1513. On the other hand, the *Life* of Serapion, who was revered in Novgorod for his generosity and charity (which Iosif deemed to be a squandering of church resources),[77] contradicts the contention of Iosif's biographers that before he died he forgave Serapion, as the ethical norms of his time dictated.[78]

Iosif's several problems came to a head in 1511, when Vasilii released Serapion from confinement, replaced Metropolitan Simon with the less friendly Varlaam (1511–22), gave Nil Sorsky's disciple Vassian Patrikeev free rein to publish on major issues of the day, but forbade Iosif to write against Vassian.[79] According to a later source, two of Iosif's disciples—Dionisii Zvenigorodsky and Nil Polev (the owner and partial scribe of the earliest extant copies of the earliest extant versions of Iosif's *Rule* and *Enlightener*), both of whom had studied with Nil Sorsky and had established hermitages near Beloozero—were temporarily confined in Kirillov Monastery after they had attempted to uncover heresy in that region.[80] On the other hand, around 1510–11, Iosif was able to reconcile Vasilii III with his politically suspect and mortally threatened brother Iurii, to promote and organize regional famine relief, and to secure Iurii's and Vasilii's aid to this end.[81] Despite the influence of Vassian Patrikeev, who reportedly 'bitterly hated Iosif and wanted to raze his monastery', the convicted heretics remained confined, and the Church kept its land. And after Iosif's death his enemies are said to have failed in an alleged attempt to have his apologetics burned.[82]

76. PIV, 329–66.

77. PIV, 206–07.

78. Savva Cherny, *Zhitie*, 475–82. Belokurov, *Zhitie*, 28, 39–43. Cf. Collins, 'Early Russian Topoi of Deathbed and Testament'.

79. L:IB, 468–69. K:VPS, 56–61. Zimin, *Rossiia,* 124–37.

80. PIV, 367–69. Cf. Kloss, 'Nil Sorskii i Nil Polev'.

81. Dosifei Toporkov, *Nadgrobnoe slovo*, 134. Savva Cherny, *Zhitie*, 482–86. Belokurov, *Zhitie*, 43. PIV. 235–36.

82. PIV 369; Dosifei, Dosifei Toporkov, *Nadgrobnoe slovo*, 137.

One of the *Lives* is attentive to Iosif's reconciliation of Vasilii and Iurii, probably because this was characteristic of Iosif's approach to political problems. In his earlier works on heresy, written when Ivan III protected dissidents, Iosif proclaimed:[83]

> If the tsar himself is ruled by . . . passions and sins, avarice and anger, wickedness and injustice, pride and fury, and, worst of all, disbelief and blasphemy, such a tsar is not God's servant but the Devil's, and not a tsar but a tyrant, . . . do not obey such a tsar, who leads you to impiety and evil, even if he tortures, even if he threatens death.

Such principled independence notwithstanding, Iosif generally held that the ruler was to be obeyed and that an 'Orthodox Tsar', the 'terrestrial god', who faithfully protected the Church, was to be heeded unconditionally. Moreover, regardless of the persuasive, supplicating, and intercessory role of the clergy and other faithful, it was essentially only the Sovereign who could protect the church and facilitate the salvation of the Orthodox.[84] Therefore, while not neglecting to render highest honors to junior members of the royal family as protectors of Christianity and as 'autocrats' in their own small principalities, Iosif extolled and placed his hopes in the 'Orthodox Tsar' and, accordingly, urged Iurii to submit completely to Vasilii and accept his judgment concerning suspected treason. In this manner, Iosif's emissaries, the eminent elders Kassian Bosoi and Iona Golova, approached Vasilii in all humility and were ready to accept his judgment, even against themselves, for having interceded. While pacifying the two princes, Iosif was thus affirming the institutionally unlimited political power of the senior prince over his four brothers, who, at that time, to protect Vasilii III's personal, dynastic interests, were prevented from marrying. The state in general was quite ruthless toward potential rivals for the throne, who, it should be noted, were likely targets for the intrigues of neighboring Poland-Lithuania. It is thus understandable that Vasilii, according to the *Life*, commanded Iosif to continue 'so to

83. AfED, 346.
84. Szeftel, 'Joseph Volotsky's Political Ideas', 19–29.

watch over us'.[85] It is similarly understandable why Iosif in his lifetime was accused of being the 'courtier of the Grand Prince.' Vasilii, according to the *Life*, accepted his responsibility as Iosif's agent in charge of observance of the Rule.[86] In the end, Iosif and his disciples succeeded in establishing a special relationship between their monastery and the royal family and in associating Vasilii with the Iosifov style of piety.[87]

All of the *Lives* praise Iosif's written Rule (here they envision his Extended Rule) for having secured the continuation of his customs and his presence within the monastery. They also note that the Rule was written to deal with problems created by the growth of the brotherhood and the monastery.[88] Without going into details, they confirm what is evident from the Rule itself: that Iosif's ways provoked opposition within and without his monastery. The Rule also records that Iosif's instructions of his monks in the 'Divine Writings'—in other words, his establishment of a quasi-academy in the his cloister—prepared many of his elders for posts in other monasteries and the episcopate. It is likely as well that antagonism toward his Rule was somehow connected to his public positions and the upward mobility in the hierarchy of his disciples.[89] For sure, the traditional notion in scholarship of two monastic-ecclesiastical parties, the 'Josephites' or 'Possessors' and the Trans-Volgans or 'Non-Possessors' may be overdrawn.[90] All the same, Nil Sorsky's pupil Vassian Patrikeev and Iosif, along

85. Savva Cherny, *Zhitie,* 485–88. The actual circumstances of Vasilii's suspicions are not known, but rumors concerning Iurii's discontent reached Poland: see above, note 74.

86. PIV, 348. Savva Cherny, *Zhitie,* 489–90, 493. Vasilii III was on his mother's side as descendent of the last Byzantine imperial dynasty and thus personally an heir to a tradition of protecting monastic rules. See below, Ch. II, note 176.

87. PIV, 95–96.

88. Dosifei Toporkov, *Nadgrobnoe slovo*, 134. Savva Cherny, *Zhitie,* 482. Belokurov, *Zhitie*, 43–46.

89. Dosifei Toporkov, *Nadgrobnoe slovo* 134. Savva Cherny, *Zhitie,* 468. These problems are discussed in detail in Chapter II, RELATIONS WITH THE TRANS-VOLGANS.

90. See, for example, Ostrowski, 'Church Polemics'.

with their respective followers, seem to have despised each other, and it is said that there developed great enmity between the elites of Iosifov Monastery and Kirillov, which had originally been one of Iosif's chief models.[91]

Iosif's last recorded acts were the final compilation of his Rule and the empowerment of the council brothers and major officials to choose the new hegumen and to administer the monastery with him.[92] The *Lives* finesse the Sovereign's supervisory role and emphasize that the brothers selected Daniil of Riazan to be Iosif's successor, Iosif's role being to approve the choice and to give Daniil special instructions.[93]

Curiously, Daniil was not among the leading elders of the monastery. He was, however, an excellent 'Josephite'. He firmly defended Iosif's positions within the Church and presided over the momentous growth of the monastery's wealth and influence, both while he was hegumen there (1515–22) and later when he was Metropolitan of Moscow (1522–39). It was also Daniil who, along with his supporters, sanctioned Vasilii's divorce and the remarriage that resulted at last in the birth of a long-awaited heir, Ivan IV. The support of Vasilii and later Ivan IV led to Pafnutii and later Iosif becoming favorite saints of the ruling house, a status that survived the advent of the Romanovs and lasted into the mid-seventeenth century.[94]

After turning the abbacy over to Daniil, Iosif became very ill and donned the Great *Schema*—a special, higher Orthodox habit signifying baptism and requiring its wearers never again to leave the cloister. His final message to the brothers exhorted them to keep the customs he had written down and not to borrow from other monasteries. He promised that if he obtained mercy from God—that is, if he died in saintly fashion—this would be a sign

91. PIV, 366–69. K:VPS, 280–81, 296.

92. PIV, 239–40, 285–86. Savva Cherny, *Zhitie,* 488–89. Also see below, XIII.33.

93. Savva Cherny, *Zhitie,* 490–92. Belokurov, *Zhitie*, 43. Zimin and others have made a good case for Daniil's having been Vasilii III's candidate: Z:KFV, 99.

94. Rybakov, 'Voinstvuiuschchie tserkovniki'.

that the monastery would always prosper. Too weak at the end even to sit up, he had to be carried on a stretcher to church for each service. He died on 9 September in his own cell during the chanting of Matins. It is said that he crossed his face and breathed three times to signify the Trinity. He was seventy-five or possibly seventy-six at the time.[95]

So rich and eventful was Iosif's life that miracles play a secondary role in his *Lives*. A few are present nevertheless. One, taking a cue from Iosif's own writings, proclaims that divine judgment was at work in the fate of some of the heretics who died miserably.[96] Iosif himself is said to have delayed the death of Prince Ivan of Ruza or to have revived him in order to administer last rites. Once, by means of prayer, Iosif expelled a 'vicious demon' from a man at Vespers. Iosif also is said to have had the power to elicit full confessions and even to have been a seer at the end of his life. Even though he was blind, he could recognize and interpret passages in books, and it is claimed that in 1514, a year before his death, he foresaw the defeat of the Muscovite army by the combined forces of Poland and Lithuania at Orsha.[97]

Only one *Life* records posthumous miracles—four of them, and they are all didactic and related to his tomb. The Novgorodian serving man, Dmitrii Vyposvky, was stricken and immobilized by tremors until cured by calling on Iosif at his tomb. Dmitrii subsequently became a monk and died in peace. The plebeian monk, Isikhei, obedient for thirty years, surreptitiously went to a neighboring village, drank a glass of the mild Russian beer known as *kvass*, and immediately fell ill. Conveyed to Iosif's grave, Isikhei confessed, partially recovered, spent his remaining days 'in tears and repentance' in the infirmary, and died in peace. Prince

95. Dosifei Toporkov, *Nadgrobnoe slovo*, 135–36. Savva Cherny, *Zhitie*, 492–93.

96. AfED, 472–73. Belokurov, *Zhitie*, 36. Cf. Goldfrank, 'Burn, Baby, Burn'.

97. Dosifei Toporkov, *Nadgrobnoe slovo*, 135–6. Savva Cherny, *Zhitie*, 470–72. Belokurov, *Zhitie*, 46. For Russian and Polish versions of the huge battle of Orsha (Orsza), which checked twenty years of steady westward advance by Moscow, see Vernadsky, *Russia at the Dawn*, 154–55, 162, and Reddaway, *Cambridge History of Poland* 1:304–305. The brief notice in Davies, *God's Playground* 1:142–43, relies on untrustworthy Polish accounts.

Andrei-Arsenii Golenin, who had richly endowed the monastery and then served humbly as a monk, could not bear Iosif's death and prayed continuously at his grave to follow him. Arsenii soon fell ill and died after a vision in which Iosif said, 'If I have obtained mercy before God, then you shall soon pass from this life'. Subsequently the monk-seer Selifont claimed to have beheld Iosif and Arsenii together in the next world. Another nobleman-monk, Andrei-Arsenii Kvashnin-Nevezhin, questioned Iosif's customs and, despite Vasilii III's advice, departed for Kirillov. Here, however, after reviling Iosif's *Rule*, Arsenii was stricken ill at the grave of Kirill, ordered back to Iosifov by the prestigious elder Gurii Tushin (another former disciple of Nil Sorsky), and only cured by praying at Iosif's tomb. Subsequently this Arsenii lived in full obedience, and his body remained whole for ten years after his death. The Volokolamsk *Patericon* has a similar tale of the Novgorodian *ieromonakh* (priest-monk) Isaiah, who disparaged the monastery, but then when he fell ill only was cured after a vision of Iosif together with the Virgin which prompted a full repentance.[98]

Iosif was canonized locally in 1579 and nationally in 1591.[99] His monastery flourished in wealth and influence through the 1560s, when a reaction against Ivan IV's domestic terror seems to have worked against the cloister.[100] Until then and well beyond the Russian Church could be defined as 'Josephite' in terms of official attitudes toward ecclesiastical land, widowed priests, ritualism, heresy, and the sanctity of an Orthodox Sovereign who protects the Church,[101] not to say the popularity of commemorations.[102] Iosif's *Rule* was the most influential such monastic instrument in

98. Dosifei Toporkov, *Nadgrobnoe slovo*, 137. Savva Cherny, *Zhitie*, 493–99. *Volokolamskii paterik*, 212–13, 215–16. Neither version of the Golenin story mentions that his mother accused Iosif of short-changing her with the specific memorial services rendered by the monastery in return for the family's grants: PIV, 179–82.

99. Golubinsky, *Istoriia kanonizatsii,* 115–17.

100. Zimin, KFV, 314; AI 1, No. 216, 410–11.

101. Zimin, *Peresvetov*, 71–101.

102. Steindorff, *Memoria*, 243–48.

sixteenth-century Muscovy and a model for other foundations and for reforming prelates.[103] In this respect Iosif may be compared to the great Byzantine reforming cœnobiarchs, such as Theodore the Studite and Timothy of Evergetis. Iosif's monastery, however, was devastated when the Poles occupied it in the early seventeenth century Time of Troubles and only reconstructed in its present dimensions in the latter 1600s[104] (and again after World War II). In the seventeenth century, however, it was only one of several important provincial cloisters.

Iosif's ideas, though, continued to be influential until the mid-seventeenth century, when Roman Catholicism started to make inroads in Muscovite theological thinking, and the culture of contracted commemorative services waned.[105] The Old Believers, who went into schism in the latter half of that century, continued to regard him as a Father because of his commitment to tradition.[106] The schismatics' opponents also owed something to Iosif. The official Church followed his strict Orthodoxy and insisted upon authority and discipline, while Tsar Aleksei (r. 1645–1676) accepted Iosif's glorification of the Orthodox Sovereign's power in the church and state. Some of the secular magnates, or boyars, were anti-'Josephite' in their opposition to a politically and economically powerful Church, as were certain prelates, among them Patriarch

103. Iosif had a decisive influence upon the monastic rules and instructions of Kornilii Komel'sky (d. 1537/38), Metropolitan Daniil (1522–39), the Archbishop of Novgorod, later Metropolitan of Moscow, Makarii (1526–42-63), and Gerasim Boldinsky (d. 1554). Kornilii composed for his monastery a Rule based largely on Iosif's. Daniil and Makarii utilized Iosif's Rule for their brief rules for monasteries under their diocesan control. Gerasim, a former leatherworker, who founded four monasteries, left an oral testament-rule with several key provisions similar to Iosif's. See Kornilii Komel'sky, *Ustav ili pravila.* Lur'e, 'Ustav Korniliia'. Zhmakin, *Daniil*, Appendix 2, 39–44. Al 1, No. 292: 531–34. Kozhanchikov, *Stoglav* 39,49–50,52. Krushel'nitskaia, 'Zaveshchanie-Ustav Gerasima Boldinskogo'. On Theodore and Timothy, see below, Ch. II, Iosif's Sources.

104. Voronin and Sakharova, 'Novye materialy', 107–08. Moshin, L.G., *et al.*, *Russkie Monastyri*, 328–33.

105. Florovsky, *Puti* (transl.), 1–113. Treadgold, *The West in Rusia and China* 1:54–83. Steindorff. *Memoria*, 236–39.

106. See Barskov, *Pamiatniki*, 391. Pascal, *Avvakum*, 469. Zen'kovsky, 364.

Nikon (1652–1666), who opposed state inference in ecclesiastical affairs and the monasteries that supported the Tsar.[107]

The 'Josephite' tradition became less relevant in the eighteenth century when the Enlightenment and secularism came to Russia and the Church lost both its autocephaly and its lands. Nevertheless, Iosif's works continued to be read and copied in monasteries into the nineteenth century, which enjoyed a revival of church activity and Russian interest in the country's past.[108] Conservative Russian churchmen tended to admire Iosif and accept his views on the controversies of the time. Liberals generally respected his talent, but favored the seemingly more 'critical' thinking, humane attitudes, and consistent otherworldliness of Nil Sorsky. Soviet Marxist scholars tended to sympathize with dissidents, free-thinkers, and heretics in the Muscovite past.[109]

Other twentieth-century scholarship has continued to build upon the interpretations of Iosif put forth in the nineteenth century. *Emigré* Russians were inclined to accept their predecessors' conclusion that Iosif's piety, with its strengths, weaknesses, and brutal fanaticism, was typical of his time and reflected his civilization.[110] At the same time, these scholars generally believed his claim that he 'collected in order to give away'. Thomas Špidlik, SJ, has researched the various points of contact between Iosif and the overall Christian monastic tradition, and thereby provided an excellent service to ecumenists as well as scholars.[111] German specialists have investigated the deep structures of Iosif's theology and the role of his monastery in the rationalization of memorial services, as well as his *Enlightener* and his inquisitorial activities.[112] American scholars have analyzed his relation to older traditions and the Western influences that became pronounced in Russia in the latter

107. PIV, 97.

108. AfED, 465

109. L:IB, 7–38.

110. Fedotov, *Mind* 2:23–315. Florovsky, *Puty*, 16–19. Kologrivof, *Essai*, 214–43. Smolitsch, *Mönchtum* 101–18. Meyendorff, 'Partisans', 28–36.

111. *Joseph de Volokolamsk*, 3–126.

112. Holzwarth, *"Prosvetitel"*. Hösch, *Orthodoxie und Häresie*. Steindorff, *Memoria*.

part of the fifteenth century, and have examined his fanaticism in the light of subsequent anti-semitism and the politics of inquisition, his political doctrines as well as his monasticism in the light of sociology of religion, and his place in the development of Russian sermonizing.[113] Soviet Russian scholars, while appearing sometime hostile to religion, private property, and anything connected with 'feudalism,' in fact made splendid studies of his manuscript tradition, his political and social ideas, and his monastery and its role as a center of learning.[114]

Iosif's individuality is still remembered by the Russian Church. His festival occupies a special place in the *Typicon* issued in 1956 by the Patriarchate of Moscow.[115] At the end of the twentieth century, under conditions of full liberty, a quasi-privileged status, and a renewed defensive stance toward other Christian churches and sects, the post-Soviet Russian Orthodox Church continues to treat him as an extraordinary figure and revere him especially for his energetic social activism and defense of Orthodoxy.[116]

113. *Inter alia*: Billington, *Icon*, 55–97. Treadgold, *West 1:* 1–23. Raeff, 'Early Theorist'. Huttenbach, 'Judaizing Heresy'. Bushkovitch, *Religion and Society*, 13–44. Goldfrank, 'Perspectives'; 'Inquisitions'.

114. The most important are Lur'e's and Zimin's publications and works: AfED, PIV, L:IB, Z:KFV, and KTsDR.

115. The 1956 Soviet Russian 'Jerusalem' *Tüpikon*, issued by the Moscow Patriarchate, has the following untypically individualistic troparion in Iosif's honor (65V-66):

As the edification of ascetics,
The beauty of the Fathers.
The bearer of mercy,
The lamp of discretion,
All the congregating faithful praise
The teacher of meekness,
The shamer of heresy,
The Russian star:
Praying to the Lord,
Have mercy on our souls.

116. See Döpmann, 'Zur Bedeutung Iosif Volockijs', 680.

II

Iosif's Rule

The Structure of the Texts

Иosif's corpus of monastic writings includes his Brief Rules written probably by 1504,[1] his Extended Rule, completed by 1514–15 (or so designed by his disciples to appear this way),[2] and several short, related pieces: a brief, formu-

1. The Brief Rule was discovered by Lur'e and published by him in PIV, 296–319, according to the earliest known copy of any of Iosif's rules, Codex No. 326/346 of the Solovetsky Monastery Collection, located in the Saltykov-Shchedrin State Public Library in Leningrad, now again St Petersburg. The manuscript was donated to Iosifov Monastery by one of the elders, Nil Polev, in 1513/1514. Following the Brief Rule in the manuscript is the earliest surviving copy of the (Brief) *Enlightener*, thought by Lur'e and others definitely to have been composed before November 1504, but recently given a 1508 *terminus ad quem* by Andrei Pliguzov: AfED, 438–47. Pliguzov, 'O khronologii', 1058.

2. The Extended Rule was published in 1868 from the official version placed by Metropolitan Makarii in his *Great Menaia* in 1552, now Codex No. 996 of the Synodal Collection, in the State Historical Museum in Moscow. The dates of the Extended Rule given here are based on several considerations. The style of the fundamental parts (Discourses I-IX) approximates that of the 'Account of the *Synodicon*' (See below, XIII/1.22 and Appendix I), written most likely in 1504–1507 and definitely before Discourse XIII was composed. The latter parts of the Rule, however, assume the stone refectory, not begun until 1506, and the monastery council, not mentioned in Iosif's Testament to Vasilii III in 1507, but spoken of in a final letter of 1514–15. See VMCh, 503,597. PIV, 239–40. K:VPS, 355–56. Iosif, Ieromonakh, *Opis'*, 20/39, 146/507. It is also possible that the final version of the Extended Rule was a late or posthumous compilation by Iosif's

laic Missive-Tradition composed for an individual monk and containing the provisions of the Extended Rule,[3] a prescript (*prikaz*) directed to the responsible elders and council brothers prohibiting intoxicating beverages,[4] and the introduction to the monastery's *Synodicon* (commemoration book)[5]. He also may have composed or edited his own Cell Rule—the formulary for the monk's daily life.[6]

The Brief Rule is simply 'Abba Iosif's Discourses to his Disciples from the Divine Writings concerning the Cœonobitic Life'. There are eleven such sermons (called here I^{B}, II^{B}, . . . XI^{B}), which comprise more a statement of principle based on Scripture and patristics than a regulatory instrument. The overall design is not complex.

The following outline describes the structure of the Brief Rule and its component parts. The translator has arbitrarily divided the Discourses into paragraphs and grouped them. The sources mentioned in the outline are discussed in the next section of this chapter.

Introduction^{B}

Int^{B}.1	List of discourses.
Int^{B}.2	Notice of general content and use.
[Int^{B}.3–6]	Donor's inscription and plea for remembrance.[7]

---

disciples in the 1520s-1530s, the date of the earliest surviving text, as Pliguzov has assumed: 'O khronologii', 1058.

3. PIV, 236–38, 284–85.

4. PIV, 238–39, 285.

5. Only the original sermon section of the 'Account of the *Synodicon*' has been published: K:VPS, pp 355–57. The rest, including Iosif's choices of patristic authority, the names of various people to be remembered, some stipulated services, and what may be more original writings of Iosif, remains unpublished.

6. Nikol'sky, 'Obshchestvennaia i keleinaia zhizn', 902–03. See below, note 23.

7. This preface, which comprises pp. 3–3^{v} of Solovetsky Codex No. 326/346, is surely not part of the original, while the preceding paragraph indicates that the Brief Rule and Brief *Enlightener* may have been copied in this form as a special edition for someone like Nil Polev to use outside of the monastery.

Discourse I^{B} Good order in the church and communal prayer.

I^{B}.1	Introduction: fidelity to the service *typicon*.
I^{B}.2–10	Hurrying to the church service—from various sources, including Chrysostom and Climacus.
I^{B}.11–23	Value and method of commmunal prayer, avoidance of leaving the service early or talking, adapted in part from Iosif's modification in the *Enlightener* of Chrysostom's Antioch sermons.
I^{B}.24–25	Disciplining talkers—also adapted from Chrysostom via the *Enlightener*.
I^{B}.26	Conclusion: safeguarding the service *typicon*.

Discourse II^{B} Foods and Beverages

II^{B}.1	Enjoinment to select the simple, from the *typica*.
II^{B}.2–8	Against eating-in-secret, from Pseudo-Basil, Symeon the New Theologian, (?Pseudo-)Pope Gregory the Great, and Nikon.

Discourse III^{B} Good order in the refectory.

III^{B}.1–3	Need for refectory reverence, from *typica* models and *apophthegmata*.

Discourse IV^{B} Garments, footwear, and other 'things'.

IV^{B}.1–14	Principles of monastic poverty, composed of citations found in Nikon.
IV^{B}.15	Requirement of perfected non-possession.

Discourse V^{B} Books and Icons.

V^{B}.1–10	Application of perfected non-possession to books and icons, from *apophthegmata* and Pseudo-Basil, partially in Nikon; with a special polemic against excluding these from the category of 'things'.

Discourse VI^{B} Against talking after Compline.

VI^{B}.1–3	Brief sermon based on the *typica* and Pseudo-Basil.

Discourse VII^{B} Against leaving the monastery without authorization.

VII.1–4 Brief sermon based on Pseudo-Basil, *apophthegmata* and *typica*.

Discourse VIII^{B} Labor, community work, and individual services.

VIII^{B}.1–15 Revision, based on *apophthegmata*, taken mainly from Nikon, to modify John Cassian's analysis of labor and despondency.

VIII^{B}.16–24 On silent labor: against jesting and joking—citations found mainly in Nikon.

VIII^{B}.25–29 Hagiographic and apophthegmatic modifications of Pseudo-Basil's strictures concerning obedience and individual offices: long morality legend from Symeon the New Theologian.

Discourse IX^{B} Against drunkenness and intoxicating beverages.

IX.1–5 Brief sermon against drunkenness, based upon the New Testament, Chrysostom, and the monastic corpus.

IX.6–9 Prohibition of intoxicating beverages, followed by polemic overruling the *typicon* traditions that allow measured amounts of wine.

Discourse X^{B} Against boys in the cloister.

X.1–7 Brief sermon based on a few *apophthegmata*, some as in Nikon, and on Pseudo-Basil, on the lustful danger of boys and adolescents to monks.

Discourse XI^{B} Against women in the cloister.

XI.1–5 Brief sermon based upon a variety of sources found mainly in Nikon.

The Extended Rule—Iosif's 'Will and Testament . . . concerning the Monasterial and Monastic Institution'—is a complex of discourses and sets of regulations whose constituent parts are structurally and thematically interrelated. It has fourteen discourses (called here Int., I, II, . . . XIV) that contain more regulations and devote relatively less space to sermons. I–IX are revision of I^{B}–XI^{B} and, together with Int.—the testamentary introduction, X—the apology for the Rule, and XI—a sermon to the successor hegumen, constitute an early recension of the Extended Rule. XII is the 'Will and Testament in Brief', a short recension of Int. and the regulations contained in I–IX. XIII—the instruction to and defense of the monastery's ruling council—is followed here by nine 'Traditions' (called here XIII/i, XIII/ii, . . . XIII/ix), which explain and amplify the regulations of I–IX and XII from the standpoint of the 'council brothers and all the monastery officials'. These are followed by protocol instructions for meetings (called here XIII/A). XIV contains nine sets of penances for infractions of the Rule. Taken together, XII, XIII/i–XIII/ix and XIV constitute a comprehensive regulatory manual, while each of these three components is itself also a 'mini-rule', as, in fact, is the table of contents (Int.10).

The following outline of the Extended Rule adheres to the same principles as the outline of the Brief Rule.

Introduction

Int.1–9	Testamentary and topical introduction based upon the opening sections of other rules and testaments going back to Pseudo-Basil of Caesarea, Climacus, Pseudo-Theodore the Studite, and others.
Int.10	Table of Contents
Int.11–15	Summary testamentary closing and transition to the Discourses.

Discourse I Good order in the church and communal prayer.

I.1	Introduction: fidelity to the service *typicon*.
I.2–10	Hurrying to the church service—from various sources, including Chrysostom and Climacus—almost the same as in I^{B}.
I.11–18	Value and method of commmunal prayer—both adapted from I^{B} (ultimately from Iosif's modification in the *Enlightener* of Chrystostom's Antioch sermons).
I.19	Section conclusion: safeguarding the service *typicon*.

I.20–30 Disciplining talkers—also from Chrysostom and Climacus, among others, but more original in relation to I^{B} and the *Enlightener*.

I.31–35 Enforcing good order in the church, based in part on the Cell Rule.

Discourse II Good Order in the refectory; foods and beverages.

II.1–6 Need for refectory reverence, seemingly expanded from III^{B}—based upon *typica* models and *apophthegmata*.[8]

II.7–18 Practice of refectory reverence—in part from the Pseudo-Basilian corpus and the Cell Rule.

II.9–27 Against eating-in-secret—revision of II^{B}, itself on part taken from Pseudo-Basil and the *typica*.

II.28–35 The dietary regimes for Iosif's three orders of monks—connected to Byzantine and Rus regulations and table customaries and to Rus customs.

Discourse III Garments, footwear, and other things.

III.1–14 Principles of monastic poverty—reproduction of most of IV^{B}, composed of citations found in Nikon.

III.15–19 Principle of perfected non-possession—adapted from V^{B}, again composed of citations found in Nikon.

III.20–22 Concretely, no possessing or other such individualistic actions without permission—in part from the Cell Rule.

III.25–31 List of clothing issued to each order of monks, based in part upon the *typicon* tradition, and defense of the tripartite division of the monks with reference to the Parable of the Seeds (Mt 13:23).

III.32–38 Responsibility toward monastic property: against theft or appropriation of community goods or found items.

III.39 Against unauthorized inscriptions in books.

8. Of course it is possible here and elsewhere that a Brief Rule section was contracted or modified from an earlier, fuller version that is reflected in the Extended Rule.

Discourse IV Against talking after Compline.

IV.1–3	Brief sermon, identical to VI^{B}.
IV.4	Provision for enforcement.

Discourse V Against leaving the monastery without authorization.

V.1–4	Brief sermon, virtually identical to VII^{B}

Discourse VI Labor, community work, obedience, individual offices.

VI.1–11	Revision of VIII^{B}—based on *apophthegmata*, taken mainly from Nikon, to modify John Cassian's analysis of labor and despondency.
VI.12	Requirement of permssion to leave work.
VI.13–17	On silent labor: against jesting and joking—shortened from VIII^{B}
VI.18–34	Modeled on Climacus' 'Step Four': hagiographical legends and *apophthegmata* emphasizing total obedience, including revision of VIII^{B} version of morality legend from Symeon the New Theologian.
VI.35–47	Revision of VIII^{B}—hagiographic and *apophthegmatic* modifications of Pseudo-Basil's strictures concerning individual offices.

Discourse VII Against drunkenness and intoxicating beverages.

VII.1–5	Same as in IX^{B}—brief sermon against drunkennness based upon the New Testament, Chrysostom, and the monastic corpus.
VII.6	Prohibition of intoxicating beverages, without the polemic of IX^{B}.

Discourse VIII Against women in the cloister.

VIII.1–5	Same as XI^{B}—brief sermon based on a variety of sources found mainly in Nikon

Discourse IX Against boys in the cloister, and other matters.

IX.1–8	Revision of X^{B}—brief sermon based on a few *apophthegmata* and Pseudo-Basil, with added delineation of the places where boys and adolescents are prohibited.

IX.9–15	Additional assorted regulations with supporting *apophthegmata*.
IX.16	Conclusion to the first nine discources.

Discourse X Apology for the Rule accompanied by a short history of early Rus (Kiev period) and Russian monasticism.

X.1–9	'Response to the censorious' and justification of the composing of 'traditions' and 'penances', with inflammatory rhetoric of Philippus Solitarius and adaptations of patristic arguments found in Nikon.
X.10–32	Exemplary tales of over thirty monks in eight monasteries, designed to create a native tradition legitimizing Iosif's own practices and monastic legislation.
X.33–43	Response (based on *apophthegmata* and *Leviticus*) to the claim, 'it is better to live . . . where there is no burden, constraint, or penances'.

Discourse XI Instruction to the successor hegumen and his flock.

XI.1–12	Variety of sources (including Scripture, Climacus, and Nikon) introducing the sanctity, reponsibility and compexity of the pastoral office.
XI.13–17	Eulogy to cœnobitic monasticism under a responsible pastor, adapted from Pseudo-Basil.

Discourse XII The Rule in brief.

XII.Int	Abbeviated version of Int.1–2.
XII.1–9	Expanded list of the regulations from I-IX, without sermons
XII.10–12	Abbreviation of Int. 11–15.

Discourse XIII Instruction to and justification of the monastery's council.

XIII.1–6	Reworking of the themes of XI, applied to the council brothers and the monastery officials.
XIII.7–11	The necessity of following the founder's traditions—based in part on Nikon.

XIII.12–17 The superior's need for help, based on Nikon, and the definition of what is 'humane', taken from Chrysostom.

XIII.18–29 Proper mode of rebuking and correcting, based on Scripture, Basil and Nikon's rendering of Chrysostom and other Fathers.

XIII.30–32 Necessity of evicting the unruly, based on Scripture and X.10–32.

XIII.33–39 Iosif's authorization for the council brothers to select his successor, based on Canon Law.

XIII.40–47 Necessity of having ten or twelve council brothers, with forced analogies from Basil, (Pseudo-)Theodore the Studite and (Pseudo-)Athanasius of Athos.

XIII.48–50 That monastery officials, as well as priests, may administer monastic penances.

XIII.51–55 Defense of structural changes occcasioned by growth and differentiation of the brotherhood and the attainment of material prosperity.

Tradition I Good order in the chuch and communal prayer.

XIII/i.1–3 Summary of XIII and introduction to the nine 'Traditions'.

XIII/i.4–9 Stationing of the council brothers during the church service-based on (Pseudo-)Theodore the Studite and (Pseudo-)Athanasius of Athos.

XIII/i.10–13 Routine for inspectors during Vigils—based on the *typica*.

XIII/i.14–17 Problems of unauthorized talking and leaving services.

XIII/i.18–21 Stationing of the council brothers when the service is in the refectory.

XIII/i.22 Offices for the Dead—reference to Iosif's separate 'Account of the *Synodicon*'.

Tradition II Good Order in the refectory; food and drink.

XIII/ii.1–11 Protocol for refectory behavior based on the *typica*, and stationing of the council brothers in the refectory.

XIII/ii.12–15 Daily routine for inspecting the cloister precincts.

Tradition III Garments, footwear, and the prohibition of unauthorized possessions.

XIII/iii.1–7 Abbreviated version of the regulatory parts of III, written for the council brothes and officials.

Tradition IV Against talking after Compline.

XIII/iv.1–2 Abbreviated version of IV, written for the council brothers and officials.

Tradition V Against leaving the monastery without authorization.

XIII/v.1–3 Practical measures to enforce enclosure.

XIII/v.4–7 Nightly routine of the sentries.

XIII/v.8–12 Daytime routine of the sentries.

XIII/v.13–14 The manner of seigneurial judicial proceedings.

Tradition VI On community work and individual offices.

XIII/vi.1–2 That council brothers and officials shall enforce productivity and decorum and control absenteeism.

Tradition VII Against intoxicating beverages and drunkenness.

XIII/vii.1–3 Revision of second part of IX^{B}—polemic overruling the *typicon* traditions that allow measured amounts of wine.

XIII/vii.4–5 Enforcing this prohibition—related to Iosif's separate *Prescript* concerning this.

Tradition VIII Against women in the cloister.

XIII/viii.1–2 Elaboration of XII.8—how to prevent unauthorized entry of women, and how to conduct women into the church.

Tradition IX Against boys in the cloister, and other matters.

XIII/ix.1–2 Iteration of the necessity of keeping boys away from the cloister.

XIII/ix.3–8 Repetition and expansion of other regulations found in IX.

XIII/ix.9–13	Assorted additional regulations to manorial officials.
XIII/ix.14–22	Elaboration of the themes raised in the Introduction; overall conclusions to XIII and the 'Traditions'.

Protocol for Meetings.

XIII/A.1–8	Protocol based on *typica* with justifications grounded in Scripture and real life.

Discourse XIV The Penances

XIV.1–3	Introduction to the Penances and principles of their application.
XIV.4–34	The nine sets of Penances, with the offenses covered, including the regulations of XII.1–9, and also some found only in Tradition V, VII and IX—modified from the *Penances* attributed to Basil and to Theodore the Studite.
XIV.35–39	Conclusion to the Penances and to the Rule as a whole.

Iosif's Sources

Iosif was both encyclopedic and selective in his use of sources. He aimed explicitly to prove that his regulations and principles were totally consistent with what late medieval Eastern Christendom called the Divine Writings—Scripture, patristic works, hagiography, and canon law. He cited more than seventy-six authorities and used at least two more Fathers without acknowledgement. His readiness to throw together a variety of sources and styles reveals a rhetorical principle analagous to the decoration of a church with diverse frescos and icons, but all contributing to the salvation of souls. His chief interests were asceticism, ritualism, and practical matters, and his choice of sources reflected these concerns.[9] They

9. Russian interest at this time in more purely spiritual literature was also keen, acceleratinng (according to a count of surviving, dated manuscripts) in 1390–1440. A secondary revival of interest occurred in about 1480–1515, the active period of Nil Sorsky, Iosif, and the alleged heretics: Prokhorov, 'Keleinaia isikhastskaia literatura', 317–24.

are almost exclusively Eastern (Egyptian, Levantine, Greek, and early Rus or Russian). The few Latin Fathers he used all date from before 720 and lack the concern for grace and for the details of administration and structure that distinguished some Latins from Greeks during the period of the undivided Church.[10] Among the hundred-odd earlier rules—Eastern and Western—which this commentator has read, Iosif's striking originality appears to have been his forays into vivid polemic and scathing rhetorical address, more characteristic of doctrinal apologetics than monastic homilies.

Scripture in itself was quantitatively less important for Iosif than were patristic writings. Nevertheless, a careful analysis of Iosif's *Rules* shows that the Bible occupied a central, although not exclusive, place as a foundation for many of the doctrines he developed on his own or took from the monastic Fathers. He grounded in the New Testament his principles regarding poverty, humility, obedience, service, labor, natural talents, temperance, confidence, mutual responsibility, fraternal admonition, and the exercise of authority, and he turned to both Testaments for ideas concerning pastoral responsibility and the afterlife.

The rather obscure, eleventh-century Byzantine Greek ex-soldier and abbot operating in Syria and known chiefly in the Slavic world as Nikon Chernogorets (Nikon of the Black Mountain), compiled two major works: his *Pandects* (*Pandekty*) and his *Taktikon*. These provided Iosif and his contemporaries with models for tracts which themselves are compiled from scripture, patristics, hagiography, and canon law. Iosif borrowed extensively from the following of Nikon's discourses: from the *Taktikon*: Nikon's *Typicon* (No. 1), on pastoral duty (No. 18); from the *Pandekty*: on teaching and admonishing (No. 8), on discipline in general (No. 10), on chastity (No. 12), on judging (No. 29), on proper

10. Compare, for example, the Augustinian and Eastern patristic concepts of original sin, or (Pseudo-)Pope Gregory the Great and Palladius's monastic histories. The Christian East lacks Augustine's 'radical individualism' according to John Meyendorff, but understands sinfulness as humanity's general state. Palladius's *Lausaic History* and other eastern *paterica* are only interested in monks. Gregory, on the other hand, wrote about Italian bishops as well as monks in his *Dialogues*. See Meyendorff, *Byzantine Theology,* 143–46.

clothing (No. 37), on labor (No. 44).[11] Iosif appears to have been faithful to these works in his *Rule*, except that he was harsher in his disciplinary strictures and not at all interested in limiting community property and wealth.[12]

The Old Russian version of the *Asceticon* of Basil of Caesarea (329?-379) included both genuine and spurious works. The most important of Basil's authentic writings for Iosif deal with authority and discipline ('Short Rules,' No. 47, 174; 'Long Rules,' No. 46, 47). Among Basil's presumed spurious writings, Iosif made extensive use of the 'Ascetical Semon and Exhortation on the Renunciation of the World'—a precis of cœnobitic principles—for a variety of problems, and of the 'Penances'. He also borrowed heavily from the preface to the 'Long Rules' and the 'Constitutions,' No. 18 and 22 (the eulogy to the common life) and No. 34 (on common property).[13] Iosif's Brief Rule, with its more stringent attitudes toward individual poverty and labor, was closer than his Extended Rule to the Basilian legacy.

The Ladder of Divine Ascent and the 'Treatise for the Pastor' of John Climacus (479–549), along with many of the seventh-to-tenth century glosses appended to them in the standard Greek copies, were included in the normal Old Russian *Ladder* (*Lestvitsa*). Iosif found in them many useful quotations, especially 'Step' No. 4, which was his model for the Extended Rule section on obedience, and the 'Treatise,' which partiallly served as a model for his Discourse No. 11 (to the successor abbot), as well as a source for his ideas on discipline and the exercise of authority.[14] His

11. For Nikon, see Irénée Doens, 'Nicon'. Porfirii, *Opisanie* 1.237–46. Allison, '*Black Mountain*': the translations in BMFD include only the first two, strictly *typicon* chapters of *Taktikon*. In 1545, the Iosifov library had three old and two new copies of Nikon's 'book': KTsDR, 31.

12. Cf. *Pandekty* 20, 21, 34, 39; AFED, 488–98 *(Prosvetitel'* 13): and below, I.20–29.

13. On the authenticity of Basil's works, see *The New Catholic Encyclopedia* 2:143–44; also Amand de Mendieta, *L'ascèse monastique de saint Basile*; a typical Russian Basilian *Asceticon* is described in *Opisanie rukopisei Solovetskago* 169/86.

14. Russian versions of the *Ladder* are described in Gorsky and Nevostruev, *Opisanie* 2.2:141–46. They contain a varying percentage of the seventh-to-tenth-

treatment of the pastoral office was much less sophisticated than John Climacus's, and the latter's mysticism did not interest Iosif.

The sermons of John Chrysostom (349?-407) were found in several Old Russian (or Old Slavonic) collections, including the *Margaritos* (Pearl)—his Antioch sermons—and the *Zlatostrui* (Golden Stream)—a selection of moral homilies. These sermons and fragments, often scrambled and reintegarted as if with a word processing cut and paste function, could be found in still other collections, one of which contained a cycle of homilies for the church year.[15] Iosif's most important use of Chryostom was to borrow from the Antioch sermons ('On I Have Seen the Lord', Hom. 1; 'On the Inconceivable', Hom. 2–5; 'Against the Jews', Hom. 4) for the basic material of the sermon on community prayer. Three versions are extant: one for all Christians in the *Enlightener* and two for monks in the Rules.[16] Iosif also utilized fragments found in Nikon and perhaps elsewhere for Chrysostom's exegesis (especailly 'On Matthrew' and 'On Ephesians') for such problems as jesting, drunkenness, and judging. Chrysostom also appears to have been Iosif's original source for the blending of monastic and lay spirituality and ethics.

The lives (*paterica*) and sayings (*apophthegmata*) of the Desert Fathers and others were available to Iosif in various forms. Certain unpublished Greek and Old Slavonic (Rus, Bulgarian, and Serbian) *paterica* contain material not found in the published Greek, Latin, and Syriac versions and translations. Thus one cannot readily

---

century glosses of Elias of Crete and others, as well as some original Russian *scholiae*. Gerasim Cherny made a copy of the *Ladder* for Iosifov in the 1480s or 1490s—codex *Eparkh*. 328(457). Among the other early Iosifov *Ladders* were copies by Simeon Stremoukhov, later Bishop of Suzdal (1509–15), and the Council Elder and calligrapher Gelasii Sukholeny (Sukholenov), as well as a gift from Archbishop Gennadii: KTsDR, 31, 348.

15. These works are described in Gorsky and Nevostruev, *Opisanie* 2.2:126, 2.3:300, and also in Titov, *Opisanie* 2:751/2129. 752/5688, 753/3842. See also Granstrem, 'Ioann Zlatoust'. One of the original Iosifov monks, Gerasim Cherny, made a copy of the *Margaritos*: KTsDR, 30.

16. See below I^B18–20,22–24, I.13–20, and AfED, 351–56 *(Prosvetitel'* 7:204–19).

ascertain the degree of Iosif's fidelity to this type of source.[17] Nevertheless Iosif seems to have referred directly to the Slavonic or Rus versions of the *Sayings of the Fathers* and the *Lausaic History* for his doctrines concerning table manners, absolute renunciation of personal possessions, unauthorized absence from the monastery, labor, obedience, and the prohibition of boys. On the other hand, he found in Nikon collated sayings concerning modesty in dress, avoidance of women, and (again) labor. Iosif's most demanding ascetic ideals, therefore, hearken directly back to the origin of Christian monasticism.

The *Paranesis* of Ephraim on Syria (ca. 306–73),[18] an Orthodox version of the *Mystical Treatises* of the seventh-century Nestorian Isaac the Syrian (Isaac of Ninenveh),[19] and many of the *Hymns*, *Catechisms*, and other works of Symeon the New Theologian (949?-1022) were popular in medieval Russia.[20] Iosif used quite a few statements attributed to them, not all of which can be located in the originals. On the other hand, some of Ephraim's purported statements are quoted and attributed to him by Nikon. Iosif, it should be noted, utilized Ephraim, Isaac, and Symeon for external

17. See Heppell, 'Slavonic Translations'. For a review of recent literature, see Heppell, *The Paterik of the Kievan Caves Monastery*, xx-xxi. Among the various *paterica* in Iosifov in 1545 were copies by Nil Polev—an alphabetized *patericon*—and the scribe Varlaam Krivoshein; these were not the same as the *Lausaic History*: KTsDR, 31–33.

18. See Arkhangel'sky, *Tvoreniia* 3:1–37, and *Dictionnaire de spiritualité* 4:788–822. The first 57 sermons of an 111-sermon Iosifov *Paranesis* from about 1500 survive—*Eparkh.* 332(465); another was copied by the Tikhon Zvorykin, the Iosifov Treasurer in 1509; and a third was donated by Gurii the Old, a Council Elder who under Iosif at times was Treasurer and Cellarer: KTsDR, 30, 347–48. Z:KFV, 118–19.

19. The typical Old Russian collection of Isaac the Syrian of Nineveh, purged of any Nestorian motifs by Greek intermediaries, is described in Gorsky and Nevostruev 2.2:131. See also *Dictionnaire de spiritualité* 7:2041–54. Nil Polev donated a 91-sermon copy of Isaac's works to Iosifov in 1513—codex *Eparkh.* 320(444); Tikhon Zvorykhin copied another: KTsDR, 32, 342.

20. An Old Russian collection of Symeon the New Theologian is described in Gorsky and Nevostruev 2.2:164, and in *Opisanie rukopisei Solovetskogo* 1:271/793. Gelasii Sukoleny copied such a collection around 1500—the codex *Eparkh.* 333(467)—Tikhon Zvorykhin another: KTsDR, 7, 31, 348.

comportment and ethical wisdom, not spirituality or mysticism.[21] In this respect it is interesting that some Slavic versions of Symeon, but not the original, commence with his *Instruction* on formal behavior in the monastery, and Iosif borrowed from it quite freely.[22]

Among the genuine rules and *typica*, with sections on ritual and discipline used by Iosif, are the *Jerusalem Typicon*, originating in Saint Sabas's Monastery; three closely related *typica*: the *Hypotyposis* (*Rule*) of Pseudo-Theodore the Studite (749–826), the *Hypotyposis* (*Rule*) of Athanasius of Mt. Athos (920–1003), and the *Typicon* in Nikon's *Taktikon*; the *Penances* of Pseudo-Basil and (Pseudo-)Theodore; and the genre of Russian *starchestvo* (*geronticon*) or cell rule—a manual containing both the rituals to be observed throughout the day and positive and negative instructions concerning behavior in church, refectory, and elsewhere. Iosif was also inspired by the *Lives* and rules of (Pseudo-) Theodore Studite and (Pseudo-)Athanasius, by Theodore's *Iambic Verses*, and by the oral and written traditions of Kirillov (Saint Kirill's/Cyril's) Monastery in Beloozero.[23] Some of Iosif's precise instructions

21. See below, II^{B}.6/II.21, IV^{B}.12/III.12, VIII^{B}.26/VI.34.

22. This *Instruction* (orig. No. 26), *O ezhe kako podobaet inokom prebyvati*, contains additions from his *Instruction* on repentance (No. 26): Cf. his *Catechisms (Catechèses, Discourses)*. To my knowledge, there has been no systematic study of the Slavic Symeon.

23. For the development of the Greek and Russian *typica* see Mansvetov, *Tserkovnyi ustav*, 83–140, 168–96, 222–27, 265–94, and now the extensive commentary to BMFD, 21–50, 193–204, 295–309, 441–53, 607–20, 859–71, 1093–1106, 1295–1302, 1483–94, as well as Gregory Meyers, 'Slavonic Witnesses', 367–72. About seventy years before Iosif entered Pafnutiev Monastery, Metropolitan Kiprian of Moscow (re. 1381–82, 1389–1408) had introduced the prevailing Byzantine 'Jerusalem Typicon'. This had supplanted the earlier 'Studite Typicon', which had combined Sabaite or Jerusalem (monastic) liturgical elemets with the Imperial 'Liturgy of the Great Church'. Characteristic examples, including Old Russian Studite and Jerusalem *typica*, are described in Gorsky and Nevostruev, *Opisanie* 3.1:380–89. According to Beck, the *Hypotyposis* attributed to Theodore is of later provenance; the *Iambic Verses, Penances,* and *Testament* are possibly, but not clearly, genuine; one scholar has considered only the first set of the *Penances* to be Theodore's (Beck, *Kirche und theologische Literatur*, 491–95). For convenience's sake, '(pseudo-)Theodore' is used throughout this work. See also Nikol'sky, *Obshchestvennaia i keleinaia zhizn'*, 897–907. The sixteenth-century Kirillov Monastery *Starchestvo* contains the cell rules from Kirillov and from Nil Sorsky's hermitage as well as *The Cell Rule of the Venerable Elders*

were very close to these sources, though his supervisory system appears to have been more elaborate, at least on paper. His penances, on the other hand, were approximately half as severe as Pseudo-Theodore's, which themselves were much lighter than Pseudo-Basil's.

In both style and substance, Iosif's regulations in general and penances in particular hearken back to original cœnobitism and the Pachomian legacy, which was unavailable to him in written form,[24] as well as to the Basilian, Sabaite (Jerusalem), Studite, and Athonite creative and reform impulses. Whether he also acquired anything peculiar to the critically important, eleventh-century Byzantine, Evergertian tradition, perhaps via the *typicon* of the Serbian Hilender (Chilandar) Monastery on Mt. Athos—the chief center for Byzantine influence in Russia via the South Slavs in the fourteenth and fifteenth centuries—is an open question. That Iosif stipulated equality of food and drink for all his monks and the public reading of the Rule means that he can be considered, among other things, as a Russian representative of the Evergetian legacy.[25]

---

of Iosifov Monastery: 82–84^{V}, 98–99^{V}. But no written rule from Kirill himself and no Kirillov rule anything like losif's is extant, only fragments contained in Kirill's *Life*: Iablonsky, *Pakhomii*, Appendix, 22–24.

24. Viellieux, *Pachomian koinonia*, especially 2:145–67 (the 'Precepts') and 3:13–48 (the Penances). Iosif also has a surprising and surely coincidental similarity in style and tone to Theodora (Theodule) Synadene of Bebaia Elpis's early fourteenth-century *Typikon* for her convent.

25. The *typicon* of Timothy of Evergetis (author's original, 1054–70, revised, 1098–1118) played a central role in Byzantine monastic reform—according to Robert Jordan, 'undoubtedly the most influential Byzantine founder's *typicon* ever written'—and was the major, often *verbatim* source for the early thirteenth-century *typicon* of Sava of Hilender, later Archbishop of Serbia. Evergetis is claimed to have been responsible for four subsequent, standard, Byzantine cœnobitic *typicon* principles, principles which Iosif also demanded: equality of food and drink for all monks, silent attentiveness to the reading at the refectory, periodic reading of the rule to the monks, and the co-governing role of preeminent monks: BMFD, 454–68, 501–06. Cf. Sava of Serbia, *Tipik*, which in the most crucial and seemingly original Evergetian element—equality of food and drink—is strangely silent, but informed Hilender monks must have known of it. (The other clearly original element, according to the surving text, is the periodic public reading of the Rule.) Among the usual Evergetian/post-Evergetian

The Old Rus and Russian nomocanons or collections of canon law (*Kormchaia kniga*—the Helmsman's Book) were quite extensive by the fifteenth century. They usually included, among other items, the Rules of the Apostles and of local and ecumenical Councils, the canons of such Fathers as Basil of Caesarea, the standard sixth-to-ninth-century East Roman compilations of laws relating to the Church—the *Syntagma of Fourteen Titles* and the *Collection of Eighty-Seven Chapters*, and specimens of Byzantine civil law.[26] Only two of six canons cited by Iosif were taken from the available nomocanons; the other four are found in Nikon. Iosif used canon law to justify his position on the mode of dress, segregation by gender, and the selection of abbots by the brotherhood, but he augmented a canon to legitimize the use of force to control behavior inside a church (I.28). Late fifteenth-century Russian monasticism itself diverged from canon law (though not Byzantine praxis) in the independence of cloisters from episcopal control and the vast seigneurial holdings—practices which Iosif energetically defended. Undoubtedly his most important recourse to canon law was his attempt to bolster the principle whereby the leading monks choose the superior (XIII.34–35).

Iosif made use of works by or attributed to Hippolytus of Rome,[27] Pope Gregory the Great—including the Life of Benedict of Nursia which was available in the Christian East,[28] Peter Damascenus, Macarius the Great, and Philippus Solitarius (not identified). Iosif used the *Lives* of Dositheus of Gaza, John Damascene,

---

subjects absent from Iosif's Rules and related documents are the following: the Hours, communion, tonsure, the special position of the cellarer (here the Russian equivalent of the Byzantine oeconomus/steward), favors to relatives, alienation of property, bookkeeping, total number of monks, inspection of cells, investiture of officials, and the novitiate. It should be noted that Iosif's Rule did not reproduce the Studite, Athonian, or Nikonian legacies in their entirely either.

26. Žužek, *Kormčaja Kniga*, 7–42. Iosif used a collection of canon law that attributed Justinian's *novellae* to Gregory of Agrigentum and Patriarch Photius's Nomocanon to Justinian. See below, XIII.34–35, Sreznevsky, *Obozrenie*, 71–99.

27. Two latter fifteenth-century codices from Iosifov with the Hippolytus 'Sermon on the End of the World' survive, including one in Iosif's hand—*Eparkh.* 357(536): KTsDR, 369–70.

28. The Iosifov monk Simeon Stremoukhov copied the *Dialogues* 1503–09: codex *Eparkh* 317(440): KTsDR, 30, 340–41.

Euthymius the Great, Febronia the Martyr, Theodosius the Great, Basil the Younger (attributed to Basil the Great), the Fathers of Kiev's Pechersky Monastery, Sergii of Radonezh, Metropolitan Aleksii of Moscow, and Kirill of Beloozero. Iosif found in Nikon selections from the works and *Lives* of Pseudo-Clement of Rome, Pachomius the Geat, John Cassian (not identified), Dorotheus of Gaza, Barsanuphius of Gaza, Patriarch Methodius Confessor, Sabas of Jerusalem, and Symeon the Stylite, as well as extracts from canon law and the *typica*. The Russian *Lives* were important for Iosif's historical section, but most of the other sources simply added insight or the weight to their authority to the doctrines of the Desert Fathers, Basil, Chrysostom, canon law, and the *typica*. John Cassian furnished the structure of Iosif's analysis of labor, and Philippus Solitarius gave Iosif some imflammatory apologetic rhetoric (X.I). His singling out of John Damascene, one of the venerated hymnographers to the Mother of God, as an example of extreme humility and obedience (I.27) is significant in the light of his also serving as Iosif's chief source for his doctrine of faith and reason and for the defense of the veneration of icons and sacred objects in the *Enlightener*—as if to lend more weight to Damascene's, and by extension Iosif's theological authority.[29] The gregorian Benedict, however, was just another monastic Father for Iosif (I^B.16/I.24). Far more important was (Pseudo-)Gregory's stand on the efficacy of prayers for the dead, which Iosif, in a mode analagous to Western arguments regarding purgatory, used in his 'Account . . . of the *Synodicon* and the Daily Commemoration'.[30]

By and large Iosif was faithful to the text, or at least to the sense of his sources and to the legacy of Byzantine cœnobitic reform impulses. He was also masterful in expressing his own thought in the words of others. When it suited his purpose, however, he amended canon law to justify clerics' using force against the unruly (I.28); he edited patristic exhortations to pastors to teach

29. AfED, 394 (*Prosvetitel'* 8:333–34). Cf. John of Damascus, *Exact Exposition*, I.4. PIV, 71–72

30. Le Goff, *Birth of Purgatory*, 52–95; cf. Clark, *Pseudo-Gregorian Dialogues*.

in order to legitimize his own composition of a Rule (X.2,9); and he rewrote Russian monastic history to create precedents for his traditions (X.10–31). His willingness to deviate from his sources was consistent with his pragmatism and common sense. It was not so much Iosif as Russian practices of the fifteenth century that differed from Greek customs and earlier Eastern Christian models. The clerical administration of corporal punishment, for example, may have been uncanonical, but it was customary (and not only in Russia). Iosif's innovativeness lay chiefly in his polemical style, his sanctioning of Muscovite ways, and his attentivenes to seigneurial affairs and to prevalent abuses, not in his choice of authorities.

The Content of the Rule

Spiritual and Monastic Lexicon

As a result of her conversion to Byzantine Christianity, Russia acquired a theological and moral vocabulary with roots going back in places to biblical Hebrew. The educated Russian monk had as part of his working vocabulary a Slavic version of the Greek monastic lexicon: for example, *blagochinie* for the ευταξία (decorum/good order), *poshchenie* for ἄσκησις (asceticism), *sokrushenie* for συντριβή (contrition). All the same, Iosif would have been hard pressed fully to explain his psycho-spiritual terms, for neither the Greek sources nor the Slavic translations were lexically consistent in describing the mind and the mental processes. Since he was an apologetic, polemical, and practical theologian, as well as a politician and ideologist, he accepted the formulations of his sources and displayed no inclination to investigate, speculate, or systematically synthesize, when he addressed moral or psychological issues.

The most difficult terms to render into English with precision and fidelity to Iosif's understanding are *pomysl'*, *dushevnyi*, *myslennyi*, and, *chuvstvennyi*.

Pomysl', besides meaning *mind/thought*, was the technical term for what Evagrius Ponticus and John Cassian termed λογισμός or *cogitatio*—a thought or state of mind or attitude in reference to one of the seven or eight 'deadly sins' or temptations—which subsequently became part of standard monastic theory. In the translation we use (*dangerous*) *thought*.

The adjective *dushevnyi*, from *dusha* (soul), can be translated by our *spiritual* only at the expense of blurring the classical, technical distinction (contrary to popular semantics) between soul and spirit (ψυχή and πνεῦμα; *animus* and *spiritus*; the Hebrew *nephesh* and *ruah*), with the underlying altogether different notions of blood/life force and wind/breath and also mind. We have avoided this problem usually by transforming *dushevnyi* into a noun that uses *soul*, but sometimes we employ *psychic*.

The pair *myslennyi-chuvstvennyi* is an Old Slavic and Rus equivalent of the Greek νοητός-αἰσθητός distinction between what is perceptible only by the mind and that which is descernible by the senses. We have used *mental* or *spiritual* for *myslennyi* and *material* or *physical* for *chuvstvennyi*.

One of Iosif's more interesting formulas, adapted from Nikon in this instance, is *viny nuzhnye s'kliuchaiushchie k spaseniiu dusham* (necessary causes which result in the salvation of souls) (XII.Title, XIII/i.1). Iosif covers under this rubric various aspects of the interior, exterior, and ritual comportment required of the monk for his salvation. The use of this logical and legalistic terminology was typical of Nikon and Iosif, but does not represent formal dialectical thinking.

The Inner Life of the Monk

Iosif devotes little space to the purely spiritual side of his charges. His focus is on community prayer in the church, for which he produced a version of his earlier adaptation of Chrysostom's Antioch sermons (I^B.18–20,22–25,/I.13–18,20–21).[31] Both Chrysostom and Iosif composed these sermons for all Christians, not simply

31. Compare AfED, 351–56, to PG 55:718, 725–6, 734, 744–6, 882, PG 56:997–1007 (ORT: VMCh, Sept., cols. 798. 807, 809, 833, 836, 971–81).

for monks, so Iosif's leitmotif in his Rules is not characterstically monastic. On the other hand, in his *Enlightener* he recommended to all Christians a mode of comportment more characteristically monkish:[32]

> You, beloved one, wherever you are: on the sea, on the road, walking, sitting, or sleeping, pray incessantly with a clear conscience: Lord Jesus Christ, Son of God, have mercy on me.

Iosif's only focused discussion of problems relating to solitary prayer, sin, and repentence occurs in his brief discourse on silence after Compline (VI^B/IV). He stated in the *Enlightener* that all people live under the power of sin, even if their life lasts only one day: hence they require repentance and the mourner's (that is the monk's) habit, it being more secure in this regard than life in the world.[33] This is Iosif's rendition of the doctrine of πένθος, which he also expressed with Chrysostom's words in the sermons on communty prayer (I^B.11,19,22–23/I.11,14,17–18). In the *Rules*, Iosif presupposed that his monks engaged in quiet, grieving, ascetic endeavor or some form of hesychastic praxis (VI^B.3/IV.3). The *Lives* claim that he succeeded.[34] To promote such activity he and his colleagues acquired for their cloister such basic monastic works as John Climacus's *Ladder*, the discourses of Isaac the Syrian and Symeon the New Theologian, and the writings of Russia's own 'great elder' (*velikii starets*) Nil Sorsky, who in a clear and logical way encapsuled and interpreted the Eastern hesychastic tradition for his countrymen and their northern clime.[35]

Fully within the cosmic drama of original expulsion from paradise and the promise of reattainment, Iosif linked observance and repentance, and warned against negligence in the strongest aphoristic terms.[36]

32. AfED, 356 (*Prosvetitel'* 7:218).
33. *Prosvetitel'* 4:158, 11:442–43.
34. Savva Cherny, *Zhitie*, 467–68. Belokurov, *Zhitie*, 28.
35. L:IB, 298–99; KTsDR, 31–32, 342–49.
36. Špidlík, *Joseph de Volokolamsk*, contains the most thorough analysis of the interconnection of monastic virtues in Iosif's writings.

> Because of negligence death came into the world (I.35). . . . On account of these words [asking for permission or forgiveness] all the Adversary's strategems collapse (XIII/ix.19).

To cap the monk's day, therefore, Iosif recommended nightly confession to the superior—a practice, which may represent his interpretation of an elastic pseudo-Basilian, Athonite, and Evergetian tradition.[37] He also credited the superior, as father confessor, with the power to absolve sins, which, according to John Meyendorff, is more typical of Western than of Eastern Christianity—the latter tending to view sinfulness as the general state of humanity and to envision repentance in ascetic and moral terms.[38] At any rate, Iosif's praise of absolute and total obedience (VI.18–34) places him within the current of Eastern spirituality known as 'witness of martyrdom'.[39]

Social and Administrative Structures

In the second half of the sixteenth century Iosifo-Volokolamsk Monastery had sixty-five officials and one hundred nineteen dependent artisans and workers.[40] The Extended Rule reflects an earlier stage of economic and administrative development, but has a clear division of labor between monastic and external estate affairs. Not all the officials presumed to have existed in Iosif's time are mentioned: those responsible for the infirmary and for marketing goods are absent.

The administration of the monastery, according to the *Rule* and other documents, was dominated by the hegumen (*igumen*)

37. Basil, *Ascetic Works,* 49. (Pseudo-)Athanasius, *Rule* (Ὑποτύπωσις) 33: 228 (Meyer, 139–40). Timothy of Evergetis 7:476–78, 502.

38. Meyendorff, *Byzantine Theology,* 195–96. While not wishing to dispute the late Reverend Professor, this author wonders if the nature of the confessor's power as expressed in medieval penetential tradition was not similar in the Eastern and Western Churches.

39. Hausherr, *Grands courants,* 129–32.

40. Tikhomirov, 'Monastyr'-Votchinnik', 148–50.

or superior (*nastoiatel'*), who served as everybody's father confessor (XIII.50), the cellarer (*kelar'*), who in Russia was often the equivalent of the Byzantine *oeconomus* (steward), and the treasurer (*kaznachei*).[41] The other cloister officials included the assistant cellarer (*podkelarnik*), the choirmaster or taxiarch (*ustavshchik*), disciplinary inspectors or supervisors (*naziratel'*), the rouser (*budil'nik*), the sacristan (*ponomar*), the butler or cupbearer (*chashnik*) and other refectory officials, the senior officials or bosses (*bol'shoi sluzhebnik*) in charge of such work places as the mills and the brewery (for *kvass*—Russia's mild beer), and the assistant or lesser treasurer (*men'shii kaznachei*). The supervisory system in the church and the refectory appear to have been based upon Athonite traditions as recorded in Athanasius's Life as well as his rules.[42]

An additional set of officials had functions that were more manorial: the stewards (*kliuchnik*), the chief groom or master of the horse (*koniushii*), the bailiffs (*posel'skii*), and other judges (*sud'ia*).[43] Typically of the lighter burdens peasants faced on monastic estates in comparison to secular lands, the stewards and bailliffs were empowered to adjudicate disputes within the villages and to exact judicial fees at one half the rates stipulated in the national Judicial Code (*Sudebnik*) of 1497 (XIII.v.13,15).[44] The monastery also employed a series of young and mature servants, laborers, and artisans, including tailors, sentries, and quasi-police officers (*pristav*), some of whom may have been monks.[45]

41. See the transactions of property in AFZKh 2. Professor Vodoff suggests that 'abbot' be used instead of 'hegumen' for *igumen*, but this translator prefers the latter, who ranks ceremonially below the archimandrite, who is also an abbot: Vodoff, 'Compte rendue' 204.

42. III.38; VI.11; XIII.1; XIII.ii.7; XIII.ix.10–12. Cf. Petit, *Vie de S. Athanase*, 135–36, and BMFD, 221–80, *passim*.

43. XIII.v.13; XIll,ix.9,10,13. The Serbian Hilender *Tipik* (30:62), reflecting a different application of common Slavic roots, used *ključar* (keeper of keys) for treasurer.

44. On the judicial code, see Dewey, 'The 1497 Sudebnik'. Kaiser, *The Growth of Law in Medieval Russia*, 40–41. A translation of the Text is found in Dmytryshyn *Medieval Russia*, 243–58, and Hellie, *Sudebniks*.

45. XIII.v.4–8,15; XIII.ix.9–10.

The clergy listed in the Extended Rule included the hebdomadary (*sviashchennik nedel'noi*), that is, the officiating priest for a given week, other priests, deacons, subdeacons (*d'iak*), cantors, and lectors, all of whom were supposed to be monks.[46]

The Extended Rule set up two types of stratification with the cloister: the division of all the monks into three sets of orders (*ustroenie*) for fasting regimens and clothing and the formal separation of the governing council brothers (*sobornye bratiia*) from the other monks. Each of these, when instituted, represented an innovation for the monastery, and Iosif had to justify them within the *Rule*.

The three orders were a departure from Russian monastic practice and the inverse of one recorded Byzantine arrangement from the eleventh century.[47] Some scholars, arguing unconvincingly from what is known about sixteenth-century Russian monastic life in general, rather than from Iosifov Monastery sources, claim that this arrangement was a cover for sumptuary privilege and inequality.[48] Yet Iosif's enemies did not attack this division. The issuance of clothing, the third order, which was the most generous, the least prestigious, and—apparently—the most common, conformed to the Byzantine cœnobitic standards attributed to Theodore the Studite (III.26).[49] One of Iosif's *Lives* claims that the strictest, first order was a serious affair.[50] It thus makes more

46. XIII.i.19. The ecclesiastical *diiak or diak* was the equivalent of the subdeacon or choirboy. Professor Vodoff prefers acolyte: 'Compte rendue', 204. In secular life in the fifteenth century, the *diak* could be as lowly as a simple scribe or as high as the head of a central bureau or of the civil administration of a province and even might be the chief advisor of the Sovereign.

47. The germ of Iosif's idea of three orders may have lain in Climacus' division of monasticism into three orders: cœnobites: two or three together: and solitaries (*Ladder* 1.24; PG 88:641C). Nikon and Nil Sorsky repeat this: *Pandekty* 57:489. *Ustav* 11:87 (Lilienfeld, *Nil Sorskij,* 253). Around 1083 a former soldier, Gregory Pakourianos established three orders for the purchase of clothing; the more prestigious monks received the higher monetary allowances, but there is no evidence that Iosif knew of this arrangement: BMFD, 535.

48. Rybakov, *Remeslo*, 587. Budovnits, *Russkaia publitsistika,* 84–85, and *Monastyri,* 244–45. L:IB, 454–55. Z:KFV, 96–97.

49. (Pseudo-)Theodore, *Rule* (Ὑποτύπωσις) 38:114–15 (PG 99:1720AB). Athanasius of Athos, *Rule* (Ὑποτύπωσις) 35:228 (Meyer, 140). Nikon, *Taktikon* 1:13V (BMFD, 406).

50. Belokurov, *Zhitie,* 44.

sense to view this structure in terms of Iosif's proclivity for regularity. Monks for whom the cloister hierarchy was unattractive or closed could seek a more purely spiritual height, that of extreme asceticism, but under all conditions they enjoyed equality of food, drink, garments, and footwear with their peers.

Neither institutionalized abbatial consultation with preeminent monks nor the specific monastery council or chapter (*sobor*) was Iosif's innovation. Consultation is ancient, and the council may go back to the rise of the Byzantine *idiorhythma* in eleventh- and twelfth-century, whereby rich monks retained their own property and servants, and everyone had his own special rule, but first appears in 1406 as a full-blown body of fifteen—that number sanctified by a spurious reference to Athanasius and his συμβουλία—in the *Typikon* of Emperor Manuel II Palaiologos (Paleologos) for the monasteries of Mount Athos.[51] If Iosif is to be believed, councils of ten or still twelve functioned at the various cloisters at Mt. Athos, Constantinople, and Jerusalem when he was completing his Extended Rule (XIII.42,44).[52]

How this institution developed in Russia is not known, but the Russian cœnobia usually had idiorhythmic traits, which invited a devolution of power. The richer monks made deposits (*vkup*, *vklad*) and tended to act as shareholders. Iosif, unlike his older contemporary, the reforming, cœnobiarch Evfrosin of Pskov

51. Kazhdan, 'Monastyr', 62–6 7; Manuel II, *Typikon* 6:1620; Meyer, *Haupturkunden*, 63, 203–07. Cf. Sinitsyna, 'Poslanie Maksima Greka', 132–34. The notion of continuous consultation with the preeminent elders is found first in Evergetis, late eleventh or early twelfth century, and is developed is several other rules. The rule for the Lips Convent speaks, like Iosif, of the preeminent (here nuns) and the officials (1294–1301): Timothy of Evergetis, *Typikon* 13:484; Theodora Palaiogina, *Typikon* 27:1273; Athanasios I, *Rule* 5:1502; Joachim of Zichna, *Typikon* 22:1606–10. Another possibility is a connection among the fifteen 'choir monks' of the St Dimitrios Kellibara Monastery of Constantinople, who had the authority to name the new abbot (1282), Manuel II's Athonite συμβουλία, and the Russian *sobor*: Michael VIII, *Typikon* 17–18:1250–52.

52. Cf. Sinitsyna, 'Poslanie Maksima Greka', 132: according to Maksim Grek, the council of fifteen still operated in the early sixteenth century. Actually Iosif does not speak of the coucil (*sobor*) *per se*, but of the council brothers.

(d. 1479), made no attempt to abolish the deposit system,[53] which was central to the financing of commemorations and public feasts in the great cloisters.[54] Rather, and as if the passage of time, Russia's hierarchical break with the Greeks in the 1440s, and the final Ottoman conquest of Byzantium in 1453 had made no difference whatsoever, Iosif claimed the authority of Mt. Athos and Constantinople, as well as canon law, when he instituted the council and granted it the right to name his successor and to impose penances upon monks for infractions of the Rule (XIII.32–48). This latter provision provoked opposition within the monastery, and Iosif responded with practical arguments based on analogies with the secular world and the requirements of a complex institution dedicated primarily to pious living (XIII.49–55).

Iosif's council, in theory selected by the entire brotherhood (XIII.i.7), was probably established around the time he testated his monastery to Vasilii III, 1507.[55] During the period 1507–17, for which we have some indication as to the persons who served on the council or its equivalent, members of the local, well-to-do gentry predominated. A few were of the high nobility, though such origin did not assure an automatic seat on the council, and a few members may have originally been commoners. Moreover, during Iosif's lifetime or right afterwards, most of the monastery's identifiable copyists of the Psalter, Chrysostom, *paterica*, and the spiritual tracts of Ephraim of Syria, Isaac of Syria, Symeon the New Theologian, and Nil Sorskii served as council elders or the equivalent.[56] The initial selection process of this intellectual as

53. Von Lilienfeld, *Nil Sorskij*, 310. The Byzantine tradition was not uniform in this regard.

54. Steindorff, *Memoria*, 205–08.

55. AFZKh 2:36,37.

56. See above, notes 14–15, 17–20; also KTsDR, 7, 28–29. AFZKh 2:36, 37, 39, 47. PIV, 239–40. Z:KFV, 112–22. Among these elders were Gerasim Cherny, Nil Polev, Arsenii Golenin, Gelasii Sukhalenov, Gurii the Old, and Tikhon Zvorykhin. Another of these transcribers, Semeon Stremoukhov, became Bishop of Suzdal in 1509. Of the four other major copyists from this period, Dosifei Toporkov, Iosif's nephew, was also a writer, and Varlaam Krivoshein may have served as a coucil brother. For a detailed study of the regional gentry, see Chernov,

well as social and administrative elite is not apparent from the text of the Extended Rule, which assumes a functioning body with the authority to coopt new members. Iosif's provision for the council's naming his successor, however, flatly contradicted his testament of 1507 that granted or accepted Vasilii III's authority to make the appointment.[57] This incongruity is evident in a missive sent by Iosif just before his death to the Grand Prince with a list of ten leading elders and a plea that he not appoint a successor from another monastery or anyone else without their approval.[58] If such equivocacy is the norm for the early phases of constitutional development or for the gray zones of political or corporate structures, the very fact of structural and constitutional consciousness, which envisions and articulates a strong superior, a co-governing council, and then consultation with the entire brotherhood in extraordinary circumstances (XIII.A), was, on paper, innovative for Muscovite Russia (but not the Byzantine world) at this time.[59]

Clothing

The list of the garments issued to the monks in the Extended Rule covers only the normal or minor habit less the girdle: the

---

Volok Lamskii. For a composite picture of central Russian provincial gentry from the following century, see Kivelson, *Autocracy in the Provinces*.

57. AI I:288.

58. PIV, 239–40.

59. The prevailing trend in recent American scholarship concerning the structure of Muscovy around 1500 favors the notion of consensus among an elite whose ceremony produced a 'façade autocracy': See Kollmann, *Kinship and Politics*, 146–51. However, no record or contemporary statement of the institutional power of the Moscow boyars of his time comes close to matching the power that Iosif granted his monastic council. In a reverse move, forty years after Iosif died, when Muscovy had experienced a good deal of strife-filled 'boyar rule' during Ivan IV's childhood and youth, Gerasim Boldinsky commanded his twelve Council Elders not to make policy without the abbot: Krushel'nitskaia, 'Zaveshchanie-ustav Gerasima Boldinskogo', 269. Byzantine *typica*, starting with Timothy of Evergetis, linked monastic autonomy to the role of the preeminent brothers or sisters, sometimes having them help in the selection of the other monastery officials; in 1406 the Emperor Manuel II opposed the both the 'democracy' of allowing anyone to govern or the 'tyranny' of abbatial monocracy: BMFD, 1620.

cowl (*klobuk*), the skull cap (*skufiia*), the cassock (*riaska*), the mantle (*manatiia*), and the tunic (*svitka*).[60] Iosif does not mention either the neophyte's attire—just the cassock and the cap—or the Great *Schema*, that is, the major habit—a special cowl cum black cloth with embroidered cross lying on the monk's back and shoulders. On the other hand the Rule does note several items required by Russia's severe climate: boots (*sapogi*), undershoes (*chiulki*), the hide or fur coat (*shuba*), and a special skull cap for winter (III.24–26).[61]

Iosif's *Enlightener*, Discourse No. 11, devoted to the defense of monasticism and the monastic habit (*obraz*) as the divinely inspired life and garb of 'repentance and mourning', provides some symbolic interpretations of the various items. The act of tonsure (*postrizhenie*) represents freedom from sensuality; the mantle, lacking arms, signifies the absence of hands that might perform evil acts; the girdle (*poias*) protects the monk from sensuality; the cowl (here—*kukol*)—a child's hat—teaches humility; the skull cap (here—*kamilavka*) is a sign of divine protection; the scapular (*paramand*) is a protective shield of salvation; and the *analabos* or *schema* embodies the cross monks must bear.[62] It is strange, in the light of both Iosif's reverence for the habit itself and the relative scarcity and cost of goods in the pre-modern era, that the Extended Rule nowhere warns or instructs the monks regarding the care of their clothing.

60. *Klobuk* derives from the Turkish *kalabak/kalpak*, *skufiia* from the Italian *scuffia* via the Greek ἡ σκούφια, *manatiia* from the Greek μαντίον and *riaska* from the Greek ῥάσον; *svitka* is a Russian word.

61. An analysis and description of the early Russian monastic vestments is found in Golubinsky, *Istoriia* 1.2:175–89, and *Arkheologicheskii atlas,* 32, plate 63.

62. *Prosvetitel'* 11:435–37. This explication undoubtedly derives from a source where the Greek terms κουκούλιον, καμελαύκιον, and παραμάντιον/παραμάνδυον (among others) were explained. The Rule has the more common Russian words. An earlier Rus explanation of the monastic habit based on the Old Testament was written by the obscure, if very competent and eloquent, Bishop Kirill of Turov (? ca. 1160s-1180s): its Byzantine sources have not been identified: 'Collected Prose', 88–91.

The Major Edifices

Iosif called his foundation the Monastery (*monastyr'*) or cloister (*obitel'*) of the Venerable and Glorious Dormition of the All-Glorified (or Immaculate—*Prechistyia*) Mother of God (*Bogoroditsa-Theotokos*).[63] It was (and is) located southwest of the Lama River, about twenty kilometers east of the town of Volokolamsk. The cloister proper was roughly a quadrilateral, about 250 meters along the west wall, 150 meters on the east wall, 190 meters along the north wall and across the middle, with an approximately 200-meter wall going northeast/southwest and connecting the southwest corner to the southeast corner. During Iosif's lifetime all the walls were of wood. There may have been (as later in the sixteenth century) seven towers: at the four corners and along the west, south, and east walls. In the middle of the north wall were the Lower (*Podol'nye*) or Water Gates leading to the nearby artificial pond mentioned in the Extended Rule (XIII.v.11). About fifty-five meters from the southeast corner along the south wall were the Holy Gates (*Sviatye Vraty*), the main entrance to the cloister.[64]

The two major buildings inside the monastery were the refectory and the church. The stone refectory (*trapeza*), built in 1506,[65] was located about sixty-five meters northwest of the Holy Gates, measured about 27 x 22 meters, and had two stories. Above was the main dining hall with a central column and vaulted ceilings. In the northeast corner of the upper story was the heated church noted in the Extended Rule (XIII.i.19), about 8 x 11 meters, with one cupola. The pantry lay in the southeast corner. The ovens and

63. See the title to the Extended Rule and XIII.44. In the Volokolamsk *Synodicon* the Monastery is called 'The Cloister of Our Most Holy Lady, the Theotokos and Eternal Virgin': *Sinodik*, 2.

64. See Pavlichenkov, 'Ansambl", 128, for a diagram of the interior of the monastery in the sixteenth century, and Baldin and Gerasimov, 'Dukhovskaia tserkov", 54, for a model reconstruction of the interior of Troitse-Sergiev Monastery in the fifteenth century.

65. Z:KFV, 54–55.

kitchens were below.[66] The refectory was heated by its ovens and sometimes served as the church (XIII.i.18–21). The Extended Rule mentions three types of seats inside the refectory: the great bench (*bol'shaia skamnia*), the great, the second, and the third benches (*lavitsa*), and the long seat (*skamia*), as well as the pantry or larder *(shchegun)* and its doors (through which monks were normally forbidden to pass), and the great doors on the west side, which had an elevated entrance with balcony (*most*), similar to the one Iosif mentions for Kirillov Monastery (X.14).

The main abbey church or *katholikon* (*sobor*), dedicated to the Dormition of the Theotokos, was located about fifty meters north and slightly to the east of the refectory. The church, of standard Russian design, was about 20x16 meters, with three apses facing east, one central cupola (and later four corner cupolas) and three main doors with elevated entrances, one each on the south, west, and north facades.[67] As in other Russian Orthodox churches at that time, as well as today, the sanctuary (*oltar*) was separated from the nave and aisles by the iconostasis[68] with three sets of doors: the Royal Doors in the center and the North and South Doors on either

66. See Pavlichenkov, 'Ansambl", 138, for a photograph of a side of the seventeenth-century Iosifov refectory, which was reconstructed on the foundation of the sixteenth-century edifice. See also *Istoriia russkogo iskusstva* 3:362,365,369, for pictures of other, similarly planned, early sixteenth-century Moscovite refectories. The term *trapeza* (from the Greek) could mean refectory table and table of oblations, as well as refectory.

67. Pictures and diagrams of a church similar to the original Iosifov *sobor* or *katholikon* of the Dormition can be found in Baldin, 'Arkhitektura Troitskogo sobora', 23–26. The Volokolamsk city *katholikon* of the Resurrection, also dating from the 1480s, is reproduced in *Istoriia russkogo iskusstva* 3:320–21. Note also the Church of the Deposition of the Robe in Moscow, built precisely in 1484–85, and the monastery Church of the Intercession in Suzdal of 1510–14 in Brumfeld, *A History of Russian Architecture*, 90, 108. Photographs of the present Iosifov *katholikon*, dating from the 1660s, are in Voronin and Sakharova, 'Novye materialy', 118. The interior of a typical Orthodox church is described and illustrated in Sokolof, 2,10,14. There is no good English rendition of the Russian *sobor*—any major church, often where services are performed every day. The popular *cathedral* is imprecise, and *basilica* would imply a larger structure than the typical Russian *sobor*.

68. On the development of the Russia iconostasis, see Cheremeteff, *Transformation*. Lelikova, *Ikonostas 1497 g.*

side. Inside the sanctuary to the north was the table of oblations. The sacrificial altar (*zhertvennik*)[69] was in the center. The slightly elevated ambo was directly in front of the iconastasis, and the two choirs (*krylos*)[70] were on the sides of the ambo. The narthex or vestibule (*pritvor*) at the west end occupied about two-fifths of the interior (in contrast to the vestibule of the typical Western church) and was used for the chanting of the little hours and Vespers when it was followed by Grand Compline. From the text of the Extended Rule it is not clear what Iosif meant by front doors (*prezhnie dveri*). The forward corners mentioned in the Rule were located in the aisles alongside the choirs. Although Iosif's sermon on the communal service archaically referred to the semantron or clapper (I^B.2, I.II), the monastery had a bell tower with its own little church by 1495, and a bell summoned the brothers to the services (XIV.4).[71]

The Extended Rule speaks of other places in and around the monastery, whose precise locations are not apparent. Certainly the cells were within the walls. The mills, the brewery for kvass, the stables, the tailors', servants' and childrens' quarters, and most other outbuildings *(dvorets)* as well as the courtyards (also *dvorets*) were located outside the walls (XII.ix.9–12).[72] The Rule also mentions the treasury or wardrobe (*kázna*), ice houses, storerooms, and fodder sheds (XIII.V.6), but not the hospital or infirmary attached to, if located away from the main monastery.[73] Unless Iosif deviated from Muscovite architectural norms—something for which we have no evidence in any other instance, the cells would have

69. *Oltar* and *zhertvennik* were used interchangeably for the sanctuary and the sacrificial altar: Sreznevsky, *Materialy* 1:890, 2:662–63.

70. *Krylos*, derived from the Greek κλῆρος, assimilated to the Slavonic *krilo/krylo* (wing, hence flank of an army and arms of a protuding or inscribed cross of a church): Sreznevsky, *Materialy* 3:1221–22, 1323.

71. Z:KFV, 54–55.

72. The term *dvorets*, which today means palace, seems to have been used by Iosif both for the courtyards or surrounding grounds and the buildings on them (IX.8, XIII.v.11,13–14). It is not clear whether the children's quarters mentioned in the Rule (XIII.ix.9) is identical with the orphanage Iosif is said to have established during the famine of 1511: Dosifei Toporkov, *Nadgrobnoe slovo*, 134–35. Savva Cherny, *Zhitie*, 482.

73. On the satellite infirmary cloister, see Belokurov, *Zhitie*, 31–32.

been rectangular, tent-roofed, one room, wooden plank houses, measuring 3.5 x 6 meters on a side, with three small sash windows in the front and with a stove, but having no cellars, rear doors or casement windows, orchards, or gardens.[74] Roughly the size of a modern, one-car garage, these cabins could house a monk or an elder with a novice. With the superior's authorization, monks might have books, icons, candles, other 'cell objects', and even cooking utensils and food, as well as clothing and working material.[75] Some of the monks were capable craftsmen, but they were forbidden to use the monastery's tools, nails, or construction wood without the superior's permission (III.32). Apparently, Iosif was worried about fires or wasting fuel, as he imposed a penance for keeping a cell heated in the monk's absence (XIV.32). The wording of Iosif's command to his council to prevent any improvements to the cells (XIII.ix.7) makes one wonder if, in contrast to Pafnutiev, the Iosifov cells were not directly visible from the superior's residence. Unlike the others in Iosifov, hegumen's and the cellarer's cells were large enough for meetings of the three top officials and the council of twelve (XIII/A.5).

The Service Typicon

Iosif took the letter of the service rubrics extremely seriously as a key to salvation (I.19). In no position critically to judge the fidelity of a given Russian service book to the Byzantine originals, he nevertheless had great respect for writings in general, which, in keeping with classical Christian rhetoric, he considered the depository of stored memory.[76] He thus insisted in the Extended

74. Sidorova, 'Realisticheskie cherty', 76–78, reproduces and analyzes sixteenth- and seventeenth-century drawings of Russian cells.

75. III.21–22,32; IX.13, XII.9. XIII.ix.7.

76. See IB.1, IX.16, X.32,34, and the introduction to the memorial section of the Iosifov *Synodicon*: K:VPS, 357. Iosif gave similar eulogies to writings and to icons for preserving records, models, and images in his apologetics: AfED, 336 (*Prosvetitel'* 7:167). Overall, in his attitude towards transmitted traditions and in his own writings, his legacy serves as testimony to the keenness of Averil

Rule that no one inscribe anything in a book without the superior's or choirmaster's blessing (III.39), and that clerics study only their own readings for the service (XIII.i.5). Unlike many Byzantine monastic rules and typica, Iosif's does not include a guide to the service typica (ordinaries), but rather assumes such a typicon to be functioning.

Iosif alluded to the various services when he discussed the supervision of monks by the council brothers and other officials in the church and the refectory (XIII.i-ii). He used both the finite divisions within the services and the Old Russian system of measuring time by day and night hours that varied with the seasons in order to indicate when inspectors would make their various rounds.[77]

The offices in Iosif's Russia were much the same as they are today in the Eastern Church, but longer. The usual monastic service typicon was a modification of that of the Laura of Saint Sabas of Jerusalem.[78] The monk's normal day began in the evening with Vespers (*vechernia*), followed after a brief rest by supper (*uzhina*); then came Compline *(povechernitsa)* or Grand Compline (*nefimon*);[79] next the long period of silent cell activities or sleep;

Cameron's recent observation (here for the time of the Classical Church Fathers) that 'the self-conscious Christian creates his own self and does so through the medium of texts, which in turn assume the functions of models': *Christianity and the Rhetoric of Empire*, 57.

77. The day in medieval Rus and Muscovy was divided into 'night hours' and 'day hours', which always added up to twenty-four, but varied according to seasonal changes. For example, in Kirillov Monastery in the sixteenth century, November and December had six day hours and sixteen night hours, but the reverse was true in May and June. Similarly the division was nine day and fifteen night hours for January and October, eleven day and thirteen night hours for February and October, thirteen day and eleven night hours for March and August, and fifteen day and nine night hours for April and July. See Nikol'sky, 'Obschchestvennaia i keleinaia zhizn", 896–90.

78. Mansvetov, *Tserkovnyi ustav*, 168ff.

79. The term *nefimon*, changed from *mefimon*, is derived from the Greek μεθήμῶν—'With us God', the opening lines to the collects at Compline. Metropolitan Fotii thought that Russians chanted too many *mefimons* in the early fifteenth century: Sreznevsky 2:134

then Matins *(zautrenie)*,[80] which was preceded by Vigils *(bdenie)* or the Midnight Office *(polunoshchnitsa)* on Sundays and Holidays;[81] after this followed a period of cell activities or community work, interrupted by Prime, Terce, and Sext (these three were not mentioned in the Rule), then a mid-day break for *kvass* (II.14, XIII.ii.9) except during November, December and January;[82] next was celebrated the Divine Liturgy (*liturgiia* or *obednia*—Mass or Lord's Supper) followed by dinner *(obeda)* in the refectory, and finally another period of rest and work before None (also not mentioned), which immediately preceded the next day's Vespers.[83]

Iosif singled out the specific parts of the Midnight Office during which the inspectors were to make their rounds (XII.i.10–12): the initial recitation of the Nicene Creed; the psalm 'Blessed are the undefiled' (Ps 119 {118 LXX})—the high point of Matins;[84] the Psalter reading that follows (probably Ps 51/50) and the fourth and ninth odes *(pesn')* of the subsequent variable canon (*kanon*).[85] He also called for tours of inspection at the beginning of Vespers, Compline, and Divine Liturgy (probably at the commencement of the Liturgy of the Catechumens, the first part of the Divine Liturgy), as well as during the Communion Hymn (*kenanik*)[86] at the end of the second part, the Liturgy of the Faithful, and at the beginning

80. *Utrenie* in modern Russian.

81. According to the Iosifov Monastery Customary of 1589–91, Vigils were chanted on the eve of Sundays and holidays: Leonid, '*Obikhodniki*', 7–22.

82. III.14, XIII.ii9. See Leonid, '*Obikhodniki*', 12.

83. See Nikol'sky, 'Obshchestvennaia i keleinaia zhizn'', for the monk's day. See Mary and Ware, *A Festal Menaion*, Hapgood, *Service Book*, and Skaballanovich, *Tolkovyi tipikon* for descriptions and analyses of the sevices. Special arrangements were also made for the officials. According to the Customary of 1591, the cellarer, head waiter, lector, lesser waiters, gatekeepers, and others legitimately absent from the main meal dined together at the 'last table' (*poslednaia trapeza*) noted in II.12, and then the assistant cellarer, chef, assistant butler, fire stoker, four assistant cooks, four refectory officials and the major refectory officials dined in the larder: Leonid, 'Obikhodniki', 6–7.

84. Skaballanovich, *Tolkovyi tipikon* 2:227–35. Mary and Ware, *Festal Menaion,* 75.

85. The eighth ode of the canon is usually omitted: Skaballanovich, *Tolkovyi tipikon,* 2.287–8.

86. *Kenanik* derives from κοινωνικόν (communional).

of one of the *moleben's*—special prayer services or litanies (like a *Te Deum*) which followed Vespers and Matins.[87]

Eastern monastic life had its own forms of non-sacramental communion, which are noted in the section of the Extended Rule concerning penances (XIV). Iosif mentioned, in addition to the communion loaf *(prosfora)* and the sacred elements (*sviatye dary*),[88] the Panaghia (*panagiia*) or Immaculate's loaf (*Prechistyi khlebets),* a triangular bread cut from the *prosfora* and set aside for a quasi-eucharistic rite held after the refectory meal (XIII.ii.9, XIV.4) This is distinct from the *antidoron*, consecrated bread used not for the Eucharist, but distributed to the faithful after the liturgy or at mealtime. In one recorded case of what might be called the popular culture of elite monasticism, an Athonite monk went so far as to claim that the Panaghia was transformed at the time of its benediction into the body of the Virgin![89] Punishments for infractions of the Rule could include denial of the sacred elements or the Panaghia, as well as a number of prostrations and/or *xerophagia*—a diet of bread, water, and dry herbs for one or more days (XIV).

The section of the Rule that deals with community meetings alludes to a song and two prayers. The song, 'It is worthy' *(Dostoino est')* is a hymn to the Theotokos found in the Liturgy of John Chrysostom and often sung today as formerly at convocations and short services.[90] One of the prayers, 'Glory and now' (*Slava i nyne*) is the common doxology, 'Glory to the Father, and to the Son and to the Holy Spirit, now and forever and unto ages and ages, Amen'.[91] The other is the *Jesus Prayer* (' . . . Jesus Christ, our God, have mercy . . .') in several forms.[92]

87. Mary and Ware, *Festal Menaion,* 74–79. Hapgood *Service Book,* 151–52. Skaballanovich, *Tolkovyi tipikon,* 2.249–56. *Tüpikon*, 2.

88. Literally: holy gifts.

89. *Tüpikon*, 9V-10. *Starchestvo*, 12v-13; Yiannias, 'Elevation of the Panaghia', 233. The Slavonic word *prechistyia* is the equivalent of the Greek παναγία (all-holy), a popular sobriquet of the Blessed Virgin.

90. Hapgood, *Service Book,* 107–08.

91. *Sluzhebnik*, 70–70V.

92. On the Jesus Prayer, see Hausherr, 'La méthode d'oraison hesychaste'.

Iosif also adduced Kremlin court ritual as a model to be emulated at cloister meetings (XIII/A.6). He had visited the royal quarters in Moscow first in 1477 and 1478 on business for Pafnutiev Monastery, and later in 1503, when he negotiated with Ivan III concerning the fate of the accused heretics and could inspect the new Palace of Facets (*Granovitaia Palata*), designed and decorated by Italians for more elaborate state receptions.[93] The assumption in scholarship that Iosif actually introduced court ritual into his monastery, however, does not make any sense at all.[94]

The Table Customary

Iosif's discussion of the food that the three orders of monks could select on various days presupposes the existence of a table customary (*obikhodnik*) (II.29–34).[95] The Rule gives general instructions for the different types of meals served and assumes the reader can make the necessary analogies and computations.

The meal system, like the liturgical cycle, was determined by three variables: the day of the week; the lunar calendar for Easter and related holidays; and the solar calendar for most anniversaries. The availability of food was also an important factor—scarcity might curtail a feast, while an unforeseen benefactor might deliver perishables at an canonically inopportune moment. Normally on Sundays and feast days there were supposed to be three dishes at dinner and two at supper. Monday, Wednesday, and Friday were fast days with no cooked food.[96]

The major feasts of the Eastern Church—in addition to Easter, the Great Day—are the Birth of the Theotokos (8 September), the

93. See Brumfeld, *A History of Russian Architecture*, 99–101: he uses the term 'Rusticated Chambers'.

94. L:IB, 458.

95. The 1589–91 table customary appears to be related to the Extended Rule, and Iosif's own table regulation could have been a source for a later sixteenth-century Kirillov Monastery Customary, though, alternatively, they all might derive from a common source: Pokrovskaia, 'Opisanie', 293.

96. Leonid, 'Obikhodniki', 5–6.

Exaltation of the Cross (14 September), the Entry of the Theotokos into the Temple (21 November), Christmas (25 December), Theophany/Epiphany (6 January), Presentation/Purification (2 February), Annunciation (25 March), Palm Sunday (One Week before Easter), Ascension (forty days after Easter), Pentecost (fifty days after Easter), Transfiguration (6 August), and the Dormition of the Theotokos (15 August). In 1591 Iosifov Monastery also celebrated New Year's Day (1 September), the death of Iosif (9 September), the Intercession of the Virgin (1 October—a Russian holiday presumably instituted by Prince Andrei Bogoliubsky in Vladimir-Suzdal to celebrate his victory in 1164 over the Moslem Volga Bolgars), the death of Grand Prince Vasilii III (tonsured as he died as the monk Varlaam under the direction of Metropolitan Daniil in 1533–4 December), the feast of John the Theologian (10 May), the birth of John the Baptist (24 June), and the feast of Peter and Paul (29 June).

The principal fasts were Advent (15 November–24 December), Lent—the Great Fast—(the seven weeks before Easter), the Fast of the Apostles (from the second Monday after Pentecost—that is, from fifty-seven days after Easter—to the eve of the feast of SS. Peter and Paul), and the Fast of the Dormition (1–14 August). Fasts were interrupted by special feast days such as the Feast of Saint John the Baptist which fell during the fast of the Apostles. In Iosifov Monastery, the eve of the Exaltation of the Cross (14 September), Ascension Thursday, the Saturday before Pentecost and the Decapitation of John the Baptist (29 August) were full or partial fast days.[97]

A typical major feast was that of Symeon the Stylite on New Year's Day (1 September). If it fell on a Tuesday, Thursday, or Saturday, each monk might have two fish fried in butter with a decoction and mustard, buttered white *kalatch* (a round wheaten bread), two *pirogs* (tasty rolled dough with filling) with eggs and pepper, and two thin pancakes (*bliny*, that is, blintzes) with honey and honey *kvass*. If the feast fell on a Wednesday or a Friday, then

97. Leonid, 'Obikhodniki', 7–23, gives the annual cycle of feasts and fasts. See also Steindorff, *Speisungsbuch*, 1–335.

the monks had cabbage soup *(shchi),* vegetable dishes with oil, soup with vermicelli, and *kalatch.*[98]

The Extended Rule demanded equality in foods for all monks (II.28) and allowed for substitutions of equivalent foods, but provided no details (II.32). Accordingly, the Customary of 1591 stipulated that on the normal Tuesday, Thursday, and Saturday, when there was one dish for supper along with the cabbage soup, boiled milk, cheese, or fresh milk, the substitute food would be three eggs or coarse *kasha* (gruel) with *pirogs.*[99] The provision for equality seems to have held, since Iosifov and Kirillov were among the only mid-sixteenth-century Russian monasteries renowned for providing all monks, from the highest officials to the lowliest servant, with the same meals.[100]

Shortcomings of Russian Monastic Life

Iosif's sermonizing style might lead the reader to conclude that his monks were always in disarray, eating-in-secret, or shirking their work. For sure he addressed several problems with such intensity as to indicate that these were deadly serious issues and not simply pretexts for preaching. Several times he articulated his fear that monks might become the laughing stock of society as a result of their unruliness.[101]

Disorder in the church, refectory, and elsewhere undoubtedly concerned Iosif; otherwise he would not have introduced the supervisory system so reminiscent of boys' camp.[102] Unauthorized leaving of the cloister was especially dangerous because temptations lurked in the lively world outside (XIII.v.1). Individuals pilfering community property and stealing from each other was no small concern to Iosif, who accused Russian monks of raging like

98. Leonid, 'Obikhodniki', 6–7.

99. Leonid, 'Obikhodniki', 6–8.

100. Kuntsevich, *Chelobitnaia.* Gerasim Boldinskii also followed this principle: Krushel'nitskaia, 'Zaveshchanie-Ustav Gerasima Boldinskogo', 269.

101. I.30; VII.6; XIII.i.15; XIII.v.i.

102. XIII.1, 4–9; XIII.ii.4–11.

beasts and litigating maliciously when they were the victims of theft.[103] Iosif claimed that his monastery had been robbed around 1507, when, as noted earlier, fifteen of his monks absconded with fourteen books and other valuables for a rival cloister, and he thereupon initiated the litigation that led to Vasilii III taking the monastery under his direct protection.[104] Such major acts of larceny may explain why Iosif threatened potential thieves with the brutal penalties of byzantine civil law (III.33), although the penances he stipulated for taking things within the monastery were rather light (XIV.14–16). He was generally afraid that his monks would live as country gentlemen[105] (or at least he wanted to appear opposed to the possibility), so he specifically forbade private servants, horses, saddles, gardens, orchards, and cellars, rear doors, and fine windows.[106]

Two issues which especially drew Iosif's attention were inebriation and the presence of boys in the monastery. Fearing that adolescents and youngsters might easily inundate his economically flourishing establishment, he made special provisions to have them supervised and kept out of the cloister,[107] except for those serving in the refectory (XIII.ii.8). Flouting Russian tradition and claiming in vivid terms that Russians cannot drink in moderation, he banned wine and strong drinks absolutely (IX^B.7–9/XIII.vii.2–4).[108] He

103. III.33; XIII. ix.8. Individuals' raiding the community's stores and implements is a problem in any group work place or unit of socialist economy. The specific issue of monks' litigating in court over property was raised by Metropolitan Fotii in a regulatory missive to a Pskov monastery in 1418. As for monks' acting like wild beasts, a Iosifov source reports the murder of an elder from the Polev family inside the monastery in the middle of the sixteenth century. See *Dopolnenie k AI* 1:186. von Lilienfeld, *Nil Sorskij,* 294–95. Zimin, 'Kratkie letopistsi', 6.

104. PIV, 185.

105. See Ivan IV, *Poslaniia,* 162–92, for his (or his ghost-writer's) upbraiding of some of the Kirillov monks for their sumptuous life styles.

106. IX.913; XII.9; XIII.ix.6–7.

107. IX.1–8; XIII.ix.1–2,9.

108. The ecclesiastical statute attributed anachronistically to (Grand) Prince Iaroslav the Wise (d. 1054), art. 48, reads: If a priest, or monk, or nun gets drunk at an inappropriate time, he or she is guilty before the Metropolitan: Kaiser, *The Laws of Rus'*, 49.

specifically lambasted the pretext that holidays were for drinking and rejected standard *typicon* provisions for one-to-three cups of wine as unworkable in intemperate Russia. In fact his most severe penances were reserved for those who imbibed outside the monastery or kept drink in their cell (XIV.26).[109] Iosif's separate *Prescript* concerning drinks is even more severe than the Extended Rule, which envisions the option of fettering as well as expulsion for recidivists.[110]

Women

If the amount of space devoted to it is any measure of the intensity of a problem, then it appears that Iosif felt less concern with women and heterosexual temptations than he did with inebriation and pederasty. Even though some of the monks evidently were not convinced of the absolute need to bar women (XIV.27), Iosif was not so harsh towards these brothers in his writings as other monastic legislators were.[111] Moreover, once the monastery became a local shrine, welfare institution, and intercessor for the deceased, he retreated from his strict prohibition and introduced regulations for the supervision of women who came to the monastery to pray.[112] Hagiographical tradition recounts that the first woman allowed inside by Iosif was the paralyzed daughter of the monk Pafnutii (Boris) Oboburov; she was cured by her prayers in the monastery to the Theotokos. A miracle on behalf of a member of the local gentry thus permitted departure from the original principles.[113]

109. See IXB. Iosif split his original Brief Rule sermon on drunkenness into two parts: the first became VII of the Extended Rule, the second became a somewhat defective second part of XIII.vii. See also PIV, 238.

110. PIV, 238–39.

111. See, for example, *Volokolamskii paterik,* 191.

112. XII.8; XIII.viii. 2.

113. *Volokolamskii paterik,* 183–84.

Russian Monastic History

The tenth discourse of the Extended Rule, probably Iosif's best piece of monastic writing, and surely the most striking for his listeners, served several functions. Commencing as a polemical defense of his having composed a Rule, it turns into a slanted, didactic history of some highlights of Rus and Russian monastic leadership. Accordingly, Iosif provides models of discreet superiors who could be either mild and irascible, as they strove to enforce their rules against unruly monks, and of stubbornly tough elders who fought against irresponsible or innovating superiors to preserve the original traditions. One problem singled out—which Iosif obviously was attempting to avert—was the selection of successor hegumens from other monasteries, either by the monks themselves or by the imposition of the sovereign prince. It was the latter possibility Iosif feared at the end of his life, as we noted above in our discussion of the monastery's council.

Iosif turned to written sources for his hagiography, but he also based his accounts on hearsay and personal experiences. For his anecdote concerning the Kievan monk-saints, the hermit Antonii (d. 1073) and Russia's cœnobiarch Feodosii (d. 1076), the founder of the Pechersky or Cave Monastery in Kiev (X.11), Iosif utilized the *Pechersky Patericon* (early 1200s)—one of the great literary legacies from the Kievan period.[114] His version of the monastic expansion spearheaded by Sergii of Radonezh (1314–92), founder of Russia's chief shrine, Troitse-Sergiev (Trinity-Saint Sergius) Monastery in Zagorsk, and of the native, patriotic Metropolitan Aleksii (1340–78), founder of two Moscow monasteries mentioned in the Rule, Spaso-Andronikov (1355) and Chudov, the Monastery of the Miracles of Saint Michael (1365), derive from existing hagiography (X.12,29–30).[115] The presentation of Iosif's mentor,

114. Abramovych, *Kyevo-Pechers'kyj Pateryk*, 43–44; transl. Muriel Heppell, *Paterik*, 49–50.

115. Epifanii, 'Zhitie . . . Sergiia', 43–46, 53–54, 60–63. Fedotov, *Treasury*, 63–70. Pakhomii, 'Zhitie . . . Sergiia', 33–35, 61–65, 82, and *Zhitie . . . Aleksiia*, 83–98, 135–38, 214–44. Iosif's main deviation from hagiographic tradition was to present Sergii as irascible as well as meek. Indeed, almost all of the Muscovite

Pafnutii and his commanding exercise of authority (X.32) is close to that of his Life, written by Iosif's brother Vassian—which may explain why Pafnutii has appeared to scholars as a forerunner of Iosif.[116] Pafutii's earlier discipleship to Nikita, founder of the Borovsk Vysotsky Monastery and a disciple himself of Sergii, allowed Iosif to appropriate for himself Sergii's prestigious legacy.

On the other hand, Iosif's tales were themselves the sources for the later hagiography of Makarii (d. 1483), founder of the Kaliazin monastery (1444) (X.31),[117] and for the period that Iona, Moscow's first autocephalous metropolitan (1448–61), spent in Simonov Monastery in Moscow (X.17–18).[118] Iosif's accounts of Savva (d. ca. 1466–70) and his brother Varsonofii of Savvin Monastery (X.20–26)[119] and of Evfrosin of Savvateev Hermitage (mid-fifteenth century) (X.27–28)[120] are their only surviving portraits. In that Kaliazin, Savvin, and Savvateev originated within the then independent Grand Principality of Tver (absorbed by Moscow

monastery founders are portrayed as meek in the *Lives,* although the conditions in the northern wilds of the country and the proximity of hostile pagans and peasants, as well as the contemporary customs, must have produced occasional severity if not also anger in these leaders. See Budovnits, *Monastyri*, 27–45. Iosif may have obtained his picture of Sergii from his informant for the history of Simonov Monastery, Spiridon, who was hegumen of Troitse-Sergiev during 1467–76. Spiridon at times resorted to drastic measures: AI 1:278.

116. See Kadlubovsky, *Ocherki*, 54–59. Lur'e, *Istoki*, 411–20.

117. Iosif is also credited as the originator of tales concerning Makarii as an exacting superior and supervisor of other hegumens in the *Volokolamsk Patericon:* Budovnits, *Monastyri*, 204–07. Kliuchevsky, *Drevnerusskie zhitiia,* 289. Kadlubovsky, *Ocherki*, 44–45. *Volokolamskii paterik,* 185–86. K:VPS, 297.

118. Makarii, *Istoriia* 6:8.

119. Barsukov, *Istochniki,* 479–84. Savva Cherny, *Zhitie*, 456–57. Kliuchevsky, *Drevnerusskie zhitiia,* 156–57. *Volokolamskii paterik,* 190. Savvin was founded in 1397, but apparently not by Savva Iara Borozdin, as Iosif claimed. Varsonofii was probably hegumen for five years between 1412 and 1420, and his brother Savva between 1416–20 and 1466–70. The plague incident (X.22) could have taken place during reported outbreaks in Tver in 1417, 1419, 1425–27, or 1448: Borzakovsky, *Istoriia*, 235–37. See also, Langer, 'Black Death'.

120. Iosif may have had some active connections with Savvateev Hermitage. His younger contemporary, Kornilii, founder of the Komelsky-Vvedensky Monastery in the Vologda region and composer of a rule based chiefly on Iosif's, spent some time as a hermit near Savvateev. See Barsukov, *Istochniki,* 492–94. Budovnits, *Monastyri*, 280–88, Also above, note 88 to Chapter 1.

only in 1485), Iosif can be viewed as a unique recorder of Tverian hagiography and traditions, which he observed as a young man and then integrated with the Muscovite. This harmonizes with the major role his monastery played at the end of his life and the next several decades in the development of a sacralized, national Russian historiography.[121]

Iosif's accounts of the Simonov and Kirillov Monasteries (founded in the early fourteenth and early fifteenth centuries respectively) are problematic for the historian. The *Life of Kirill* is Iosif's source for the early history of both and possibly the only record of Kirill's rule or traditions, which Iosif claimed to have followed.[122] The loss by fire of the Simonov archives in 1455 precludes any identification of the archimandrites and elders he mentioned.[123] Crediting as his source Spiridon, an allegedly severe hegumen of Troitse-Sergiev (1467–76), Iosif produced the only known tale about a certain Varfolomei, depicted as an exacting administrator (*stroitel'*) of Moscow's Simonov from the early fifteenth-century (X.17–18).[124]

The survival, on the other hand, of Kirillov Monastery documents in a later copybook reveals more superiors than Iosif's story would allow:[125]

Kirillov Sources	*Extended Rule (X.13–16)*
Kirill (d. 1427)	Kirill
Innokentii (1427)	Innokentii
Khristophor (1428–34)	Khristophor
Login (1434)	The first bad superior
Trifon (1435–47)	
Kassian (1448–64/65)	

121. See Kloss, 'Iosifo-Volokolamskii monastyr' i letopisanie kontsa XV-pervoi poloviny XVI v. *Nikonovskii svod i russkoe letopisanie XVI-XVII vv.*, 81–88.

122. See above, notes 23, 24.

123. ASEI 2:337–38, 696.

124. Barsukov, *Istochniki,* 591–92.

125. Pakhomii, *Zhitie . . . Kirilla*, 39–48. ASEI 2, 694.

Filofei (Trifon's brother) (1464/65–65/66)	The second bad superior
Kassian again (1465/66–70)	
Ignatii (1471–75)	
Nifont (1475–82)	
Serapion (1482–84)	The third bad superior
Gurii Tushin (1485)	

Evidence from the elders whom Iosif lists as opposing the unsatisfactory hegumens and from the chronicles indicate that the brothers Trifon and Filofei were the first two villains of Iosif's tale. Trifon, as suffragan archbishop of Rostov (1462–67), tried to impose Filofei on the monastery, whereas Kassian was the choice of the monks, including Simon (Kartmazov) and Mikhailo (Treparev), named by Iosif as the leaders of the opposition.[126] The third culprit clearly was Serapion. Iosif noted the temporary, demonstrative departure of the (fifteen) major elders, also recorded in a brief Kirillov annal under August 1483-March 1484. Whether the issue of Kirill's traditions actually caused any or all of the struggles against the superiors, as Iosif claimed, is debatable.[127]

These stories introduce incidents from the careers of princes, metropolitans, leading elders, and iconographers, as well as the eminent founders and priors and several contemporary elite families. (Grand) Prince Iziaslav Iaroslavich (1054–73, 1076–78) of Kiev figures in the Pechersky tale (X.11). Grand Prince Vasilii I (1389–1425) of Moscow is mentioned as having appointed Varfolomei administrator of Simonov (X. 18). Evfrosin of Savvateev is said to

126. ASEI 2, 67–97, 100, 104, 124, 148, 150, 151, 173, 187, 188, 315, PSRL 4:185, 23:153, 157–58. The first villain abbot could also have been Login, whose term was very brief.

127. L:IB, 57. Tangental evidence that Iosif sided with the elders against Serapion is provided by Iosif's relations with Serapion's predecessor Nifont, who welcomed Iosif to Kirillov in 1477–78 and who later as Bishop of Suzdal, apparently supported Iosif against Metropolitan Zosima and the heretics. Scholars at various times have posited as the basis for the elders' departure Serapion's acquisition of lands for the monastery (although Nifont acquired some as well), differences over Ivan III's centralizing policies which affected Beloozero, or, as Iosif claimed, fidelity to Kirill's overall traditions.

have cured Maria, the daughter of the Grand Prince Boris of Tver (1425–61). Since she was at that time betrothed to the future Ivan III of Moscow, Evfrosin is credited with having preserved the peace between Tver and Moscow (X.28). This otherwise unrecorded event, if true, must have occurred between 1447, the time of the betrothal of the seven year-old prince and the five year-old princess Mariia, and 1452, when they were married. At this time a civil war raged within the ruling house of Moscow, and Boris opted to support Vasilii II over the latter's cousins.[128]

Aleksii and Iona are not the only metropolitans mentioned in the Rule. The energetic Metropolitan Fotii (Photios, 1408–31), Russia's last reigning chief prelate from Byzantium, appears in Iosif's narrative turning to the learned Varsonofii of Savvin Monastery for interpretations of Scripture or patristics (X.23).[129] Metropolitan Gerontii (1473–89), whom Iosif elsewhere castigated for not attacking the heretics due to fear for Ivan III,[130] is cited as contemporary to the departure of the fifteen elders from Kirillov; the local prince, Mikhail Andreevich of Verea (1432–85), is credited for having supported them (X.16). In fact both Gerontii and Mikhail backed the elders against their suffragan archbishop, Vassian Rylo of Rostov (1467–81), and Mikhail's overlord and sovereign, Ivan III, in a conflict that has intrigued several historians.[131]

Among the families noted by Iosif, the Kartmazovs, the Treparovs, and the Oboburovs (X.14) were all active in the sixteenth century; the Oboburovs included a Volokolamsk branch with ties to Iosif's monastery during his lifetime and afterwards. The Byvaltsovs from Tver were benefactors of and participants in the Kaliazin Monastery (X.31), and the Borozdins, also from Tver, had connections with both Kaliazin and Iosifov Monasteries (X.23).[132]

128. Borazkovsky, *Istoriia*, 194–203. On Moscow's civil war, see Crummey, *The Formation of Muscovy*, 62–82.

129. On Fotii's pastoral activities, see Golubinsky, *Istoriia* 2.1:389–410. Fennell, *A History of the Russian Church to 1448*, 162–69.

130. AfED, 471 (*Prosvetitel'*, Introduction, 21).

131. L:IB, 50–66.

132. AFZKh 1.81, 91, 102, 2.32, 284, 321. ASEI 1.50, 151, 444, 2.400, 505, 3.170,172–73. Buganov, *Razriadnaia kniga,* 44. Zimin, *Tysiachnaia kniga*, 317, 364–65, 411. Z:KFV 113–14. *Volokolamskii paterik,* 183–84.

Iosif's glorification of the outstanding early fifteenth-century Russian iconographers, Andrei Rublev and Daniil Cherny (both d. ca. 1427–32), can be interpreted several ways (X.29). On one level Iosif was attributing the greatest achievements of Russian iconography to native monastic piety as he understood it. On another level he was presenting a neo-hesychastic theory of iconography with an implicit reproach of contemporary painters for too much formalism and insufficient inspiration on their work.[133]

Creating Hagiography

Iosif's historical excursus allows us to witness an early stage of the crafting of hagiography—the recording of miracles. In a simple and straightforward case, Evfrosin of Savvateev prayed to the icon of the Virgin and arranged *molebens* to both the Virgin and Saint Nicholas, the favorite saints in Russia, to cure the young Mariia of Tver (X.28).[134] In another, a reverent nobleman has a vision of the desceased, lame, tireless disciplinarian, Varfolomei of Simonov (X.19). Savva of Savvin in Tver, another exacting disiciplinarian, completely tamed a possessed man by forgiving his vicious personal assault (X.21). Savva also miraculously delayed the death of several plague-stricken brothers in order to hear their final confessions and grant them absolution (X.22). After his death he appeared in a dream to an unworthy successor and physically beat him into fleeing the monastery (X.26). His erudite sage-hermit brother Varsonofii, in a throwback to regional political mythology, declares a copy of the Vladimir Theotokos icon the protectress of his valuable books, and then mirculously with his

133. Kuzmina, 'Drevnerusskie pis'mennye istochniki', 103–24. Goleizovskii, "Poslanie ikonopistsu", 233.

134. For representative of such Nicholas and Mother of God icons, see Belaiev, *Ikon Bozhei Materi Umileniia*, and *Istoriia russkogo iskusstva* 3:189. Also Gormin and Yarosh, *Novgorod*. No. 168. For representative *molebens* to the Theotokos for personal intercession, see van den Baar, *Kanonnik*, 64–79, and Mohyla, *Eukhologion*, 3:326–27. For a *moleben* to St Nicholas, see *Sobranie akafistov* 3:27–50v.

guilt-ridden tears revives the mortally smitten thief, who had taken them (X.23–24).[135] Iosif's account of the deaths of the inseparable iconographers, Andrei Rublev and Daniil Cherny—with one summoning the other to eternal bliss—is another specimen of incipient hagiography (X.29).

Eschatological Visions

The Rules contain several colorful eschatological visions, which are perplexingly and probably unavoidably contradictory, granted the liminal nature of the afterlife. In the opening section of the Extended Rule, Iosif attributed to Basil of Caesarea the opinion that even the great saints were not able to pass the 'demonic tollbooths' without being subject to vicious inquests (Int. 7). Iosif should have credited the *Life of Basil the Younger* (d. 944), in which the latter's disciple Gregory explains a vision of the soul's passing after death through twenty-one such stations. In them are demons conducting investigations over the following sins: 1) slander, 2) abuse, 3) envy, 4) falsehood, 5) anger and fury, 6) pride, 7) bad language, 8) usury and deceit, 9) indifference and vanity, 10) avarice, 11) drunkenness, 12) implacability or unforgivingness, 13) sorcery, 14) gluttony, 15) idolatry and heresy, 16) sodomy and pederasty, 17) adultery, 18) homicide, 19) theft, 20) fornication, and 21) stinginess and

135. This in fact was an adaptation of words attributed to Prince Andrei Bogoliubsky of Vladimir (1155–74), one of the founding fathers of the distinctive northern Rus (Russian) principality that developed into Muscovy. Prince Andrei is said to have exclaimed upon seeing in a southern Rus church the celebrated Byzantine icon now known as the Virgin *(Theotokos)* of Vladimir: 'If you will be the protectress of the Rostov (north Russian) land, . . . then all shall be according to your will'. The original legend claims that the icon assured both Andrei's safe return and a major victory over the Muslim Volga Bolgars. This became the occasion for the institution of the Feast of the Intercession of the Virgin 1 October as an important Russian holiday. Later the Vladimir icon—a tender Mary holding the Christ child against her breast—became a model for others, including those typically found in monks' cells. For a Muscovite depiction of monastic cells with copies of the icon ofthe Virgin of Vladimir, see Sidorova, 'Realisticheskie cherty', 78, plate 5. For the surrounding legends and their ideological context in Iosif's time, see Hurwitz, *Andrej Bogoljubsky,* 54–59, 69–78. Miller, 'Legends'.

hard-heartedness. This frightening peregrination of the soul—the 'minor judgment'—precedes its finding its resting place to await the Last Judgment.[136]

The apophthegmatic tradition, which Iosif readily utilized, has by and large a simpler notion of the passage of the soul, namely, that it is taken away after death by angels or demons, depending upon one's merits. In one striking example, Iosif borrowed from Symeon the New Theologian a colorful tale of two blood brothers personifying moral opposites, whom 'death takes to that fearful day'. The sinner, before being 'dispatched to the eternal fire', glances upward and sees his brother 'in great glory with Christ' (VIII^{B}.28, VI.34). Here the two judgments appear combined and may well reflect a central unifying aspect of monastic and non-monastic popular religious culture, which is depicted in the elaborate Last Judgment iconography of the time.[137]

Iosif's justification of his three orders in the Extended Rule, resting partly on the Parable of the Seeds (Mt 13:8,23) and partly on an unpublished eschatological work attributed to Hippolytus of Rome, introduces quite a different notion of the Christian nirvana (III.29–30). Using ideas found in Paul, Pseudo-Paul, and John of Patmos, Hippolytus or Pseudo-Hippolytus separately hypostatized the paradise and heaven of 2 Cor 12:2–4 and the heavenly Jerusalem of Rev 21:2–4. The three places then become the domiciles of the souls whose value has been reckoned equivalent to the thirty-, sixty-, and one hundred-fold yields of the parable. This passage also contains an affirmation of the ultimate resurrection of the body and an emphasis on the material-sensible aspects of future life at the expense of the mental-spiritual. In contrast, the chief textbook of Orthodox theology for Russia, John of Damascus's *Exposition*,

136. See Halkin, *Bibliotheca,* 93–94. For more details concerning the mystery of how the Greek twenty-one tollbooths became twenty in Russia, see Goldfrank, 'Who put the Snake on the Icon?', 180–81, 190–92. For the published Early Modern Russian version of this vision, still the official version for the Russian Church, see KZhS for March 15–31, 104–15. On the intriguing problem of the intermediary period between death and the Last Judgment in late pre-Christian Judaism and early Christianity, see Le Goff, *The Birth of Purgatory*, 19–55. Bernstein, *The Formation of Hell*, 131–266.

137. See below, Ch. II, Aspects of Iconography.

claimed that paradise is duplex in nature, spiritual and material, while some other Orthodox theologians and monastic theorists focused on the mental-spiritual aspects of beatified afterlife.[138]

The Brief Rule lacks any explicit eschatology, but contains, rather, a picturesque apocryphal exegesis on *Genesis*—taken from Nikon—with roots in biblical pseudepigrapha and the monastic apophthegmatic tradition. God's command to the fallen and expelled Adam that he till the ground (Gen 3:24) is seen as a defense against lust and the devil's temptations (VIII^{B}.13).

Heresy and Authority

A monastic rule may not appear to be the proper place to address questions related to heresy, but Iosif's Rules and his *Enlightener* have parallel themes. In Iosif's typically medieval vision of the universe, the devil and his army of demons with their tricks *(kovarstvo)* lurked behind sinful urges and enticements into not only dissident thinking, but also deviant practices.[139] Accordingly, parallel vigilance, control systems and outright scare tactics were necessary to protect monks from infractions of the Rule and to guard society from heresy. Iosif's concept of pastoral authority was roughly the same for abbots and for prelates, and he used several of the same Biblical and patristic citations in addressing bishops in general and his successor hegumen in particular.[140] He believed that the flourishing of monasteries and the survival of

138. See John of Damascus, *Exact Exposition,* 2.11, 4.24; PG94:909D-918D. Nicetas Stethatos, *Le Paradis spirituel,* ed. Chalendard, 40–59. Philippus Solitarius, *Dioptra*, 229–34; PL 127:866C-867C. All of these were available in fifteenth-century Russia. The Pseudo-Hippolytus work is not the *Slovo ob antikhrista* published by Nevostruev in 1868. Golubinsky noted an unpublished *Slovo* on *Revelation* attributed to Hippolytus and designated for reading on December 31: *Istoriia* 4:270.

139. This motif is found in the opening paragraphs of several of the *Prosvetitel'* discourses.

140. Cf. IX.13, XI.1–2,7–8, and AfED 474, and *Prosvetitel'* Introd.47 12.469–72, 15.494, 16.549–50. Iosif uses some of the same principles as 'a little negligence intercedes to cause a great calamity;' 'the whole world is not worth a soul . . . ;' and 'Son of Man, I have made you a watchman for the house of Israel . . .' (Ez 3:17–19) in the Extended Rule and *Prosvetitel'*.

a proper Christian kingdom, not to say general deliverance from eternal damnation, were dependent upon adherence to monastic rules and to inquisition-backed Orthodoxy,[141] and that sometimes only fire could purify a person or a place of sin or of heresy.[142] In both the monastery and in society at large, moreover, Iosif felt one had a duty to inform upon transgressors.[143]

That Iosif's doctrine of monastic authority is closely connected with the public controversy over the prosecution and persecution of heretics should not be surprising. More responsible than anyone else for the executions and imprisonments of 1504–05, Iosif was severely rebuked for this by Vassian Patrikeev and other 'Trans-Volgan elders', whose stated notions of authority were less severe.[144] Iosif, as a monastic theorist, thus needed to demonstrate that his ecclesiology held for the monastery as well. Accordingly, as he established the authority of the monastery council in his Rule, he took up some of the same issues he first aired in his defense of the condemnation of heretics, which he wrote in 1504–05. He even may have been using the Rule concretely to reply to arguments, based on the New Testament, against the condemnation of dissidents: 'Judge not, that you be not judged' (Mt 7:1) or 'Do not judge anything prematurely before the Lord comes' (1 Cor 4:5).[145] For in the Rule Iosif followed his own earlier advice from 1504–05, during the controversy over his inquisitorial tactics, to

141. Cf. I.15,34,45; XIII.7–11,555, AfED 502, and *Prosvetitel'* 14:507, 16: 544–51. Iosif also applies Jer 48:10 ('Cursed be he who does the work of the Lord negligently') to princes who fail in their inquisitorial duties, as well as to monks in general: *Prosvetitel'* 16:546.

142. *Volokolamskii paterik*, 181. Late in the seventeenth century, many devotees of the older rituals responded with self-immolation to the official church's innovations, seen as the advent of the Antichrist: Crummey, *Old Believers*, 39–57—though a fair amount of cynical fraud involved in enticing victims appears to have been involved in these tragedies. See Michels, 'Self-Immolation'.

143. XIII.19, XIV.34. First the Synod of 1490 and then Iosif claimed that anyone knowing of heretics and not reporting them was in fact in communion with them: AfED 386, and 491–92, 501–10 (*Prosvetitel'* 13–14, 485, 503–09).

144. K:VPS, 250–52. On dating and attribition problems, see Pliguzov, 'Polemika o novgorodskikh eretikov i "Otvet Kirllovskikh startsev" '. Vassian himself, according to one not necessarily trustworthy record, could be a murderous brute: PIV, 368

145. XIII.16,19,23–25,28–29,31.

use Discourse No. 39 of Nikon's *Pandects* as the ultimate authority on this subject (XIII.23–26).[146] Iosif's disciple Nil Polev utilized similar arguments to justify the Moscow synod's excommunication and confinement of Archbishop Serapion in 1509 over his treatment of Iosif.[147]

Curbing heretics required secular authority and force. Discipline inside a monastery did not, and Iosif simply adopted the story of the driving of the money-changers from the Temple as a precedent for clerics themselves to use physical coercion (I.25,27). To bolster his case, however, he did not shrink from perverting an apostolic canon and Nikon's exegesis by adding that it is proper for a bishop or priest personally to strike those who talk in church (I.28). The sense of the original, of Nikon's use of it, and of Vassian Patrikeev when he was upbraiding Iosif, is that the cleric must turn his other cheek.[148]

Iosif touched upon the general problem of heresy or schism twice in the Extended Rule. One was his stricture against unauthorized inscriptions in books: 'From these arise: disturbances, trouble and the corruption of the Divine Writings, discord and cliques and then curses and anathemas' (III.39). His formula is close to one attributed by Nikon to Basil of Caesarea concerning levels of dissent: 'discord, cliques, and heresy'.[149] In the Rule, Iosif appears to have been more concerned with schisms over minutia than with heresy over doctrine. All the same, he seems to have had an insight into the mentality that would produce and exacerbate the great seventeenth-century Russian schism (*raskol*), which resulted in part from minor ritual changes introduced by Patriarch Nikon (1652–67) without any attempt to achieve consensus among the faithful.[150]

146. XIII.23–25; AfED, 488 (*Prosvetitel'* 13:456–57).

147. Zhmakin, 'Nil Polev', 192–93.

148. Cf. Apostolic Canons 27; *Councils,* 595 (Mansi 1:33), as in Nikon, *Pandekty* 15:118. Iosif was also elastic in his interpretation and rendition of Chrysostom's disciplinary strictures: see 1.20 and the source noted.

149. Nikon, *Taktikon* 20:121V.

150. Michael Cherniavsky, 'The Old Believers and the New Religion', *Slavic Review* 25.1 (March, 1966) pp. 4–5. Note here Iosif's reported unwillingness or inability to compromise with the Pafutiev monks over the cœobitic reform indicates a rigid, doctrinaire character within Orthodoxy.

On the other hand, Iosif could be pragmatically flexible over non-essentials. At the end of the Rule he is quite clear: the formula that a country's customs have the force of law holds, but it applies only to such effects of geography and climate as food and clothing, not to faith or general deeds (XIV.39).

The one place where the Rules touch upon a doctrine allegedly held by the heretics is in the Hippolytus/pseudo-Hippolytus fragment, with its affirmation of the resurrection of the body (III.29). According to Iosif's invectives, Metropolitan Zosima not only protected free-thinkers, but actually denied the heavenly kingdom of the saints and the general resurrection of the body.[151] Thus, especially in the light of the role of memorial services in the monastery's economy, the affirmation in the Rule of a key element of Orthodox eschatology may not have been accidental. Hippolytus/Pseudo-Hippolytus was one of Iosif's principle sources for his analogical equating of Zosima with the Antichrist in a rhetorically brilliant missive.[152]

Relations with the Trans-Volgans

The relationship between Iosif and the group of monks known, perhaps mistakenly, as the Non-Possessors was as complex as its reflection in the Rules is many-sided. What has traditionally been considered as the Muscovite Non-Possessor movement entailed a diverse group of people with grounds to oppose the existence or growth of monastic estates and villages. The core of this faction was a set of monastic elders north of the upper Volga River—hence their own sobriquet 'Trans-Volgans'. It began with Nil Sorsky's advocacy of hesychastic prayer as the chief concern of all monks and his protests against all worldly concerns, attachment to

151. PIV, 161.

152. Goldfrank, 'Who Put the Snake on the Icon?', 195–96. *Missive to Nifont*, PIV, 162–72: neither of the surviving versions have endings which justify the rhetorical aim of the main body, in contrast, say, to his earliest surviving composition, his *Missive to Archimandrite Vassian on the Trinity*, which is rhetorically sound throughout: PIV, 139–44.

things, and carnal thinking among monks.[153] Subsequently a few of his followers, while staying within the confines of Orthodoxy, attacked Iosif and his faction at almost every turn: his inquisitorial program, his defense of monastic lands, his personal case against Prince Fedor and Archbishop Serapion, his Rule, and his disciples' qualifications as theologians.[154]

All the same, Nil and Iosif appear to have been rather close in several respects. They had a common foundation in monastic theology, a belief in written and human authority, and even a structural and stylistic dependence upon Nikon of the Black Mountain.[155] Some of Iosif's monks had a keen interest in Nil's writings.[156] In the ininital phase of the campaign against dissidence, Archbishop Gennadii of Novgorod expected the aid of the leading Trans-Volgan elders, within the scetes and hermitages, as well as the great northern monasteries.[157] Iosif himself, as he was attacking the heretics and Metropolian Zosima's circle, claimed to be speaking for the monastic order as a whole, including the anchorites.[158] He lauded the Kirillov Monastery of his day for 'shining like a candelabrum' with the founders teachings and traditions (X.13). In this light it is significant that Iosif's rendition of the third struggle within Kirillov Monastery sympathized with the bloc led by Nil's follower, Gurii Tushin (X.16).[159]

On the other hand, almost every aspect of Iosif's differences and conflicts with the Trans-Volgans is reflected in his Rules: his theory and style of inner monastic life, his attitude toward possessions, his success in having established himself as an authority, and his treatment of heretics.

153. Nil Sorsky, *Ustav*, Introduction 11–15, 5:46–57,59, 10:80–84, 11:90.

154. PIV, 336–66. K:VPS, 223–84. Zhmakin, 'Nil Polev'. L:IB, 226–29.

155. Compare Nil Sorsky, *Predanie*, his *Ustav*, Iosif's Brief Rule, *Prosvetitel'* 1, and Nikon's writings, especially *Taktikon*, Introduction.

156. L:IB, 298.

157. AfED, 320.

158. AfED, 474 (*Prosvetitel',* Introduction, 43).

159. Gurii, who had been tonsured by Iosif's future political ally Nifont, was a leading literary Trans-Volgan in the early sixteenth century, and, according to Iosifov traditions, considered Iosif's Rule to have been based on Kirill's: Kazakova, 'Knigopisnaia deiatel'nost'', and Savva Cherny, *Zhitie*, 496–97.

Iosif's perspective on inner spiritual life centered on community prayer, labor, obedience and the fulfillment of commandments, all of which secured salvation. Hesychastic prayer was only one among several recommended activities for the daily quiet period in the cell; his *Lives* emphasize instead ascetic feats, which in one place the Rule claims to produce 'the illumination of the divine light'.[160] Nil likewise believed in the acquisition of virtues and the avoidance of vices, but he focused on hesychastic praxis above all else. The two theologians, moreover, expressed different concepts of salvation itself. Iosif understood salvation in this world and the next basically as a state of glorifying God in a sanctified assembly. For Nil the goal was greater knowledge of God; his paradise was at least as mental and individualistic as physical and communal.[161]

The issue of possessions existed on two levels—the individual and the institutional—and was related to questions of lifestyle. Iosif's stance on personal possessions evolved, although in both Rules he theoretically adhered to the ideal of absolute non-possession (III.19). The Brief Rule has a specific polemic against the notion that books and icons are not the of same genre as other 'things' one is forbidden to possess (V^{B}.9). The Extended Rule, on the other hand, allows monks to keep books, icons, handicraft materials, and even money with the superior's permission (III.21,38). How Iosif actually handled this issue in the early period of the monastery's history is not clear. Around 1507, however, when the Extended Rule was more or less operational, he did permit the personal possession of valuable books and icons.[162] The superior could rescind this permission, as seems to have happened under his successor Daniil. Curiously, the monks whose books and icons had been confiscated, appealed to the elder Iona Golova, whom they 'held in Iosif's place'. They argued, as if contesting Iosif's Brief Rule, that many monastic fathers, including Iosif himself when he left Pafnutiev Monastery, had owned books and icons.

160. II.29, VIB.3/IV.3. Savva Cherny, *Zhitie*, 467–68.

161. Compare Iosif's understanding of paradise and divine illumination in IB.23/I.18, II.29, III.30, X.29, and *Prosvetitel'* 4:166, to Nil Sorsky, *Ustav*, Introduction, 15, and 9:79 (von Lilienfeld, 204, 247).

162. PIV, 212.

Maintaining that they kept their books and icons by licence of the monastery, the monks seem to have felt that they had the right to receive the superior's blessing for this, as if it were unwritten monastic customary law.[163] And so it probably was.

Nil Sorsky argued for poverty, but the small communities or scetes which he advocated were *idiorhythmic*; there the monks had to keep necessities on hand, but were enjoined to avoid any excess.[164] Nil directed his major complaint against the prevalent attachment to worldly affairs, adornments, property, and villages among rich *cœnobia*.[165] Iosif, to the contrary, promoted and praised the acquisition of institutional wealth (only some of which was directly used for charitable works—just as in the case of modern, tax-exempt 'foundations') in a special introduction to the monastery's *Synodicon* (*sinodik/senanik*), the ledger book of commemorative prayers and feasts for the dead. It is mentioned in the Rule in a special paragraph in which he insisted that the memorials be read every day (XIII.i.22). His separate *Account of the Synodicon* so clearly links this-worldly and other-worldly success that one might imagine he had read Max Weber on how medieval asceticism leaves the cloister and conquers the world.[166] Iosif also stated that obedience is a virtue superior to nonpossession (VI.29) and that poverty can most readily be practised in a cœnobium that provides the monks' basic needs (III.16).

The Extended Rule, when compared with the Brief Rule and coupled with the *Account of the Synodicon*, reflects the degree to which Iosif's foundation had become precisely that type of monastery which Nil opposed. Iosif's original Brief Rule sermon on labor underscored that monks work for charity as well as for themselves (VIII^{B}.22). In the Extended Rule, the ethical interest in charity is replaced by the emphasis on humility and total obedience (VI.18–30). The *Account*, moreover, unabashedly praises the acquisition of property and fine things, as well as necessities, all of them resulting from the sale and performance of memorial services.

163. Zhmakin, *Daniil*, Appendix 19:55–57.

164. Nil Sorsky, *Ustav* 11:89 (von Lilinenfeld, *Nil Sorskij,* 254).

165. Nil Sorsky, *Ustav* 5:59 (von Lilienfeld, *Nil Sorskij,* 234).

166. See below, Appendix I. Weber, *Economy and Society* 2:1167–73. Cf. Goldfrank, 'Perspectives', 294–96.

The accompanying feasts and their charitable side are of secondary interest.[167] For Nil Sorsky, poverty was superior to charity, and the true charity of monks was spiritual.[168] This is quite different from charity of the memorial feasts, where, according to Ludwig Steindorff's astute observation, the 'socially dead' recipients would in return pray for the souls of the donors.[169] In a somewhat ironic twist, Nil Sorsky's writings were among those that pious monks and prelates might give to the monastery to finance designated requiems. In other words, Nil's works enjoining Russian monks to avoid personal possessions became commodities that enriched Iosif's (and not only Iosif's) cloister.[170] In the light of prevailing eschatological notions in Russia around 1500, it probably could not have been otherwise. If Francis Clark is correct concerning the late seventh-century origin of Pope Gregory the Great's *Dialogues*, then we have an interesting parallel. Just like Pseudo-Gregory and his milieu, Iosif stretched tradition to innovate with commemorations at the expense of compromising some of the stricter principles of monastic poverty.[171] In the end, the writings of 'Nil of Beloozero' or 'Nil the Trans-Volgan' simply joined those of other monastic fathers among the valued treasures of a monastery library.[172]

Vassian Patrikeev's attacks on Iosif followed Nil's general indictment of possessions. Using the ethical authority of the New Testament, Vassian lambasted Iosif for completely neglecting Evangelical principles in his acquisition of wealth and power. As if assailing Iosif's regulation that peasants be judged outside the monastery's walls, Vassian also accused Iosif and his followers of a gamut of abuses normally attributed to high-handed, venal state officials or estate stewards collecting taxes and rents:[173]

167. See below, Appendix I; also XIII.i.22.

168. Nil Sorsky, *Predanie*, 6–7 (von Lilienfeld, 198). Nil's position going back to Isaac of Nineveh, is close to and may derive from Nikon, *Pandekty* 20:150. Cf. Isaac, *Mystic Treatises*, 18:99–101.

169. Steindorff, *Memoria*, 16, 50. Cf. Hasenfratz, *Die toten Lebenden.*

170. Int^{B}.3.

171. Clark, *Pseudo-Gregorian Dialogues*, 643–50: Clark notes, among other things, the authentic Pope Gregory's manifest hostility to monastic wealth.

172. KTsDR, 34, 37, 80, 81, 96.

173. K:VPS, 265.

> Those who have renounced fear of God and of their salvation order that those who have difficulty in paying back monastery debts be tortured mercilessly and investigated, with the aid of various punishments—but, significantly, not inside the monastery, rather somewhere outside, in front of the gates. They have considered it to be an act without sin to punish the peasant outside the monastery.

One section of the Rule, on the other hand, appears to have been directed against Vassian. Scholars have assumed that Iosif had Vassian in mind in the beginning of the tenth discourse:

> And if someone is overweening, very boastful, stiff-necked presumptuous, querulous, and censorious, and says: 'In earlier times our holy Fathers instituted in writing the cœnobitic teachings and traditions; it is not proper to do so now, but only to teach by word, . . .'

The issue at hand, however, was not that Iosif had composed his own traditions; Nil Sorsky had also done that. The real concern for Vassian was Iosif's power and influence, and Iosif's response was to combine in one discourse his defense of the legitimacy of composing a rule with a tendentious account of Russian monastic history to justify his own style of monasticism (X.1–44). At the same time he identified his own style as the Russian tradition, which he singled out for such achievements as the thirty wonderworkers recorded in the Kiev Pechersky Monastery's *Patericon* (X.II), or the decision by the Greek Metropolitan of Moscow Fotii to turn to the Russian elder Varsonofii of Savvin Monastery for advice (X.23). And, as if to counter the Trans-Volgans' reliance on the authority of Mt. Athos, Iosif had one of his elders proclaim: 'It is possible for those living here to be saved: for here everything is done just as in the cœnobia of the Holy Mountain'(X.31).

The tenth discourse also has some anomalies that would link it to the quarrel with Vassian. Iosif never states that his monastic predecessors in Russia actually composed any rules or traditions, but rather emphasizes exemplary lives, miracle-working powers and fidelity to standard community regulations. His initial enumeration of Russian founders (X.10), moreover, does not correspond precisely to those whose tales he tells. Savva and Varsonofii of Savvin, Evfrosin of Savvateev, Metropolitan Aleksii, Makarii of Kaliazin, and Pafnutii of Borovsk are missing. Instead Iosif lists, in addition to Antonii, Feodosii, Sergii, and Kirill, who are discussed, the following five: Varlaam (d. 1192, founder of Khutynsky Monastery near Novgorod), Dmitrii (d. 1391, founder of Spaso-Prilutsky Monastery in the suburbs of Vologda); Dionisii (d. 1437, founder of a colony of monasteries including Glushitsky near Lake Kubensky); Avraamii (founder of four monasteries including Chukhlomsky near the northern Galich; and Pavel (Obnorsky or Komel'sky, co-founder of two monasteries in the Vologda region).[174] Almost all these names are associated with the Church's conflict with Vassian Patrikeev over monastic villages: Vassian claimed that these saints did not own any villages, while spokesmen for the Church (including by tradition, if not necessarily fact, Iosif in 1503) claimed that they did.[175]

The institution of the council with its authority to name the successor hegumen and the examples given of elders' defending the founder's customs were also politically defensive measures. In the light of Vasilii III's power to appoint the successor and his forbidding Iosif to write anything against Vassian, Iosif firmed up his council as a means of preserving his overall political and ideological legacy.[176]

Iosif's monastic Rules, however, were not primarily directed against Trans-Volgans, whom he and his disciples attacked else-

174. Barsukov, *Istochniki,* 6, 10, 79–81, 156–58, 163–66, 416–18.

175. K:VPS, 233, 242, and PIV, 325. On the problem of dating Vassian's works, see Pliguzov, '"Prenie s Iosifom"'; 'Tekstologicheskaia istoriia "Sobraniia nekoego startsa"'; and 'Vstuplenie Vassian Patrikeev v polemiku o monastyrskikh zemliakh. This list, of course, could serve as evidence of later tampering with Iosif's original history of native monasticism. For the argument that the '1503' response was composed around 1551, see Ostrowski, 'Church Polemics'.

176. Goldfrank, 'Perspectives', 299–301. Late Byzantium had a tradition of emperors protecting monastic autonomy. Emperor Michael VIII Palailogos (r.1259–81) wished the Imperial Monastery of St Michael on Mt. Auxentios to remain autonomous under the superior and 'certain members of the spiritual brotherhood selected because of their age, way of life, and, it may be, surpassing the rest in learning', while St Demetrios was to remain autonomous under the superior and entire commiunity: *Typikon* . . . Auxentios 2:1217–18. *Typikon* . . . Kellibara 15:1249–50.

where in their defenses of monastic land and Russia's inquisition.[177] Iosif's chief targets within the Rules were the lax, the lazy, the unruly, the idle, the inebrious, the lascivious, the avaricious, the dishonest, and those who opposed his specific monastic innovations: his three orders, his council, and authority system, his prohibition of strong drinks, and, at an early stage, his theoretical rejection of any personal possessions whatsoever.

Aspects of Iconography

Paintings, either as frescoes or as icons, were central to the religious life of the devout in early Rus. Since disputes over icons were an essential element of the dissidents' challenge to the Church,[178] it would be surprising if the positive side of iconography and its veneration did not figure in his monastic writings. And indeed we find not only that icons play a role in the healings effected by Evfrosin of Savvateev and Varsonfii of Savvin, but that Iosif promoted the work of two of Russia's greatest masters, Andrei Rublev and Daniil Cherny, as examples of monastic sanctity and mystical prowess. In Iosif's words, their success as painters came from their elevation 'of mind and thought to the immaterial and divine light . . . and their sensible eye to the images, painted from material pigment, of the Lord Christ, his Immaculate Mother, and all the saints . . . would gaze fixedly upon them and be filled with divine joy and illumination'. Iosif further adapted for them the hagiographic trope of the vision of the first of a pair who die summoning the second to eternal bliss (X.29).

Unfortunately, the damage done to Iosifov during Russia's Time of Troubles (early seventeenth century) left no traces of the original frescoes executed around 1485 by the master Dionisii. Fortunately, though, Dionisii's slightly later murals at Ferapontov Monastery near Beloozero have survived in quite a remarkable state. We

177. AfED, 486–510. *Prosvetitel',* 13–16. Malinin, *Filofei*, Appendix, 128–44.

178. AfED, 322–73, 382–86 (*Prosvetitel'* 5–7: 170–332).

may therefore imagine that the soft blues, golds, yellows, whites, burnt reds, and light, spiritual, often optimistic figures found on the restored Ferapontov frescos also adorned Iosifov. Moroever, according to standard iconographic programs, almost all of Iosif's major sources would have been on a wall, ceiling or column frescoes or on the iconostasis, some more than once.[179] In the main Ferapontov church, consecrated to the Birth of Mary, a good deal of space is devoted to illustrating the popular *Akathistos* (Hymn) to the Virgin. As Iosifov was dedicated to Dormition of the Virgin, Dionisii may have painted the same or a parallel iconographic program for Iosif. One might wonder as well if Iosif commissioned an iconostasis icon or fresco similar to the Ferapontov one of the *Anastasis* (Descent/Resurrection), that figured so heavily in his apologetics—this one having the victory of symbolic angels over paired demons representing the defeat of evil, calamities, and vices (such as the fall of man, death, hate, arrogance, filth etc.), by the positive (the resurrection, life, love, humility, and purity).[180]

The Introduction to the Extended Rule, alludes directly to the standard Last Judgment fresco found on the western walls or their equivalents of most churches. Iosif, as we have noted, foregrounds the 'demonic tollbooths' which the souls of the deceased must traverse (Int.7). Curiously it was just at this time, around 1500, that a snake curling from hell up to Christ's judicial tribunal and having rings with demons to represent these tollbooths began to appear in Russian Last Judgment iconography. Whether Iosif was influenced by this development or caused it to occur is impossible to determine.[181] The standard Last Judgment tableau, which conflates the immediate ('minor') and final judgments and in the lower registers and, depicts the bliss of paradise on the viewer's left

179. Danilova, *Freski Ferapontogo monastyria.*

180. Gove, *The Slavic Akathistos Hymn.* Smirnova, *Moskovskaia ikona*, 291, pl. 145. V.K. Laurina argued that this icon expressed the ideals of Nil Sorsky's writings: 'Vnov' raskrytaia ikona "Soshestvie vo ad" ', 174–77; but, as we have seen, Iosif included the spiritual ideals of the Neo-Hesychasts under his own umbrella. Around 1550, Iosifov possessed about ninety icons painted by Dionisii and his disciplies. Z:KFV, 54.

181. For details, see Goldfrank, 'Who Put the Snake on the Tollbooths', 190–99.

(Christ's right) and the torments of hell of the viewer's right, as well as the damned being led or pulled directly into the fire,[182] serves as an implicit illustration of the above-mentioned morality tale of the two brothers, one lazy, the other diligent (VIII^{B}.28, VI.34). The frequent references to John Climacus, moreover, probably brought to mind among readers and listeners the standard depiction illuminated manuscripts of monks ascending a thirty-rung ladder, summoned by the saint, cheered on from below and above, but with a few being pulled off toward Hell by demons.[183]

The standard Dormition icon, which emblematized Iosifov and many other cloisters and *katholika* or cathedrals, can also be related to Iosif's Rule, whose very title suggests this mysterious representation. The depiction below the 'sleeping' Virgin of the severed hand of the guard, which will be restored when he changes heart and believes in her—all effected by the archangel Michael—expresses the drama of repentance and forgiveness. Above in heaven, borne by Angels in the heaven around the enthroned Virgin, are the twelve Apostles, who in the Extended Rule symbolize the monastery council (XIII.43).[184]

The protocol for general meetings in the main church or, during winter, in the refectory stipulates a ceremony to celebrate the resolution of the problem at hand, whereby the superior turns, faces the iconostasis, and recites the liturgical formula :'It is worthy that in truth we bless thee, [O Mother of God . . .] '(XIII/A.5).[185] It is

182. For depictions, see Smirnova, *Moskovskaia ikona*. pl. 113. Danilova, *Freski Ferapontova monastyria*, left side, pl. 57. Gormin and Yarosh, *Novgorod Art Treasures*, pl. 175, 197. Also Goldfrank, 'Who Put the Snake on the Tollbooths', pl. 5–8, 11.

183. For an earlier such depiction from Mt. Sinai, see Evans and Wixom, *Glory of Byzantium*, 376, pl. 247. For one from sixteenth-century Russia, see Grabar, *Istoriia russkogo iskusstva* 6: 293.

184. For such representations from Iosif's time, see Smirnonva, *Moskovskaia ikona*, 285–87, pl. 124, 130–31; for earlier, simpler versions, without the floating apostles above or the drama of the doubting guard below, pl. 7, 30; and the front cover on this book. Smirnova connects the lower depiction to the struggle against dissidence. Her tentative date for the first such elaborated Dormition icon, 1479, corresponds roughly to Iosif's first known foray into doctrinal apologetics (1476–77) and precisely to the foundation of his monastery.

185. See above, Ch. 2, note 90, and text to it.

also perhaps no mere coincidence that, so far as it is known, the period of Iosif's major activities witnessed the appearance of an original four-part icon dedicated to the Mother of God and leading off with 'It is worthy' (*dostoino est'*).[186]

This brief review only scratches the surface of the multiplicty of visual images, which Iosif's words must have invoked in his listeners and readers, surrounded as they were by icons and frescoes in their sacred indoor public space.

Doctrine of Man and Salvation

Iosif's basic theological work was not his Rule(s), but his *Enlightener*. Written for all Orthodox Christians, it was nonetheless permeated with a monastic mentality which justifies our using it as a summation of his ideas concerning man and the divine plan for salvation:[187]

> Just as the Father, Son, and Holy Spirit (*dukh*) are eternal and infinite, so man, created in God's image, carries within himself the likeness of God: a soul, a word, and a mind (*um*). And if man comes out of a body, that trinity in him which is the likeness of God, the soul, the word, and the spirit (*dukh*), sings and glorifies the Lord, as it has learned in the body—piously to make supplications, prayers and other good actions, not with reveries, but in truth. . . . Indeed, down to today an innumerable multitude has been saved thanks to his kindheartedness and mercy: some by means of the divinely beloved and pure life, others through repentance and tears, others with steadfast and warm faith; and others have obtained mercy after their death, because of prayers, offerings of the divine mysteries, and alms for the poor.

This is Iosif at his most optimistic, which, nevertheless, was dangerous for those who disagreed with him. He made no secret of his penchant for external practices including almsgiving (and receiving), nor would he omit the materially lucrative prayers for

186. Smirnonva, *Moskovskaia ikona*, 304–05, pl. 106.
187. *Prosvetitel'* 1:90, 4:166.

the dead, But all actions had to be performed, *not with reveries but in truth*. For there was no coercion involved in adhering to the rule (Int.11). Such was the fundamentalist piety of the leading spokesman and teacher of the Russian Church in the early sixteenth century.

In the translations which follow, the division of the Discourses and Traditions into paragraphs (indicated by the numbers in parentheses at the left side of the page) and into sections (indicated by the double margins between paragraphs) is solely the work of the translator and editor.

Part II

The Texts of the Rule

The Brief Rule

[Int^{B}.1] TABLE OF CONTENTS

[Int.^{B}.2] Let it be known, that in this book there are 11 Discourses, the works of Hegumen Iosif, the founder[1] of the Cœnobium of the Immaculate Mother of God, near the city of Volokolamsk, his cœnobitic traditions to his disciples taken from the Divine Writings. There are also his 11 Discourses and

1. *ktitor* — owner or founder, but Iosif, until 1507, shared ownership with his territorial prince and, to some extent, the brotherhood.

Introduction against the godless heretics.[2] If anyone reads though these discourses and protests that these are not suitable for everyone, but only for leaders and other philosophers desirous of opposing heretics and debating with them—it is not as he gripes, because they are comprehensive and suitable for everyone: prelates, gentlemen, commoners, and idiorrhythmic, cœnobitic, scete, and solitary monks. And if anyone reads these with attentiveness and true faith in God and the Savior, he will benefit greatly. Indeed they are excellent, because by these divinely inspired works the entire truth from the Divine Writings of the Prophets, the Evangels, and the Apostles are manifested, and the entire Judaic and godless deceit and the superstitions of all the godless heretics are exposed.

[Int.^{B}.3] In the year 7022[3], this book was donated by the monk Nil Polev for three souls, Kseniia,[4] the monk Mark, and the monk Nil. Their names are to be inscribed after they die in the daily list of the Cloister of the Venerable and Glorious Dormition of the Mother of God, in the foundation of our reverend father Iosif, near Volokolamsk.

[Int^{B}.4] We implore you, our lords and fathers who read through this book while we are alive and after our death, that you remember our complete love for you and they you memorialize our souls in your holy prayers.

[Int^{B}.5] And I have given eight books for myself for the daily list and three rubles in money for three forty-day requiems.[5] so that for the sake of God after each of our deaths forty masses with vigils—that is to say, the forty-day requiems shall be chanted without interruption.

[Int^{B}.6] We pray with tears and entrust our lord, the Christ-loving Prince Arsenii Golenin, the elder Kassian, my elder Iona Golova,

2. That is, the brief *Enlightener*, which is heavily biased towards a 'judaic' interpretation of the religious dissidents of the time.

3. 1 September 1513–31 August 1514.

4. Probably Nil Polev's mother. Cf. Chernov, *Volok Lamskii*, 174–77.

5. *Sorokoust*, the Greek τεσσαρακοστὴ/σαρακοστὴ, the forty-day requiem, contrived as a succor for the soul, which according to Orthodox (and related Jewish and Muslim) traditions, may wander for forty days after terrestrial death before finding its place to await the Last Judgment (or its equivalent).

and the elder Gerontii Rokitin[6] to execute this after the transit of our souls, and we hope that with love we obtain mercy from the Lord God.

6. Nil and these four represented half of the monastic council in 1514: PIV, 239–40.

Abba Iosif's Discourses to his Disciples from the Divine Writings on the Coenobitic Life.

Discourse I. On the Community Prayer.

Give a blessing, Father.

[I^B.1] First of all it is proper for us, brothers, to display much zeal and struggle so that everything in the cloister proceeds gracefully and according to order, and most important, the Order of the church offices, so that nothing great of small in the typicon be overlooked for any cause whatsoever.[1] Rather the order and the structure of the church offices shall be preserved without any damage or change, just as they have been handed down to us by the Holy Fathers by writing and tradition.[2] Therefore, let us receive them and renovate them in our hearts, so that they in no way, through the long course of time, fall into the depths of oblivion, become obscure, perish, and then soon come to nought. If we behold written models, and they still from day to day become corrupted and approach insignificance,[3] then how much worse would it be if we began to be indifferent about them and through laziness and despondency make the divine office indecent and thus petition for a curse for ourselves instead of a reward.

[I^B.2] Therefore first of all we strive so that *when the clapper sounds*[4] *let us quickly put aside everything in our hands and let us rush together very zealously and seriously to the divine and beautiful shelter of the church, as Peter and Paul ran to the Lord's tomb.*[5] *Let us not wait until the cessation of the clapper and the completion of the introit, and let us not say or think, 'if I arrive*

1. Cf. Theodora/Theodule Synadene, *Typikon* VI:1537–38.
2. Cf. John of Pantelleria, *Typikon* 10: 62–63; Timothy of Evergetis, *Typikon* 42:497.
3. Cf. AfED, 336 (*Prosvetitel'* 7:267).
4. John of Pantelleria, *Typikon* 1:61.
5. Jn 20:3–4, Lk 24:12.

early, then I shall have to wait a long time and shall sit in vain and to no profit'.[6]

[I^B.3] Athanasius the Great says: *'Holy angels stand in front of the altar. They observe the indifferent and the serious, recognize the reverent, identify those who do not so act, and mark those who curse, chatter idly, and converse'*.[7]

[I^B.4] Saint Ephraim says:[8] *'Be aware that when you walk toward the good, you will obtain your reward for each and every good word and each and every step. Likewise, when you walk toward evil, you will answer on the Day of Judgment for each step and idle word'*.[9] Again he says: *'When the brother claps, come quickly to life: diligently and zealously hurry to the church, life up your hand to God, and bow down to his throne of grace, as if you were a chamois*[10] *who had escaped from a snare or a bird from a net. Thus the lazy person, upon seeing your diligence and harmony, will lift up his soul and become cheerful, and you will be like unto the divine lips, for if someone takes forth the precious from the vile, he shall be as my mouth'*.[11]

[I^B.5] The longer you remain standing and waiting in the church, the more worthy you shall be of grace from God. The first to come to church is the first to obtain mercy from the Lord God. Whosoever comes to the earthly king always remains standing or seated at the palace first, awaits the king's procession, tarries, and is always patient. He who so acts is beloved by the king. But if someone arrives indifferently, with contempt, and last of all, he will be sent away as lazy and indifferent from the presence of the king. Similarly, if we become indifferent toward the rule for the church, arrive last and leave first, we shall be rejected by God as indifferent.

6. Source not identified: attributed to Chrysostom in the Extended Rule, I.2. For unattributed use of Chrysostom for instruction concerning the communal prayer, see Theodora/Theodule Synadene, *Typikon* VIII-IX:1539–41.

7. Source not identified.

8. Source not identified. Cf. Nikon, *Pandekty* 28:195.

9. Cf. Nikon, *Pandekty* 36:269^V.

10. *serna/sr'na*: a type of antelope.

11. Jr 15:19. Cf. below, Extended Rule Discourse XI.2, Discourse XIII.4.

[I^{B}.6] Therefore, brothers, let us cast off every earthly affair and responsibility, laziness and sleep. Let us strive always to hurry to prayer before everyone else, and thus we shall always be there at the beginning. Let us not wait until we have finished this or that piece of business or until the others have assembled and then go. But let us all race and compete against one another as if we were plundering booty. Just as whoever arrives there first is most enriched, similarly whoever comes first here is most enriched with heavenly riches.

[I^{B}.7] The holy Fathers say: *If anyone is doing anything when the hour for prayer arrives, and he does not abandon his ongoing activity, he is being mocked by demons. For the wicked devil knows we inherit the heavenly kingdom as a result of small labors. If someone strives and forces himself upon God's activity, and begins to arrive early at the divine temple and to pray and to hear divine words, then the devil introduces the opposite notion. He says: 'Wait until the brothers have assembled and then go'. Sometimes he advises us to finish certain legitimate and necessary things first and then go. When somebody is sleeping, he sometimes creates extraordinary dreams and other times submerges them in sleep. He carries this out in order to steal an hour of our prayer time and thus to incite indignation in God toward us. He knows that if the foundation is shoddy, then everything will be rejected and disgraced.*[12]

[I^{B}.8] Just as Cain made an offering first to himself and then to God and was cast off and spurned,[13] similarly he who now wants to arrange his vain, perishable and earthly affairs and thus does not arrive for the beginning of the divine chant will be cast off from God and be loathsome. So let us cut off this type of negligence, for 'cursed is he who does the work of the Lord negligently'.[14] This habit demands a savage remedy. Therefore let us first of all compel ourselves and enact for ourselves a law and commandment

12. Climacus, *Ladder* 19.3; PG 88:937BC; cf. Nikon *Pandekty* 30:214.

13. Gn 4:3–4. Cf. below, Extended Rule Discourse VI.32

14. Jr 48:10. Cf. below, Extended Rule Discourse I.26, Discourse VIII^{B}.25/VI.36, Appendix I.6.

for good deeds: always to hurry and to be the first to one to the divine activity, and with great zeal to rush to the food for the soul. If we merely lay our foundation and begin to act, God will not abandon us.[15] He will grant us mercy and send us help from his holy heights. For he surely loves us and wants to save us.

[I^{B}.9] And know this: the sober man makes a profit and the lazy man loses. Just as in the case of a sweet dish on the table or a gold piece thrown on the crossway, whoever comes first is the most satisfied or enriched. Godly words in the divine church are sweeter than honeycombs and dearer than a thousand gold pieces, according to holy David.[16] He who arrives first will enjoy grace first, but he who arrives lazily and carelessly is a stranger to grace and will be condemned like the wicked and lazy slave.[17]

[I^{B}.10] When the trumpet sounds for battle, no one puts off going, but everyone strives to be first before the king. He who[18] comes first achieves honor first. Here the trumpet blows for the heavenly king and summons us to the divine and beautiful shelter of the church. Therefore let us not wait or delay until the chanting commences.[19] Let us strive with joy, rush with love, anticipate one another and urge one another on to the doxology of our Savior Jesus Christ.[20]

[I^{B}.11] When we thus arrive in the divine church and stand as if with the powers on high of heaven itself, let us not merely display physical elegance, but let us also concentrate our minds with the sensations of our hearts and not whisper, banter, or speak vanities. Instead clasp your hands, join your legs, shut your eyes, concentrate your minds, and elevate your thoughts and your heart toward heaven. In this manner, with tears and moaning, call to

15. Seemingly adapted from Symeon, *Catechisms* 26.20–42.

16. Ps 19:10.

17. Mt 25.26. Cf. below, Extended Rule Introduction.11 (Int.11), Discourse XIII.55. Appendix I.6.

18. The printed *nizhe*=neither (PIV, 299) should probably be *i izhe*=and he who.

19. Cf. Symeon, *Catechisms* 26.24–25.

20. That is, the commencement of the Matins, not the formal "doxology" of the Liturgy, but the initial praising of God: Petras, *Typicon, 21, 24*. For this use, see Symeon, *Catechisms* 26.111.

God for mercy, and absolutely do not leave the assembly without an urgent need.[21]

[I^{B}.12] The Divine Writings speak in this manner in the *Patericon: When the priest Ammon was performing a liturgy of the divine office in the church, he saw an angel sitting to the right of the altar and writing down in a book the names of those who entered. He erased the names of those who left out of laziness, and they died thirteen days later.*[22] And Saint Dorotheus likewise speaks in his writings of the angel who distributes gifts to the monks who toil at vigils.[23]

[I^{B}.13] And the blessed Eulogius saw an angel distributing gifts to the monks who toiled at all-night vigils: to one he gave a gold piece with an image of Our Lord Jesus Christ, to another a silver piece with a cross, to another a copper piece, to another a bronze piece, and to another nothing. The others who had remained in the church remained empty-handed. It was revealed to him that the ones who had obtained the gifts are those who toil at vigils and are diligent in prayers, supplications, psalms, chants, and readings. Those who received nothing or who left the church empty-handed are those who are heedless of their salvation, are enslaved to vainglory and the clamors of life, and stand feebly and lazily at vigils and whisper and jest.[24]

[I^{B}.14] So know this, brothers: do not creep out of the church before the dismissal prayer, for he who exits from the divine chant or converses or whispers has been seduced by demons, as the Divine Writings bear witness.

[I^{B}.15] Indeed, Saint John Climacus says: *Some are forced by demons to make conversation in the church, others to joke and whisper, and still others to leave before the end.*[25]

[I^{B}.16] Saint Benedict is a witness to this, having had in his monastery a certain brother who left the chanting. The saint prayed to God to reveal who was taking that monk from prayer, and he

21. Seemingly adapted from Symeon, *Catechisms*, 26.25–62.
22. Source not identified: Geronticon in I.32.
23. Source not identified.
24. Source not identified.
25. Cf. Climacus, *Ladder* 19.3; PG 88:937.

saw a demon in the form of a Moor, taking that monk by his robe and dragging him from the church. Blessed Benedict beat him with his staff and he thus stopped leaving.[26] And there is a great deal of about this in the Divine Writings.

[I^{B}.17] So, fathers and brothers, let us force ourselves upon the godly activity. Let us be concerned first over physical elegance and good order and then over internal observance and attentiveness. Let us lovingly keep this as the most venerable activity: always to hurry to the divine chanting and doxology, not to leave in haste before the dismissal, and not to whisper or jest, lest we intercede for the wrath of God instead of divine mercy.

[I^{B}.18] As the divine Chrysostom teaches:[27] *Let no one relax: let no one utter or consider vain and perishable things. Rather drive every earthly thing from your mind; turn your whole self toward heaven, be sober, and stand with a lively soul before the Lord*[28] *Christ. When an archer desires to shoot his arrows successfully, he first takes great pains over his posture, aligns himself accurately with his mark and with zeal releases his arrows.*[29] *It should be the same with you, who are about to shoot the head of the wicked devil.*[30] First be concerned about the good order of sensations and then for the good posture of inner thoughts.

[I^{B}.19] *What is required of us for which we shall be called to account? To stand with much fear, with restrained and adorned reverence, with elevated thought, and with a contrite heart; and then visibly to display the character of your heart by means of posture, good order of the hands, and a meek and quiet voice. Indeed the Lord loves the calm and the meek: 'The man on whom I look', He says, 'is a meek and silent one, who trembles at my words'.*[31]

26. Pope Gregory the Great/Pseudo-Gregory, *Dialogues* 2,4; PL 66:141AC.

27. For the rest of this discourse, see Iosif's original version in AfED 351–56 (*Prosvetitel'* 7:204–18).

28. *vladytse* (*vladyka*, instead of *gospod"*), from the Greek δέσποτας. PG 48:734.

29. The original reads: and releases his arrows.

30. Adapted from *De incomprehensibili* 4; PG 48:734 (VMCh 1:819–20).

31. Is 66:2. Cf. Neilos Danilos, *Testament and Typikon* 12:1474–75. Also below, Extended Rule Discourse XIII/A.5.

[I^{B}.20] *When someone is talking with the earthly king, he contrives in every possible way to display great reverence for him. Thus chiefly and*[32] *by means of clasped hands, joined legs, and control over the whole body, he chooses his words from among those the latter desires. If he dares bring up something contrary to the latter's will, he receives the ultimate punishment. You are standing before the heavenly king before whom the angels tremble as they stand. You have abandoned your conversation with him and are talking about dung and dust and spider webs. How will you endure the penalty for your act of contempt? And why, o wretched one, do you neither fear nor tremble? Do you not understand that invisibly you are standing before the King of heaven and earth, who tests every mind and tries every conscience, and that angels stand before him in fear? But you do not consider this. Rather you carry on with such negligence and indifference, and you do not know what you are talking about. And why do you talk? Have you no fear, o wretched and lusty fellow? You are not afraid to say in the church what is heard in the market place, to surround yourself with 'disorderly howls',*[33] *to utter useless noises at that fearful time, to think about vanities, to be lazy, and to yawn and to be heedless of yourself?*[34]

[I^{B}.21] When a certain demon sees an idle, mucky, and doorless temple, he enters it with great fearlessness, as if it were a deserted cloister. If he sees anyone standing with sobriety, fear, and trepidation, completely extended and elevated, suspended from the very heavens, and releasing wellsprings of tears from his eyes, then the fiend no longer dares to look.[35]

[I^{B}.22] *Thus the Prophet sings out with fear. 'Out of the depths have I cried to you, O Lord'.*[36] *Note that we are to speak and pray from the depths of the heart, and with diligence, a grieving soul, and contrite thought. Such a prayer indeed goes up to heaven.*

32. *glavnym obrazom i*, a confused or ambiguous translation of διὰ τοῦ τῆς κεφαλῆς σχήματος: PG 56:101.

33. *Tüpikon*, 37^{V}.

34. Section [I^{B}.19–20] is adapted from Chrysostom, *In laudem* 1: PG 56:99–106 (VMCh 1:971–72, 977, 982).

35. Source not identified.

36. Ps 129:1/130:1.

When waters flow on flat lands, they do not move upwards. When they have been dammed up from their course, they collect and press together, and many spurts of water quickly shoot up high. Similarly, so long as human thought remains without fear and heedless of itself, it flows and runs off in many directions. When it is oppressed from below,[37] *by afflictive things and sad circumstances, it is greatly compressed and sends up on high pure and powerful prayers. That is why the Prophet said: 'In my distress I cried unto the Lord and he heard me'.*[38]

[I^B.23] *Let us warm our conscience with all of this, and let us become afflicted and oppressed. He who is always so afflicted while praying can attract to his soul the divine sweetness that originates in tears. The motion of clouds darkens the atmosphere, but when the rain releases many drops and falls, it makes the whole place calm and radiant. It is similar with sadness. So long as it is inside, it darkens our thoughts. When it relieves itself with the words of prayer and the accompanying tears*, and detaches itself from vain and alluring worldly conversation,[39] *it deposits much light in our soul with God's assistance, as if some beams of light were being sent by God into the soul of the person in prayer.*[40] *For the light of prayer is just like the light of a candle. And if you train yourself to pray with precision, you will not require instruction from your comrades, as God, without any mediator, enlightens your thought.*[41] At the time of our devotions, therefore, let us collect our wits, face ourselves, drive away laziness, chase every earthly and perishable thing away from our thoughts, and not be concerned about things earthly, perishable, and vain.

[I^B.24] *Someone may say that there is evil in unsettled affairs and concerning the real needs of our lives, but we shall not say this at all. This pretext is demonic and the enticement of the Devil, and*

37. The printed text *odole* should be, with modern spacing, *o dole* (orig. κάτωθεν).

38. Ps 119:1/120:1.

39. The original reads: 'and dissipates outside'.

40. Sections [I^B.22–23] to this point are Chrysostom, *De incomprehensibili* 5; PG 48:746, 744 (VMCh 1:836, 833).

41. I^B.24 from the last note is Chrysostom, *De incomprehensibili* 3; PG 48:725–6 (VMCh 1:807).

this word is vain. Indeed God, when scorned, scatters the assembly. Although we have a great deal to arrange in our lives, there are other times to hold meetings about them.[42] If someone speaks in church about these things—it is better not to come than to irritate the Lord. If someone comes, that wretched one labors in vain; for he is loathsome and unclean before God, since he has converted the divine temple into a robbers' den.[43] Let us unanimously be concerned about good order and, if it is possible, reprimand him. *If he is disobedient, bridle him as a calumnator of our salvation and drive him from the church enclosure,*[44] for our Lord Jesus Christ revealed himself as he raised his whip and drove them from the church.[45] *If he is insulting, spits, or speaks more sharply, do not abandon the treatment, beloved one. If someone is treating a man with a deranged mind and suffers great want and does not quit,*[46] then how much more proper is it for us, brothers, for the profit of our souls, to endure great afflictions and calamities and to gain them? *For the ill man has often ripped the doctor's clothing, dishonored, abused, and spat upon him, but the doctor was not embittered over these vexations, nor did he become wroth toward the sick man, as I remember, but he only wanted to see the sick man healthy. How can it not be absurd, that those who are so diligent to provide for bodies be indifferent toward the souls of those who perish? If he is displeased now, he still cannot harm you in any way and he will later be grateful to you. If he is your enemy today, tomorrow he will be your friend; and if he is your enemy tomorrow, then God will still be your friend.*[47]

[I^B.25] *Because in so acting, we save the brother, obtain clemency for our own sins and much free access to God. And we obtain an even greater reward than the man who prays, for the latter*

42. Chrysostom, *In laudam* 1: PG 56:102–3 (VMCh 1:976–7).
43. Cf. Mt 21:13.
44. Chrysostom, *In laudam* 1: PG 56:106 (VMCh 1:982).
45. Cf. Mt. 21:12.
46. Chrysostom, *De incomprehensibili* 2: PG 48:718 (VMCh 1:797). Cf. Nikon, *Pandekty* 54:449^V.
47. Chrysostom, *Adversus Judaios* 4:PG 48:882 (VMCh 1:879). Cf. Phoberos, *Typikon* 18:904.

only benefits himself, but he who bridles the disorderly benefits the many—first of all those who would stand before God and serve him with a humble heart and then those who would be unruly. Let us obtain for ourselves a double profit and have among us the Lord himself who gives a crown to each of the orderly ones.[48] This is what Saint John Chrysostom teaches and commands.

[I^{B}.26] Let us strive as much as possible, with fear and with love, not to deprive the office of the smallest item. We know full well that if we safeguard the office in keeping with the traditional *typicon* and canon, we will be granted physical and spiritual health to serve the living and true God in the present age. And in the future age, you can await the day when you shine like the sun with the saints, and in return for these meager little labors, you will obtain the joy of the heavenly kingdom, in Jesus Christ our Lord, to whom is the glory for ever and ever.

48. Chrysostom, *In laudem* 1: PG 56:106–07 (VMCh 1:982).

An account from the divine writings concerning food and drink

Discourse II

[II^{B}.1] Just as we have said concerning the office in the church, that it is proper for us to conduct ourselves in the divine church with much zeal and attention cum fear and to bear responsibility for good order, in the same manner concerning food and drink, select the simple and inexpensive.[1]

[II^{B}.2] And keep yourself from eating in secret and in no way dine alone or with anybody, for all evils are born from this.[2] And these are seeds from the devil, which appear to be nothing, but which contain within themselves a hidden poison.[3]

[II^{B}.3] Basil the Great says: *If you control your stomach, you will enter paradise; if you do not control it, you will be devoured by death.*[4] Again he says: *Keep yourself from eating in secret, for if craving for a little taste of something can place in your stomach the passion of madness, it will shamelessly give you over to death. I have seen many possessed by passions and then cured by repentance, but I have not seen one secret-eater or glutton who desisted or repented. Rather they either withdrew from the life of abstinence and rotted in the world or they concealed themselves from the continent ones and dined while the devil aided them with voluptuousness. Outwardly they were among the saved; actually they were among the doomed.*[5]

[II^{B}.4] And it is written *in the Life of Saint Theodore Sanctified, the disciple of Pachomius, that one day, when he was lecturing to the brothers, he said: 'When some monks were fasting as is customary, an unclean spirit came, found a thirsting and weakening monk,*

1. Copied from *Tüpikon*, 46, Nikon, *Taktikon* I:13.

2. Pseudo-Basil, *Ascetical Discourse*, 26–27; PG 31:641BC. Cf. *Starchestvo*, 33–34; Symeon, *Catechisms* 26.13–16.

3. Cf. Jas 3:8.

4. *Ascetical Discourse* 26; PG 31:641B. Cf. Nil Sorsky, *Ustav* 5:42.

5. Ascetical Discourse 24–25; PG 31:640A. Cf. Climacus, *Ladder* 14, *Scholia* 20; PG 88:877BC.

placed a thought within him, and inflamed his thirst. For it is the custom of demons to resettle as a passion of a man and attack him. He immediately made him steal some bread and eat surreptitiously, and now that monk-thief sits among us, a transgressor of his vow'.[6]

[II^{B}.5] Saint Symeon the New Theologian says: *Nothing profits us, my brothers, if we restrain the great passions and are controlled by the little ones. I say, if we preserve unsullied flesh, and we master fury, theft, and all filth, and we remove ourselves from laziness, despondency, contumacy, disobedience, murmuring, and the consumption of great amounts of wine, we take no profit, when we eat some bread or something else without the superior's command.*[7]

[II^{B}.6] And Saint Gregory, Pope of Rome, bears witness to this: *There was a certain monastery,* he says, *called 'The Galatians',*[8] *in which there was a certain monk, who was considered by everyone to be saintly. When he was found to be sick, all the brothers assembled about him, and were waiting to hear something great from such a holy man. Forced to depart from his body, he was crying and trembling, and he said this: 'You believed that I was fasting with you, but hidden away from you I used to eat. And now, therefore, I have been given as food to the Serpent, who has bound my legs and knees with his tail, has placed his head inside my mouth, and is pulling out my dying spirit'. Having said this, he immediately died. And this shows that God willed that it be told for our profit, lest we so perish, for that one did not escape the Adversary to whom he had been consigned.*[9]

[II^{B}.7] And Saint Nikon writes similarly in his missives: *A certain elder,* he said, *collected a brotherhood. Having boldness towards God, he prayed that he might see his deceased disciples. Seeing two in a very terrible place, he interrogated them. The first answered: 'I had an unconfessed thought, and therefore they*

6. Nikon, *Pandekty* 57:474.
7. Cf. Symeon, *Catechisms*, 26.170–242; *O ezhe kako podobaet*, 16^{V}-17.
8. Slavic *galatiiskii*; published Greek των γαλάτων and Latin τῶν γαλατῶν.
9. *Dialogues* 4:40; PL 77:393BC, perhaps as in Nikon, *Pandekty* 34:240^{V}.

have brought me here'. The second one answered: 'gluttony has destroyed me'.[10]

[II^{B}.8] Lo and behold, we have heard that no one should consider this to be a trifle. Not one virtue is profitable, if one is indifferent toward this one. Rather those who have neglected this are horribly tormented and utterly destroyed. Therefore our first struggle is to contain our stomach and concentrate our heart on fear of hell and our desire on the heavenly kingdom, so that in fearing hellfire and enjoying the beauty of the heavenly kingdom, we cut off the fiercest passion of all and the origin of all evil, which is eating in secret. We do not forbid nourishment which is necessary for life, but we cut off the voluptuous root, the originator and perfecter of all evils, the demonic habit of eating-in-secret.[11] Otherwise we cannot escape the demon of gluttony. Therefore we are diligently diligent and soberly sober, so that if we become slightly ill, the Lord will immediately aid us and not allow a passionate stomach to operate within us, by the grace of his Holy and life-creating Spirit, Amen.

10. *Taktikon* 38:200–200^{V}, attributed to *Starchestvo*.
11. Cf. Nikon, *Taktikon* 1 (72), BMFD, 405.

That one should not converse at the table.

Discourse III

[III^B.1] It is proper that there be great precision, so that at the refectory table no one speak any word whatsoever other than the verse and the lection. When it becomes necessary, then only the superior or the refectory servant shall speak, with restraint and reverence. For the divine Fathers say concerning this: The holy sacrifical altar and the brotherhood's table at dinner time are equivalent.[1]

[III^B.2] It is said in the *Patericon: An elder said: 'Once I was sitting with Father John Colubus and a certain elder was eating with him. The elder spoke once, and Abba John was tacit. He spoke a second time, and the elder was tacit. He spoke a third time, and Abba John said to him: "Behold, Abba, since this one sat at the table, God has been taken from me, and noise has entered". And he got up, took his basket, and began to work. The elder was grieved and left right away. I said to Father John: "Why, Abba, have you shocked the man in such a way that he went away grieved?" He said to me: "It is much more excellent, good, proper, and suitable not to anger God and not to grieve the holy angels, for it is written: 'I spake before kings and was not ashamed'.*[2] *If we honor the One, they shall all honor us; if we are negligent of the One who is God, they shall all neglect us, and we shall go to perdition. He who reveres the One, does not fear the many; rather the many fear the One. A man who converses at the table is in no way different from a pig or a cat, for a pig slurps when he feeds, and a cat purrs when he eats. I shall go to that elder and make a prostration, and beg forgiveness. He shall profit, I shall sit untroubled, and you who are in no way harmed shall go to your cell" '.*[3]

1. *Tüpikon*, 43^V. Nikon, *Taktikon* 1:6 (BMFD, 394). Entire paragraph almost *verbatim* from Nikon.

2. Ps 118/119:46

3. Source not identified.

[III^{B}.3] Again it is said that Abba Isaac, the *hegumen* of Scete, said: *A monk who sits at table and does not pray in his mind, but converses and utters any word at all—such a man is physical, not spiritual. He who at table chatters, laughs, or reviles the food, has withdrawn from God and God has withdrawn from him. His prayer is not welcome, and his labors are futile.*[4]

4. Source not identified.

An account from the Divine Writings concerning garments and footwear

Discourse IV

[IV^B.1] Just as we have said concerning foods and beverages, that it is good to select the simple and unexcessive and to do everything with the counsel of the spiritual superior; by the same model, have clothing that is necessary, simple, very mean, and appropriate for the place and climate, and do not by means of demonic cunning seek out the very expensive and excessive.[1]

[IV^B.2] The Canons of the Seventh Ecumenical Council say: *Bishops*, monks,[2] *or clergymen who have adorned themselves with colorful and bright clothing should on this account be reprimanded. If they persist, they shall be given a penance. If someone laughs at those wearing worthless garments, it shall be corrected with a penance. Indeed from the first years, every monastic and priestly man passed his life in humble and worthless garments.*[3]

[IV^B.3] The most supreme Peter said to his disciple Clement: *Clement, you have not understood my life, that I only eat bread, olives, and the most worthless vegetables and that my coat is this old robe, and I do not need another. For my mind always beholds the eternal and good out there and does not regard anything here.*[4]

[IV^B.4] It is said in the *Life* of Chrysostom that after his elevation to the archbishopric of Constantinople, that his food was strained, ground barley, which was placed in water for a day, and he took a correctly measured quantity. His garment was a hair-shirt, and he did not have a third one for changing.[5]

[IV^B.5] Saint Gregory the Theologian says of Basil the Great:

1. Nikon, *Taktikon* 1:13^V (BMFD, 406). Cf. *Tüpikon*, 46.

2. 'Monks' is not in the original or Nikon, and may have been added by Iosif.

3. Nicea 2.16; *Councils*, 566 (Mansi 14:754AC), as found in Nikon, *Pandekty* 37:283^V-284.

4. Pseudo-Clement *Homilies* 12:6:293; PG 2:305BC, as found in Nikon, *Pandekty* 37:282^V-283.

5. Cf. Nikon, *Pandekty* 37:283^V.

Basil the Great said to the prefect: 'I am not afraid of pillage, for I have nothing unless you need one of my hair-shirts'.[6]

[IV^{B}.6] And again Father Isaiah says: *Do not vainglory in clothing, but remember the sheepskin of Elijah and the sackcloth of Isaiah, and do not forget the Baptist's garment, which was of camel's hair.*[7]

[IV^{B}.7] It is written of Arsenius the Great that when he was in the world, he wore the brightest of all clothing, and when he was a monk he wore the most worthless.[8]

[IV^{B}.8] When Sabas the Great went to the emperor, they drove him from the palace as a beggar, for he was wearing an old and tattered shirt.[9]

[IV^{B}.9] The holy Fathers say that all luxury and adornment is alien to the priestly and monastic habit.[10] Therefore from the earliest years all the saints went about deprived, grieving, and maltreated in sheepskins and goatskins, *and the whole word was not worthy of them.*[11] 'He who is adorned with clothing in the worldly life obtains glory from man; he who has humble and very worthless clothing in the monastic life prepares glory for himself and in the heavens'.[12]

[IV^{B}.10] Father Isaac said: *Our fathers wore old rags. Now you wear the most expensive clothing. Go away from here, for you have devastated this place.*[13]

[IV^{B}.11] Saint Ephraim said concerning this: *He who loves bright garments is stripped of divine clothing, and our robe spoils love of goodness in that it has nothing in common with the heavenly kingdom; the beauty of our garment signifies that we are stripped of*

6. *Funeral Oration*, 411; PG 36:560C, as found in Nikon, *Pandekty*.

7. Nikon, *Pandekty* 37:281^{V}, attributed to Ephraim, before a citation attributed to Isaiah.

8. Arsenius, *Sayings*, 8: PG 65:88C, probably as in Nikon, *Pandekty* 37:281^{V}.

9. Cyril, *Zhitie*, 270–73, as in Nikon, *Pandekty*, 37:283^{V}.

10. Nicea 2.16; *Councils* 566 (Mansi 13:754B), as in Nikon, *Pandekty*, 37:281^{B}.

11. Heb 11:38.

12. Nikon, *Pandekty* 37:281, attributed to Ephraim.

13. Isaiah 7; *Sayings* 85; PG 65:225B, as in Nikon, *Pandekty* 37:281.

that glory. Again he says: *For you the Lord accepted abuses on the cross, and you, wretched one, adorn yourself with garments! Does you heart not tremble? Is you mind not horrified when you hear this? The Impassible One suffered passion, that you might adorn yourself not with the rotten garments, foods, or meals of common people, but with those proper to monks. The crucified Lord will seek out an answer for all of your indifference; for you, who are now listening, are now indolent, eating luxuriously, adorning yourself with vestments, and laughing. When the great and terrible day comes, you will cry incessantly in the fire and will wail with the weakness of your soul!*[14]

[IV^{B}.12] Saint Symeon the New Theologian says: *We, the passionate and wretched, who have abandoned the great and the admirable and have entered a monastery, now love shiny garments, belts, cutlery, sandals, and drapery, sweet foods and drink, and apples and beautiful fruits. In loving them we fall away completely from Christ the King and become his enemies.*[15]

[IV^{B}.13] The holy Fathers say that a debauched demon observes the monk's vestments to see if he has the best one for the sake of conversation. This is a *typicon* for debauchery, and we shall therefore be condemned with the publicans and sinners and with the rich, who have lived in debauchery.[16]

[IV^{B}.14] Let us, then, exert ourselves with all our strength to abstain from avarice, adornment of garments, and passion for things, and not only not have possessions, but also not even desire them.[17]

[IV^{B}.15] The unknown incursion of death, moreover, must always be before our eye, lest Our Lord come at an unexpected hour and find our conscience polluted by avarice and materialism and say to us what is said to the rich man in the Gospel: 'Fool, this night your soul shall be required of you and these things which you have

14. Source not identified.

15. Symeon, *Catechisms* 5:806–14; *O ezhe kako podobaet*, 10–10^{V}.

16. Attributed to Isaiah in Nikon, *Pandekty* 37:281^{V}. Cf. Symeon, *Catechisms* 5.81–19; *O ezhe kako podobaet*, 10^{V}.

17. Cf. Nil Sorsky, *Ustav* 5:47.

prepared, whose will they be?'[18] On this account, our holy Fathers, all having the same understanding, handed down to us as a tradition that one cannot lay any firm foundation for the perfection of virtues if one does not exercise perfected non-possession,[19] from which are born humility and compunction.

And this is enough of that for now.

18. Lk 12:20. Cf. Cf. Heppell, *Paterik . . . Kiev.*, 62. Also John of Phoberos, *Typikon* 24:911.

19. *nestiazhanie*: the Greek ἀκτησία, sometimes rendered as 'non-acquisition'.

An account from the Divine Writings concerning holy icons and books, how one must have them

Discourse V

[V^{B}.1] We shall speak of holy icons and books, how one must possess them.

[V^{B}.2] The Divine Writings of the holy Fathers say concerning this: *Abba Theodore of Pherme had three good books, and so informed Macarius, saying: 'I profit from them, and the brothers take them and profit from them. Tell me, what am I supposed to do about them?' The elder said: 'The thing is good, but non-possession is the highest good of all'.*[1]

[V^{B}.3] Abba Evagrius says:[2] *A certain brother had one Gospel and sold it and gave to the poor, saying: 'I sold what says to me directly: "Sell what you have and give to the poor"'.*[3]

[V^{B}.4] *A brother asked Father Serapion: Tell me, how can I be saved? The elder said to him: 'What can I say to you, who have taken what you should give to the widows and orphans and placed it on a window sill'? For he had seen a multitude of books in his cell.*[4]

[V^{B}.5] A brother asked Father Poemen, saying: 'I desire to live in a cœnobium'. The elder said: *'If you desire to live in a cœnobium, renounce everything, and do not have dominion over even a cup, and thus shall you be saved in a cœnobium'.*[5]

[V^{B}.6] Basil the Great speaks similarly: *It is not proper for an ascetic who lives in a cœnobium to have material possessions, but he shall be free from all personal possessions.*[6] *In possessing anything great or small in a cœnobium, one makes oneself alien to God's church, and similarly one has alienated oneself from God's*

1. Theodore of Pherme 1; *Sayings*, 63 (PG 65:188A).
2. Source not identified. Cf. *Sayings*, 54–5 (PS 65:173A-176A).
3. Cf. Mt. 19:21.
4. Serapion 2; *Sayings*, 190 (PG 65:416C).
5. Poemen 152; *Sayings* 158; PG 65:360B, cited in Nikon, *Pandekty* 4:30.
6. Cf. Pseudo-Basil, *Constitutiones* 34 (PG 31:1424C-25C).

love. It is better to live with a few intelligent people than with many who are negligent of the Lord's commandments. Those in holy monastic garb who live in a cœnobium must not say the words, 'yours', 'mine', 'this one's', or 'that one's', in relation to anything. When there are people who sow weeds and think in such a manner, it is not proper to call it a cœnobium, but a mob of brigands,[7] *full of all sacrilege, wickedness, and evil. Cœnobia are so named, because everything is held in common.*[8]

[V^{B}.7] *Everywhere the rules of the common life write: 'Do not acquire any personal possessions, nor do anything in secret to the detriment of the brotherhood, or become a bad model for those who are predisposed to salvation. When someone has scorned fear of God and the laws of the Holy Spirit* and wants to have some personal possessions, he has become enslaved to materialism and possessions. Similarly *he produces evidence of disbelief against himself; he does not trust that God spiritually and physically comforts those gathered in his name, for "if two or three are gathered in Christ's name, he is among them",* [9] *Indeed no needed thing will be wanting when Christ is our superior if it is wanting for the sake of testing us, then it is better to be wanting and to be with Christ than to become rich in all worldly goods and to be without communion with him'.*[10] and be condemned with them, for our Lord Jesus Christ says: 'Whoever will come after me, let him take up his cross and follow me'.[11] Likewise, 'Whoever of you does not renounce all that he has cannot be my disciple'.[12] We who have renounced everything deceive ourselves with imaginary hopes that we have joy and security in our collected goods.

7. Close to the 'den of theives' formulation of Mt 21:13. Cf. Athanasios the Meteorite, *Canonical Rule* 9:1460.

8. Cited in Nikon, *Pandekty* 4:28^{V}; used by Bishop Dionisii of Suzdal in his statutory missive to the Pskov Snetogorsk Monastery in 1382 and by Evfrosim of Pskov in his Rule: AI I:5; Von Lilienfled, *Nil Sorskij*, 288–89, 298–99. The last sentence reads: *sego bo radi naritsaiiutsia obshchaa zhitia, da vsia obshcha imut'*.

9. Mt 18:20. Cf. below, Extended Rule Discourse XIII/A.5.

10. Nikon, *Pandekty* 3:28–29, quoting Basil, *Constitutiones* 34; PG 31: 1425BC.

11. Mt. 16:14; Mk 8:34.

12. Lk 14:33.

[V^{B}.8] Let us be on guard against this immense stupidity. We have abandoned the great and the admirable, that is to say, father and mother and other beloved ones, and the whole world and what is beautiful and sweet in it. We abide in afflictions and calamities and wrestle with physical passions day and night, as if against a lion and a serpent, and we always taste death.[13] Shall we again be bound to trifles and little nothings, in this life be dead to conscience, and in the future life obtain God's wrath instead of God's mercy?[14]

[V^{B}.9] If someone says: 'Holy icons and books are not "things", and therefore it is proper for "non-possessors" to have their own'. If that were so, then Macarius the Great would not have said to Saint Theodore: 'Non-possession is the highest of all'; that brother would not have sold his holy books and given to the poor; and Serapion the Great would not have scorned the brother who had many books. Notice that they honored non-possession before anything else, not only in the cœnobium, but also those living in hermitages, where the needs are many, great, and unavoidable. Did they really not have books in hermitages? They did have them, but not their own, as the blessed Peter Damascenus bears witness: *I never had my own books, but I borrowed them from devotees of Christ, read them, and returned them.*[15] In a cœnobium there is no need, but through the grace of Christ, his servants live together with abundance of all good things.

[V^{B}.10] Therefore let none of those, who have not falsely renounced life, walk in opposition to the commandments. Rather honor the narrow over the wide, poverty over wealth, infamy over glory, and endurance of pain over joy here and now, so that in the present life he will illuminate life with a light, and in the future we shall inherit the kingdom which cannot be taken away, which is Christ, 'the light and the life'.[16] And no one here has a more beloved or honorable mind than his.

And this is enough of that for now.

13. Cf. Climacus, *Ladder* 26:41; PG 88:1088C.

14. Similar to a longer passage in the Introduction to the Extended Rule (Int.6) attributed to Ephraim of Syria, but close in places to Pseudo-Basil, Climacus, and Symeon the New Theologian.

15. Cf. *Dobrotoliubie* 3:5^{V}.

16. Cf. Jn 1:4.

Concerning not conversing after Compline

Discourse VI

[VI^{B}.1] After Compline, as the God-bearing Fathers discerned, it is not proper to stand and converse in the monastery or to assemble in the cells.[1] Only the *hegumen* may speak out about the needs of the cloister, but for the sake of good order he shall speak in a cell.[2] Nor should anyone drink water, except for the sick. For Compline has been established by the holy Fathers as the conclusion and the fulfillment of the whole day.[3]

[VI^{B}.2] And in case someone happens to have transgressed during the night or day,[4] it is therefore proper after the conclusion of the Compline chant not to speak foolishly of the vain and perishable or to criticize or slander somebody. Rather with humility and contrition of the heart, make a prostration at the foot of the superior, as if at the very feet of Christ, and confess to him everything you did in the preceding night and day: deeds, words and thoughts.[5] The holy Fathers required hourly confession. If that is not possible, then certainly do not let an evening come, when you do not confess these[6] out of fear of death, because many have gone to sleep at night and not gotten up the next day. 'In the state I find you', says the Lord, 'shall I judge you',[7] either in repentance and compunction or in negligence and merriment. Indeed there is no other consolation at the time of death than repentance and confession.

1. Cf. *Tüpikon*, 18–18^{V}. Petit, *Vie de s. Athanase*, 40.
2. Cf. Joachim of Zichna, *Typikon* 17:1602.
3. Cf. Nikon, *Taktikon* 1:13.
4. Professor Wladimir Vodoff, following Lur'e's punctuation, suggested an alternative reading: For Compline has been established by the holy Fathers as the conclusion and the fulfillment of the whole day, especially in case someone happens to have transgressed during the [preceding] night or day. ([VI^{B}.2] would follow, beginnning with: It is therefore proper after the conclusion of the Compline chant . . . . See PIV, 309); Vodoff, 'Compte rendue', 203–04.
5. Apparently from Basil, *Longer Rules* 37:310; PG 31:1056. Cf. Timothy of Evergetis, *Typikon* 7:475–6. Archbishop Sava *Tipik* 7:49–50. Gregory Pakourianos, *Typikon* 13:537
6. Cf. Theodora/Theodule of Synadene, *Typikon* XX:1553–54.
7. Cf. Ez 21:30.

[VI^{B}.3] And having thus received absolution from the superior[8] as if from God himself, one should flee in silence into one's cell and not speak to anyone. And so one should apply oneself with quietness[9] in prayer or handicraft or reading, be soberly mindful of oneself with prayers and tears, and repent and confess all transgressions to the Lord. Then his soul can rest from the burden of having transgressed in the preceding night and day. If it happens that he die that night, he will not be disregarded by the Lord God, because he will have been found in repentance and confession. For the Lord himself sings out through the Prophet: 'In the state I find you, I shall judge you'.[10] To him is the glory.

8. Cf. Joachim of Zichna, *Typikon* 22:1606.

9. *bezmolvie*, the equivalent of the Greek ἡσυχία—the quieteness of the Hesychasts.

10. Ez 21:30.

An account from the Divine Writings, that it is not proper for monks to go outside the monastery without a blessing.

Discourse VII

[VII^B.1] It is necessary to know that it is improper, better to say, calamitous, for monks to go outside the monastery without the superior's blessing. For if we need to go outside for some food, clothing, or work, will we not obtain his blessing? If it is necessary, then it is especially proper to go with a blessing, lest our labor be in vain; for every deed without a blessing is cursed.[1] If it is good, then why go without a blessing? If we go outside for something evil, that is, to banter and laugh and make idle chatter and eat and drink, these manifestly dispatch our souls to hell.

[VII^B.2] When a monk starts to be negligent about himself and to wander outside the cloister without the superior's blessing, then the devil traps him, hurls him toward sin, or hands him over to death. If he indeed hurls him into sin, then he immerses him in the despair that there is no longer hope for salvation, and he is drowned in disgrace and shame over the lack of that boldness towards the father which comes from obedience. Thus he seduces him in the world to the ultimate destruction of his soul, just as the elder who was ninety years old bears witness. Though being of such age, he went off to the city without the father's blessing, fell into fornication, and was not able quickly to repent because of his disgrace. Rather he put it off until they brought the child to Scete, and he cried inconsolably in front of everybody.[2]

[VII^B.3] Many indeed have despaired to the ultimate joy of the Adversary. If he entraps someone to his death, obviously the latter is being condemned by God as a transgressor of the patristic commands, just as we have found in the Divine Writings of the Fathers. A certain elder lived for fifty years without going outside

1. Cf. Pseudo-Basil, *Ascetical Discourse* 20; PG 31:633B.

2. Attributed in the Extended Rule, Discourse V.2, to the *Otechestvo* (*Patericon*); source not identified.

the monastery and wore his black robe well. The devil envied him, tempted him to leave the monastery without a blessing, and then fettered his foot and smashed him against a rock, so that he died. They told the *hegumen* about the death, and he, not guessing the Adversary had tempted that one to leave the monastery without a blessing, told the brothers to pray for the deceased brother. When they were praying for him day and night, a voice came to them: 'Do not register as part of the brotherhood him who did not heed his vow. Rather bind his foot with a rope and throw him in a ditch'. And they did so. Thus the holy Fathers forbade giving such a person a burial or offering an oblation for him, because he was a transgressor of his vow. He had vowed at his renunciation of the world to remain in the monastery until his last breath, and he had vowed to preserve his obedience to the superior even until death.[3]

[VII^B.4] Therefore, brothers, let us exert ourselves wholeheartedly to flee, as if from a stench and deadly sting, individualism, insubordination, and wandering outside of the cloister without the command of the superior, and let us struggle even until death. Let us place our souls along the single line of God's commandments, and let us keep as our tradition the measure and typicon throughout—in motions, words, and deeds.[4] To our God.[5]

3. Cf. *Paterik skitskii* (VMCh 4:2657–58), found in the Old Russian *Lausaic History*.

4. Cf. *Tüpikon*, 42^v; Nikon, *Taktikon* 1:6^v (BMFD, 392).

5. A mid-seventeenth century copy adds: is the glory now and always and for ever and ever. Amen.

An account from the Divine Writings, that it is proper for everyone to exert himself in community work

Discourse VIII

[VIII^{B}.1] It is proper to know that it is necessary here also to talk about community work.

[VIII^{B}.2] It is proper for everyone to exert himself in community work. *Indeed the holy Apostle Paul says: 'We command you, brothers, in the name of our Lord Jesus Christ, that you withdraw yourselves from any brother that walks disorderly*[1] *and does nothing'. 'Similarly we command you, brothers, and we exhort you in Christ Jesus that you work quietly and eat your own bread'.*[2] *And 'if anyone will not work, let him not eat'.*[3] Therefore the holy Fathers, instructed by these apostolic teachings, counsel monks, especially the young, never to be idle.

[VIII^{B}.3] And Macarius the Great says: *Nor can an idler be faithful.* And again: *Idleness has taught much evil.*[4]

[VIII^{B}.4] And again it says: *The worker wrestles with a single demon, and the idler is imprisoned by a thousand demons.*[5]

[VIII^{B}.5] And again it says: *He who can work and does not work will be condemned with the robbers.*[6]

[VIII^{B}.6] And again it says: *A monk who lives in a cœnobium must have these three: humility, obedience, and exertion in his work for the community.*[7]

[VIII^{B}.7] Saint Ephraim says: *This is the origin of arrogance and*

1. 2 Thes 3:6.

2. 2 Thes 3:12. Cassian, *Institutes* 10.7; PL 49:373–75, as in Nikon, *Pandekty* 44:345.

3. 2 Thes 3:10. Cassian, *Institutes* 10.22; PL 49:388–93, as in Nikon, *Pandekty* 44:347. Cf. Si 33:38.

4. Attributed to Lot by Nikon, *Pandekty* 44:348^{V}. Cf. Si 30:27; Symeon, *Catechisms* 26.75; 'Izbornik 1076', 52.

5. Cassian, *Institutes* 10.23; PL 49:393–94, as in Nikon, *Pandekty* 44:347.

6. Attributed in the Extended Rule to the *Geronticon*. Cf. Eph 4:28.

7. Attributed to Poemen in the Extended Rule: Poemen 103; *Sayings*, 152 (PG 65:348A).

loftiness, not to desire to labor with the brotherhood in keeping with one's strength. Such a person shall not eat. As we set forth, let us not be long-winded, but our zeal shall be directed only toward our original goal.[8]

[VIII^{B}.8] And in the *Holy Ladder* it is said: *As much as faith blooms in the heart, the body hurries to serve.* And again: *Heartily give the labors of your youth to Christ, and you will rejoice in old age over the wealth of impassibility; for that which is gathered in youth feeds and comforts exhausted old age.* And again: *Let us young ones labor in heat. Let us run soberly. Death is uncertain. In truth we have gruesome, wicked, deceitful, atrocious, strong, vigilant, immaterial, and invisible enemies, who are keeping fire in their hands starting to burn the divine church due to the flame which is in them.*[9]

[VIII^{B}.9] The Fathers said: *Once when Anthony was sitting in the desert he was in a state of despondence and mental gloom, and he said: 'Lord, I want to be saved, but these states of mind will not leave me'. A little later he saw another, sitting and weaving baskets, then standing and praying, again sitting and weaving baskets, and again standing and praying. It was an angel of the Lord sent to correct him. And Anthony heard a voice say to him: 'Do like this, and you shall be saved'. Hearing this he had great joy and boldness, and he so acted and was saved.*[10]

[VIII^{B}.10] Abba Matoes said: *I prefer light work that abides for a long time to heavy work that I quickly stop doing.*[11]

[VIII^{B}.11] Abba Isidore, the priest of Scete, said: *Brothers, did we not come here for the sake of labor? We no longer have any labor. I have readied a sheepskin and I shall go to where there is labor, and there I shall find tranquility.*[12]

[VIII^{B}.12] Ammoes said: *We once went to Abba Achilles, and we listened to him teach with the words: 'Jacob, fear not to go down*

8. Cited in Nikon, *Pandekty* 10:74.
9. Climacus, *Ladder* 1.24; PG 88:641BC.
10. Anthony 1; *Sayings* 1 (PG 65:76AB), as in Nikon, *Pandekty*, 44:346^{V}.
11. Matoes 1; *Sayings* 121 (PG 65:290C).
12. Poemen 44; *Sayings* 145 (PG 65:332D).

into Egypt'.[13] *And he for a long time kept saying these words. And when we knocked he opened to us. We found him working at night and making many baskets, and we asked him: 'Tell us something'. He said: 'From evening up to now I have woven twenty fathoms, and in truth I do not need any, but I fear God may be wroth with me and say: "Why, if you can work, have you not worked"? Therefore I labor with all my might'. And we profited immensely.*[14]

[VIII^B.13] An elder said: *There are four virtues incumbent upon a man: fasting, praying to God, physical chastity, and manual labor. The devil countered these four and drove out Adam. First he bound him with food. Secondly he shamed him and made him hide and not come before God, lest Adam at some time come before God and have his transgression forgiven. Just as Adam was driven out as an idler, the devil, wanting to attract him to himself, wanted him to aspire to another transgression by his idleness—despair. The humane Lord, having foreseen the devil's evil machinations, gave work to Adam and said: 'Till the ground whence you were taken',*[15] *in order that so long as Adam bore responsibility for his work, he would repel the devil's evil cunning. Then the devil, completely vanquished, prepared the vessel of fornication, joined the daughters of man to the sons of God, and led them into the desire of the flesh. Indeed the devil struggles against fasting and manual labor, since manual labor cuts off his great evil cunning. And he struggles against virtuous chastity. If someone is honored with the action of these four virtues, then he possesses all virtues.*[16]

[VIII^B.14] An elder said: *The novice does not need any activity other than obedience and physical labor.*[17]

[VIII^B.15] A brother asked an elder: 'Tell me, how can I be saved'? The elder responded: 'Let us strive to work and not be lazy, and we shall be saved'.[18]

13. Gn 46:3.

14. Achilles 5; *Sayings* 25 (PG 65:125AB), as in Nikon, *Pandekty* 44:349.

15. Gn 3:23; cf. 'Slavic vita Adae et Evae', *Apocrypha and Pseudepigrapha* 2:134–38.

16. Attributed to *Starchestvo* (*Geronticon*) in Nikon, *Pandekty* 44:346–46v.

17. Source not identified.

18. Source not identified.

[VIII^B.16] An elder said: *It is proper for a man to safeguard his work lest he destroy it, for if someone works a great deal but does not safeguard it, then there is no profit. If he creates a little and is observant, the work remains intact.*[19]

[VIII^B.17] And indeed nothing squanders good works so much as to speak, jest, and laugh. Saint John Climacus says: *I have seen some, who priding themselves in their skill in lying and exciting laughter by their jests and idle chatter, have destroyed the tenderness of those listening to a lamentation.*[20]

[VIII^B.18] Basil the Great says: *It is proper to move far away from jesting, for it happens that those who often engage in it lose the right word, often tread this evil path, and end their days in filthy language, improprieties, and corrupt communication.*[21]

[VIII^B.19] The Apostle says: *Let no corrupt communication proceed out of your mouth, and do not grieve the Holy Spirit, by whom you are sealed.*[22] And what evil it is to grieve the Holy Spirit!

[VIII^B.20] It is said in the Divine Gospel: *A good man out of the good treasure of his heart brings forth good; an evil man out of the evil treasure of his heart brings forth evil, For out of the abundance of the heart the mouth speaketh.*[23] And again he says: *'For every idle word men speak they shall give an account on the day of judgement'.*[24] *An idle word means uncoerced lying that is to say, a lie or slander. Some say that an idle word is one which excites unruly, filthy, shameless, or illicit laughter.*[25]

[VIII^B.21] And Saint Poemen says: *There is a man who is considered to be a silent one, but in his heart he criticizes others. That one is always speaking. There is another who talks from*

19. Source not identified.
20. *Ladder* 12:4 (PG 88:856A), cited in Nikon, *Pandekty* 10:74^V.
21. Cited in Nikon, *Pandekty* 10:74.
22. Cf. Eph 4:29–30; Pachomius, *Instructions* 2:34–35.
23. Mt 12:34.
24. Mt 12:26.
25. Chrysostom, *Matthew* 42:269–70; (PG 57:453), as in Nikon, *Pandekty* 10:74.

morning to night and keeps his silence, that is to say, except for what is useful, he says nothing.[26]

[VIII^{B}.22] Saint John Chrysostom says: *Nothing is more shameless than the jester, for his mouth is full of disease, bitterness, and deceit; let us drive away such habits from our tables. There are*, he says, *some who teach this to the poor. How disgusting! And they make those in afflictions jest. I speak, indeed, and I shall show a multiplication of evil. I am shamed, but again I speak. I know that I shall raise a laugh, but I shall say what I have heard. It happened that a man was with another, whose intelligence was that of a great thinker, and they made a toast: 'Go to it children: take and eat, lest your belly be angry'. And again, others said: 'Misery to you, Mammon, and those who do not possess you'. Soul, these expressions are devoid of reverence, and these expressions are not even worth a thunderbolt. Thus I exhort you in every way, that we drive away such habits, speak what is proper, and not let our holy mouth make conversation and disgraceful and filthy words:*[27] What communion does light have with darkness?[28]

[VIII^{B}.23] From banter—idleness; from idleness—negligence; from negligence—unruliness; from unruliness—laughter and boldness; and laughter and boldness are the ruination of the soul, monks! And Saint Ephraim says: *If you see yourself in this, o monk, you see yourself in the ultimate perdition.*[29]

[VIII^{B}.24] *The Apostle wisely shows us the cause of laughter and boldness, for he calls the jester and those who do not work 'unruly'.*[30] *The unruly and the jester become irreverent, bold in word, ready for contumely, incapable of quietness, and a slave to despondence. Therefore the Apostle commmands us to preserve ourselves from that as from a feverish illness, and not to 'eat bread for naught', but to work 'with labor and travail day and night that we need not be chargeable to anyone'.*[31] *And work not only for your*

26. Poemen 27; *Sayings*, 143 (PG 65:329A), as in Nikon, *Pandekty* 10:75.
27. *Ephesians* 17:131 (PG 62:120), as in Nikon, *Pandekty* 10:74–74v.
28. 2 Cor 6:14.
29. *Quod non oporteat ridere*; ed. Assemiani 1:254; ed. Thwaites, 157.
30. 2 Thes 3:11.
31. 2 Thes 3:8–12.

own needs, but also for the lowly, the wandering, the enfeebled, and the aged, for such benevolence is a welcome offering to God.[32]

And this is what concerns community work.

[VIII^{B}.25] Let us speak now of the other offices, which are in the cloister, of how it is proper with zeal and with fear of God to bear responsibility for each office, to which one has been assigned, as Basil the Great says: *Perform the work of your office gracefully and diligently, as if serving Christ:*[33] *for cursed is he who does the work of the Lord negligently.*[34] *Fear the fruits of wicked negligence more than ineptitude, even if your work seems bad, for God is inspecting.*

[VIII^{B}.26] *The work of the office is great and intercedes to the heavenly kingdom. It is a dragnet for virtues which bears in itself all the divine commandments. The very first of all these is humility, which delivers a multitude of blessings. Next is 'I was hungry and you gave me food; I was thirsty and you gave me drink; I was a stranger and sick and in prison', and you served me,*[35] *especially when the duty is performed with humble-mindedness, without loftiness, anger, or murmuring. In the daily steps of your office, make ready along with the actual physical labor a word of consolation for the beloved one served, so that your service be welcome, combined with salt. And do not forsake the work imposed upon you for others to do, lest the reward be taken from you and given to another, and lest another be glorified with your riches, while you are humbled.*[36]

[VIII^{B}.27] Likewise it is said in the *Patericon* that a certain father asked father Zeno: 'Tell me, father how can I discern whether my service has been welcomed by God'? The elder responded: *'The first sign for the serving man is benign thoughts, love of God, and fear. The second sign is humble-mindedness in the face of*

32. Cassian *Institutes* 10.8,22; PL 49:376, 393, as in Nikon, *Pandekty* 44:346–47.

33. Cf. Eph 6:7.

34. Cf. Jer 48:10. Cf. above and below, Discourse I^{B}.8/I.8, Extended Rule Discourse I.26, Appendix I.6.7

35. Cf. Mt 25:35.

36. Pseudo-Basil, *Ascetical Discourse*, 29, 21; PG 31:645BC, 633BC.

everybody; consider that you are serving not men, but angels, and that in keeping with the Lord's words, "Wherever I am, there shall my servant be also",[37] *you are standing before Christ's sacrificial altar. The third sign: words of compunction, speech without murmurs, sighs from the heart, the flowing of tears, fear of God, desire of future blessings, precision in your charges, so that nothing be arranged unseasonably or be materially excessive, but everything with faith and fear of God. If you behold and feel these in yourself, the service is welcome and pleasing to God, angels, and men. But if your service is accompanied by wickedness, deceit, stupidity, murmurs, troublemaking, bitterness, any stinginess with food, unnecessary laziness in prayer, solitary eating, fullness of sleep, extravagance with fearlessness, neglect of brothers in your charge, avoidance of elders, reviling of novices, contumely towards the great, desire for worldly people and readiness to eat and drink with them—such a servant is a friend of vainglory, a disciple of arrogance, and a seeker of praise. He does what is forbidden by the leader; he is no counselor of the superior's representative, but does everything by himself concealed from the superior; squanders; cheers up the devil; destroys himself; becomes a friend of Achar of Israel, a companion of Gehazi, a disciple of Judas the renegade, and a brother of Annias and Sapphira.*[38] *Such a servant is without reward and, deprived of his reward, forfeits his labor. Such as servant is a lamb by day and a wolf by night. Such a servant is a monk in form and among the worldly in understanding. Such a servant is a dry spring, a house without cover. Such a servant feeds upon vainglory from the devil, imbibes arrogance, dresses in turpitude, studies disputation, and is shod in wickedness. The mind of such a servant becomes murky; his thought darkens; his heart hardens; and he is titillated towards beauty by debauched thoughts*[39] *and freefalls into masturbation. Such a servant has surpassed Hellenic sacrifices in his vanity, for the Hellenes offered*

37. Jn 12:26. Cf. below, Extended Rule Discourse XI.2.

38. See Jos 7:16–26; 2 Kgs 5:21–27; Acts 5:1–11; Mt 26:14–15,47–49, 27:3–5; and parallels.

39. Cf. Climacus, *Ladder* 14.36; PG 88:869D.

animals and were disciples of demons; this one not only offers birds and animals and is a friend of demons, but makes a whole offering of himself, with the touch of the hand and the relaxation of the mind clothes himself completely in the voluptuousness of the devil. Such a servant is replete with irascibility, filled up with bitterness, agitated by anger and controlled by malice.[40] *Why should I talk so much? He has fallen from the heavenly kingdom, if he does not correct himself through fasting, vigils, prayer, confession, and humble-mindedness,* and if he does not carefully exert himself to take responsibility for the office he has been given.

[VIII^{B}.28] Saint Symeon the New Theologian speaks similarly: *Two brothers by blood,* he said, *rejected the world. Both were young and pure regarding every bodily sin. One was humble, readily submissive, and obedient, and worked as it for God, not men, and had a humble and contrite mind-set, and so never thought of himself, and said to those who questioned him: 'In the world, venerable Fathers, I could hardly obtain food with much labor. Having come here, why would I want to neglect work, feed off the monastery's bread gratis, and be called to account for it on the Day of Judgment? Because now I have come here to slave for God, I am striving with all my strength to increase my work, rather than my food, and I shall submit to my director and to all my brothers without a murmur, even unto death, as if to Christ himself'. The other brother was overcome with pride, insubordination, and laziness, and said: 'God has now sent me a house, bread, and wine, and I am now among the first, and I am a brother to all, willy-nilly, and I shall eat and drink to my full. What need have I henceforth to work? So that I labor and others acquire the fruits of my labor'? When they ordered him to work, he alleged debility, by crying and shrieking, claimed weakness of the knees, and responded: 'I feel murky—my head is troubled with bile', so that he could eat, curse, and blaspheme from morning on, and he contradicted all commands and murmured. And if they gave him any work or office, he similarly neglected it. And under these circumstances,*

40. Source unknown, but found separately in a mid-sixteenth-century codex in the St. Petersburg State Public Library: *Rogozhskii* 530:32v-34.

death came and took both of them to that fearful day. The one who was evil was naked, and shamed, and standing to the left, and he immediately looked up and saw on the right the one who had once lived with him and ate and drank with him, and who was now in great glory with Christ. And what could he then say or answer? But groaning, and shaking, and gnashing his teeth, he was dispatched to the eternal fire.[41]

[VIII^{B}.29] *Another father told us this, saying: When I went to the cœnobium for a visitation with the fathers, I was there for an ample number of days to observe their life. Once I beheld the œconomus*[42] *enter the kitchen. He saw a few lentils strewn on the floor and did not disdain this as if it were a little thing, really nothing, but summoned the brother whose responsibility it was to do the cooking, gave him a penance for having slighted the office bestowed upon him by God, and set his conscience straight.*[43] They safeguarded their offices with such faith and so much zeal that those things which we suppose to be trifles and unseemly, they preserved them as if they were holy objects of some kind. If they saw a vessel or anything else in the wrong place, they put it in its place with fear, believing that they would receive a reward from God for this.

41. From Symeon, *Catechisms* 5.861–967; *O ezhe kako podobaet,* 12–15.

42. *Ikonom* (Greek: οἰκονόμος), the functional near equivalent of the cellarer in Russia.

43. Source not identified. Editor's surmise of the end of the citation and commencement of Iosif's commentary.

An account from the divine writings that it is not proper for drinks which cause drunkenness to be in the cloister

Discourse IX

[IX^{B}.1] As drunkenness is the beginning and end of all evil, our Lord Jesus Christ therefore says: 'Watch over yourselves, lest your hearts be weighed down with overeating and drunkenness'.[1] And the Apostle Paul says: 'Do not get drunk with wine, wherein is debauchery'.[2]

[IX^{B}.2] And Basil the Great says: '*Just as smoke drives away bees,*[3] *so drunkenness drives away the Holy Spirit, because drunkenness is the door to passions, the commander of pollutions, the worker of debauchery, billows of smut, a sea of thoughts, an abyss of indescribable filth, profanity, insensitive banter, audacity, insatiability, psychic analgesia, non-remembrance of death, lack of hope, and despair, the most gruesome of all,*[4] which generates psychic ruin and mental derangement.

[IX^{B}.3] And Saint John Chrysostom says: '*The Holy Apostle Paul indeed spoke well: "For I have told you often and now tell you weeping that they are enemies of the cross of Christ, whose God is their belly and whose glory is their shame".*[5] *So he who fills his belly excessively and lives in fornication and drunkenness is an enemy of Christ, for the glutton and the drunkard destroys his body and his soul'.*[6]

[IX^{B}.4] *Do you see how the drunkard is more hateful than the demoniac? For the demon drowns man with God's sufferance, but the drunkard destroys himself by his own will. His saliva is*

1. Lk 21:34.
2. Eph 5:18.
3. Cf. Antiochus, *Pandectes* 4; PG 69:1444C (VMCh 4:1878).
4. Climacus, *Ladder* 14.36; PG 88:869D; see also 27.41 (1108CD).
5. Phil 3:18–19; Cf. *Philippians* 13:242; PG 62:275. See Titov, *Opisanie* 2:751–53.
6. Cf. *Ephesians* 19.2:138; PG 62:129.

inflamed and he gives off a stench and an evil belch like an animal. Consider this, how the soul of a drunkard wallows in the body as in a pit and in a swamp.

[IX^{B}.5] Many stupid people say: 'This holiday is venerable; let us drink and be merry'. You fools, do you understand what you are saying here, that you have forsaken the divine festival and are pleasing the devil, as if you preferred working for the devil rather than for Christ? For you are not venerating God's holiday but the devil's when you overeat, get drunk, and debauch. If you enter a church, how can you glorify God? Since the drunkard belches out a stench, God hates a drunkard as much as we loathe a stinking dead dog. Let him who would be free from all of this abhor drunkenness and thus cut off the serpent's head and crush his whole body.[7]

[IX^{B}.6] First of all, therefore, it is proper to have much responsibility and zeal so that no drinks which cause drunkenness be in the cloister, the refectory, or the cells.

[IX^{B}.7] If it is written in the *typica* and *Lives* of the holy Fathers that monks may drink wine at the proper times, sometimes one cup and sometimes two or three,[8] and that they had wine in all the monasteries, both in the early and the present ones, yet they did not drink to drunkenness. As many noble men and monks who have been in Constantinople and on Holy Mount Athos and other places bear witness, not only monks, but also all Orthodox Christians hate and loathe drunkenness. Not only the Orthodox, but the unbelievers flee and hate drunkenness.[9] They all have wine, but they flee from drunkenness as from a putrescent disease. Such is the custom of

7. Sections [4]-[5] appear to have been inspired by Chrysostom, if not taken directly from the Chrysostom/Pseudo-Chrysostom corpus.

8. Cf. Nikon, *Pandekty* 57:485–89. (Pseudo-)Theodore, *Rule* (Ὑποτύπωσις) 29–30:109–11 (PG 99 1713C-1716C). (Pseudo-)Athanasius *Rule* (Ὑποτύπωσις) 22–26:226 (Meyer, 137–39). BMFD, 109–11; *Tüpikon*, 41^{V}.

9. Note here the indirect reference from the (as reflected in *Prosvetitel'*) very intolerant Iosif not only to differences between drinking customs among Orthodox and Christians in the southern and northern parts of Eastern and East-Central Europe, but also to Jewish calls for moderation and, perhaps, Islamic strictures on abstinence.

that land, and the custom of the land is unwritten law, as we have stated earlier.[10]

[IX^{B}.8] As for Russia, there is another custom, another law: if we have drinks which cause drunkenness, we cannot abstain, but we drink to drunkenness. What the holy Fathers commanded regarding one cup, two, or three, this we do not wish to hear. Nor do we know the measure of their cup. Instead, this is our measure: when we are so drunk that we do not recognize or remember ourselves, then we stop drinking.

[IX^{B}.9] On account of this custom, destructive ethic, and sinful habit, it is not proper for us to have drinks which cause drunkenness in the cloister, lest we fall into ultimate perdition, the pit of fornication, which results from drunkenness.

To our God be glory now, always, and forever and ever. Amen.

10. Actually this is discussed only at the very end of the Extended Rule [XIV.38–39], indicating that the Brief Rule, as it survives, is not Iosif's earliest such composition.

An account from the divine writings that it is not proper for boys to live in the cloister

Discourse X

[X^B.1] The Divine Writings say about boys: *Not God, but our adversary, the devil brings boys into the monastery to trouble active monks.*[1]

[X^B.2] And again Father Isaac said: *Brothers do not bring children into the cœnobium, for I have seen three churches deserted on account of children.*[2]

[X^B.3] Again a great elder came to a cœnobium, saw that there were boys there, and therefore did not enter to sleep. He said: *'If it only enters my mind that some of them are here, I shall immediately be troubled. Why should I take on an unnecessary battle'*?[3]

[X^B.4] Saint Ephraim says: *It is a great calamity for boys to be in a cœnobium.*[4]

[X^B.5] And again Abba Poemen says: *A man who has a boy living with him, fights with a passion to keep from him, and does not drive him away is like a man with a cornfield which is devoured by worms.*[5]

[X^B.6] And again it is said in the *Patericon*: *Once a demon came to the brothers in a cœnobium, saw a boy in the cœnobium, and said: 'I do not need to be here, because he will be much more troublesome here than I'.*[6]

[X.^{B}.7] In wanting to be saved, therefore, let us move far away from them as from a flame. Let us not turn toward them in a house or in a place where no one sees us. Let us sit far away from them on benches and not look them in the face, lest in some way, by looking in their faces, we get the seed of lust from the Adversary and harvest a sheaf of corruption and perdition. Let us not believe

1. Source not identified.
2. Cf. Isaac 5, *Sayings*, 85 (PG 65:226B).
3. Source not identified.
4. Cited in Nikon, *Pandekty* 4:34.
5. Poemen 176; *Sayings*, 161 (PG 65:365A); Cf. Nikon, *Pandekty* 4:34^V.
6. Source not identified.

the deceitful thought. which suggest to us that this is not tempting. Rather the beholding itself and the cohabitation is reckoned to be a temptation, because the devil has scorched many this way and surrendered them to eternal fire.[7]

7. Pseudo-Basil, *Ascetical Discourse*, 23–24; PG 31:638BC (entire paragraph).

An account from the divine writings that it is not proper for women to enter the cloister

Discourse XI

[XI^{B}.1] The great Chrysostom says concerning women: *Any act of love, either living with or frequently conversing with women, is an act of fornication for monks. Are you really a stone? You are a man, of the common nature, subject to falling, and you are tending a fire in your bosom. Will you not set yourself ablaze? Do you place a candle on top of the hay, as if hay will not burn? For you eat with women and drink, laugh, and converse with them; yet you would call yourself a celibate? Tell not me, but Him who knows what is concealed, and who will later come to collect deeds, thoughts, and words!*[1]

[XI^{B}.2] The divine canons and civil laws enjoin that *neither a woman nor a nun enter a monastery for funeral or any other causes.*[2] *In doing this we do not despise nature or kinship, but whenever they come near us they bring a collection of passions, they confuse and darken the mind, and incite a host of thoughts.*[3]

[XI^{B}.3] Thus the blessed Marcian speaks well: *It is better to converse with the devil than with shameless women, and better to frequent the devil than graceful and adorned women. Human nature is readily mutable: when it has neglected the good, it easily turns toward evil.*[4]

[XI^{B}.4] Therefore it is well said in the *Holy Ladder*: *Fleeing we flee, so as not to see or hear the fruit we vowed not to taste. I marvel then that we consider ourselves more steadfast that the prophet David, which is impossible.*[5]

[XI^{B}.5] On this account it is proper for us all-zealously to submit to the admonition of our holy Fathers and to preserve ourselves

1. Cf. Nikon, *Pandekty* 12:86^{V}, attributed to Chrysostom, *Liber de virginitate.*
2. *Trullo* 47. *Councils*, 387 (Mansi 11:965DE), as in Nikon, *Pandekty* 12:88^{V}-89.
3. Attributed to Basil in Nikon, *Pandekty* 12:88^{V}-89.
4. Cf. Nikon, *Pandekty* 12:85^{V}.
5. Climacus, *Ladder* 15, *Scholia* 36: PG 88:917AB.

from little things—beholding or talking—lest we fall into the great. Thus shall we be saved in Christ Jesus our Lord, to whom is the glory, honor, and worship, now, always, and for ever and ever. Amen.

The Extended Rule

The Will and Testament of the Reverend Hegumen Iosif concerning the Monasterial and Monastic Institution, authentic, detailed, and in keeping with the Witness of the Divine Writings, 'to the Spiritual Superior who follows me and to all my Brothers in Christ, from the first down to the last', from the Cloister of the Venerable and Glorious Dormition of the All-Glorious Mother of God in whom we dwell.

Give a blessing, Father.

[2] In the name of the Father, the Son, and the Holy Ghost. I, the wretched and unworthy hegumen Iosif, in keeping with my strength and for the sake of the love of Christ and of my own and all my brothers' in Christ salvation, openly make my testament to the spiritual superior who follows and to all my brothers in Christ, from the first down to the last. I have issued these writings while I am still alive, in order that you treasure them while I am with you and after my departure.

[3] The years have approached old age, and the mortal cup[1] is prepared. I have fallen sick with numerous and diverse illness, and

1. Cf. von Lilienfeld, *Nil Sorskij,* 282. AfED, 324 (fragments of Nil/Pseudo-Nil or Iosif/Nil: Letter to Anonymous, Letter to the Iconpainter).

nothing summons me, but death and the terrible judgment of my Lord, Christ God.[2]

[4] Therefore I fear and tremble, for I hear the Divine Writings say: *The superior shall be called to account for all who are under him. If he is able to cut them off from evil, but fails to do so, God will demand their blood from his hand,*[3] *and he himself will perish with them as indifferent and lazy. If he rebukes and forbids them and is still unable to cut them off from evil, then he has delivered his own soul, and they will die in their own sin.*[4]

[5] Therefore, I, your unworthy brother and servant, exhort you, my fathers and brothers and beloved sons,[5] for the love of our Lord Jesus Christ who gave himself for our sins. Let us be responsible for our souls. Let us grieve for the transience of our lives. Let us struggle for future blessings, lest we pass our lives lazily and indifferently and be condemned at the terrible Second Coming of the Lord. How will we be able to look with our eyes upon the great day of the Lord and upon the terrifying face of Christ, which shines more brightly than the sun and grants inexpressible blessings to the righteous and tribulations and torments to the sinful? What is more wretched than this? And what is more bitter than these afflictions and sorrows?[6]

[6] And Saint Ephraim speaks similarly: *We see laymen who live with wives and children, are concerned over worldly affairs, and achieve the heavenly kingdom. We have abandoned everything: father, mother, wife, children, and other beloved ones-the whole world and what is beautiful and sweet in it.*[7] *We abide in afflictions and calamities and wrestle day and night with physical passions,*

2. Cf. the Testaments/Rules of (Pseudo-)Theodore, (Pseudo-)Athanasius, Kirill of Beloozero, Iosif (1507): PG 99:1813. Meyer, 123. BMFD, 75, 274. ΛSEI 2.314. AI 1.288. VMCh Sept., 490.

3. Cf. Ez 3:20

4. Climacus, Liber *6, Scholia* 6; PG 88:1181AB. Cf. Ezk 3:19; *Prosvetitiel'*, 16:549–50; and below, Discourse X.5, Discourse XI.6–7.

5. Cf. Symeon, *Catechisms* 26.42–43. (Pseudo-)Athanasius, *Testament* (Διατύπωσις), 274 (Meyer, 123).

6. Cf. Pseudo-Basil, *Introduction to Longer Rules,* 223; PG 31:889B-891B.

7. Adapted from Symeon, *Catechisms* 5.690; *O ezhe kako podobaet,* 7.

as if with a lion and a serpent.[8] *Shall we be condemned with fornicators, publicans, and sinners on account of a little negligence and the weakness of disobedience? Let us therefore be on guard against the immense stupidity of abandoning the great and the admirable only to be tempted by the transient, the mean, and the illusory, and thus fall away from the love of the universal King, Christ God. For at the frightful time of death we shall be called to account as lazy and indifferent.*[9]

[7] Basil the Great speaks similarly: *I think that neither the great illuminators and Spirit- bearing Fathers nor the holy martyrs passed the demonic toll-houses at the terrible hour of death without an inquest.*[10] Therefore, brothers, if even such great men, engaged in such great toils, can expect to be called to account at the hour of death, how can we, the passionate and the wretched, escape these terrible inquests?

[8] And what sort of clemency shall we obtain? We anger God every hour. We dwell in complete joy, tranquility, and security. We have everything on hand, food and drink, garments and footwear, and all the things we need. And still we do not wish to be concerned over our souls. Not only have we no memory of how and why we cast off the world and vowed to Christ to endure every affliction and to maintain humility, obedience, and Christ-like poverty, but we do not even bear responsibility for our little rule for good behavior in the church, the cell, and refectory, for food and drink, garments and footwear, and things which we keep in our cells without a blessing. No, we live simply as laymen, without so much as a care for our salvation. We are really vain and renounce the world only in word—in deed, not in the slightest. We do not fear the future torments, the terrible hour of death, or that we, like our fathers and brothers, shall soon die and stand before Christ's impartial tribunal and account for ourselves—for our deeds, words, and thoughts. In truth, the indifferent and the lazy shall receive a terrible and

8. Cf. Climacus, *Ladder* 26:41; PG 88:1088C.

9. Source not identified. Cf. Discourse V^{B}.8.

10. Adapted from the *Life* of Basil the Younger: Vilinskii, *Zhitie*, 21–41. See above, Ch. 2, ESCHATOLOGICAL VISIONS.

merciless sentence! *If the righteous shall scarcely be saved, where shall the ungodly and the sinner appear?*[11]

[9] Therefore, from now on let us be concerned about the evangelical commandments, the patristic writings, and the following traditions, which are here written down with the testimony of the Divine Writings, namely:

[10] An Exact Account of the Chapters Listed Below

1. How it is proper for the superior and all the brothers to take responsibility for good order in the church and concerning the community prayer.
2. How it is proper to take responsibility for reverence and good order in the refectory, and concerning foods and drinks.
3. How it is proper to have garments and footwear and other things, in keeping with the superior's blessing.
4. That it is not proper to converse after Compline or to go from cell to cell.
5. That it is not proper for monks to go outside the monastery without a blessing.
6. That it is proper to take responsibility for the communal and particular offices to which each has been assigned.
7. That it is not proper for drinks which cause drunkenness to be in the cloister.
8. That it is not proper for women to enter the monastery.
9. That it is not proper for boys to be in the monastery, and concerning other necessary causes.[12]
10. The Response to the Censorious and a Brief Account of the Holy Fathers from the Russian Monasteries.
11. That it is proper for the superior to teach and admonish those under him.
12. The Second Will and Testament, in brief, of the sinful and miserable hegumen Iosif, 'To my fathers and brothers' who

11. 1 Pt 4:18.

12. On this quasi-Scholastic formula, see above, Ch. 2. SPIRITUAL AND MONASTIC LEIXCON.

would hear in brief about everything which is here written concerning the monasterial and monastic institution.

13. How it is proper for the council and senior brothers, to whom the direction of the monastery has been entrusted, to bear responsibility together with the superior and in the absence of the superior, for the causes, pertaining to the church and monastery, which necessarily result in the salvation of souls.
14. How it is proper for the council and the senior brothers, together with the superior or in the absence of the superior, to administer penances to those heedless of the cœnobitic traditions which are here written down—from *the Asceticon* of Basil the Great and the *Typicon* of Saint Theodore the Studite.[13]

[11] Lo and behold, we have mentioned here in brief that it is proper for us to bear responsibility for good order in the church, refectory, and monastery; how it is proper for us to have garments, footwear, and other things; and also other necessary causes. Anyone who wants to know exactly and in detail how it is proper for us to bear the responsibility for these things should read the following piece of writing: for the first heading, the first discourse; for the second heading, the second discourse; and thus for all the fourteen headings written here, read the fourteen discourses in order. He will then know that the one who keeps and treasures these traditions will obtain the delight of the heavenly kingdom and will be a partaker of the eternal blessings, and that those who are heedless of them will be condemned as an *indifferent and lazy servant,*[14] for there is no coercion involved in keeping and treasuring them.

[12] Indeed it is well known that the way is smooth and wide[15] because of the weakness of this last generation.[16] If someone so wishes, he can keep them, for Christ's holy Testament grants him

13. See above, Chapter 2: Iosif's Sources.
14. Mt 25:26. Cf. above and below, Discourse I^{B}9/I.9, XIII.55, Appendix I.6.
15. Cf. Mt 7:13. Cf. below, Discourse II.29.
16. Heppell, *Paterik . . . Kiev.*, 25.

total security[17] and frequent joy and cheer. He who does everything in keeping with the blessing and command of the superior will live in paradise, better said, in the heavens,[18] and does not fear death. What is more elevated or more beneficial for our souls than the fact that when someone strives for this and is wholeheartedly concerned, he need not fear death? '*For at the time of death, not he but the superior will be called to account*'. Thus it is said in the *Holy Ladder*.[19]

[13] The holy martyrs submitted their bodies to many lashes, bloodshed, and violent deaths. Similarly, our holy Fathers shed blood by their asceticism, mortification, and bloody sweat,[20] so that they would not be put on trial at the terrible hour of death.[21] We need not shed our blood or bloody sweat, but must merely cut off a few trivialities and unnecessary nothings and be concerned over these traditions in a meek and prudent manner.

[14] If someone does not wish to accept or keep them, he shall answer for himself at the terrible tribunal of Christ.[22]

[15] So much for this. Let us speak further about the above-mentioned topics.

17. Cf. Matthew I, *Testament* A1:1633.

18. Cf. below, Discourse III.30.

19. Climacus, *Ladder* 4:50; PG 88:705B; also below, Discourse XII.10.

20. Cf. Lk 22:44; Pachomius, *Instructions* 2:34. Cf. AfED 341 (*Prosvetitel'* 7:272–73).

21. See above, Ch. 2, Eschatological Visions.

22. Compare the close of Iosif's brief *Prescript* or *Tradition* in missive form, which also has the standard testamentary appeal to Christ's tribunal: PIV, 288. Cf. DDG, 1, 89.

How it is proper for the superior and all the brothers to take responsibility for good order in the church and concerning the community prayer.

Discourse I

[1] First of all, it is proper for the superior himself and for all the brothers to display great zeal, responsibility, and struggle, so that everything in the cloister and, most important, the order of the church offices, proceed gracefully and according to order as the Divine Writings command.

[2] Sacred Chrysostom says: *Our foremost endeavor is this: when the clapper sounds let us quickly put aside everything in our hands and let us rush together very zealously and seriously to the divine and beautiful shelter of the church, as Peter and John ran to the Lord's tomb.*[1] *Let us not wait until the end of the clapper and the completion of the introit, and let us not say or think, 'if I arrive early, then I shall have to wait a long time and shall sit in vain and to no profit'.*[2]

[3] Athanasius the Great says: *'Holy angels stand in front of the church. They observe the indifferent and the serious, recognize the reverent, identify those who do not so act, and mark those who curse, chatter idly, and converse'.*[3]

[4] Saint Ephraim says:[4] *'Be aware that when you walk toward the good, you will obtain your reward for each and every good word and each and every step. Likewise, when you walk toward evil, you will answer on the Day of Judgment for each step and idle word'.*[5] Again he says: *'When the brother claps, come quickly to life: diligently and zealously hurry to the church, lift up your hand to God, and bow down to his throne of grace, as if you were*

1. Jn 20:3–4. Lk 24:12.
2. Source not identified.
3. Source not identified.
4. Source not identified. Cf. Nikon, *Pandekty* 28:195.
5. Cf. Nikon, *Pandekty* 36:269^{V}.

a chamois[6] *who had escaped from a snare or a bird from a net. Thus the lazy person, upon seeing your diligence and harmony, will lift up his soul and become cheerful, and you will be like unto the divine lips, for if someone takes forth the precious from the vile he shall be as my mouth*'.[7]

[5] The longer you remain standing and waiting in the church, the more worthy you shall be of grace from God. The first to come to church is the first to obtain mercy from the Lord God. Whosoever comes to the earthly king always remains standing or seated at the palace first, awaits the king's procession, tarries, and is always patient. He who so acts is beloved by the king. But if someone arrives indifferently, with contempt, and last of all, he will be sent away as lazy and indifferent from the presence of the king. Similarly, if we become indifferent toward the rule for the church, arrive last and leave first, we shall be rejected by God as indifferent.

[6] Therefore, brothers, let us cast off every earthly affair and responsibility, laziness and sleep. Let us strive always to hurry to prayer before everyone else, and thus we shall always be there at the beginning. Let us not wait until we have finished this or that piece of business or until the others have assembled and then go. But let us all race and compete against each other as if we were plundering prisoners. Just as whoever arrives there first is the most enriched, similarly whoever comes here first is most enriched with heavenly riches.

[7] The holy Fathers say: *If anyone is doing anything when the hour for prayer arrives, and he does not abandon his ongoing activity, he is being mocked by demons. For the wicked devil knows that we inherit the heavenly kingdom as a result of small labors. If someone strives and forces himself on God's activity, and begins to arrive early at the divine temple to pray and to hear divine words, then the devil introduces the opposite notion. He says: 'Wait until the brothers have assembled and begun to chant and then go'. Sometimes he advises us to finish certain legitimate and necessary*

6. *serna/sr'na*, a type of antelope.

7. Jer 15:19. Cf. below, Discourse XI.2, XIII.4.

things first and then go. When somebody is sleeping, he sometimes creates extraordinary dreams and other times submerges them in sleep. He carries this out in order to steal an hour of our prayer time and thus to incite indignation in God toward us. He knows that if the foundation is shoddy, then everything will be rejected and disgraced.[8]

[8] Just as Cain made an offering first to himself and then to God and was cast off and spurned,[9] similarly he who now wants to arrange his vain, perishable and earthly affairs and thus does not arrive for the beginning of the divine chant will be cast off by God and be loathsome. So let us cut off this type of negligence for 'cursed is he who does the work of the Lord negligently'.[10] This habit demands a savage remedy. Therefore let us first of all compel ourselves and enact for ourselves a law and commandment for good deeds: always to hurry and to be the first one to the divine activity, and with great zeal to rush to the food for the soul. If we merely lay our foundation and begin to act, God will not abandon us.[11] He will grant us mercy and send us help from his holy heights. For he surely loves us and wants to save us.

[9] And know this: the sober man makes a profit and the lazy man loses. Just as in the case of a sweet dish on the table or a gold piece thrown on the crossways, whoever comes first is the most satisfied or enriched. Godly words in the divine church are sweeter than honey and honeycombs and dearer than a thousand gold pieces, according to holy David.[12] He who arrives first will enjoy grace first, but he who arrives lazily and carelessly is a stranger to grace and will be condemned like the wicked and lazy slave.[13]

[10] When the trumpet sounds for battle, no one puts off going, but everyone strives to be first before the king. He who comes first achieves honor first. Here the trumpet blows for the heavenly king

8. Climacus, *Ladder* 19.3; PG 88:937BC; cf. Nikon *Pandekty* 30:214.

9. Gn 4:3–4. Cf. below, Discourse VI.32.

10. Jer 48:10. Cf. below, Discourse I.26, VI.6, Appendix I.6; also Dicourse VIII^{B}.25.

11. Seemingly adapted from Symeon, *Catechisms* 26.20–42.

12. Ps 19:10.

13. Mt 25:26.

and summons us to the divine and beautiful shelter of the church. Therefore let us not wait or delay until the chanting commences.[14] Let us strive with joy and rush with love, anticipate one another and urge one another on to the doxology of our Savior Jesus Christ.[15]

[11] When we thus arrive in the divine church and stand as if with the powers on high in heaven itself, let us not merely display physical elegance, but let us also concentrate our minds with the sensations of our hearts and not whisper, banter, or speak vanities. Instead clasp your hands, join your legs, shut your eyes, concentrate your mind, and elevate your thoughts and your heart toward heaven. In this manner, with tears and moaning, call to God for mercy, and absolutely do not leave the assembly without an urgent need.[16]

[12] Therefore, fathers and brothers, let us force ourselves upon the godly activity. Let us be concerned first over physical elegance and good order and then over internal observance. Let us lovingly keep this as the most venerable activity: always to hurry to the divine chanting and doxology, not to leave in haste before the dismissal, and not to whisper or jest, lest we obtain the wrath of God instead of divine mercy.

[13] Therefore the divine Chrysostom teaches:[17] *Let no one relax: let no one utter or consider vain and perishable things. Rather drive everything earthly from your mind; turn your whole self toward heaven, hold firm, and stand with a lively soul. When an archer desires to shoot his arrows successfully, he first takes great pains over his posture and aligns himself accurately with his mark. It should be the same for you who are about to shoot the head of the wicked devil.*[18] Let us be concerned first for the good order of sensations and then for the good posture of the inner thoughts.

14. Cf. Symeon *Catechisms* 26.24–25.

15. That is, the commencement of the Matins, not the formal 'doxology' of the Liturgy, but the initial praising of God: Petras, *Typicon, 21, 24*. For this use, see Symeon, *Catechisms* 26.111.

16. Seemingly adapted from Symeon, *Catechisms* 26.25–62.

17. For Sections [13] through [20], and the beginning and end of Section [21], see AfED 351–56 (*Prosvetitel',* 7:204–18).

18. Adapted from *De incomprehensibili* 4; PG 48:734 (VMCh 1:819–20).

[14] *What is required of us for which we shall be called to account? To stand with much fear, with restrained and adorned reverence, with elevated thought, and with a contrite heart, and then visibly to display the character of your heart by means of posture, good order of the hands, and a meek and quiet voice. Indeed the Lord loves the calm and the meek: 'the man on whom I look', He says, 'is a meek and silent one, who trembles at my words'.*[19]

[15] *When someone is conversing with the earthly king, he contrives in every possible way to display great reverence for him. Thus chiefly*[20] *by means of clasped hands, joined legs, and control over the whole body, he chooses his words from among those the latter desires. If he dares to bring up something beyond the latter's volition, he receives the final punishment. You are standing before the heavenly king before whom the angels tremble as they stand. You have abandoned your conversation with him and you are talking about dung, dust, and spider webs. How will you endure the penalty for your act of contempt? And why, wretched one, do you not fear and tremble? Do you not understand that invisibly you are standing before the King of heaven and earth, who tests every mind and tries every conscience, and that the angels stand before him in fear? But you do not consider this. Rather you carry on with such negligence and indifference, and you do not know what you are talking about. And why do you talk? Have you no fear, o wretched and lusty fellow? You are not afraid to say in the church what is heard in the market place, to surround yourself with 'disorderly howls'*[21] *to utter useless noises at that fearful time, to think about vanities, to be lazy, and to yawn!*[22]

[16] It is impossible for us to be saved, brother, when we act this way and do not fear God's terrible threat and righteous anger.

19. Is 66:2. Cf. below, Appendix I.6.

20. *glavnym obrazom i*, a confused or ambiguous translation of διὰ τοῦ της κεφαλῆς σχήματος (by the position of the head): PG 56:101.

21. *Tüpikon*, 37^{V}.

22. Section [14–15] is adapted from Chrysostom, *In laudem* 1: PG 56:99–106 (VMCh 1:971–72, 977, 982).

And it is terrible to fall into the hands of the living God,[23] for he investigates hearts and tests wombs and flights of the mind.

[17] *Thus the Prophet sings out with fear, 'Out of the depths have I cried to you, O Lord'.*[24] *Note that we are to speak and pray from the depths of the heart, and with diligence, a grieving soul, and contrite thought. Such a prayer indeed goes up to heaven. When waters flow on flat lands, they do not move upwards. When they have been dammed up from their course, they collect and press together, and many spurts of water quickly shoot up high. Similarly, so long as human thought remains without fear and heedless of itself, it flows and runs off in many directions. When it is oppressed from below*[25] *by afflictive things and sad circumstances, it is greatly compressed and then it sends up on high pure and powerful prayers. This is why the Prophet said: 'In my distress I cried unto the Lord and he heard me'.*[26]

[18] *Let us warm our conscience with all of this, and let us become afflicted and oppressed. He who is always so afflicted while praying can attract to his soul the divine sweetness that originates in tears. The motion of clouds darkens the atmosphere, but when the rain releases many drops and falls, it makes the whole place calm and radiant. It is similar with sadness. So long as it is inside, it darkens our thoughts. When it relieves itself with the words of prayer and the accompanying tears,* and detaches itself from vain and alluring worldly conversations,[27] *it deposits much light in our soul with God's assistance, as if some beams were being sent by God into the soul of the person in prayer.*[28] *For the light of prayer is just like the light of a candle. And if you train yourself to pray with precision, you will not require instruction from your comrades, as God, without any mediator, enlightens your*

23. Heb 10:31. Cf. AfED 496 (*Prosvetitel'* 13:497).

24. Ps 129:1/130:1.

25. The printed text *odole* should be, with modern spacing, *o dole* (orig. κάτωθεν).

26. Ps 119:1/120:1.

27. The original reads: 'and dissipates outside'.

28. Sections [17] and [18] to this point are Chrysostom, *De incomprehensibili* 5; PG 48:746, 744 (VMCh 1:836, 833).

thought.[29] At the time of our devotions, therefore, let us collect our wits, face ourselves, drive away laziness, chase every earthly and perishable thing away from our thoughts, not be concerned about things earthly, perishable and vain.

[19] Let us strive as much as possible, with fear and with love, not to deprive the office of the smallest item. We know full well that if we safeguard the office in keeping with the traditional *typicon* and canon,[30] we will be granted a healthy body and soul to serve the living and true God in the present age. And in the future age, you can await the day when you will shine above with the saints, just like the sun, and in return for these meager little labors, you will obtain the joy of the heavenly kingdom.[31]

[20] *Someone may say that there is evil in unsettled affairs, but we shall not say this at all. This pretext is demonic and the enticement of the devil. Indeed God, when scorned, scatters the assembly. Although we have a great deal to arrange in our lives, there are other times to hold meetings about them.*[32] If someone speaks in the church of perishable and vain things—it is better not to come than to irritate the Lord—let us all unanimously be concerned over good order in the church and reprimand him. *If he is disobedient and if it is possible, let us drive him from the church enclosure.*[33] *If he is insulting or speaks more sharply, do not abandon the treatment, beloved one.*[34] *If he is your enemy today, tomorrow he will be your friend; and if he is your enemy tomorrow, then God will be your friend.*[35]

[21] *In so acting, brothers, we obtain clemency for our own sins and much free access to God. And we obtain even greater reward than the man who prays, for the latter benefits only himself, but the other benefits many-first of all, those who would stand before God*

29. Section [18] from the last note is Chrysostom, *De incomprehensibili* 3; PG 48:725–6 (VMCh 1:807).

30. Cf. Theodora/Theodule Synadene, *Typikon* VI:1537–38.

31. Cf. above, Discourse I^{B}.1.

32. Chrysostom, *In laudem* 1; PG 56:102–3 (VMCh 1:976–7).

33. Chrysostom, *In laudem* 1; PG 56:106–7 (VMCh 1:982). Cf. below, Discourse I.31.

34. Chrysostom, *De incomprehensibili* 2; PG 48:718 (VMCh 1:797).

35. Chrysostom, *Adversus Judaeos* 4; PG 48:882 (VMCh 1:879).

and serve him with a humble heart and then, those who would be unruly. Let us obtain for ourselves a double profit and have among us the Lord himself, who gives a crown to each of the orderly ones,[36] who stand before him with sobriety, the fear of God, and trepidation, and let forth wellsprings of tears. And the Evil One cannot hold him in contempt.

[22] If at that fearful time, someone is negligent and indifferent, utters useless things, speaks vanities, and is heedless of himself—a certain demon saw an idle, mucky, and doorless temple, and he quickly went in it as if into an empty cloister—the Evil One makes him first hold conversations about perishable and earthly matters during prayer and then jests. Finally he dragged him from the chanting to laughter and idle chatter.[37]

[23] It is said in the *Holy Ladder: The spiritual trumpet signifies that the brothers are congregating visibly and the demons are congregating invisibly. In order to bring down God's wrath upon us, some of them stand by our bed and tell us to lie down again until the chanting has completely begun, and others tell us to make conversations during the chanting and to joke and whisper.*[38]

[24] *The Dialogues* speak similarly: *A certain brother,* it says, *who lived in the monastery of Saint Benedict, loved to jest at the time of the chant and to leave the chanting. Saint Benedict saw a demon in the form of a Moor, jesting with that monk. The saint then beat him with his staff and subsequently he desisted from that evil habit.*[39]

[25] Now nothing is more evil or more destructive to our souls than this, and nothing else can so bring down God's wrath upon us. Saint Isidore says concerning this: *God spares neither his churches nor his holy mysteries, but renders them desolate on this account. Indeed he consigned the Ark of the Tabernacle and the Holy of*

36. Chrysostom, *In laudem* 1; PG 56:106–7 (VMCh 1:982). Cf. Phoberos, *Typikon* 18:904.

37. Source not identified; note the different mixture in Discourse I^{B}.21.

38. Cf. Climacus, *Ladder* 19:3; PG 88:937.

39. (Pseudo-)Gregory the Great, *Dialogues* 2,4; PL 66:141AC. Discourse I^{B}.16 is faithful to Gregory's text.

Holies, along with the priests, to the fire. And our Lord Jesus Christ first drove the unruly Jews from the Temple with a scourge and then for this reason consigned the city and the Temple to plundering and desolation.[40]

[26] A similar tale is told in the *Geronticon: A certain saintly father lived in an hermitage near Jerusalem. In a dream, he saw himself inside the Church of the Holy Resurrection near the tomb of our God, Christ. An unbearable stench was*[41] *in the church. There were two priestly elders there and he questioned them: 'Where is the stench coming from?' They answered him: 'from the lawlessness of the clerics who live here'. The elder said to them: 'Then why have you not cleaned it up'? And they answered him: 'Trust in this, brother, that it is impossible to purify them, except by fire'. Shortly afterwards the Persians came, destroyed the church and the city, and set the lawless priests ablaze.*[42] Indeed the Prophet says concerning this: *Cursed is he who does the work of the Lord negligently,*[43] and who does not piously honor the divine.

[27] Our Lord Jesus Christ was meek and humble, suffered his shoulders to be lashed, his cheek to be smitten, and his face to be spat upon, and never in any way was he incited to a violent word. When he saw someone in the divine church engaged in perishable and earthly affairs, he could not endure it, but took up the scourge and began to lash him. He did not struggle with fury or anger, but he gave us a model for action. When we see someone in the divine church engaged in earthly and perishable affairs, let us in no way be silent, but let us reprimand and forbid him. If it is possible, let us drive him from the church, for Chrysostom so commands.

[28] The sacred canons speak similarly: *It is not proper for a bishop or a priest to strike a sinning believer or non-believer. If they see someone making noise about perishable and vain things*

40. Source not identified.

41. Corrected as in *Prosvetitel'* 7:281, *byvshu*, from *slyshit"* (he hears).

42. Cf. Nikon, *Taktikon* 19:112. AfED, 344 (*Prosvetitel'* 7:281). Attributed in the *Prosvetitel'* version to *Starchestvo*.

43. Jer 48:10. Cf. above and below, Discourse I^{B}.8/I.8, Discourse VIII^{B}.25/VI.36. Appendix I.6.

in the church, however, then it is proper for the bishop or the priest with his own hands to strike and drive him from the church.[44]

[29] It is said in the *Holy Ladder: When that great pastor was standing at prayer, he noticed several of the brothers making conversations during the prayer. He banished them for seven days and ordered them to stand outside the church and to bow to those entering and leaving. What was marvelous is that there were clerics who were banished for a very long time.*[45]

[30] If there happens to be a layman or a guest monk with us at the communal prayer, even if he is a nobleman, then it is especially proper for us not to make conversation during the prayer, so that we avoid censure and do not attract God's wrath upon ourselves.[46] For it is the custom of laymen to censure and deride unruly monks. Let us not tempt anyone, for *he who creates temptations for laymen will not behold the light.*[47] But if it is necessary, let us make the requisite bow or kiss, say the customary 'peace', and return to our original silence. If he begins to converse, let us meekly reprimand him, for nothing is of such profit to laymen as the good order and reverence of monks.

[31] Thus none shall speak during the chant, except the superior, the cellarer, the choirmaster, and the inspector.[48] They shall briefly say what is necessary for good order in the church, not in a loud voice, but rather in a whisper, lest others be disturbed. If they see anyone saying or doing anything which is outside these traditions, they shall in no way be silent, but shall reprimand and forbid him. For the divine Chrysostom says that it is proper not only to reprimand the idle chatterers, but also *to drive them out of the sacred enclosure'*.[49] And the sacred canons likewise dictate.[50]

44. Cf. *Apostolic Canons* 27; *Councils* 595 (Mansi 1:33), perhaps as in Nikon, *Pandekty* 15:119, which Iosif completely twisted; also above, Ch. 2, HERESY AND AUTHORITY.

45. Cf. Climacus, *Ladder* 4.37; PG 88:701 BC.

46. See Ch. 2, SHORTCOMINGS OF RUSSIAN MONASTIC LIFE.

47. Nikon, *Pandekty* 33:248, attributed to Isaac of Syria.

48. See above, Ch. 2, SOCIAL AND ADMINISTRATIVE STRUCTURES.

49. Chrysostom, *In laudem* 1; PG 56:106–7 (VMCh 1:982). Cf. above, Discourse I.20.

50. See above, Discourse I.28.

[32] If it is urgent that one say something, then it is proper to leave the chanting or to say it after the chanting. But do not leave the church before dismissal, except for illness and for necessary monastery activities. For it is said in the *Geronticon: When the Priest Ammon was performing a liturgy in the church, he saw an angel sitting to the right of the altar and writing down in a book the names of those who entered. He erased the names of those who left out of laziness, and they died thirteen days later.*[51]

[33] So know this, brothers, that it is not proper for us to exit from the church before the dismissal from the divine chanting or to move from place to place. Symeon the New Theologian says: *Brothers, when we are standing for the prayer of lamentations, we should in no way forget, but should stand with trepidation.*[52]

[34] And let us not stand with our legs apart, move from place to place, lean on a wall or a column, mingle with each other, whisper, or joke.[53]

[35] And if someone must leave the chanting, he shall go to his cell and not stand or sit in front of the church or in front of the refectory.[54] Idle chatter and neglect of the divine chant occur for this reason, and *because of negligence, death came into the world.*[55] If someone needs to leave the chanting, he shall go silently to his cell and then quickly return to the communal prayer. If, having left, he begins to sleep or engage in idle chatter, he will quickly fall into the hands of his enemies. For the Divine Writings say: *Do not scorn the divine office, lest you be surrendered into the hands of your enemies.*[56]

Enough of this for now.

51. Source not identified: Patericon I^{B}.12.

52. Adapted from Symeon, *Catechisms* 26.116–19.

53. Cf. *Starchestvo,* 6–6^{V}.

54. See below, Discourse V.4, Tradition IX.13 (Discourse XIII.ix.13). Cf. Irina Doukaina Komnene, *Typikon* 49:693, where disobedience is the original cause of death.

55. Source not identified.

56. Source not identified.

That it is proper to take responsibility for reverence and good order in the refectory and concerning food and drink.[1]

Discourse II

[1] It is proper to know that after the final prayer, when the brothers exit the church, they shall enter the refectory[2] to eat together with the superior, be on time for the benediction, and sit each in his own place with reverence and silence and in order. *It is proper that there be great precision, so that at the refectory table no one speaks any word whatever other than the verse and the lection. For the divine Fathers say concerning this: 'The holy sacrificial altar and the brotherhood's table at dinner time are equivalent'.*[3] Therefore it is proper to eat silently and prayerfully and to attend to the lection in the refectory just as when we chant in the divine church.[4]

[2] It is said in the *Patericon: An elder said, 'Once I was sitting with Father John Colubus in the refectory and was eating with a certain other elder. The elder spoke once, and Abba John was silent. He spoke a second time, and Abba John was silent. He spoke a third time, and Abba John said to him: "Behold Abba, since this one sat at table God has been taken from me, and noise has entered", and he got up and left'. And he also said: 'A monk who converses at the table is no different from a pig or a cat, for a pig slurps when he feeds, and a cat purrs when he eats'.*[5]

[3] Again, it is said that *when Saint Niphont was walking, he saw a man sitting and eating, and he saw several beautiful beings in bright robes, standing in front of those who were eating in that house, and equal in number to them. God revealed to him that these were angels of God who stand at dinner time before those*

1. Cf. (Pseudo-)Theodore Studite, *Rule* (Ὑποτύπωσις) 28, PG 99:1713BC (BMFD, 109).
2. See above, Ch. 2, The Major Edifices.
3. *Tüpikon*, 431. Nikon, *Taktikon* 1:6 (BMFD, 406).
4. Cf. *Starchestvo*, 6^{v}-7.
5. Source not identified.

who eat. When idle, shameful, or slanderous talk or fables begin, something improper is said or someone starts to revile the food, then just as smoke drives away bees, the evil conversations drive away the angels of God. When the holy angels of God depart, a dark demon arrives and plants a foul-smelling smoke among those who are eating.[6]

[4] Similarly it is said in the *Geronticon* that a saintly monk saw several others sitting at a table and eating honey: *'When they began to talk, make idle chatter, and revile the food, then I saw them eating manure'*.[7]

[5] Again it is said that Abba Isaac, the *hegumen* of Scete, said: *A monk who sits at table and does not pray in his mind, but who utters any word at all, chatters, laughs, or reviles the food, has withdrawn from God and God has withdrawn from him. His prayer is not welcome, and his labors are futile.*[8]

[6] Now we have heard from the Divine Writings that if someone makes conversation at table, he has withdrawn from God, and God has withdrawn from him; his prayer is not welcome, and his labors are futile. Therefore it is not proper for anyone to speak at table except the superior, the cellarer, the assistant cellarer, and the cupbearer, and they shall say in brief and in a whisper what is necessary for good order in the refectory.[9] If someone begins to do or to say anything not in keeping with the custom of a reverent brotherhood, they are to reprimand and forbid him. If anyone does not obey, Basil the Great says of these: *'Cast out', it is said, 'the pest from the assembly, and his contention shall go out'*.[10]

[7] And do not sit at another's place[11] and move from place to place, because the audacious, shameless, and unruly shall be judged!

6. Cf. Titov, *Opisanie* 2:38 ff. and 751/2129; *Kir.-Bel.* 22/1099, 437^{V}-38: Kagan et al., 'Opisanie . . . Efrosina', 98. In this version, which goes back to Chrysostom, the man is eating with his wife and children.

7. Source not identified.

8. Source not identified.

9. Cf. Timothy of Evergetis, *Typikon* 9:478–79. Archbishop Sava, *Tipik* 9:50–52.

10. *Longer Rules* 47:325; PG 31:1037A, citing Prv 22:10. Cf. below, XIII.31.

11. Timothy of Evergetis, *Typikon* 9:479. Archbishop Sava, *Tipik* 9:50.

[8] And do not make gifts at table or away from the table.[12] This causes vainglory, disturbances, and unruliness. For Basil the Great so speaks: *The proud, the unruly and the troublemakers become malignant joy for demons and fodder for hell.*[13]

[9] And no one shall bring anything of his own to table, neither food nor drink; for all the Divine Writings and cœnobitic traditions so dictate.[14]

[10] And do not take the food and drink from in front of another brother, or place your own in front of a brother.[15] For Basil the Great so speaks: *If you give someone your food and drink at the table or take something from someone, you will not avoid sin; either you make your brother liable for gluttony, drunkenness, and disobedience, or you yourself so suffer.*[16]

[11] At the table there shall be equivalent food and drink for everybody. The Divine Writings dictate this to cœnobites and forbid that some have a lot, some a little, some the sweet, and some the sour. This causes turmoil, troubles, and quarrels, not only among laymen, but also among spiritual persons.

[12] And no one shall go to the 'last table' except officials,[17] and only when necessary.

[13] And brothers not engaged in particular offices, who are late to the refectory, shall ask the hegumen or cellarer for forgiveness.[18] The Divine Writings say: *For each idle word or deed or act of disobedience it is proper to ask for forgiveness; on account of this word, all of the Adversary's stratagems collapse.*[19]

[14] And when the brothers drink *kvass* in the refectory or by the cellar, then after having drunk they shall go in silence to their

12. Cf. Petit, *Vie d S. Athanase,* 40. Pomialovsky, *Zhitie . . . Afanasiia*, 36.

13. Cf. (Pseudo-)Theodore Studite, *Testamentum* 26; PG 99:1824A (BMFD, 79).

14. Cf. *Starchestvo*, 13^{V}.

15. Cf. Petit *Vie d S. Athanase,* 40; Pomialovsky, *Zhitie . . . Afanasiia*, 36.

16. Cf. Timothy of Evergetis, *Typikon* 9:479. Archbishop Sava, *Tipik* 9:51

17. Cf. Petit, *Vie d S. Athanase,* 40; Pomialovsky, *Zhitie . . . Afanasiia*, 36.; and above Ch 2, note 83. Cf. Timothy of Evergetis, *Typikon* 9:479. Archbishop Sava, *Tipik* 9:52.

18. Cf. Petit, *Vie d S. Athanase,* 40. Pomialovsky, *Zhitie . . . Afanasiia*, 36.

19. Source not identified. Cf. Discourse XIII.IX.19, below.

cells and not remain standing or seated. Indeed from this come idle chatter and jesting, and we shall answer to God for every silly word.[20]

[15] It is proper to act in this manner towards the sick: comfort the sick man who cannot walk with food, drink, and clothing.[21] Do not afflict him in any way respecting his needs, for *he who afflicts an ill man irritates his Creator and in the time of his own afflictions will not find anyone to help him.*[22] *He who neglects this sick man shall not gaze upon the light. His day is darkened who turns his face from a sick man.*[23]

[16] And any sick man who can walk, but cannot be satisfied by the refectory food, shall tell the truth to the hegumen, not a lie.[24] 'For each lie is from the Evil One, and lips which lie are abominable to the Lord'.[25] 'And you will destroy all who tell lies', says the Prophet.[26] And the hegumen shall command the officials to refresh him in his cell, not in the refectory.[27]

[17] And do not take any drinks or vessels from the refectory without a blessing. Thus speaks Saint Theodore the Studite: *It is indeed theft to take something without a blessing; thieves not only fail to inherit the heavenly kingdom, but they will also be condemned to eternal darkness.*[28]

[18] And no one shall remain in the refectory after the meal and the chanting[29] or go into the pantry without a blessing and without an urgent need. For Basil the Great says: *After rising from table, do not stand and converse with anyone, do not give your ears to each and every babbler, and do not respond to anyone who is making a merry conversation. Rather strive to hurry on quick wing to your*

20. Cf. Mt 12:36.

21. Cf. (Pseudo-)Athanasius of Athos, *Rule* (Ὑποτύπωσις) 31:227 (Meyer, 139). Timothy of Evergetis, *Typikon* 26:490–91.

22. Kozhanchikov, *Stoglav* 49, attributed to Isaac of Dalmatos.

23. Source not identified.

24. Cf. *Starchestvo*, 14^{V}.

25. Prv 12:22.

26. Ps 5:6.

27. Cf. *Tüpikon*, 43. Leoniid, 'Obikhodniki', 7.

28. Cf. Nikon, *Pandekty* 4:29, attributed to Basil.

29. Cf. *Starchestvo*, 10–10^{V}'.

cell, as if you were some innocent dove going back to the ark which has released you, and bearing on your lips the mercy of Christ.[30]

[19] It is proper for the superior and the brothers to take this responsibility: except when the superior and the brothers have given a command specifying what and where, and *even if this is due to abstinence, a major struggle, another good reason,*[31] debility, or urgent needs, no brother shall eat or drink in a cell or any other place. This is what the cœnobitic traditions dictate.

[20] *And keep yourself from eating in secret and such drinking, in no way dine with anyone or alone, for all evils are from this.*[32]

[21] Saint Symeon the New Theologian says: *If we preserve unsullied flesh and we master envy, fury, theft, and all filth and we secretly eat some bread or something else without the superior's command, we profit nothing; even if we restrain the great passions, we are controlled by the little ones.*[33] He who conquers the great but is vanquished by the small will be condemned like Ananius and Sapphira, who placed many riches before the Apostles' legs, but were vanquished by some little things, and because of them were tormented with death.[34]

[22] Therefore it is not proper in any way to eat or drink alone or with someone else, for no virtue can help us if we are conquered by gluttony. Indeed all evils spring from such doings,[35] and they are diabolical actions which appear to be nothing, but contain a fatal poison.[36]

[23] Saint Isaac says: *He who has friendship with his stomach is a wolf who dines on carrion. Flee this loathsome love and this indecent and unclean way of life. Flee, o brother, those who have such a habit, and do not eat with them at all, even if it is*

30. *Ascetical Discourse,* 27,23; PG 31:641C, 637B. Cf. *Starchestvo,* 33–33^{V}, and Gn 8:9.

31. *Tüpikon* 45^{V}'. Nikon, *Taktikon* 1:13 (BMFD, 405).

32. Pseudo-Basil, *Ascetical Discourse,* 26–27; PG 31:641BC. Cf. *Starchestvo,* 33–33^{V}; Symeon, *Catechisms*, 26,13–16.

33. Cf. Symeon, *Catechisms*, 26.170–242; *O ezhe kako podobaet,* 16^{V}-17.

34. Acts 5:1–11.

35. Cf. *Starchestvo,* 33^{V}-34.

36. Cf. Jas 3:8.

necessary for you. Their table is loathsome, and they have demons for servants. Friends of Christ's betrothed do not dine on this.[37]

[24] Basil the Great says: *If you control your stomach, you will enter Paradise; if you do not control it, you will be devoured by death.*[38] *And again he says: Keep yourself from eating in secret, for if craving for a little taste of something can place in your stomach the passion of madness, it will shamelessly give you over to death. I have seen many possessed by passions and then cured by repentance, but I have not seen one secret-eater or glutton who desisted or repented. Rather they concealed themselves from the continent ones and dined while the devil aided them with voluptuousness. Outwardly they were among the saved; actually they were among the doomed.*[39]

[25] And Saint Gregory, Pope of Rome, bears witness to this; *There was a certain monastery*, he says, *called 'The Galatians'*,[40] *in which there was a certain monk, who was considered by everyone to be saintly. When he was found to be sick, all the brothers assembled about him, and were waiting to hear something great from such a holy man. Forced to depart from his body, he was crying and trembling, and he said this: 'You believed that I was fasting with you, but hidden away from you I used to eat, and now, therefore, I have been given as food to the Serpent, who has bound my legs and knees with his tail, has placed his head inside my mouth, and is pulling out my dying spirit'. Having said this, he immediately died. And this shows that God willed that it be told for our profit, lest we so perish, for that one did not escape the Adversary to whom he had been consigned.*[41]

[26] And Saint Nikon writes similarly in his missives: *A certain elder*, he said, *collected a brotherhood. Having boldness towards God, he prayed that he might see his deceased disciples. Seeing two*

37. Source not identified.

38. *Ascetical Discourse,* 26; PG 31:641B. Cf. Nil Sorsky, *Ustav* 5:42.

39. *Ascetical Discourse,* 24–25; PG 31:640A. Cf. Climacus, *Ladder* 14, *Scholia* 20; PG 88:877BC.

40. Slavic *galatiiskii*; published Greek text τῶν γαλάτων, and Latin text τῶν γαλατῶν.

41. *Dialogues* 4:40; PL 77:393BC, perhaps as in Nikon, *Pandekty* 34:240^{v}.

in a very terrible place, he interrogated them. The first answered: 'I had an unconfessed thought, and therefore they have brought me here'. The second one answered: 'gluttony has destroyed me'.[42]

[27] Therefore our first struggle is to control our stomach and concentrate our heart on fear of hell and our desire on the heavenly kingdom, so that in fearing hellfire and enjoying the beauty of the heavenly kingdom, we cut off the fiercest passion of all and the origin of all evil, which is eating in secret. We do not forbid nourishment which is necessary for life, but we cut off the demonic habit, the voluptuous root and the originator and perfecter of all evils, namely, eating in secret.[43] Therefore we are diligently diligent and soberly sober, so that if we become slightly ill, the Lord will immediately aid us and not allow a passionate stomach to operate within us—by the grace of his holy and life-giving Spirit, Amen.

[28] It is proper to know that if in value, quality, and quantity, the same food and drinks are to be on the table for all the brothers, everyone does not have the same ascetical regulation, nor is there one measure for everyone, because not everyone has the same strength.[44] We have placed them therefore into three orders: the first, the middle, and the last.[45]

[29] The first order is just as the holy Fathers say: *always one kind of food from among those present.*[46] According to the custom of our land and the local climate this is 'one kind'. When there are three or two foods at the table, one eats one of these with bread or *kalatch*,[47] and does not abstain from any of them as evil. The holy Fathers handed down the tradition of dining on one kind of food because it is impossible for us to partake of all and not be sated, and because this striving cuts off desire. *Let us walk the narrow and afflictive path of fasting, which leads to a life of purity*,[48] and

42. Taktikon 38:200–200^{v}, attributed to *Starchestvo*.
43. Cf. Nikon, *Taktikon* 1 (72), BMFD, 405.
44. Cf. John of Phoberos, *Typikon* 5:889.
45. See above, Ch. 2, Social and Administrative Structures.
46. Source not identified.
47. Wheaten bread. See above, Ch. 2, The Table Customary.
48. Cf. Climacus, *Ladder* 14.29; PG 88:869AB, and Mt 7:13–14.1. Cf. above and below, Extended Rule Introduction.12 (Int.12), Discourse III.24.

we shall receive the illumination of the divine light,[49] when we observe the holy Fathers' traditional limits for abstinence—that is, to receive food and drink, and when there is a desire for a little more, to abstain. Such asceticism with humility, as if by golden wings, lifts the soul up to heaven and makes it worthy of the heavenly kingdom.[50]

[30] The second order. When there are three foods on the table, one shall have two with *kalatch,* shall not eat the third, and shall do everything with the blessing of the superior. Thus he will shortly renounce satiety of the gut, as it is said in the *Holy Ladder: Cut off first the fattening foods, then the heating, and then the seasoning, and restrain your stomach before it controls you, and then you will abstain with the aid of shame.*[51] Therefore we must have not only bodily abstinence, but also contrition of the heart, and thus shall we obtain eternal blessings.

[31] The third order. If someone does not have the will to practice the first or second orders, he may eat his fill at table, according to the monastery's custom. Otherwise he shall not eat or drink anything or overeat. If we steadfastly safeguard these traditions and do not infringe them, then we shall, as guardians of the patristic traditions, be worthy of the mercy of the Lord God--*we, who do not keep our own wills, but who tread along a path, even if it is the last.*[52] Especially if one goes with humility, he shall reach up to the gates of the eternal blessings.

[32] If one must substitute, he should substitute in this manner. When there are two foods at the table along with the soup, and someone does not eat a food which happens to be on the table, then give him two portions of what he eats. And there shall be no other foods except for those two which are on the table. And at supper it shall be as at dinner. And when there is one food with the soup at the table, and someone does not eat that kind of food, then give him another similar to that one.

49. See above, Ch 2, RELATIONS WITH THE TRANS-VOLGANS.
50. Source not identified.
51. Climacus, *Ladder* 14.12,17; PG 88:865BC.
52. Cf. Nikon, *Pandekty* 18:182.

[33] And when Tuesday and Thursday are days of fasting, give *kalatch* or another similar food at table to whoever does not eat a certain food. And when Monday, Wednesday, and Friday are not days of fasting and when there is cooked food on the table, if someone does not eat a certain kind of food, then for his needs give him *kalatch.*[53]

[34] When there are two fish dishes for the brothers, then there shall be no substitutions. When there is one fish dish and the other food is not fish, and someone wants fish in place of the other food, do not give it to him.

[35] And whoever wants to abstain and eat the worst shall eat the most worthless foods that are [set out] for the brothers. For the holy Fathers say: *If you are given food and drink, leave the excellent; drink the good and the most worthless for the sake of the Lord, who dined for your sake on vinegar and bile.*[54]

Enough of this for now.

53. Cf. (Pseudo-)Theodore Studite, *Rule* (Ὑποτύπωσις) 29; PG 99:1713C-1716A (BMFD, 109–10).

54. Source not identified.

How it is proper to have garments and footwear and other things, and how it is not proper for anyone to take anything anywhere, neither an object belonging to the monastery nor that of any brother, without the superior's or the cellarer's blessing.

Discourse III

[1] Just as we have said concerning foods and beverages that it is good to select the simple and unexcessive and to do everything in keeping with the counsel of the spiritual superior; by the same model have the clothing that is necessary, simple, very mean, and appropriate for the place and climate, and do not by means of demonic cunning, seek out the very expensive and excessive.[1]

[2] The Canons of the Seventh Ecumenical Council say: *Bishops,* monks,[2] *or clergymen who have adorned themselves with colorful and bright clothing should on this account be reprimanded. If they persist, they shall be given a penance. If someone starts to laugh at those who are wearing worthless garments, it shall be corrected with a penance. Indeed from the first years, every monastic and priestly man passed his life in humble and worthless garments.*[3]

[3] The most supreme Peter said to his disciple Clement: *Clement, you have not understood my life, that I eat only bread, olives and the most worthless vegetables, my coat is this old robe, and I do not need another, for my mind always beholds the eternal and the good out there and does not regard anything here.*[4]

[4] It is said in the *Life* of Chrysostom that after his elevation to the archbishopric of Constantinople, his food was strained ground barley, which was placed in water for a day, and he took a correctly

1. Nikon, *Taktikon* 1:13^{V} (BMFD, 405–06). Cf. *Tüpikon*, 46.

2. 'monks' was added to the original and to the text found in Nikon.

3. Nicea 2.16; *Councils*, 566 (Mansi 13:754AC), as found in Nikon, *Pandekty* 37:283^{V}-284.

4. Pseudo-Clement *Homilies* 12.6:293; PG 2:305BC, as found in Nikon, *Pandekty* 37:282^{V}-283.

measured quantity. His garment was a hair-shirt, and he did not have a third one for changing.[5]

[5] Saint Gregory the Theologian says of Basil the Great: *Basil the Great said to the prefect: I am not afraid of pillage, for I have nothing, unless you need one of my hair-shirts.*[6]

[6] And again, Father Isaiah says: *Do not seek vain glory in clothing, but remember the sheepskin of Elijah and the sackcloth of Isaiah, and do not forget the Baptist's garment, which was of camel's hair.*[7]

[7] It is written of Arsenius the Great that when he was in the world he wore the brightest of all clothing, and when he was a monk, he wore the most worthless.[8]

[8] When Sabas the Great went to the emperor, they drove him from the place as a beggar, for he was wearing an old and tattered shirt.[9]

[9] The holy Fathers say that all luxury and adornment is alien to the priestly and monastic habit.[10] Therefore from the earliest years all the saints went about deprived, grieving, and maltreated in sheepskins and goatskins, *and the whole world was not worthy of them.*[11] 'He who is adorned with clothing in the worldly life obtains glory from man; he who has humble and very worthless clothing in the monastic life prepares glory for himself in the heavens'.[12]

[10] Father Isaac said: *Our fathers wore old rags. Now you wear the most expensive clothing. Go away from here, for you have devastated this place.*[13]

[11] Saint Ephraim said concerning this: *He who loves bright*

5. Cf. Nikon, *Pandekty* 37:283^{V}.

6. *Funeral Oration*, 411; PG 36:560C, as found in Nikon, *Pandekty* 37:283^{V}.

7. Nikon, *Pandekty* 37:281^{V}, attributed to Ephraim, before a citation attributed to Isaiah.

8. Arsenius 4; *Sayings,* 8; PG 65:88C, probably as in Nikon, *Pandekty* 37:2811.

9. Cyril, *Zhitie,* 270–73, as in Nikon, *Pandekty* 37:283^{V}.

10. Nicea 2.16; *Councils* 566 (Mansi 13:754B), as in Nikon, *Pandekty,* 37:281^{V}.

11. Heb 11:38.

12. Nikon, *Pandekty*, 37:281, attributed to Ephraim.

13. Isaiah 7; *Sayings* 85; PG 65:225B, as in Nikon, *Pandekty*, 37:281.

garments is stripped of divine clothing, and our robe spoils love of goodness in that it has nothing in common with the heavenly kingdom; the beauty of our garment signifies that we are stripped of that glory. Again he says: *For you the Lord accepted abuses on the cross, and you, wretched one, adorn yourself with garments! Does your heart not tremble? Is your mind not horrified when you hear this? The Passionless One suffered passion, that you might adorn yourself not with the rotten garments, foods, or meals of common people, but with those proper to monks. The crucified Lord will seek out an answer for all of your indifference, for you, who are listening, are now indolent, eating luxuriously, adorning yourself with vestments, and laughing. When that great and terrible day comes, you will cry incessantly in the fire and will wail from the weakness of your soul!*[14]

[12] Saint Symeon the New Theologian says about this: *We, the passionate and the wretched who have abandoned the great and the admirable and have entered a monastery, now love shiny garments, belts, cutlery, sandals, and drapery, sweet foods, and drink, and apples, and beautiful fruits. In loving them, we fall away completely from Christ the King and become his enemies.*[15]

[13] The holy Fathers say that a debauched demon observes the monk's vestments to see if he has the best one for the sake of conversation. This is a typicon for debauchery, and we shall therefore be condemned with the publicans and sinners and with the rich, who have lived in debauchery.[16]

[14] Let us, then exert ourselves with all our strength to abstain from avarice, adornment of garments, and passion for things, and not only not have possessions, but also not even desire them.[17]

[15] Basil the Great says, *in writing the rules of the common life: 'Do not acquire any personal possessions, nor do anything in secret to the detriment of the brotherhood, or become a bad model for those who are predisposed to salvation. When someone*

14. Source not identified.

15. Symeon, *Catechisms*, 5.806–14; *O ezhe kako podobaet*, 10–10^{V}.

16. Attributed to Isaiah in Nikon, *Pandekty* 37:281^{V}. Cf. Symeon, *Catechisms*, 5:81–19; *O ezhe kako podobaet*, 10^{V}.

17. Cf. Nil Sorsky, *Ustav* 5:47.

has scorned fear of God and the laws of the Holy Spirit and wants to have some personal possessions, he has become enslaved to materialism and possessions. Similarly, he produces evidence of disbelief against himself; he does not trust that God spiritually and physically comforts those gathered in his name for "if two or three are gathered in Christ's name, he is among them".[18] *Indeed no needed thing will be wanting when Christ is our superior; if it is wanting for the sake of testing us, then it is better to be wanting and to be with Christ than to become rich in all worldly goods and to be without communion with him'.*[19]

[16] Indeed if it was to laymen that the Apostle said: 'Having food and clothing, let us be content; but they who desire to be rich will fall into temptations and the snares of demons',[20] then how much more proper is it for monks not to desire riches but to love non-possession and Christ-like poverty. It is not easy for those who are not in a cœnobium, where we have security regarding our most basic needs, to exercise this virtue.[21]

[17] The unknown incursion of death, moreover, must always be before our eyes, lest Our Lord come at an unexpected hour and find our conscience polluted by avarice and materialism and say to us what is said to the rich man in the Gospel: 'Fool, this night your soul shall be required of you and these things which you have prepared, whose will they be'?[22] On this account, our holy Fathers, all having the same understanding, handed down to us as a tradition that one cannot lay any firm foundation for the perfection of virtues if one does not exercise perfected non- possession, from which are born humility and compunction.

[18] He who desires to be worthy of divine grace in the present age and in the future must have perfected non-possession and

18. Mt 18:20. Cf. Timothy of Evergetis, *Typikon* 33:492. Archbishop Sava, *Tipik* 33:63.

19. Nikon, *Pandekty* 3:28–29, quoting Basil *Constitutiones* 34; PG 31: 1425BC.

20. Cf. 1 Tim 6:8–9; and below, Tradition IX.16 (XIII/ix/16). 'of demons' is not in 1 Tim.

21. Cf. Symeon, *Catechisms*, 12.141–43.

22. Lk 12:20. Cf. Heppell, *Paterik . . . Kiev.*, 62. Also John of Phoberos, *Typikon* 24:911.

Christ-like poverty, just as the Lord Christ himself says: 'The Son of Man has nowhere to lay his head';[23] and I came down from heaven, not to be served but to serve:[24] I am among you as one who serves'.[25] And again it is said: 'He took a towel and washed the disciples' feet and said, "Just as I, your Lord and teacher, have washed your feet, you ought also to wash one another's feet. For I have given you an example that you should do as I have done'.[26]

[19] Therefore it is proper for all of us to imitate that humility and poverty, especially those of us who have renounced the world and vowed to endure every affliction for the sake of the heavenly kingdom. Saint Poemen says: *If you desire to live in a cœnobium, renounce everything, and do not have dominion over even a cup, and thus shall you be saved in a cœnobium.*[27]

[20] In like manner the Lord Christ says: 'I have a commandment, what I should say and what I should speak',[28] and 'I do not do my own will, but the will of the Father who sent me'.[29] He who created the land and the sea and everything visible and invisible by his Word, displayed such humility to give us a model; so it is even more proper for us not to have our own wills, but to do everything in keeping with the superior's blessing.

[21] Consult the superior about what, when, and how it is proper to eat and drink foods and drinks, and also about what quantity and value to have of clothing and footwear, holy icons, books, and all things, and silver coins, and for working handicrafts, buying and selling, and writing and sending letters, or if anyone is sent a letter or anything else.[30]

[22] In like manner, the officials are not to buy for themselves anything special with the monastery's money without the superior's or the cellarer's blessing. And they shall distribute and take

23. Mt 8:20; Lk 9:58.
24. Jn 6:38; Mk 10:45.
25. Lk 22:27.
26. Jn 13:4–5,14–15.
27. Poemen 152; *Sayings* 158; PG 65:360B, cited in Nikon, *Pandekty* 4:30.
28. Jn 12:49.
29. Jn 6:30.
30. Cf. *Starchestvo*, 5–5^{v}. (Pseudo-)Athanasius of Athos, *Rule* (Υποτύπωσις) 34:228 (Meyer, 139–40). Manuel II Palaiologos, *Typikon* 2:1618–19.

back and do everything in keeping with the superior's blessing and not have or consider anything their own. Rather, everything belongs to the monastery. For all the Divine Writings and cœnobitic traditions dictate to those living in cœnobia to act in such a manner.

[23] We have more to say concerning garments and footwear, and we shall also place these in three orders.[31]

[24] The first order. If someone wants to have perfected non-possession according to the words spoken by Christ: 'Do not acquire a second coat',[32] then he shall have one mantle, one cassock, one skin coat, two or three tunics, one of each type of clothing—everything being mean and ragged—and one of each cell object—everything being mean and uncomely.[33] Such a person is a perfect disciple of Christ and an imitator and emulator of the saints, who suffered winter, coldness, nakedness, calamities, labors, and coercion for the sake of Christ, and on his account walked 'the narrow way, that leads to life'.[34] This person can say to Christ with boldness: 'We have forsaken all and followed you'.[35] To him the Lord says: 'If anyone serves me, he must follow me; wherever I am, there shall my servant be also'.[36]

[25] The second order. One shall have one big untattered mantle and one cowl, cassock, and skin coat—not vaingloriously or cravingly. This person walks along a blessed way, follows the first, and knows not if he has reached the end.[37]

[26] The third order. We are not legislating details but rather setting limits on account of those who are greedy for things, possess in excess, and know no measure.[38] *Therefore, if someone wants to have more than this, the superior and the brothers shall not allow this to be, but let them have these: one new mantle and a second old one; one new cowl and a second old one; one new cassock and*

31. Cf. Gregory Pakourianos, *Typikon* 9:535. Also above, Ch. 2, CLOTHING.
32. Lk 3:11.
33. See above, Ch. 2, CLOTHING.
34. Mt 7:14. Cf. above, Discourse II.29.
35. Mt 19:27.
36. Jn 12:26. Cf. below, Discourse VIII^{B}.27/VI.40, Discourse XI.12.
37. Source not identified.
38. Cf. *Tüpikon,* 41^{V}. Nikon, *Taktikon* 2:21.

a second old one; three tunics-one new and two old; one new pair of boots and a second dilapidated pair; several under-shoes; two winter caps and two summer caps, one new and the other old.[39]

[27] It is proper to have 'simple and inexpensive' garments in the storeroom just as the Divine Writings dictate.[40]

[28] It is proper for the treasurer, while issuing garments and footwear, to make an inquiry. If someone has two garments and he wants a third, do not give it to him. When someone takes a new garment from the storeroom, he is to give back the old one, and if he does not surrender it, then do not issue him a new one. If someone wants to exchange apparel, and he really needs three skin coats, then he should surrender a cassock or a mantle and take the skin coat.[41] Likewise if he wants another garment, he is to surrender something which he does not need of similar value. Everyone shall have the equivalent of two of each garment, one in good condition and one old, except in cases of debility and the offices which take place outside the monastery.

[29] And it is according to the witness of the Divine Writings that I have established three orders for food and drink and garments and footwear. *For all are not equal, because of lack of zeal and exhaustion of strength.*[42] Indeed our Lord Jesus Christ has said in the holy Gospel in the parable of the seeds: 'Others', he said, 'fell on good ground and brought forth fruit, some an hundred-fold, some sixty-fold, and some thirty-fold'.[43] Notice that they fell into the same ground and yielded unequal fruits. And it is not the case that anyone who did not create an hundred-fold fell down; rather sixty-fold is welcomed, and thirty-fold is not rejected.

[30] The sanctified martyr Hippolytus interprets similarly: *At*

39. Cf. Nikon, *Taktikon,* 1:13^{V} (BMFD, 406). (Pseudo-)Theodore Studite, *Rule* (Ὑποτύπωσις) 37:114–15 (PG 99:1720B). (Pseudo-)Athanasius of Athos, *Rule* Ὑποτύπωσις 35:228 (Meyer, 140). See above, Ch. 2, CLOTHING.

40. *Tüpikon*, 46.

41. Cf. Timothy of Evergetis, *Typikon* 25:490. Archbishop Sava, *Tipik* 27:61.

42. Cf. *Prosvetitel'* 4:160, and below XIII.2. Also Gregory of Sinai, *Praecepta; PG* 150:1336A, possibly as in Nil Sorsky, *Ustav* 2:26.

43. Mt 13:8,23. Cf. Budge, *Paradise*, 1005–6. John II Komnenos, *Typikon* 19:749.

that time there shall be a difference in keeping with each one's deeds. Some yielded an hundred-fold, some sixty, and others thirty. Some of them will go up to heaven, others are reckoned to live in paradise.[44] *For paradise has been materially constituted, although not temporally.*[45] *Rather it has eternal delight. Similarly man's flesh is now mortal, but at that time it will be immortal. Paradise was not mentioned in the parable, but Paul saw it after five thousand years; having been carried thither and having heard the mysteries of the Church, he went from there up to the third heaven.*[46] *Others will make merry in the holy city which John the Theologian saw; for he says: 'I saw the city of God, Holy Jerusalem, coming down from God out of heaven, and a voice saying, "Behold the Tabernacle of God and men are making merry and God shall be with them, and he shall remove all the tears from their eyes, and there shall be no more death. And the City will not need the sun or moon, but God's glory will illuminate"*[47] *whoever is worthy of seeing him'. For Jerusalem, the mother of cities, now is perishable and temporal, but it was selected as the domicile of the by nature imperishable and eternal God. He who is completely insignificant, subsequently will be imperishable and has been proclaimed by God to be reborn as a righteous one, in merriment and joy.*[48]

[31] And in the *Holy Ladder* it is said: *It is impossible for everybody to be free from passion, but it is possible for everybody to be saved.*[49]

And this is enough of that for now.

[32] It is proper here to speak of this. Without the superior's or cellarer's blessing, no one in the brotherhood shall take anything: not from the church, not from the refectory, not from the other workshops, not from the cells in the monastery, and not from outside the monastery; no garment, no boots, no other such item;

44. Cf. 2 Cor 12:2–4.
45. See above, Ch 2, Eschatological Visions.
46. Cf. *The Revelation of Paul*; ANF 8:575.
47. Rv 21:2,3,23.
48. Source not identified. See above, Ch. 2, note 138.
49. Climacus, *Ladder* 26:82; PG 88:1029D.

none of the iron objects, namely pole axes, knives, nails, awls, needles and similar things; none of the woodworking objects, namely logs, planks, squared beams, and roofing boards for cells and other buildings; and nothing belonging to the monastery, or anything belonging to a brother.

[33] If anyone finds anything anywhere, he shall report it to the superior or the cellarer and shall absolutely not keep it for himself. For if he keeps it for himself, then obviously he has stolen it. This is how the civil law judges laymen and inflicts gruesome punishments upon them; so how much more are monks liable to just the same![50] *Every deed done in secret and without blessing is an act of sacrilege:*[51] thus speak the Divine Writings. Thieves are hated and loathsome in the worldly life, and not only in the worldly life, but also in monasteries they are hated and receive gruesome punishments.[52] For if under the Old Law Achar and Gehazi[53] and under the Apostles Ananius and Sapphira were condemned to death for theft,[54] then how much more proper is it that we keep ourselves from theft.

[34] If someone says: 'In a cœnobium everything is common, and therefore we may take needed items without a blessing', then let him hear Basil the Great speak: In a cœnobium, *he who does anything secretly and without a blessing is nothing other than the devil's man; he becomes his subordinate and will be condemned with him to the 'outer darkness'*[55] *on account of theft. Therefore the Apostle says: 'Nor shall thieves inherit the kingdom of God',*[56] and what is done without a blessing and a command is robbery.[57]

[35] Saint Theodore the Studite speaks similarly in his cœnobitic traditions: *It is proper for a monk who lives in a cœnobium to do*

50. Cf. Justinian, *Digest* 46.2.43.

51. Cf. Pseudo-Basil, *Ascetical Discourse,* 20; PG 31:633B.

52. See Freshfield, *Manual*, 152–57.

53. Jos 7:16–26, Cf. below, Discourse XIII.24.

54. Acts 5:1–11. Cf.(Pseudo-)Athanasius of Athos, *Rule* (Ὑποτύπωσις) 36: 228 (Meyer, 140). Also above, Discourse II.21.

55. Mt 25:30. Cf. below, Discourse XIII.55.

56. 1 Cor 6:10.

57. Cf. Pseudo-Basil, *Ascetical Sermon*, 20; PG 31:633B, and *Constitutiones* 34, PG 31:1024C-1025C.

everything with a blessing, for every deed that is not blessed is cursed.[58] In the common life, much more than in individual life, it is proper to act with a blessing, lest we be condemned like Gehazi and Achar.

[36] Accordingly, we should contemplate how we are really being insulted by demons when we take another's things. When we are indicted, then we say, 'In a cœnobium everything is common'. But when someone takes our personal things, then we do not say: 'In a cœnobium everything is common', but we become like wild beasts towards our neighbor; we bite and we sting, and we are not afraid to quarrel and litigate, just like malicious laymen.

[37] Therefore, it is not proper for us to act like that, but if someone takes something from us, we should not make any trouble, but gently and calmly report this to the superior. And let no one of us dare to take anything in any way from any place without the superior's or the cellarer's blessing. And if we find anything, let us not conceal it; rather let us report to the superior or the cellarer, lest we be condemned in the present age and in the future, as has been previously said.

[38] Similarly, no one shall take anything in the holy church: not a book, not a candle nor any other object without the sacristan's blessing.

[39] And also no one shall inscribe anything in a book without the superior's or the choirmaster's blessing: from this arise disturbances and trouble and the corruption of the Divine Writings, and discord and cliques, and then curses and anathemas.[59] He who would escape all of this, should do everything with a blessing, so that he may therefore be worthy of divine grace and mercy in the present and future age. Amen.

58. Source not identified; Cf. Basil *Shorter Rules* 48; PG 31:1037B.

59. See above, Ch. 2, Heresy and Authority.

Concerning not conversing after Compline.

Discourse IV

[1] After Compline, as the God-bearing holy Fathers discerned, it is not proper to stand and converse in the monastery or to assemble in the cells.[1] Only the hegumen may speak out about the needs of the cloister, but for the sake of good order, he shall speak in a cell.[2] Nor should anyone drink water, except the sick, for Compline has been established by the holy Fathers as the conclusion and fulfillment of the whole day.[3]

[2] If it happens that someone has transgressed that night or day,[4] it is therefore proper after the conclusion of the Compline chant not to speak foolishly of the vain and perishable or to criticize and slander somebody. Rather, with humility and contrition of heart, make a prostration at the feet of the superior as if at the very feet of Christ, and confess to him everything you did in the passing night and day: deeds, words, and thoughts.[5] The holy Fathers required hourly confession. If that is not possible, then certainly do not let an evening come when you do not confess[6] these faults out of fear of death, because many have gone to sleep at night and not gotten up in the next day. 'In the state I find you', says the Lord, 'shall I judge you',[7] either in repentance and compunction or in negligence and merriment. Indeed there is no other consolation at the time of death than repentance and confession.

1. Cf. *Tüpikon*, 18–18^{V}. Petit, *Vie de S. Athanase,* 40.

2. Cf. Joachim of Zichna, *Typikon* 17:1602.

3. Cf. Nikon, *Taktikon,* 1:13.

4. Professor Wladimir Vodoff, following Lur'e's punctuation, suggested an alternative reading: For Compline has been established by the holy Fathers as the conclusion and the fulfillment of the whole day, especially in case someone happens to have transgressed during the [preceding] night or day. ([VI^{B}.2] would follow, beginning with: It is therefore proper after the conclusion of the Compline chant. . . .) See PIV, 309; Vodoff, 'Compte rendue', 203–04.

5. Apparently from Basil, *Longer Rules* 37:310; PG 31:1056. Cf. Timothy of Evergetis, *Typikon* 7:475–6. Archbishop Sava, *Tipik* 7:49–50. Gregory Pakourianos, *Typikon* 13:537

6. Cf. Theodora/Theodule of Synadene, *Typikon* XX:1553–54.

7. Cf. Ez 21:30.

[3] And having thus received absolution from the superior[8] as if from God himself, one should flee in silence into one's cell and not speak at all to anyone. And so one should apply oneself with quietness[9] in prayer and handicraft or reading, be soberly mindful of oneself with prayers and tears, and repent and confess all transgressions to the Lord. Then his soul can rest from the burden of having transgressed in the preceding night and day. If it happens that he die that night, he will not be disregarded by the Lord God because he will have been found in repentance and confession. For the Lord himself sings out: 'I am not come to call the righteous, but the sinners to repentance'.[10]

[4] After the conclusion of Compline, the inspector of the church shall walk about the monastery, and if he sees anyone standing in the monastery, walking from cell to cell, or going beyond the monastery, he shall reprimand him and report him either to the superior or the cellarer. If the gates are not bolted, he shall order the gates to be bolted in his presence: *for from a little negligence, we fall into great sins.*[11]

8. Cf. Joachim of Zichna, *Typikon* 22:1606.

9. *bezmolvie*, the equivalent of the Greek ἡσυχία—the quietness of hesychasm.

10. Mt 9:13.

11. Source not identified; cf. below, Discourse IX.13.

That it is not proper for monks to go outside the monastery without a blessing.

Discourse V

[1] It is necessary to know that it is improper, better to say, calamitous, for monks to go outside the monastery without the superior's blessing. For if we need to go outside for some food, a vestment, or a task, will we not obtain his blessing? If it is necessary, then it is especially proper to go with a blessing, lest our labor be in vain; for every deed without a benediction is cursed.[1] If it is good, then why go without a blessing? And the good is not good when there is no blessing. If we go outside for something evil, that is, to banter and laugh and make idle chatter and eat and drink, these manifestly dispatch our souls to hell.

[2] When a monk starts to be negligent about himself and to wander outside the cloister without the superior's blessing, then the devil traps him, hurls him towards sin, or hands him over to death. If he indeed hurls him into sin, then he immerses him in the despair that there is no longer hope for salvation, and he is drowned in disgrace and shame over the lack of that boldness towards the father which comes from obedience. Thus he seduces him into the world to the ultimate destruction of his soul, just as that elder who was ninety years old bears witness. It is said about him in the *Patericon,* that though being of such age, he went off to the city without his father's blessing, fell into fornication, and was not able quickly to repent because of his disgrace. Rather he put it off until they brought the child to Scete, and he cried inconsolably in front of everybody.[2]

[3] Many indeed have despaired to the ultimate joy of the Adversary. If he entraps someone to his death, obviously the latter is being condemned by God as a transgressor of the patristic commands, just as we have found in the Divine Writings of the Fathers. A certain elder lived for fifty years without going outside

1. Cf. Pseudo-Basil, *Ascetical Discourse,* 20; PG 31:633B.
2. Source not identified.

the monastery and wore his black robe well. The devil envied him, tempted him to leave the monastery without a blessing, and then fettered his foot and smashed him against a rock, so that he died. They told the hegumen about the death, and he, not guessing the Adversary had tempted that [monk] to leave the monastery without a blessing, told the brothers to pray for the deceased brother. While they were praying for him day and night, a voice came to them: 'Do not register as part of the brotherhood him who did not heed his vow. Rather bind his foot with a rope and throw him in the ditch'. And they did so. Thus the holy Fathers forbade giving such a person a burial or offering an oblation for him, because he was a transgressor of his vow. He had vowed at his renunciation of the world to remain in the monastery until his last breath, and he had vowed to preserve his obedience to the superior even until death.[3]

[4] Therefore, brothers, let us exert ourselves wholeheartedly to flee, as if from a stench and deadly sting, individualism, insubordination, and wandering outside of the cloister without the command of the superior, and let us struggle even until death. Let us place our souls along the single line of God's commandment, and let us keep as our tradition the measure and typicon throughout—in motions, words, and deeds.[4]

Enough of this for now.

3. Cf. *Paterik skitskii;* (VMCh 4:2657–58), found in the Old Russian *Lausaic History*.

4. Cf. *Tüpikon*, 42^{V}. Nikon, *Taktikon*, 1:6^{V} (BMFD, 393).

That it is proper to bear responsibility for the community and particular offices to which each has been assigned.

Chapter VI

[1] It is necessary also to talk about community work.

[2] It is proper for everyone to exert himself in community work. *Indeed the holy Apostle Paul says: 'We command you, brothers, and we exhort you in Christ Jesus that you work quietly and eat your own bread';*[1] *and 'if anyone will not work, let him not eat'.*[2] *Thus the holy Fathers were admonished by these apostolic teachings, and they enjoin monks, especially the young, never to be idle.*3[3]

[3] Makarios the Great says: *Nor can an idler be faithful.* And again: *Idleness has taught much evil.*[4]

[4] And it is said in the *Geronticon: He who can work and does not work will be condemned with the robbers.*[5]

[5] And in the *Holy Ladder* it is said: *As much as faith blooms in the heart, the body hurries to serve.* And again: *Heartily give the labors of your youth to Christ, and you will rejoice in old age over a wealth of impassibility; for that which is gathered in youth feeds and comforts exhausted old age.* And again: *Let us young ones labor in heat. Let us run soberly. Death is uncertain. In truth we have gruesome, wicked, deceitful, atrocious, strong, vigilant, immaterial, and invisible enemies, who are keeping fire in their hands and are starting to burn the divine church because of the flame which is in them.*[6]

[6] Isidore the priest of Scete said: *Brothers, did we not come here for the sake of labor? We no longer have any labor. I have*

1. Thes 3:12.

2. 2 Thes 3:10. Cassian, *Institutes* 10.7; PL 49:373–75, as in Nikon, *Pandekty* 44:345.

3. Cassian, *Institutes* 10:22; PL 49:388–93, as in Nikon, *Pandekty* 44:347. Cf.Si 33:38.

4. Attributed to Lot by Nikon, *Pandekty* 44:348[V]. Cf. Si 30:27. Symeon, *Catechisms* 26.75. 'Izbornik' of 1076, 52.

5. Cf. Eph 4:28.

6. Climacus, *Ladder* 1:24; PG 88:64IBC.

readied a sheepskin and I shall go to where there is labor, and there I shall find tranquility.[7]

[7] An elder said: *The novice does not need any activity other than obedience and physical labor.*[8]

[8] A brother asked an elder: 'Tell me, how can I be saved'? The elder responded: 'Let us strive to work and not be lazy, and we shall be saved'.[9]

[9] The holy Fathers say: *The worker wrestles with a demon, and the idler is imprisoned by a thousand demons.*[10]

[10] Saint Poemen says: *A monk who lives in a cœnobium must have these three: humility, obedience, and exertion in his work for the community.*[11]

[11] Saint Ephraim says: *This is the origin of arrogance and loftiness, not to desire to toil in manual labor with the brotherhood in keeping with one's strength. Such a person shall not eat. Let us condescend rather than be long-winded, but our zeal shall be directed only toward our original goal.*[12]

[12] If it is necessary to leave work, one should ask for the blessing of the superior; when the superior is absent, that of the foreman.[13]

[13] An elder said: *It is proper for a man to safeguard his work lest he destroy it, for if someone works a great deal but does not safeguard it, then there is no profit. If he creates a little and is watchful, the work remains intact.*[14]

[14] And nothing indeed squanders good works so much as to speak, laugh, and jest. Basil the Great says: *It is proper to move far away from jesting, for it happens that those who often engage in it lose the right word, often tread this evil path, and end their days in filthy language, improprieties, and corrupt communication.*[15]

7. Poemen 44; *Sayings* 145; PG 65:332D.
8. Source not identified.
9. Source not identified.
10. Cassian, *Institutes* 10:23; PL 49:393–94, as in Nikon, *Pandekty* 44:347.
11. Poemen 103; *Sayings,* 152; PG 65:348A.
12. Cited in Nikon, *Pandekty* 44:347.
13. *bol'shoi sluzhebnik*, literally, major official.
14. Source not identified.
15. Cited in Nikon, *Pandekty*, 10:74.

[15] Saint John Chrysostom says: *Nothing is more shameless than the jester, for his mouth is full of disease, bitterness, and deceit; let us drive such habits away from our tables. Soul, these expressions are devoid of reverence.*[16] *Thus I exhort you in every way, that we drive away such habits, speak what is proper, and let not our holy mouth make conversation with disgraceful and filthy words from which Christ departs.*[17]

[16] From banter—idleness; from idleness—laughter and boldness; and laughter and boldness are the ruination of the soul, monks! And Saint Ephraim says: *If you see yourself in this, o monk, you see yourself in ultimate perdition.*[18]

[17] Therefore the Apostle commands [us] to work: *with labor and travail day and night,*[19] *in humility and silence, for such work is an offering welcome to God.*[20]

[18] If we want our work to be well-received by God and our offering to be considered pleasing to him, let us display such great zeal and struggle that we not only work with humility and silence, but also arrive earliest of all. As at prayer in the divine church, he who comes earlier is earlier worthy of divine grace. Similarly at work, he who comes earlier receives a great reward. *For as much as faith blooms in the heart, the body hurries to serve.*[21] And he who was in disbelief, that is to say, in disobedience, stumbled and fell; for it is normal for disobedience to destroy any profit.

[19] Therefore blessed is he who has completely killed his own will and has given up responsibility for himself to his teacher in the Lord.[22] That person stands at the right hand of the Crucified One.[23] Let all of us who would fear the Lord struggle with all our strength

16. The original reads: 'These words are from a soul without reverence'.

17. *Ephesians* 17:131; PG 62:120, as in Nikon, *Pandekty* 10:74–74^{V}.

18. *Quod non oporteat ridere;* ed. Assemiani 1:254; ed. Thwaites, 157.

19. Cf. 2 Thes 3:8.

20. For Section [17], cf. Nikon, *Pandekty* 44:246–47; adapted from Cassian, *Institutes* 10.8,22; PL 49:376, 393.

21. See above, Discourse VI.5 (Discourse VIII^{B}.8).

22. Climacus, *Ladder* 4:44; PG 88:704D. Cf. (Pseudo-)Athanasius of Athos, *Rule* (Ὑποτύπωσις) 27:257–58 (Meyer, 111).

23. Climacus, *Ladder* 4:49; 705B.

completely to kill our will, just as did our reverend Fathers who lived in obedience and humility. On this account they shone here like luminous stars, and they duly obtained as an inheritance the heavenly kingdom in the future age—and of them we shall now briefly speak.

[20] This is written in the *Geronticon* concerning blessed Mark, the calligrapher, the disciple of Father Silvanus: *One day while he was doing calligraphy, his elder summoned him for a mission. At that moment he was writing an* ω, *and he had already written a half* υ, *but he left the other half and got right up and ran to work.*[24]

[21] And also that blessed John the Sabbaite, who changed his name to Antiochus, played the fool *for the sake of Christ,*[25] *and never was idle at work; indeed they commanded him to do all the monastery's hard labor, and he zealously did it all.*[26]

[22] Similarly of Acacius it is written in the *Ladder* that his teacher not only tried him with insults and indignities, but also tormented him every day with strokes.[27]

[23] And Abbacyrus was humiliated and abused, banished from the refectory many times for seventeen years, remained the whole day without food, and spoke thus: *'The fathers are testing me and are not doing this in real earnest'*.[28]

[24] And Dositheos, who was a disciple of Saint Dorotheos, it appears, never performed his own will right up until his death. Rather when the blessed Dorotheos, to joke with or to test him, would command him to do something, he did everything without a second thought.[29]

[25] It is written concerning John Colubus, that his teacher placed a dry tree six miles from his cell and commanded him to water it every day. After three years he brought the tree back to

24. Mark 1; *Sayings,* 123 PG 65:296A. Cf. Nikon, *Pandekty* 2:10.
25. I Cor 4:10.
26. Climacus, *Ladder* 4.11; PG 88:721AD. Cf. Nikon, *Pandekty* 2:10.
27. Climacus, *Ladder* 4.11; PG 88:72OB-721A, as in Nikon, *Pandekty* 2:10^{V}.
28. Cf. Climacus, *Ladder* 4.29; PG 88:693CD, and in Nikon, *Pandekty*, 2.10^{V}.
29. Nikon, *Pandekty,* 2.10^{V}. Cf. *Vita S. Dosithei* 17–19; *Acta SS* Feb 3:389–90 (later ORT KZhS, Feb 13–38, pp. 38,44; French trans., Regnault and Préville, *Sources chrétiennes* 92:137).

life and created fruit, and the fruit of the tree was called 'the fruit of obedience'.[30]

[26] The pastor commanded Saint Isidore, who had been a prefect, to stand before the gates for seven years, and commanded him to prostrate himself before all who entered and exited and to say: 'Pray for me, for I am an epileptic'.[31]

[27] And that great Saint John Damascene, most renowned for his great wisdom, was commanded by the elder to clean up the monks' filthy latrine with his own hands. Once the elder commanded him to walk to Damascus, where he had previously been glorious and great to sell maniples, and he did everything without a second thought.[32]

[28] Anthony the Great once commanded blessed Paul the Simple to draw water for the whole day and then let it flow for no purpose. Another time, having torn his robe, he commanded him diligently to sew it up again. Once again the saint told him: 'Stand and pray while I fetch some work for you', and Paul remained steadfast for a whole week and was roasted by the burning sun. Then the saint came, moistened some palm leaves, and said to him: 'Sit and weave plaits'. Paul wove thirty yards before the ninth hour. The saint said to him: 'You wove badly; unweave it, and weave again'. He then unwove all that work and wove it again. Paul had not eaten for seven days. The saint set up the table and pieces of bread and said to Paul, 'Watch, but absolutely do not touch what is lying on it'. Then he said to him, 'Stand up and pray, and go to sleep'. Then he sent him into the desert to walk about and come back after three days. When several brothers came to the elder, he said to Paul, 'Serve the brothers in silence'. He was silent, and then the saint commanded him to talk to the brothers. Another time someone brought the saint a jug with honey, and he said to Paul, 'Take the vessel, break it, and spread the honey out on the ground'. And when that had been done, the elder said to Paul, 'Gather the

30. Nikon, *Pandekty*, 2.1O^{V}. Cf. Cotelier, *Sanctorum senum* 1:468–69.

31. Climacus, *Ladder* 4:23; PG 88:689D, as in Nikon, *Pandekty*, 2.10^{V}. Epileptic—literally 'fall about the moon'.

32. Cf. John of Jerusalem, *Vita S. Joannis Damasceni; Acta SS Maii* 2:116–18.

honey in a dish, and do not leave any of it there'. Paul created no trouble or difficulty whatsoever, but accomplished everything with humility and without a murmur.[33]

[29] Thus did our holy, sainted, and God-bearing Fathers possess obedience and humility, for they knew that nothing is greater or more profitable for our souls. It is so said in the *Patericon: An elder said: 'He who is settled in obedience to his spiritual father will have a greater reward that he who is settled in the desert and lives by himself'. He said that one of the fathers said: 'I saw four orders in heaven. The first order is sick of man and praises God. The second order has hospitality, occupies itself with it, and serves. The third order lives in the desert and does not look upon man. The fourth order is settled in obedience to a spiritual father and submits to him for the sake of the Lord. Those who had obedience wore a gold torque and a gold armlet and had greater glory than the others'. I said to my guide: 'What does "has greater glory than the others" mean'? He answered: 'The hospitable one does his own will. Similarly he went off to the desert of his own will. This one, who had obedience, has abandoned his own will completely to depend upon God, his*[34] *Father'.*[35]

[30] Once four monks from Scete who were dressed in skins approached the blessed Father Pambo, and each one reported the virtue of his comrade. One fasted very often; the second was non-possessor; the third had acquired a tremendous capacity for love; and they said to him concerning the fourth: 'He has been obedient to his elder for twenty-two years'. Father Pambo responded: 'I say unto you that his virtue is greater than yours, for as each of you acquired his virtue, you kept your own will, but this one cut off his own will and performed another's will. Such are confessors, if they hold fast to the end'.[36]

33. Cf. Butler, *Palladius und Rufinus*, 93 (21.3–4). Iosif's version is a melange of the long and brief redactions according to Butler's division of the text.

34. Originally: and his.

35. Cf. Rufus 2; *Sayings,* 177; PG 65:389C-392D, (VMCh 8:336).

36. Pambo 3, *Sayings,* 165; PG 65:365AB.

[31] Saint Syncletica says: *Those in monasteries should acquire more obedience than asceticism. The latter teaches pride; while the former teaches humble-mindedness.*[37]

[32] If we indeed want to be worthy of divine mercy, let us strive to become emulators and imitators of those blessed and aforesaid holy Fathers of everlasting memory. Then our work will be a well-received offering, pleasing to God, and similar to Abel's, who offered first to God the most esteemed, and then to himself the worst.[38] If we begin to arrive last of all, leave first of all, work murmuringly and disobediently, and play the jester and make idle chatter, then our work, like Cain's offering, will not be well-received or pleasing to God. For Basil the Great says:[39] *The work of the man who works negligently, disobediently, and with murmuring is unacceptable to God, for Scripture says: 'The lawless person who sacrifices a calf to me is like him who kills a dog; and he who offers fine flour is like the person who offers swine's blood'.*[40]

[33] Saint Ephraim bears witness concerning those whose work was like Cain's offering he said: *A certain monk, he said, by the name of Palladius, lived in the monastery of a certain saintly elder and remained always at his own work, and regarded neither the community's nor the monastery's work, but only his own, for he was possessed by avarice. When the holy elder summoned him to work, he vowed to go, but did not go with the elder. When the elder had a little meal with the brothers, Palladius came and ate with them and again went to his own work. The saintly elder exhorted and admonished him not to disregard his salvation, but he did not submit to the good admonition of the saintly elder. And he*

37. Syncletica 16; *Sayings,* 196; PG 65:425D-428A, also Pseudo-Athanasius of Alexandria, *Vita . . . Syncieticae 100;* PG 28:1549. The original Greek for 'pride' is ὑπεροψία (arrogance, contempt). Cf. (Pseudo-)Athanasius of Athos, *Rule* (Ὑποτύπωσις) 38:260–61 (Meyer, 116): 'The reward of obedience is greater than what one achieves by abstinence'. This apothegm appears earlier in Pseudo-Basil, *(Another) Ascetical Discourse*, 142 (PG 31:884C).

38. Cf. Gn 4:3–4. Cf. above, Discourse I^{B}.8/I.8.

39. *Longer Rules* 29:292 PG 31:989D-992C.

40. Is 66:3.

remained thus to the end. As he had removed his thoughts far from God's succor, a demon vanquished him; and having destroyed his mind, he thus ended his days.[41]

[34] Saint Symeon the New Theologian speaks similarly: *Two brothers by blood,* he said, *rejected the world. Both were young and pure regarding every bodily sin. One was humble, readily submissive, and obedient, and said to the brotherhood: 'In the world, venerable Fathers, I could hardly obtain food with much labor. Having come here, why would I want to neglect work, eat the monastery's bread for free and be called to account for it on the Day of Judgement? Because I came here to slave for God now, I am striving with all my strength to increase my work, rather than my food, and I shall submit to my director and to all my brothers without a murmur, even unto death, as if to Christ himself'. And he strove to be the first to come to prayer and to all monastic work; he left after everybody; and he worked with humility, quietness, and contrition of the heart. The other brother was overcome with pride, insubordination, and laziness. When they ordered him to work, he alleged debility, by crying and shrieking, claimed weakness of the knees, and responded: 'I feel murky; and my head is troubled with bile', so that he could eat, curse, and blaspheme from morning on, and he contradicted all commands and murmured. When he was summoned to work, he arrived last of all, left first of all, worked with murmuring and bitterness and said: 'In the world, Fathers, I never saw work. I did not come here to be anyone's slave, to toil and have others enjoy the fruits of my labor'. And under these circumstances death came and holy angels took the soul of the humble, meek, readily obedient brother and carried it off to a luminous place, the domicile of the righteous, while dark and filthy demons pulled the soul out of that ferocious, disobedient, proud, and haughty brother and led it off to a domicile in hell. And he immediately looked up and he saw the one who had been born with him, grown up with him, once lived with him and who was now totally in great glory with Christ. There was nothing he could*

41. *Paranesis;* ed. Assemani 2:114; ed. Thwaites, 276.

say or answer, but groaning, shaking and gnashing his teeth, he was dispatched to the eternal fire.[42]

[35] Behold, we have seen how disobedience and disdain intercede for us. So, beloved ones, let us not disdain the fear of the Lord and our own salvation. Let us submit ourselves under his firm hand and work for him with humility and obedience.

And this is enough about community work.

Concerning individual offices.

[36] Let us speak now of the individual offices which are in the cloister, of how it is proper with zeal and with fear of Cod to bear responsibility for each office to which one has been assigned, as Basil the Great says: *Perform the work of your office gracefully and diligently as if serving Christ: cursed is he who does the work of God negligently.*[43] *Fear what results from wicked negligence more than ineptitude, even if your work seems bad, for God is inspecting.*[44]

[37] Therefore it is proper for the officials to have great zeal and careful responsibility lest one of those who normally perverts the truth with his weakness and offends and perverts others and has something extra apart from the brothers, eats and drinks more than the brothers, is enslaved to avarice and materialism, or has more clothing and footwear than the brothers, then does not exert himself. Therefore, not only should the officials themselves observe and safeguard the traditions and commands here written, but they should admonish and teach the others under them to safeguard and observe them, and they should not condescend to the weakness[45] of those who would eat and drink anything extra, have possession of extra objects or perform any other deeds not in keeping with the tradition here written, lest they suffer, as many others have suffered, and of whom we now shall briefly speak.

42. From Symeon, *Catechisms* 5.861–967; *O ezhe kako podobaet,* 12–15. The Brief Rule (VIII^{B},28) is closer to the original.

43. Jer 48:10. Cf. above and below, Discourse I^{B}.8/I.8, Appendix I.6.

44. Pseudo-Basil, *Ascetical Discourse,* 29; PG 31:645B.

45. Cf. below, Discourse XIII.52.

[38] It is said in the *Life* of Euthymius the Great that after the departure of Saint Euthymius, a monk by the name of Paul was brought to his monastery from the Monastery of Martyrs because he was being tormented by a vile spirit. They laid him by the tomb of Saint Euthymius, and he immediately became healthy. They inquired of him how he was cured and he said: *When I was in the monastery, they entrusted me with a refectory office. I did not think about fear of God, nor did I fear sin. Sometimes I took things for myself, and other times I distributed things to others. I ate and drank without restraint, in spite of the custom and the typicon of the monastery. Once I drank wine and fell asleep, and immediately the thought of fornication entered me. While having such thoughts I felt murky and was tormented for many days by a demon. The brothers saw me suffering, brought me here, and laid me by the tomb of the saint. I started to pray to him with bitter tears and right away I saw the saint shining as a light and speaking to me with fury: 'Have you trusted that nothing can be concealed from God? Have you perceived how great a calamity it is to neglect service to Christ? And have you contemplated that everything in a monastery is holy and is consecrated to God; and those who are negligent of this go off to perdition; and what kind of perdition is fitting this present age and in the future for those who drink and eat without the command and counsel of the superior, and who are enslaved to avarice and materialism? I swore with tears to the living God never to do this again. Then the saint took me by the hand and tore off my hirsute cowl. In his hand it was like a little Ethiopian, and fire was coming forth from the eyes. There was a large ditch in front of him and he tossed the Ethiopian into it and said to me; "Look! You are well; sin no more, lest worse things happen to you".*[46] *Since that time nothing evil has befallen me, thanks to the grace of Christ and the Prayers of Saint Euthymius'.*[47]

[39] Similarly it is said in the *Life* of Macarius the Great of Egypt, that when Macarius built his hostel, he received visitors, sick

46. Cf. Jn 5:14.

47. From Schwartz, *Kyrillos*, 72–74. Pomialovsky, *Zhitie Evthimiia,* 83–86. Cf. Symeon Metaphrastes, *Vita*; PG 114:712C-717A.

persons, and strangers, and honored each of their needs. To minister to them he assigned a certain Abraham,[48] who was good at first and administered according to the father's command. Subsequently, however, alas! Abraham was entrapped by the ruse of avarice, and he stole what was brought by the devotees of Christ for the poor, the strangers, and even the sick. He hoped that from this he could nourish himself and relax until the day of his death. Macarius the Great rebuked, forbade, and exhorted him, but when he saw that he was unsubmissive and insubordinate, he said to him: 'Because you desire vain and rotten wealth, know for sure that you will not be allowed this, and that after my death you shall get the leprosy of Gehazi[49] and even a greater illness than his'. After the passing of the blessed father, the body of the wretched man was completely infected with leprosy. Soon he was separated from men and had destroyed not only the property he had collected, but also—woe is me—his own soul![50]

[40] Likewise it is said in the *Patericon* that a certain father asked father Zeno: *'Tell me father, how can I discern whether my service has been welcomed by God'? The elder responded: 'The first sign for the serving-man is benign thoughts, love of God, and fear. The second sign is humble-mindedness in the face of everybody; consider that you are serving not men, but angels, and that in keeping with the Lord's words, "Wherever I am, there shall my servant be also,"*[51] *you are standing before Christ's sacrificial altar. The third sign: words of compunction, speech without murmurs, sighs from the heart, the flowing of tears, fear of God, desire of future blessings, precision in your charges, so that nothing be arranged unseasonably or be materially excessive, but everything with faith and fear of God. If you behold and feel these in yourself, the service is welcome and pleasing to God, angels, and men. But if your service is accompanied by wickedness, deceit, stupidity, murmurs, troublemaking, bitterness, any needless*

48. In the original: John.
49. 2 Kgs 5:20–27.
50. From Palladius, *Lausiac History*, 17.4; PG 34:1043C.
51. Jn 12:26. Cf. above and below, Discourse III.24, Discourse XI.2.

stinginess with food, laziness in prayer, solitary eating, fullness of sleep, extravagance with fearlessness, neglect of brothers in your charge, avoidance of elders, reviling of novices, contumely towards the great, desire for worldly people and readiness to eat and drink with them—such a servant is a friend of vainglory, a disciple of arrogance, and a seeker of praise. He does what is forbidden by the leader; he is no counselor of the superior's representative, does everything by himself, concealed from the superior; squanders; cheers up the devil; destroys himself; becomes a friend of Achar of Israel, a companion of Gehazi, a disciple of Judas the renegade, and a brother of Ananius and Sapphira.[52] *Such a servant is without reward and, deprived of his reward, forfeits his labor. Such a servant is a lamb by day and a wolf by night. Such a servant is a monk in form and among the worldly in understanding. Such a servant is a barren tree, a dry spring, a house without cover. Such a servant feeds upon vainglory from the devil, is sated with arrogance, dresses in turpitude, studies disputation, and is*[53] *shod in wickedness. The mind of such a servant becomes murky; his thought darkens; his heart hardens, and he is titillated toward beauty by debauched thoughts*[54] *and falls into the calamity of masturbation. Such a servant has surpassed Hellenic sacrifices in his vanity, for the Hellenes offered animals and were disciples of demons; this one not only offers birds and animals, and is a friend of demons, but makes a whole offering of himself, with the touch of the hand and the relaxation of the mind clothes himself completely in the voluptuousness of the devil. Such a servant is replete with irascibility, filled up with bitterness, agitated by anger, and controlled by malice.*[55] *Why should I talk so much? He has fallen from the heavenly kingdom if he does not correct himself through fasting, vigils, prayer, confession, and humble-*

52. See Jos 7:16–26; 2 Kgs 5:20–27; Acts 5:1–11; Mt 26:14–15,47–49, 27:3–5, and parallels.

53. corrected from *am (esm")* to *is (est")*.

54. Cf. Climacus, *Ladder* 14.36; PG 88:869D.

55. Source not identified. This passage is found separately in a mid-sixteenth-century codex in the St. Petersburg (Leningrad) State Public Library/Russian National Library: *Rogozhskii* 530:32^{v}'-34.

mindedness, and if he does not carefully exert himself to take responsibility for the office he has been given.

[41] As it has been stated in the *Geronticon: 'When I went to the cœnobium for a visitation with the fathers, I was therefore an ample number of days to observe their life. Once I beheld the œconomos*[56] *enter the kitchen. He saw a few lentils strewn on the ground and did not disdain this as if it were a little thing, really nothing, but summoned the brother whose office it was to be responsible for the cooking, gave him a penance for having slighted the office bestowed upon him by God, and set his own conscience straight.*[57] *They safeguarded their offices with such faith and so much zeal that those things which we suppose to be trifles and unseemly they safeguarded with every precaution, as if they were holy objects of some kind. If they saw a vessel or anything else lying out of place they put it in its place with fear and with the belief that if someone worked disdainfully, negligently, or simply haphazardly, he would receive condemnation, and that he who works with fear of God and with reverence will receive and obtain the heavenly blessings'.*

[42] Basil the Great says: *The work of the office is great and intercedes to the heavenly kingdom. It is a dragnet for virtues which bears in itself all the divine commandments. The very first of all these is humility, which delivers a multitude of blessings. Next is 'I was hungry, and you gave me food; I was thirsty, and you gave me drink; I was a stranger and sick and in prison,' and you served me,*[58] *especially when the duty is performed with humble-mindedness, without loftiness, anger, or murmuring. In the daily steps of your office, make ready along with the actual physical labor a word of consolation for the beloved one served, so that your service be welcome, combined with salt. And do not forsake the work imposed upon you for others to do, lest the reward be taken from you and be given to another, and lest another be glorified with your wealth, while you are humiliated.*

56. *Ikonom* (Greek: οἰκονόμος), the functional near equivalent of the cellarer in Russia.

57. Source not identified. Editor's surmise of the end of the citation and commencement of Iosif's commentary.

58. Cf. Mt 25:35.

[43] *Therefore if you are a nobleman, do not exalt yourself over your nobility of flesh and honor, and require more tranquility than others. Rather suppose yourself to be the most dishonorable and sinful of men, a stranger and a sojourner. Strive to be last of all and a servant to all'.*[59] Indeed our Lord Jesus Christ said: 'Whoever would be first among you shall be the last of all and servant of all'.[60] Another time he said: 'You should do as you have seen me do'.[61] Another time he said: 'I am among you as one who serves, while you are reclining'.[62] And again he says: 'Learn from me, for I am meek and lowly of heart'.[63] Therefore condemn loftiness and accept serving, especially humility.[64] If you begin this way and end this way, you will in a short time, by God's grace, enter into paradise to rejoice with Christ forever and ever.

59. Pseudo-Basil, *Ascetical Discourse,* 29, 21 PG 31:645BC, 633BC.
60. Mk 10:44.
61. Jn 13:15.
62. Cf. Lk 22:27–28.
63. Mt 11:29.
64. The printed text is not clear: *sego radi v"znoshenia vinu slugovanie priimati no pache smirenie.*

That it is not proper for drinks which cause drunkenness to be in the cloister.

Discourse VII

[1] As drunkenness is the beginning and the end of all evil, our Lord Jesus Christ therefore says: 'Watch over yourselves, lest your hearts ever be weighed down with overeating and drunkenness';[1] and the Apostle Paul says: 'Do not get drunk with wine, wherein is debauchery'.[2]

[2] And Basil the Great says: '*Just as smoke drives away bees,*[3] *so drunkenness drives away the Holy Spirit, because drunkenness is the door to passions, the commander of pollutions, the worker of debauchery, billows of smut, a sea of thoughts, an abyss of indescribable filth, profanity, nonsense, insensitive banter, audacity, insatiability, psychic analgesia, non-remembrance of death, lack of hope, and despair, the most gruesome of all,*[4] *which generates psychic ruin and mental crime*'.[5]

[3] And Saint John Chrysostom says: '*The holy Apostle Paul indeed spoke well: "For I have told you often, and now tell you even weeping that they are the enemies of the cross of Christ, whose God is their belly and whose glory is in their shame."*[6] *So he who fills his belly excessively and lives in fornication and drunkenness is an enemy of Christ, for the glutton and the drunk destroys his body and his soul*'.[7]

[4] *Do you see how the drunkard is more hateful than the demoniac? For the demon drowns man with God's sufferance, but the drunkard destroys himself by his own will. His saliva is*

1. Lk 21:34.
2. Eph 5:18.
3. Cf. Antiochus, *Pandectes* 4; PG 89:1444C (VMCh 4:1878).
4. Climacus, *Ladder* 14.36; PG 88:869D; also 27.41 (1108CD).
5. Source not identified: mental 'crime' (*prestuplenie*) is 'derangement' (*istuplenie*) in the Brief Rule.
6. Phol 3:18–19. Cf. *Philippians* 13:242 PG 62:275. See Titov, *Opisanie* 2:751–753.
7. Cf. *Ephesians* 19.2:138 PG 62:129.

inflamed and gives off a stench and an evil belch like an animal. Consider this, how the soul of a drunkard wallows in the body as in a pit and in a swamp.

[5] *Many stupid people say, 'This holiday is venerable; let us drink and be merry'. You fools, do you understand what you are saying here, that you have forsaken the divine festival and are pleasing the devil as if you preferred working for the devil to [working] for Christ? For you are not venerating God's holiday but the devil's when you overeat, get drunk, and debauch. If you enter a church, tell me, how can you glorify God? Since the drunkard belches out a stench, God hates the drunkard as much as we loathe a stinking dead dog. Let him who would be free from all of this abhor drunkenness, and thus cut off the serpent's head and crush his whole body.*[8]

[6] First of all, therefore, it is proper to have much responsibility and zeal so that no drinks which cause drunkenness be in the cloister, the refectory, or the cells, lest we become the laughing stock of our enemies and subject to their physical and mental profanation of us.

Enough of this for now.

8. Sections [4]-[5] appear to have been inspired by Chrysostom, if not taken from the Chrysostom/Pseudo-Chrysostom corpus.

That it is not proper for women to enter the monastery.

Discourse VIII

[1] The great Chrysostom says concerning women: *Any act of love, either living with or frequently conversing with women is an act of fornication for monks. Are you really a stone? You are a man, of the common nature, subject to falling, and you are tending a fire in your bosom. Will you not set yourself ablaze? Do you place a candle on top of the hay, as if hay will not burn? For you eat with women, and drink, laugh, and converse with them; yet you would call yourself a celibate? Tell not me, but Him who knows what is concealed, and who will come later to collect deeds, words, and thoughts!*[1]

[2] The divine canons and the civil laws enjoin that *neither a woman nor a nun enter a man's monastery for funeral or any other causes.*[2] *In doing this, we do not despise nature or kinship, but whenever they come near us, they bring a collection of passions, they confuse and darken the mind, and incite a host of thoughts.*[3]

[3] Thus the blessed Marcian speaks well: *It is better to converse with the devil than with shameless women, and better to frequent the devil than graceful and adorned women. Human nature is readily mutable: when it has neglected the good, it easily turns toward evil.*[4]

[4] Therefore it is well said in the *Holy Ladder: Fleeing, we flee, so as not to see or hear the fruit which we vowed not to taste. I marvel then that we consider ourselves more steadfast than the prophet David, which is impossible.*[5]

[5] On this account it is proper for us all-zealously to submit to

1. Cf. Nikon, *Pandekty* 12:86V, attributed to *Liber de virginitate.*
2. *Trullo* 47; Councils, 387 (Mansi 11:965DE), as in Nikon, *Pandekty* 12:88^{V}-89.
3. Attributed to Basil in Nikon, *Pandekty* 12:86^{V}–87^{V}.
4. Cf. Nikon, *Pandekty* 12:85^{V}.
5. Climacus, *Ladder* 15, *Scholia* 36; PG 88:917AB.

the admonition of our holy Fathers and to preserve ourselves from little things—beholding or talking—lest we fall into great. Thus shall we be able to be saved in Christ Jesus our Lord.

That it is not proper for beardless boys to live in the monastery and concerning other necessary causes.

Discourse IX

[1] It is not proper for beardless boys to live in the monastery. Father Isaac said: *Brothers, do not bring children into the cœnobium, for I have seen three churches in Scete deserted on account of children.*[1]

[2] And again it is said in the *Patericon: Once a demon came to the brothers in a cœnobium, saw a boy in the cœnobium, and said: 'I do not need to be here, because he will be much more troublesome here than I'.*[2]

[3] In wanting to be saved, therefore, let us move far away from them as from a flame. Let us not turn towards them in a house or in a place where no one sees us. Let us sit far away from them on benches and not look them in the face, lest in some way, by looking in their faces, we get the seed of lust from the Adversary and harvest a sheaf of corruption and perdition. Let us not believe the deceitful thought, which suggests to us that this is not tempting. Rather the beholding itself and the cohabitation is reckoned to be a temptation, because the devil has scorched many this way and surrendered them to the eternal fire.[3]

[4] There we shall now speak of this: that it is not proper for lay deacons to sing, read, chant the canon, or read the psalms in the church.

[5] The Divine Writings say: *Not God, but our adversary, the devil, brings boys into the monastery to trouble active monks.*[4] Therefore beardless children shall not serve in the refectory, and the children who do serve shall be dismissed from the refectory together and not be left in the refectory for any work whatever.

1. Isaac 5, *Sayings*, 85; PG 65:226B.
2. Source not identified.
3. Pseudo-Basil, *Ascetical Discourse*, 23–24; PG 31:638BC.
4. Cf. Nil Sorsky, *Ustav* 5:46.

[6] It is said in the *Geronticon: It is not proper for those who would be saved to be in a house or any other place where there are children, because for monks, children are more evil than women.*[5] Therefore children shall not work in the cells, and beardless children shall not be allowed in the cells or in the monastery for any work. If any brother must have something done in his cell, then send him someone his own age, not a beardless one.

[7] It says in the Patericon: *A great elder came to a cœnobium, saw that there were boys there, and therefore did not enter the cœnobium to sleep.*[6] See what caution our holy Fathers had! Therefore there shall be at the monastery a guard who shall not allow children into the monastery and shall give them bread outside the monastery. And whenever children bring something to sell, he shall fix a place for them where we can buy from them.

[8] Saint Ephraim says: *It is a great calamity for boys to be in a cœnobium.*[7] Even if we converse with them about chastity, we are stabbed in the heart. Therefore do not receive beardless children in the monastery or in the out-buildings: no serving men,[8] clerks, artisans or laborers.

[9] Likewise, do not keep your own personal serving men, horses, saddles, or sleighs in the cells or the outbuildings of the monastery. One is enslaved by his own conqueror; so a monk who submits to materialism is enslaved to it. The holy Fathers say: *He who removes himself from things comes near the immaterial; he who loves things removes himself from the immaterial, that is to say, from God; and those who are removed from God perish.*[9]

[10] Likewise, the brothers shall not stand or sit in the monastery. If it is necessary to say something, then say it briefly and go to a cell to say it. Indeed, Saint Symeon the New Theologian says: *If you are walking and you see a brother alone some place or conversing*

5. Source not identified.
6. Source not identified.
7. Cited in Nikon, *Pandekty* 4:34: source not identified.
8. Cf. Timothy of Evergetis, *Typikon* 24:490. Archbishop Sava, *Tipik* 26:61.
9. Source not identified.

with someone, never stand or sit with prattlers, but make a bow and walk past in silence, for it is said: 'Do not direct your ears towards worldly conversations and blush with laughter, but woe to the laughing, for they shall lament'.[10]

[11] Do not judge peasants at the monastery. This generates turmoil, and temptations in the brotherhood, and *woe to that man by whom the temptation comes.*[11]

[12] Likewise, the monk-bailiff shall not live in the villages, for it is said in the *Geronticon: As fish die on land, so also a monk who frequents the world dies a psychic death.*[12]

[13] And there shall be no rear doors or windows; *for a little negligence intercedes to effect a great calamity.*[13]

[14] All the monastery gates shall be bolted at night, so that during the night no one may leave the monastery or enter the monastery. On account of such negligence, we fall into great calamities of soul and body.

[15] Likewise, the brothers shall not walk about the monastery without a cowl and a mantle; for the Divine Writings and the cœnobitic traditions so enjoin.

Enough of this for now.

[16] Now everything that has been said here concerning good order in the monastery and the church, food and drink, garments and footwear, and objects is in keeping with the Divine Writings and the cœnobitic tradition. Thus for each tradition I have put down the witness of the Divine Writings, so that the readers understand that we have not dared to do anything of our own volition, but have followed the Divine Writings in everything. Novices who do not know the Divine Writings should read them, not only for the aforesaid reasons, but also because I have compressed a great deal from the Divine Writings into a few words which direct

10. Cf. *Starchestvo*, 8–10.

11. Mt 18:7.

12. *Starchestvo,* 172 (Cotelier, *Sanctorum senum* 1:342CD; Antony 10; *Sayings* 2; PG 65:77B; Budge, *Paradise,* 1055).

13. Source not identified; cf. above, Discourse IV.V, and below, Tradition IX.13 (Discourse XIII/ix.13); also *Prosvetitel'* 16:546.

us to improvement and near to salvation. Those who know the Divine Writings and read through these will remind themselves of whatever is written here.

A RESPONSE TO THE CENSORIOUS[1] AND A BRIEF ACCOUNT OF THE HOLY FATHERS OF THE MONASTERIES OF RUS'

DISCOURSE X

[1] *All of you, fathers and brothers in Christ, who have read through these writings:*[2] although they are crude, they are in keeping with the witness of the Divine Writings. *Let no one suppose in any way that conceit is the cause or that I am hunting for glory among men. That is not so; no, not at all; let Christ be my witness!*

[2] *And if someone is overweening, very boastful, stiff-necked, presumptuous, querulous, and censorious and says:*[3] 'In earlier times our holy Fathers instituted in writing the cœnobitic teachings and traditions; now is it not proper to do so, but only to teach by word'[4]—if this were so, then why does our reverend father Nikon say: *Just as in ancient times, now it is proper that each superior, especially in his own cloister, compose or render, by words and writings, precepts and admonitions which are consonant with the teachings of the Divine Writings. It is not proper for the flock to be contentious or to act or to speak adversely. Rather, they should do only that which has been said by the father. For if the superior acts and teaches, what kind of response will the disobedient give?*[5]

[3] This is said in the *Holy Ladder: It is proper for the pastor to teach with words, and he need not feel shame; for it is the nature of pastors to shun what is shameful. But they should not refuse to formulate instructions for the students, and they should begin with writings and point out the necessary information.*[6]

1. Cf. Gorsky and Nevostruev, *Opisanie* 2.1.170:455.
2. Cf. Philippus, Ἡ Διόπτρα, 224.
3. Cf. Philippus, Ἡ Διόπτρα, 224–5 (from the last part of Discourse X.1).
4. See above, Ch. 2, RELATIONS WITH THE TRANS-VOLGANS.
5. *Pandekty* 8:63; attributed to Nicea 2: cf. *Councils*, 566 (Mansi 13:748).
6. Climacus, *Liber ad pastorem* 6; PG 88:1180A.

[4] And Saint Symeon the New Theologian says: *It is proper for the pastor to teach and preach and leave in writing the words of God and his own desires and commands. These words will stand fast when the Lord comes to judge and to recompense each according to his deeds; for the pastor will be found without fault.*[7]

[5] Thus says the Lord through the prophet Ezekiel: 'Behold, I shall demand an account of my sheep from the shepherds'. and again: 'Son of Man, I have made you watchman for the house of Israel; if you warn and speak, he shall die in his sin, and you will have saved your soul'.[8]

[6] And the divine Chrysostom says: *If the superior*[9] *orders his life well, but is indifferent toward those under his hand, he will go off with the wicked to hell.*[10] *Although Eli the priest arranged his own life well, he let his children do iniquities, and therefore was condemned by God along with his children.*[11]

[7] Therefore, when I see the magnitude of misfortune, let me counsel and speak to my brothers in Christ. Let me, a wretched person, by the prayers of the saints be worthy of the voices of those in the *Divine Ladder*: *'Such ones were an example, that wallowed there in dung, but they taught the passers-by, and thus for the sake of the salvation of others, the Almighty delivered even these ones from the dung.* And again that one says: *'Do not be a bitter judge of those who teach by word, when you behold that they have been lazy in deeds, for many times the word of profit has made up for the want of deeds'.*[12]

[8] And Saint John Chrysostom says in his commentary on the Gospel of Matthew: *You should have invested with the bankers, which is to say; you should admonish and counsel with teachings*

7. Source not identified.

8. Ez 3:17,19; 33:7–9. Cf above, Introduction.4 (Int.4), and below, XI.7, XIII.28. Also PIV, 144 ('Iosif to the Pafnutiev Monastery Monks', 1479–80).

9. Originally: priest.

10. Nikon, *Pandekty* 8:57: attributed to John: ultimate source not identified.

11. Cf 1 Sm 3:13–14.

12. Climacus, *Ladder* 26.14,155; PG 88:1016C, 1068C. From 'Let me . . .': Nikon, *Taktikon*, Introduction, 9–9[v]. Cf. Nil Sorsky, *Predanie*, 4; but contrast with Si 37.19: 'Izbornik of 1076', 57.

and writings.[13] And another of everlasting memory said: *Judge those under you; do not judge those outside of you.*[14]

[9] And all the Divine Writings command to teach and write traditions and penances, and it is nowhere stated that in ancient times it was proper but now it is not proper, to act in some manner. For if in ancient times, when men were steadfast, a writing, an admonition, a tradition, and a penance were necessary and profitable, then how much more are they now!

[10] If someone begins to say: 'Although the ancient holy Fathers admonished with traditions, penances, writings, and words, our holy Fathers in Russia did not write traditions and penances for monks, but only admonished them with words', let us respond to them: 'Our holy Fathers, who shone forth in Rus[15]—Antonii and Feodosii Pechersky, Sergii, Varlaam, Kirill, Dimitrii, Dionisii, Avramii, Pavel, and the others, their disciples, were of steadfast mind, and they had understanding and perfect love for God and their neighbor.[16] And just as the blessed Anthony and Pachomius and others who were monks in ancient times treasured all of God's commandments, so in our country the blessed Antonii, Feodosii, Sergii, Varlaam, Kirill, and the other aforesaid holy Fathers executed all of God's commandments and became worthy of the grace of the Holy Spirit. The *wonders and the healings which they worked and which they still now work,*[17] because they lived virtuously and in a manner pleasing to God[18] and similarly taught and admonished those under them, bear witness'. He who would contemplate this exactly and truthfully should read through their *Lives* and he will comprehend how they lived very pain-racked and toil-stricken lives and what kind of grace they became worthy of obtaining from the Lord Christ.

13. Cf. *Matthew* 78; PG 58:714, as in Nikon, *Pandekty* 8:60^{V}, and *Taktikon,* Introduction, 9^{V}. Mt 25:27. Iosif added: and writings(!).

14. Cf. Nikon, *Pandekty*, 8:60^{V}.

15. Cf. Heppell, *Paterik . . . Kiev.*, 143; 'Lesson on the Life of Boris and Gleb', 7; Dn 12.3, and below, Discourse X.13.

16. See above, Ch. 2, note 174. Cf. Heppell, *Paterik . . . Kiev.*, 108.

17. Cf. *Prosvetitel'* 4:159, 168; cf. 'Lesson on the Life of Boris and Gleb', 18.

18. Symeon, *Catechisms*, 5.828–32.

[11] This we know from the Divine Writings, from the book called *The Pechersky Patericon,* concerning Saints Antonii, Feodosii, and the other saints who were in Pechersky Monastery.[19] At one time there were thirty wonder-workers and perfect saints who could exorcise demons, heal sicknesses, and work many wonders and miracles.[20] When we read through all the Divine Writings, we do not find at one time in any other monastery so many wonder-workers and so many and such terrifying wonders and miracles connected with the divine church and the holy and reverend fathers of the monastery. What asceticism, mortification, struggle, and Christlike poverty they had—not only then, at that time, but also earlier—and later these monks were given to fasting and traversed this very pain-racked and toil-stricken life. And what responsibility they took for monastic good order, reverence, and firmness! No one can now demonstrate in word or deed how they then acted. Indeed the monastery was never open, but always locked, and watchmen always stood before the gates, so that they did not give entrance without the superior's blessing even to the Sovereign, the devotee-of-Christ, Grand Prince Iziaslav himself, son of Iaroslav and grandson of the blessed and most renowned Vladimir.[21]

[12] We have also heard about the blessed Sergii and the other saints from honest witnesses who were their contemporaries. They had such ardor and zeal for their flock that they did not disregard any little act of negligence or disobedience. They were indeed lenient when it was proper, irascible when it was necessary, and they rebuked and forced sinners toward good things. They did not forsake the disobedient to follow their own wills, but in every way reprimanded them and banished them from the church and from the refectory. They had such poverty and non-possession in the monastery of blessed Sergii that they did not write even books on

19. See above, Ch. 2, Russian Monastic History and Creating Hagiography, for commentary on Discourse X.11–32 and for further identification of Iosif's *dramatis personae*.

20. Heppell, *Paterik . . . Kiev.,* 146–47.

21. Heppell, *Paterik . . . Kiev.*, 49–50.

parchment, but rather on birch bark.[22] The blessed Sergii himself wore such worthless and ragged vestments that many times he was not recognized by visitors, but they supposed that he was one of the beggars. He was adorned with all the virtues, those of the soul, it is said, and those of the body, and because of this he was worthy of great gifts from the Lord God.

[13] And of Saint Kirill, why should I write and speak out? His traditions and teachings, now kept in his cloister which shines like the light of a candelabrum[23] in the present times, are a witness to the degree of his responsibility in this regard. And just as the blessed Kirill himself bore such caring responsibility for the monastery and the monks' good order, so did his disciples who came after him. They imitated him, held his traditions in their hearts, and in no way allowed others to be unruly, overweening, nonobservant, and heedless of Saint Kirill's traditions. They always struggled over this, not only against monks like themselves, but also against superiors, when they saw something irregular, perverse, and not executed according to the norms of the patristic traditions.

[14] After the demise of the blessed Kirill and his disciples, Innokentii and Khristofor, there was in his monastery in our lifetime a superior from another monastery, one who did not treasure some of Saint Kirill's traditions and laws and put them into a state of neglect. There was at that time in Kirillov Monastery an elder by the name of Dosifei, called Nevedomitsin. He and other of the active elders who loved Saint Kirill's traditions—namely Symon Kartmazov and Mikhailo Treparev, Irinarkh Sukhoy, Feognost Oboburov, Feodot Proskurnik, and others—were in no way silent, but reprimanded and talked back. The blessed Dosifei so suffered at the hands of the superior that he received blows from him many times. Once when he was telling the superior that he must not pervert the traditions of Saint Kirill, the latter threw him off the refectory balcony, and he fell down on the ground almost dead.

22. To the knowledge of the editor, no such birchbark books, in contrast to simple writs, have survived.

23. Cf. Heppell, *Paterik . . . Kiev.*, 108; also Dan 12.3, and above, Discourse X.10.

When he recovered his health, he said to the superior: 'Even if you want to surrender me to death, I shall not cease to speak to you of this'.

[15] After the departure of that superior, they again chose their hegumen from another monastery. He acted as the former one and put several of Kirill's traditions into a state of neglect. Moreover he loved to make conversation and speak needlessly in the church and in the refectory when they ate. The elders there at that time—Ilia Chapey, Ignatii Burmak, and others like them—likewise reprimanded and talked back. Many times he rushed against them in anger and wanted to strike them with his staff, and sometimes he did strike them. They did not submit, however, but reprimanded him for his unruly custom until he became ashamed of his brutality and departed from them.

[16] Then during the tenure of Metropolitan Gerontii, they selected for themselves a hegumen who had been tonsured in Kirillov, but had lived for many years in other monasteries. He also began to pervert many of Saint Kirill's traditions. The elders here at the time were greatly afflicted over this, and they spoke to him of this at the council and individually. He neglected their words; so then the senior, major elders, unable to endure beholding Saint Kirill's traditions trampled upon and despised, all fled the monastery until the prince heard of it and commanded him to be driven from Kirillov Monastery. And again all those elders assembled in the monastery of Saint Kirill.

[17] We have heard like things from that great elder Spiridon, the former hegumen of Sergiev Monastery, concerning that saintly elder Varfolomei, who was the administrator of Simonov Monastery. After the departure of Feodor, who was the founder of Simonov Monastery, to the Rostov bishopric, and after the departure of the successor archimandrite, Saint Kirill, to Beloozero, there were there some archimandrites who perverted some of the customs and traditions of blessed Feodor and Kirill. At that time the custom of that monastery was this: they neither ate nor drank in the cells; nor did they go outside the monastery without the blessing of the superior; nor did boys live in the monastery or in the outbuildings;

rather everything there was in keeping with the Divine Writings and the cœnobitic traditions.

[18] When the blessed Varfolomei and the elders there—one of them from the monastery was Ioann, called Zlaty, and there were Ignatii the iconographer, Iona, who was then young and afterwards became Metropolitan, and others like them—saw that the customs of the monastery were altered and that good order was despised, they were not silent, nor did they neglect these customs, but they reprimanded and did not allow unruliness and disturbances to occur. They obtained much affliction and grief from the archimandrites of that time, especially the blessed Varfolomei, who had been entrusted with the administration by the Autocrat and Grand Prince Vasilii Dmitrievich. Even if, therefore, the superiors were often possessed by fury and anger and rushed against him to strike him with their staff, they feared the sovereign. The blessed Varfolomei continuously applied himself to administering the monastery, first spiritually and then corporeally. He incessantly went about inspecting everywhere—in the monastery, the refectory, the cook-house, the bakery, the outbuildings and the cells. If he saw something being done not in keeping with their customs, but irregular and perverse, he was not silent about this, but spoke and exhorted, at first meekly and lovingly. He did not suffer the disobedient, but reprimanded and forbade. And he drove from the cloister those who would not desist from their wicked customs.

[19] And thus the blessed one struggled on for many years and never gave himself tranquility but always made the rounds, taught, and admonished, forcing good things. He was lame in one foot, but on this account did not weaken, nor did he desist from the divine work. And because of his labors and those of the brothers who suffered with him, everything in that monastery was in good order, reverent, meek, and peaceful. Therefore the Lord Christ did not abandon that one's labors, nor did he place them in oblivion. Instead, many years after his death, he showed him standing in the church in the place where the blessed Varfolomei habitually prayed, to a certain reverent and noble man, just as he showed the holy martyr Febronia and Saint Basil, the disciple of Theodosius the

Great, after their passing, standing in their places in the church.[24]

[20] And we saw the blessed Savva who had been in Savvin Monastery in the territory of Tver for fifty years or more. He had such zeal and responsibility toward his flock that he used to stand, staff in hand, in front of the church doors. And if any of the brothers did not arrive for the beginning, left before the dismissal, made conversation during the chanting, went over from his place to another, or if someone left the chant by himself, he was in no way silent, but rather reprimanded and forbade, for he would not disregard even little sins and acts of unruliness. He sometimes struck with a staff and sometimes sent to the dungeon those who talked back and were unruly. He was brutal when necessary and lenient when proper, as the next discourse will demonstrate.

[21] Once when he was admonishing an unruly brother, he exposed his beard at the window. Prodded by some demon, the brother grasped the beard with both hands, pulled it all out, leaving very little. The brothers seized him, led him to the blessed Savva and asked him: ‘How do you command us to avenge this’? He said to them: ‘I strike monks with my staff and dispatch them to the dungeon on account of their unruliness in the monastery and offenses against the brotherhood. It is proper for me not to avenge offenses against myself, but to endure everything’. When he saw the brother repenting his transgression, he quickly forgave him. The brother, having obtained forgiveness, remained in that monastery in repentance and compunction until the day of his death.

[22] Once there was a great plague. The priests died from it and only the blessed Savva was left to be responsible for all the brothers, to visit the ailing, administer penance, and bury those departing to the Lord. Whenever he was visiting one of the ailing brothers, and another brother came and reported that such and such a brother was dying and needed to repent, the blessed Savva answered: ‘Go, brother, and tell the dying one that he is not yet to die but must await my visitation’. Then the brother spoke to the dying brother according to the command of the father, and immediately the one

24. Cf. Theodore Of Petra, Βίοσ . . . θεοδοσίου, 23–24 (VMCh 5:578–59).

dying felt alleviated until the blessed Savva arrived. And when he had administered Divine Communion and absolution to him, the brother died.

[23] And it was not like this only for one or for two, but it was like this for many. So we have heard from the reverent elders who told this and especially from that great elder Varsonofii, called Neumo, who was the brother of the blessed Savva and whom the earlier Savva Borozdin, called Era, the founder of that monastery, installed as superior when he himself departed to the Holy Mountain.[25] The blessed Varsonofii remained five years as hegumen and then departed to a hermitage, gave the abbacy to this Savva and commanded him to obtain the priestly rank. (He himself witnessed for him that he was pure from the womb of his mother and worthy of such grace.) He lived in the hermitage for forty years and in those years he had no work other than praying, chanting, and reading books. He accepted books from devotees of Christ, read them, returned them, and took from others. The blessed one was such that he possessed nothing of his own, not even one copper coin, for he truly loved non-possession and Christlike poverty. Because of his great attention, silence, prayers, and reading, he was worthy of so much divine grace that he could remember all the Divine Writings, carry them on his tongue, and render no scant amount to all who were in need. Many came to him from all parts, monks and noble laymen, some for a profitable word, others seeking an analysis of the Divine Writings. Even that great high priest Fotii,[26] Metropolitan of All Russia, himself had to send to him to analyze some unknown words of the Divine Writings which had been a bone of contention between himself and some others.

[24] The fathers there told me this on oath, that when he was still living in the hermitage, a brother from Savvin Monastery came to him and exhorted him to go to Savva to forgive several transgressions. When the blessed Varsonofii arrived at the monastery, he looked at the icon of the Immaculate Mother of God standing

25. Mt. Athos.

26. Rus word *arkhier*, from the Greek αρχιερεύς—hierarch (literally, high or chief priest).

in his cell and spoke thus; 'Most Holy Lady, Mother of God, you shall be the guardian of my books!' After his departure, that brother was tempted by a wicked plot. He put all those books in his bosom and wanted to flee, but as he came close to the doors of the cell, an invisible force struck him, and he was dead. Now when the blessed Varsonofii arrived, he discovered the dead brother and the books in his bosom and started to cry and lament and said: 'I am guilty of the brother's death'. Then they carried the brother off to the monastery to inter him. When they started to chant over him, the blessed Varsonofii began to cry so much over the brother that the whole place where he stood was soaked from the tears. When they were about to kiss the dead brother, the dead one started to move. They uncovered his head and unbound him, and the dead man immediately sat up. The brothers raised him up and started to inquire: 'What did you see and hear'? He said: 'I neither saw nor heard anything'. That brother remained living in virtue at that monastery until the day of his death.

[25] When the blessed Varsonofii attained a very old age, Saint Savva commanded him to be brought to the monastery. His arrival was joyful and delightful for all the brothers, for he was a healer and a doctor for the sufferings of the body and the soul. So long as the blessed Savva and Saint Varsonofii and their supporters remained alive, everything in that monastery was done in good order and in a meek, calm, and peaceful manner, because of their admonitions and teachings. When someone had a perverse habit, they did not allow him to do as he wished.

[26] When the blessed Savva and Saint Varsonofii and the other elders who loved the patristic traditions passed, the brothers selected an hegumen from another monastery. He began to live at variance from the custom of that monastery and not in keeping with the tradition of those holy elders. Their tradition was the following: no one was ever to eat or drink except at table, or go outside the monastery without a blessing; boys were not to live in cells or in the outbuildings; no woman was to enter the monastery; rather everything was to be in keeping with the witness of the cœnobitic traditions. That hegumen, just after coming to them, perverted all of these and put them into a state of neglect. Then after a short

while Saint Savva appeared to him in a dream and so said to him: 'Wretched man why have you been not in the least bit responsible for the monastery's and the monks' good order and reverence, but have instead trampled upon and annihilated everything'? And he beat him so amply with his staff that he could not rise from his bed. When he recovered and recognized his incorrigibility, he did not dare to remain the superior, but he quickly departed to the place from which he had come.

[27] I saw at that time in Savvateev Hermitage another holy elder named Evfrosin, who lived in a hermitage in the back woods. He was by birth a Prince Teprinsky. This blessed man lived for sixty years at the hermitage and did not go outside anywhere. Many monks, laymen, princes, and boyars visited him and interrupted his quiet. He became indignant and fled from there to Great Novgorod, found an island in the great Lake Nevo,[27] settled there, and lived for many years. When the local Christians who lived in the villages heard of him, they visited him with their wives and children. He then fled back to Savvateev Hermitage.

[28] Upon his arrival, the autocrat of that land, Grand Prince Boris Aleksandrovich, sent to him his young daughter, who was then betrothed to the Grand Prince Ivan Vasilevich. Many archimandrites, hegumens, and boyars came along with her and began to exhort the blessed Evfrosin to pray for the girl, for she was possessed of a powerful disease. They carried her in their arms into the hermitage to the blessed Evfrosin, but he refused, would not do it, and called himself unworthy and sinful. They fell on the ground and all begged him with tears to pray for her and said: 'If she revives on account of your holy prayers, Father, then you shall have reconciled two kingdoms'. Just as they had said this, she fell into such a sickness that everyone thought she was dying. When they saw this, they all began to mourn. The blessed Evfrosin then instructed them to carry her off and place her in the church at Savvateev Hermitage. He himself came quickly to the monastery, entered the church, and saw the girl lying down and hardly able

27. Lake Ladoga, the immediate source of the River Neva, at whose mouth St. Petersburg now stands.

to breathe. The blessed Evfrosin then stood before the icon of the Immaculate Mother of God bearing the Eternal Child in her arms, began to pray with many tears and lamentations, and commanded them to chant prayer services to the Immaculate Mother of God and to Nicholas, the great wonder-worker. When they finished chanting the prayer service, the girl recovered her sight and sat up. Then they raised her up. All of a sudden she was healthy and on that very day they brought her back to her father. Seeing that, they glorified God, who glorifies his worshipers.

[29] And that noble elder Spiridon told us how the Right Reverend Aleksii the New Wonder-worker founded the two monasteries called Andronikov and Chudov. He took the blessed Andronik from Saint Sergii to be hegumen at Andronikov Monastery. The blessed Andronik shone with great virtues, and with him were his disciples Savva and Aleksandr, and those wondrous and most renowned iconographers, Daniil and his disciple, Andrei. Also many others who had like great virtues were there. They displayed such exertion in the ascetic and monastic life that they were worthy of divine grace, and they so excelled in divine love that they never engaged in things earthly, but always elevated mind and thought to the immaterial and divine light and always lifted their sensible eye up to the images, painted from material pigments, of the Lord Christ, his Immaculate Mother, and all the saints. Also on the very festival of the brilliant Resurrection, they would sit on their benches with their all-venerable and divine icons; and they would gaze fixedly upon them and be filled with divine joy and illumination.[28] And not only did they act this way on that day, but also on other days when they did not apply themselves to painting. On this account, Christ the Master glorified them even at the ultimate hour of death. First Andrei passed, and then his fellow ascete Daniil fell ill; during his last breath he saw his fellow ascete Andrei in great glory and joyfully summoning him to eternal and endless bliss.

[30] Likewise the blessed Metropolitan Aleksii also saw noble elders in Chudov Monastery. He had sought some of them from

28. See above, text to Ch 2, note 133, and ASPECTS OF ICONOGRAPHY.

Saint Sergii and others from the other monasteries that were under his authority.[29] They lived in such a venerable, holy, monkish, and spiritual way that all men, old and young, came to them to receive something profitable from them. For example, under the influence of their teaching and admonition, Spiridon himself, who was still young, rejected the turmoil of the world and rushed to the monastic life.

[31] And I saw that blessed elder, the hegumen Makarii, founder of Kaliazin Monastery, who told me the following: 'When', he said, 'I came to this place, along with seven elders from Klobukov Monastery, they were so perfected in virtues and in the ascetic and monastic life that all the brothers visited them to receive instructions and something of profit. They enlightened everybody, taught them what was profitable, strengthened those living in virtue, reprimanded and forbade those who leaned towards unruliness, and did not allow them to follow their wills'. The reverence and good order of that monastery was of such renown—for they did everything in keeping with the witness of the patristic and the cœnobitic traditions—that the great elder Mitrofan Byvaltsov was astonished. He had just returned from the Holy Mountain of Athos. He had lived on the Holy Mountain nine years. He said to the brothers: 'I labored in vain and to no avail, for I walked such a long way to the Holy Mountain and bypassed Kaliazin monastery. It is possible for those living here to be saved, for here everything is done just as in the cœnobia of the Holy Mountain'.[30]

[32] We did not see the earlier holy Fathers who shone in our land namely, the great Sergii, Varlaam, Kirill, and the others like them, but I saw many who were their disciples. They had such great virtues, labor, asceticism, humility, and mortification because they had read through the writings of the earlier holy Fathers, Anthony, Pachomius, and the others. They kept these as a living model and a seal on their hearts *which cleansed them not only of sins, but also of passions*[31]—just what we saw in our own father, Saint

29. Literally, in his hands.
30. Cf. Heppell, *Paterik . . . Kiev.,* 18–23.
31. Cf. *Prosvetitel'* 4:158.

Pakhnotii,[32] who was a disciple of Sergii's disciple, the elder Nikita, the Archimandrite of Vysotsky Monastery. We lived with him for an ample number of years, and we saw his labors, mortifications, struggles, sweat, worthless clothing, firm faith in God, and his confirmed hope in the Immaculate Mother of God, whose trust he had always in his mind, and whose food for the tongue he had always in his mouth. On this account he obtained the grace to be able to foresee the future, to tell the secret thoughts of the brothers' hearts, and to cure sicknesses, and he received everything that he requested from the Lord God and from the Immaculate Mother of God. Truly he was far from the men of the present age in all habits. He was lenient when it was proper and brutal and irascible when it was necessary. And we saw many others and heard of still others, who were holy, venerable, and lived as monks should, in all the monasteries in Russia.

[33] Now in truth we are exhausted; as the Scripture says: we are unworthy of the grace of the Holy Spirit which is present among us of the lazy generation at the end of the ages. And we have loved the sweet things of this world, because of our laziness, great indifference, and lack of what is good.[33]

[34] And let no one consider that I condemn all the monks or revile the monasteries of the present time. Absolutely not, fathers and brothers, absolutely not! But as I wrote not to all monks, but to myself and to those under me, so now I speak and write not about everybody, but about myself and those under me. Since only the form of monasticism now exists among us, but not the smallest deed, *therefore we are not easily brought to virtue,*[34] and we hardly struggle for a little direction to our lives, while we need a great many instructions and admonitions, parables and tales, and writings and traditions to constrain us. Indeed, if with instructions, admonitions, and writings, we behold the ideal models and then in the course of a short time fall into the depths of forgetfulness,

32. Pafnutii.

33. Sources for X.33 not identified.

34. Nikon, *Pandekty* 30:215, attributed to Basil, *Homilia in Psalmum* I; cf. PG 29:217.

then how much worse would it be if the writings were not written? They would quickly be forgotten and come to naught.[35]

[35] We have come to so much darkness, blindness, laziness, and negligence that I hear some people shriek and say: 'It is better to live where laws and canons do not exist, and where there is no burden, constraint, or penances. Rather one should live as he wishes; for not the place, but good will promotes salvation'. These have been stated for those who are perfect and excel in the fear of God. Such is alien to us.

[36] It is said in the *Holy Ladder: It is proper to run away from sinful places as from a fire and a serpent. Sinful places are where there are wine, women, and boys; there, there is no need for Satan.*[36]

[37] And the holy Fathers say, *A man who lives away from sinful places is like a man who stands far from a ditch. When the Adversary wishes to throw him into the ditch, he is unable. The one who lives in sinful places is like a man who stands near the ditch; when the Adversary wishes it, he can hurl him down.*[37]

[38] It is said in the *Holy Ladder: I have seen in schools simple and very good children, who have come for the sake of wisdom, admonition and profit, and they learned nothing there except savagery and evil from their intercourse with the others.*[38]

[39] Saint Isaac says: *Do not let him who says: 'Nothing we hear or see can harm us, for we are the same everywhere', trick us. Those who say this would not understand that they were being stabbed.* Again he says: *Do not dwell with a man of ill repute, lest you acquire his habits.*[39]

[40] Now where are those who say: 'It is better to live where there is no burden, constraint, or penances; one should instead live as he wishes'? What shall we say to them? They themselves have already demonstrated that they are more wretched than malicious worldlings, for worldlings will be called to account regarding the

35. Indeed, if . . . , cf. above, Discourse I^{B}.1.

36. Climacus, *Ladder* 3.9; PG 88:665A.

37. Cf. *Starchestvo,* 174–174^{V}, attributed to Poemen. Cf. Heppell, *Paterik . . . Kiev.*, 29, 159; Ἀνδρῶν ἁγίων βίβλος, 99, lines 14–23.

38. Climacus, *Ladder*, 4.114; PG 88:724C.

39. Source not identified.

Lord's commandments, and monks even more so. And what does it mean to become dead to the whole world and to take up the crucified life? Each monk vows at the time of his tonsure to endure all afflictions and constraint for the sake of the heavenly kingdom. How then can anyone say, 'It is more profitable to live where there are no laws and canons'? Why then did Saint Ephraim say: '*There is a great calamity where laws and canons do not dwell*'?[40]

[41] Again, he says: *If you, wretched one, because of your weakness and craving hate afflictions, flee from endurance, malign your Lord's light burden as being brutal and heavy, and say: 'I cannot bear it', it will be gruesome for you, wretched one! Who will have mercy on you, who have destroyed yourself. A thief is better than you, and a brigand and fornicator is of more good than you, for if they pray, they shall be saved. Men extol you as a righteous person, but you mendaciously live the good life, love the pleasures and the lusts of this world, and have abhorred the heavenly kingdom.*[41]

[42] Likewise it is said in the *Holy Ladder: It is better to drive the disobedient from the cloister than to abandon them to perform their own will. He who would now condescend to the weakness of some will have caused him to be damned at the time of departure, because he tricked them and did not assist them.*[42]

[43] Basil the Great says: *If we do not observe the divine commandments and the patristic traditions, demons enter us and create whatever they want, namely a craving gaze, the wicked longings we have in our hearts, filth and unclean thoughts, laziness and indifference in prayer, hatred and enmity toward one another, love of the world, love of glory, avarice, materialism, sexual longing, pride, disobedience, and other soul-killing passions.*[43]

[44] From now on therefore let us be responsible for our souls. Let us mourn and lament when we see our laziness and our

40. Cited in Nikon, *Pandekty* 10:115, *Taktikon* 1:7^{V} (BMFD, 397) and *Tüpikon*, 42^{V}

41. Source not identified.

42. Climacus, *Liber* 14; PG 88:1200B, perhaps as in Nikon, *Taktikon*, Introduction, 11. Cf. Nil Sorsky, *Predanie*, 5, and below, Discourse XIV.2.

43. Source not identified. The translation loses the poetics of 'love of the word . . . materialism': *miroliubie, slavoliubie, sreboliubie, veshcheliubie*.

weak and impotent attitude toward every good thing. And let there be observance, attentiveness, affirmation, and a measure for everything—meals, drink, objects, sleep, and the things which may not be pleasing to God. Let us observe for ourselves, brothers, how we must live and how we must walk with care. Let us ready ourselves always for obedience to the evangelical life. Let us cleanse our hearts for the reception of the indescribable light of Christ. And let us not gather anything for ourselves in the spirit of avarice or materialism, 'for we brought nothing into the world, and it is certain that we cannot take anything out'.[44] Let us be content with what there is and let us consider nothing to be our own, nor fear want, desolation, or mortification. Rather, let us give thanks to the Lord, because he himself said, 'I will not abandon you'.[45]

[45] Therefore, let us not even be heedful of necessities, for he is the dispenser of what we need, as has been displayed in action to many. If we have forsaken everything else, let us only look to please God, for the Lord himself says: 'If you walk in my statutes and keep my commandments I will take care of you and bless you and multiply you, and you will eat your bread to the full'.[46] Let us nourish ourselves, rejoicing and giving thanks to him, and the Lord will grant us a peaceful and quiet life and will enable us to complete our life without pain or harm, and in the future we shall attain the eternal goods through his philanthropy and his grace. 'And if you will not listen to me', says the Lord, 'and will not keep my commandments, I shall send desolation upon you, and you will sow your seeds in vain; and your enemies shall eat your labors and you shall flee when no one pursues you, and when you are hungry and thirsty no one will satisfy you'.[47] Therefore it is proper that everyone harmoniously and unanimously be responsible, so that we all together, pastor and flock, look only to please God, and we shall obtain the delight of the eternal goods in Christ Jesus our Lord, to whom is the glory.

44. 1 Tim 6:7.
45. Cf. Jn 14:18.
46. Cf. Lv 26:3–9.
47. Cf. Lv 26:14,32,16; 27:36,26.

An account from the divine writings, that it is proper for the superior to teach and admonish those under him.

Discourse XI

[1] It is proper for the superior to display all his zeal and to provide and care for the souls given him by God. 'For the whole world is not worth one soul; the one passes, the other is imperishable and abides'.[1]

[2] On this account pastors and teachers have received from the Lord Christ the authority to bind and loose on earth and in heaven. For the Lord said to them: 'Whomever you shall bind on earth shall be bound in heaven'; and 'whomever you loose on earth shall be loosed in heaven;[2] he who hears you hears me, and he who rejects you rejects me';[3] and again: 'you are the light of the world; you are the salt of the earth'.[4] Again he says: 'Well done, you good and faithful servant; you have been faithful regarding a few things, I shall set you over many; enter into the joy of your Lord:[5] for wherever I am, there shall be my servant also'.[6] And again he says: 'If you extract the precious from the vile, you shall be as my mouth'.[7] And the supreme Apostle Peter says: 'Tend the flock which is in your charge, not by constraint, but willingly, and not for shameful gain; so the pastor shall be a complete example for the flock'.[8] Then there will be no constraint but free will instead.

[3] Therefore let us exert ourselves not to be scornful or indifferent towards our brothers or to abandon them to sinning. Rather let us exert ourselves, as if gathering calm water with a

1. Cf. Climacus, *Liber* 13; PG 88:1196D: also below, Discourse XIII.45. Cf. AfED 474 (*Prosvetitel'*, Introd. 47).

2. Mt 16:18–19.

3. Lk 10:16.

4. Mt 5:14,13.

5. Mt 25:21. Cf. below, Discourse XIII.3.

6. Jn 12:26. Cf. above, Discourse III.24, Discourse VIII^{B}.27/VI.40.

7. Jer 15:19. Nikon, *Taktikon* 18:106, attributed to Climacus, *Liber*: cf. PG 88:1189C; and above and below, Discourse I^{B}.4/I.4, Discourse XIII.4.

8. 1 Pt 5:2–3. Nikon, *Taktikon* 18:106.

soft sponge, to prevail over conceit and cleanse haughtiness. And do not abandon your treatment. If you do not cure him today, then tomorrow morning; if he does not submit in the morning, then he will accept a sermon tomorrow evening; and if he shuns the sermon in the evening, then he will not abide in such depravity but when he recollects the penance, he will be frightened, hesitate, and censure himself. This is the origin of salvation: that one censure oneself. And if we do not bring him to recognize his sins, then do not withdraw, but be firm by intimidating and forbidding him by yourself and with many others.[9]

[4] It is proper for the pastor to be flexible: meek and savage, humble and haughty.[10] If everyone were good, then only goodness would be needed. If this is not so, then fear is necessary, since goodness affirms what is good, while fear bridles evil.[11]

[5] And in the *Holy Ladder* it is said: *It is not fitting for the pastor to be foolishly humble or to elevate himself irrationally.*[12]

[6] It is said in the *Geronticon: An elder said: 'One shall be called to account for those under his control as to whether he thoroughly investigated possible transgressions and forbade them. If he is unable to cut them off from evil, they will die in their sin, and he delivers up his own soul; if he is able to cut them off and does not, he shall perish with them as indifferent and lazy'.*[13]

[7] And the Lord cried out to the prophet Ezekiel: 'Son of Man, I have made you a watchman over the house of Israel; and if you warn the wicked and he does not turn from his way, he shall die in his own sin, but you have saved your soul; if you do not warn him, I shall demand his blood from your hands'.[14]

[8] Jude, the brother of the Lord, says: 'But you, beloved, for

9. From Nikon, *Pandekty* 55:459^V: attributed to Chrysostom, *Margaritos*: see above, Discourse I^B.20.

10. Cf. Nikon, *Taktikon* 18:105–105^V': attributed to Chrysostom.

11. Cf. Nikon, *Taktikon* 18:105^V: attributed to Chrysostom's disciple Isidore.

12. Nikon, *Pandekty* 55:456: attributed to Climacus; source not identified.

13. Cf. Climacus, Liber *6, Scholia* 6; PG 88:1181, as in Nikon, *Pandekty* 55:457. See and above, Extended Rule, Introduction [4] (Int.4).

14. Ez 3:17,19; 33:7–9. Cf. Nikon, *Pandekty*, 55:456^V-57; *Prosvetitiel'* 16: 549–50; above, Introduction [4] (Int.4), Discourse X.5, and below, Discourse XIII.28.

some have compassion, using discretion and others save with fear'.[15] And the great Apostle Paul, writing to Timothy says: 'Reprove',[16] he said, 'and rebuke, so that others also may fear'.[17] Therefore it is proper for the pastor to be righteous so that he may be able to comfort with rightful teachings, to rebuke the contumacious, and to shun all wrath and iniquitous judgment.

[9] It is also proper for the pastor not to seek his own profit, but the profit of the many, that many be saved.[18] And when from one there arises detriment to the many, then it is not proper to forebear,[19] because the improvement of many is better than the harm to one.[20]

[10] The blessed Pachomius says: *It is proper that the pastor rather than the flock carry the cross of Christ and safeguard the canons of the brothers more than his own, so that they shall be observant and he should never think: 'I am the brothers' father; for God is everybody's sole father and master'.*[21]

[11] And blessed Mark the Hermit says: *If you happen to be commanding the brothers, be obvious about what is pleasant, but mention what is brutal by means of a riddle. If you are teaching about the Lord, and you are misunderstood, do not be troubled. He who is troubled over affairs is inexperienced.*[22]

[12] John Climacus says: *We shall not quickly lay a hand upon anyone, lest one of the sheep, unable to endure the burden, go back into the world. Moreover, to have laid a hand precipitously is not without danger from God's side.*[23] And again he says: *Seek several extra virtues, for no one beholds the Lord. First simulate a child (but not their smooth and feminine faces) in all traits which are necessary and beloved by God, and let the superior provide and be responsible.*[24]

15. Jude 20,22–23. Cf. *Prosvetitel'* 12:470–71, 13:491.
16. 2 Tm 4:2. Cf. below, Discourse XIII.25,31.
17. 1 Tm 5:20. Cf. below, Discourse XIII.25,31.
18. 1 Cor 10:33.
19. Cf. Antiochus, *Pandectes* 111; PG 89:1176C (VMCh 4:2122).
20. Climacus, *Liber* 11; PG 88:1189C.
21. From Nikon, *Pandekty* 8:58.
22. *Opuscula* 2.120,164; PG 65:948,955.
23. *Liber* 13; PG 88:1193A.
24. From *Liber* 13; PG 88:1192D-1193A.

[13] The business of the righteous and true pastor is to provide and be responsible for all; the business of the flock is to submit completely to the director and teacher and in no way murmur, be contumacious, or disobey, but rather wholeheartedly and seriously to have obedience and complete veneration, submission, and benevolence. Indeed: 'Whoever opposes authority opposes God's ordinance',[25] says the Apostle. And again: 'Let every soul be subject to authority and to those more powerful'.[26] And again he says:[27] 'Submit yourselves to your directors, for they watch over your souls'.[28]

[14] If the director carries out God's legislation with precision, he is none other than one who has the persona of our Lord, becomes a mediator between God and men, and, in banishing turmoil and contentiousness and making everything communal souls, bodies, and customs, and whatever they have for nourishment and comfort—makes a sacred offering to God for the salvation, love, humility, and unanimity of those submissive to him. God is communal, labors are communal, salvation is communal, and the crowns are communal.[29]

[15] What is more blessed and what is more joyful than this for souls and bodies? Men from different nations and countries have assembled in such unity and are united in such a loving union, as if one soul could be seen in many bodies. He whose body ails has many who ail with him; he who is sick has many who have been cured, when they work for one another and submit to one another. Such from the beginning has God wanted us to be. They are precise imitators of the Saviour; they imitate his life in the flesh; they imitate the life of angels; they are eager for the life of the angels: for there is no strife, jealousy, or hatred among the angels, but they all treasure the good within themselves and have immaterial possessions and spiritual wealth. They have nothing

25. Rom 13:2.

26. Rom 13:1.

27. Heb 13:17.

28. For the entire paragraph, cf. Pseudo-Basil, *Constitutiones* 22; PG 31: 140IC-1404c.

29. Pseudo-Basil, *Constitutiones* 22, 18; PG 31:1408C-1409A, 1381C.

of their own, but everything is God's and one another's, and they have executed perfect non-possession and every virtue.[30]

[16] And what is like this good combination, where one father imitates the Father on high, and many children strive against each other with benevolence for victory before the superior, and all have unanimity among themselves? In truth, the devil himself would give up in the face of such a contingent, as he is no match for so many champions who are protected by so much love for one another and whom celestial love has combined and united to one another. Of these the prophet David speaks in his songs: 'Behold how good and pleasant it is for brothers to dwell together in unity'.[31]

[17] The cause of all this is the pastor's zeal, diligence, and love for his flock, and the flock's obedient, symphonic, and warmest unanimity with the pastor and faith and love such that when the Lord comes, he will take joy in the pastor, revel in the sheep, and honor them with the blessed and sweet voice which summons the worthy and righteous to the heavenly, praiseworthy, and blessed kingdom, which all of us shall obtain through the grace and philanthropy of our Lord Jesus Christ, to whom is the glory forever and ever. Amen.

30. Cf. Pseudo-Basil, *Constitutiones* 18; PG 31:1381D-1384C. Ps 132/133:1. (Pseudo-)Athanasius of Athos, *Rule* (Ὑποτύπωσις) 38:260 (Meyer, 115).

31. Cf. Pseudo-Basil, *Constitutiones* 18; PG 31:1385A-1388A. Ps 132/133:1.

The second Will and Testament of the sinful and miserable hegumen Iosif, to my fathers and brothers who would hear in brief about everything written here concerning the monasterial and monastic institution.

Discourse XII

[Int.] In the name of the Holy, monophysitic, and life-giving Trinity, the Father, it is said, the Son, and the Holy Spirit, the inseparable and tri-hypostatic godhead, through whom everything was, and we as well. Lo, it is I, the sinful and unworthy hegumen Iosif. I write this will and testament in full control of my mind. I testate and reveal to all of my brothers in Christ, from the first down to the last, the following: on how it is proper to be responsible for monastery's and monks' good order, and especially for reverence in the church.[1]

1. First, on good order in the church and concerning the community prayer.

Everyone shall be on time at the beginning of the chant.
Do not move from your place to another.
Do not leave the church or refectory during the chant before the dismissal without a blessing, unless there is an urgent need.
Do not converse or laugh during the chant.
Do not remain behind in the church or refectory after the chant.[2]
And the clerics shall be responsible for the chant, lection, and psalms in the church.

2. Second, on reverence in the refectory and on food and drink.

Be on time for the benediction in the refectory.
And do not converse at the table or laugh.
And do not eat before dinner.

1. See above, Introduction, Title.
2. Cf. *Starchestvo,* 7.

And do not sit at another's place.

And do not take anything, food or drink, from in front of a brother.

And do not give your food or drink away.

No one shall take a vessel or a dish out of the refectory without a blessing.

And do not bring your own food or drink or vessel to the refectory.

No one shall go to the 'last table' except the officials.

After dinner, no one shall remain behind in the refectory.

And no one, except the officials, shall go into the pantry.

And do not enter the refectory before dinner, after dinner, after Vespers, or after Compline unless there is an urgent need.

And do not eat or drink in the cells or send food or drinks to the cells without the blessing of the superior.

Serving men and boys shall not stay in the refectory at dinner time.

3. Third, on garments and footwear.

Have garments, footwear, and other things in quantity and quality as it is written above in the *Great Will and Testament*, Discourse III.[3]

And if someone is given a vestment or any other thing from the monastery's wardrobe he shall not exchange, sell, or give it away without a blessing.

And no one shall ever take anything from anywhere without a blessing: not from the refectory, not from the monastery, not outside the monastery, and not from work.

And if someone finds anything anywhere, he shall report it to the superior.

Likewise, no one shall take anything from the church: no icon, no book, no candle, no incense, and no other thing, without the sacristan's blessing.

Likewise, no one shall inscribe anything in a book without the superior's or the choirmaster's blessing.

3. See above, Discourse III.24–26.

4. That it is not proper to converse after Compline.

After Compline, it is not proper to stand in the monastery to converse or to meet in the cells.

Only speak of the needs of the cloister, and, for the sake of good order, speak in a cell.

Nor shall anyone, except the disabled, drink water.

Nor shall anyone go outside the monastery, except for the elder to whom the outbuildings have been assigned.

After dismissal from Compline, the inspector of the church shall go around the monastery, and if he sees someone standing in the monastery, going from cell to cell, or going outside the monastery, he shall reprimand him. And if someone is disobedient, he shall tell the superior or the senior brothers.

5. That it is not proper for monks to go outside the monastery without a blessing.

It is not proper for monks to go outside the monastery without a blessing: not to the hamlets, the villages, the outbuildings, or anywhere else.

6. On community work.

It is proper that everyone arrive on time for community work; and everybody should leave together.

And do not engage in idle chatter, laugh, or quarrel at work.

And if someone leaves work before the brothers, he shall ask the blessing of the superior or of the elder who has been assigned this responsibility.

7. That it is not proper for drinks which cause drunkenness to be in the cloister.

It is not proper for drinks which cause drunkenness to be in the cloister.

If such drinks are brought to someone's cell, he shall report it to the superior or the cellarer, and he himself shall not taste it.

8. That it is not proper for women to enter the monastery.

It is not proper for a woman ever to enter the monastery.

If a woman desires to go into the church for the sake of prayer, then send a report to the superior about this. The superior shall send two or three brothers, and they shall lead her into the church. After she prays, they shall lead her out of the monastery. Never allow them to go into the refectory, past the cells, or near the work sites.

9. That it is not proper for young boys to live in the monastery or at the monastery's outbuildings.

It is not proper for young boys to live in the monastery, the cells, or the monastery's outbuildings.

Nor shall they be given alms in the monastery.

Nor shall they be allowed in the cells.

And a monk shall not live in the villages, but he shall ride over to supervise [them].

And judge peasants, not in the monastery, but in the monastery's outbuildings.

No monks shall have their own private serving men, horses, saddles, or sleds.

And neither the monastery outbuildings nor the cells shall have rear doors or a large casement window;

Nor shall there be storerooms in the cells, but only in the outbuildings.

And do not plant apple trees or other fruits in the courtyard near the cells.

Do not go about the monastery without a mantle and a cowl, except for heavy labor.

And do everything in keeping with the superior's blessing.

[10] Anyone who in reading through and putting these into action holds and treasures these traditions shall be an heir to eternal blessings. Anyone who is heedless of them shall be condemned like the indifferent and lazy slave, for there is no constraint involved in holding and treasuring them. Indeed the way is smooth and wide because of the weakness of this last generation. If someone so chooses, he can keep them. He who does everything in keeping with the blessing and the command of the superior will live in

paradise, better to say, in heaven, and does not fear death: *For at the time of death, not he but rather the superior will be called to account.* So it is said in the *Holy Ladder*.[4]

[11] If someone transgresses something written here, it is proper for him to beg forgiveness of the superior, and the superior shall forgive him in keeping with the witness of the Divine Writings, which are written down here in Discourse XIV.[5]

[12] If it is proper to read these at an assembly before all the brothers, then do it. For although it is brief, everything is said here.[6]

Let this be enough for now.

4. See above, Extended Rule, Introduction.12 (Int.12).
5. See below, Discourse XIII.48, Discourse XIV.1–2.
6. Cf. Timothy of Evergetis, *Typikon* 43:498. Archbishop Sava, *Tipik* 43:69.

That it is proper for the council and senior brothers, to whom the direction of the monastery has been entrusted, and for the monastery officials, together with the superior or in the absence of the superior, to be responsible for the causes pertaining to the church and monastery, that necessarily result in the salvation of souls.

Discourse XIII[1]

[1] Because we have written earlier in the *testament protocol,*[2] Christ, from the first down to the last', in the *Will and Testament 'to all my fathers, brothers, and beloved children in Christ with Witness from the Divine Writings',* that everybody shall be responsible for good order in the church and the monastery,[3] now I write for the senior and council brothers, to whom I entrust responsibility for the monastery. Enough has been said in the *Will and Testament* on how it is proper for everyone to be responsible for the monasterial and monastic institution. How to carry out what has been stated in the earlier sections will be stated here.

[2] If the Divine Writings command everyone in the cloister to be responsible for our good order, then it is excellent, good, and kind to the Lord, that everyone be responsible. However, *everyone is not equal in every way, because of want of zeal and exhaustion of strength.*[4] Some are steadfast; some are weak-willed; some are painstaking; and others are lazy. Indeed it is said in the holy Gospel: 'Many are called, few are chosen',[5] and: 'Little flock, it is the Father's good pleasure to give you the kingdom of heaven'.[6] And

1. Discourse XIV in the printed text.
2. Cf. Nikon, *Taktikon*, Introduction 3^{V}.
3. Cf. Extended Rule Introduction (Title, and Int.11).
4. See above, Discourse III.29.
5. Mt 20:16.
6. Mt 22:14.

elsewhere it is said: 'Many come to the monastic life, but few bear its yoke'.[7]

[3] Therefore, my fathers and brothers, I, your unworthy brother, the miserable hegumen Iosif, beseech you with Christ's acts of generosity—and I do not speak to you as to children, for I deem you worthy as fathers—that you accept, possess, and safeguard the things I have written for your benefit, not on my own, but in keeping with the witness of the Divine Writings. The senior and council brothers, who have received the direction of the monastery together with the superior or in the absence of the superior, shall themselves accept and possess these instructions and also constrain the other brothers and instruct and counsel them to accept and possess them, so that at Christ's terrifying advent, you shall hear from the Lord Christ: 'Well done, you good and faithful servant; you have been faithful regarding a few things, I will set you over many; enter into the joy of your Lord'.[8]

[4] Nothing is more venerable or more profitable for our souls than to desire the profit of your brother as if it were yours and his success as if it were yours; indeed, 'If you extract the precious from the vile, you shall be as my mouth'[9] And it is said in the *Holy Ladder: The whole world is not worth one soul; the one is transient, the other abides forever.*[10]

[5] In truth, therefore, blessed are they who are participants in this virtue and are good workers of the Lord's commandments. For the benevolent Lord so desires, delights, and takes joy, not just when someone struggles only for his own soul, but when he does this for his neighbor, locks up a typicon for perfect love within himself, obtains bliss from it, benefits his own and his neighbor's soul, and goes off to where the righteous shine as the sun.[11] Therefore, let us model ourselves upon the imitation

7. Pseudo-Basil, *Ascetical Discourse,* 30; PG 31:645C; also (VMCh 1: 149).
8. Mt 25:21. Cf. above, Discourse XI.
9. Jer 15:19. Cf. above, Discourse I^{B}.4, Discourse I.4, Discourse XI.2.
10. Climacus, *Liber* 13; PG 88:1196D (cited above, Discourse XI.1).
11. Mt 13:43.

of God.[12] For Christ says: 'Father, I desire that they also whom you have given me be with me where I am that they may behold my glory'.[13]

[6] The cause of all this is the responsibility, diligence, and love for the flock, and also the obedience to one another and to the pastor, and the humility and unanimity of the senior and council brothers, who have received the direction of the monastery, together with the superior or in the absence of the superior, and of all the monastery officials, that together they can harmoniously be responsible for good order and reverence in the church, monastery, and refectory.[14]

[7] If we remain negligent and unruly, then we shall surrender ourselves to desolation in this age and shall therefore be condemned as indifferent and lazy in the age to come. Basil the Great says: *Because we do not treasure the divine commandments and the patristic traditions, demons enter us and create whatever they want*. And again he says: *Let us attend to ourselves, brothers, for as a result of negligence and unruliness, cities have been razed, monasteries desolated, and churches consumed by fire*.[15]

[8] Saint Isaac says to the brothers: *If you treasure the divine commandments and the patristic traditions, God will send his grace to you and guard this place. If you do not treasure them, he will make this place desolate and you shall not remain here*.[16]

[9] And Saint Nikon says: *Let us carefully attend to ourselves, brothers, lest being negligent and unruly we surrender ourselves to desolation, as it has been said in the Life of Saint Symeon, the Thaumaturge of the Wondrous Mountain. Saint Symeon appeared in a revelation to the senior priest in his cloister. Lord Symeon said to him: 'If the few of you who are really pleasing to me safeguard my traditions and are responsible for yourselves and for the monastery's and the monks' order and reverence were not here, I would allow enemy troops to raze and disperse you'. After*

12. This first plural is placed in the text before the third singular phrase, 'locks up a typicon', as if the scribe or typesetter made a simple cut-and-paste error.

13. Jn 17:24.

14. See above, Discourse XI.17.

15. Source not identified; cited above, Discourse X.43.

16. Source not identified.

a while, those who maintained the saint's traditions departed to the Lord, and those who remained neglected Saint Symeon's tradition. The saint immediately sentenced the monastery to ultimate perdition, for Saracens came, burned the monastery, slaughtered the brothers, and turned the church into a mosque.[17]

[10] The cause of all these calamities, the desolation of the monastery and the slaughter of the brothers, was neglect and contempt for the ordering of the monastery, church, and monks on the part of the superior and the council brothers, who had received the direction of the monastery. For in the monastery of Saint Symeon the Thaumaturge, when there were preeminent brothers who treasured the patristic traditions and had a great sense of responsibility toward the monks' good order and reverence, then the monastery was not sentenced to desolation. But when those monks who treasured the tradition of that righteous one departed to the Lord, and those who came after them neglected the patristic traditions, then they were sentenced to immolation and the monastery to desolation. And not only did that monastery so suffer and obtain such a sentence on account of negligence and unruliness, but countless monasteries and divine churches were sentenced to desolation for no other reason than the unrulineness and negligence of the pastors and especially the senior and council brothers to whom the direction of the monastery was entrusted.

[11] Therefore, brothers, upon hearing this, let us take to fear and trembling, lest we likewise suffer afflictions, calamities, and the devastation of the monastery here, and in the future age be condemned as indifferent and lazy. So let us display all our zeal and struggle for the monasterial and monastic institution and reverence.

[12] The superior alone cannot manage this if other brothers do not sympathize with him, especially those who have received the direction of the monastery and all the monastery officials. And if everybody is responsible for this, together with the superior or in the absence of the superior, then all defects will quickly be corrected and we shall all quickly excel in the fear of God and in good order and reverence. If it is not this way, no reverence,

17. Cf. *Taktikon* 12:62, 19:119^{V}.

regularity, or good order is possible. All the Divine Writings bear witness to this.

[13] It is said in the *Holy Ladder: Without the aid of the oarsmen, the helmsman alone cannot save the ship on the open sea; likewise the pastor alone cannot administer the flock without the aid of the flock.*[18]

[14] Elsewhere it is said: *The general alone cannot overcome the enemy or establish order during civil turmoil without the army's aid; likewise the pastor alone cannot establish order out of monastic turmoil or create good order if the brothers are not sympathetic.*[19]

[15] Therefore the divine Chrystostom says: *It is proper for the brothers to sympathize with the father in everything, for not everything lies with the superior alone, but also with the brothers. I am telling you to be angry along with the rulers at those towards whom he is righteously indignant. When you see someone punished, all of you should shun him more than the superior does. Let the transgressor fear you more than the superior. If he fears only the teacher, then he will transgress more readily. If he fears so many fathers and so many mouths, then he will be more composed. For if the transgressor sees that he was punished by the eldest, but flattered by the brothers, he will be even lazier. Therefore when the superior punishes righteously, then you become angry too. 'For if I build up and you pull down, then what have we achieved besides toil'?*[20]

[16] *If someone says: 'Be humane towards the brothers', this is how it is proper for Christians to be humane. Let them learn that he who is angry is more humane than he who allows another to perceive what is sinful. This is just as when someone has compassion for a man possessed with fever and insanity and then fills him with undiluted wine and food; does he not think he is being humane, while he is producing a more gruesome illness? And just as when we see a horse running down a steep slope, we bridle,*

18. Climacus, *Liber* 7; PG 88:1184A, perhaps as in Nikon, *Taktikon* 18:102.
19. Source not identified.
20. Si 34:23.

stop, and strike him many times, similarly this torment is a cause of salvation. You do just this: punish the transgressor until he is kind to God. Let no one suppose this to be savagery and inhumanity, but rather ultimate meekness, extraordinary treatment, and great beneficence.[21]

[17] Also Saint Ephraim says: *It is proper for us, brothers, that the strong lift up the weak, the diligent comfort the pusillanimous, the vigilant arouse the dream-ridden, the capable admonish the incapable, the reverent instruct the unruly, the abstinent forbid the fearless, and the healthy suffer with the sick. In thus controlling ourselves and teaching each other what is profitable, we shall unanimously shame our adversary and glorify God, and the angelic orders will revel over us and upon hearing of us, will be amazed and will glorify God.*[22]

[18] Therefore it is proper for the council brothers who have received the direction of the monastery, and for all the monastery officials, together with the superior or in the absence of the superior, to bear responsibility for this, so that it be just as the Divine Writings have said in the foregoing pages. If they see someone irregular or perverse, they shall rebuke and forbid or report him to the superior.

[19] If it is said: 'When someone reports a brother's transgression to the superior it is slander, and when someone undertakes to forbid or rebuke a brother, it is condemnation', then let him hear the perfect truth: it is not calumny or condemnation, but perfect love. For the divine Apostle Paul commands and says: 'Now I exhort you, brothers, to admonish the unruly, comfort the faint-hearted, and support the weak'.[23] Again he says: 'If a man falls into a transgression, you who are spiritual should restore him in a spirit of meekness'.[24] Concerning the unsubmissive he states this: 'If any man does not obey you, with this epistle take note of and

21. Source for both paragraphs [XIII.15–16]: *Second Corinthians* 14:349; PG 61:501–02, as in Nikon, *Pandekty* 51:4161–417.

22. Cf. Rom 15:1. Source for Ephraim citation not identified.

23. 1 Thes 4:14.

24. Gal 6:1.

have no company with him, so that he may be ashamed'.[25] Now if worldly people were told this, to warn the unruly, forbid the insubordinate, and not keep their company lest they be ashamed, then it is still much more proper for the senior and council brothers and all the monastery officials, who have been so ordered, to forbid the unruly.

[20] However, those who have not been so ordered shall not rebuke or forbid, for this is condemnation and calumny. Rather, if they see someone doing something improper, they shall correct him with humility and love and without abuse. Indeed it is said in the *Geronticon: A certain Father said: 'There is no greater commandment than to correct your brother without abuse'*.[26]

[21] And if with this he does not reform, then do not condemn, slander, or abandon him to perish, but do just as Barsanuphius the Great says: *When the brothers transgress, say to them: 'Take heed of yourselves, brothers, for we are condemned for this and destroy our souls'. If he is slow witted, say to him: 'Believe me, brother, that this merits chastisement; if I tell the father, he will surely chastise you'. If he submits, very well. If he is angry, tell the father and he will forbid that brother; but do not make a prostration to him, for you will give him the idea that you have transgressed, and he will fight you even more'*. He also says: *If you see something bad happening, speak with humility and state again how it should be, but only in your own monastery, and nowhere else, for those in a cœnobium are as one body.*[27]

[22] Similarly, Saint Dorotheos speaks of this: *If someone happens to see his brother doing something improper, he shall not slander him, be silent, or leave him to perish, but shall say to him with meekness and humility: 'Forgive me, brother, that I have seen your perversion; in truth, what has been done here is not good'. Say this without wanting to abuse or eject the brother, but to benefit him. If he does not obey, then speak to someone with the power to*

25. Cf. 2 Thes 3:14.
26. From Nikon, *Pandekty*, 10:70.
27. From Nikon, *Pandekty*, 9:67–68.

correct him or tell the superior, and in the absence of the superior, tell the council brothers and then let the matter rest.[28]

[23] Basil the Great says: *The Lord once said: 'Judge not, that you be not judged',*[29] *and another time also said: 'If your brother sins against you, go and tell just him his fault; if he does not listen, tell it to the church; if he refuses to listen even to the church, he shall be to you as a heathen and a tax-farmer'.*[30] *Therefore we are in no way forbidden to judge, but we have been instructed to be flexible regarding whom it is meet to judge and whom it is not. It is not proper to be silent towards those under one's authority and trust, but otherwise it is not proper to judge one's brother, for it is stated by the Apostle: 'Therefore do not judge anything prematurely, before the Lord comes'.*[31]

[24] *There is an undeniable need to avenge those who are negligent of the divine commandments, lest we who are silent obtain the wrath of God along with them.*[32] *Eli the High Priest was not silent to his sons about their transgressions, but he failed to avenge or display the proper irritation against them. Thus he provoked such divine wrath that his people and his sons were destroyed, the divine ark was taken by foreigners, and Eli himself died a bitter death.*[33] *And if those who reprimanded and bore witness against transgressions and only failed to avenge kindled so much wrath, then what is to be said of those who know and are silent? And the Apostle likewise cried out against those who know and are silent; 'Why have you not mourned, for he who has done this deed might be taken away from you'.*[34]

28. From Nikon, *Pandekty*, 10:71. Cf. AfED 502 (*Prosvetitel'* 14:506).

29. Mt 7:1. Cf. below, Discourse XIII.26.

30. Mt 18:15–17. Cf. below, Discourse XIII.26,31. Also used, and attributed to Basil, by Iosif in his *Missive to I.I. Tretiakov* (ca. 1509) against Archbishop Serapion: PIV, 203.

31. 1 Cor 4:5.

32. Discourse XIII.23–24 to this point is adapted from *Shorter Rules* 164; PG 31:1189B-1192A. Cf. Nikon, *Pandekty* 39:290.

33. Cf. Jos 7:16–26. Cf. above, Discourse III.33.

34. 1 Cor 5:2. Discourse XIII.24 from note 30 is adapted from *Shorter Rules* 47; PG 31:1113C-1116A.

[25] And the divine Chrysostom says: *What? It is not proper to rebuke the sinner? Then why did the Apostle say: 'Reprove, rebuke, exhort',*[35] *and 'Rebuke those who sin in the presence of everybody, so that others may also fear'?*[36] *If it were proper for everyone to rebuke, then instability would follow, and if they held back, all good order and reverence in cities and in homes would be ruined, and they all would be filled with mutinies, troubles, confusion, stealing, drunkenness, and fornication. Indeed if the lord does not judge the slave, the lady the handmaiden, the father the son, and the friend the friend, they are surrendering them to evil. Let us then attend precisely to what has been said about who properly may not judge and who properly may. It is not proper for anyone to judge or rebuke who himself is guilty of myriad evils and would be harsh towards the transgressions of those being judged. For if a man is himself unruly and immoderate and makes idle chatter and jokes or does something else improper, then how can he teach others reverence, good order, moderation, and the other virtues? Of such the Lord says: 'You hypocrite, first cast the beam out of your own eye'.*[37] *Behold that he does not forbid judging, but orders us first to cast the beam out of our own eye and then to correct others.*

[26] *How is it proper to correct others? Listen! It is proper not to abuse or attack, but to teach; do not slander, but advise; do not attack with vainglory, but correct with love. When you leave your neighbor's transgressions alone, by not laboring, you make yourself liable for his transgressions. When with consideration and mercy you examine the transgressions of others, as a result of the examination you have furnished yourself with great mercy. 'What', he says, 'if someone fornicates or does some other improper thing? Neither say that fornication is evil nor correct the obscene man'? Indeed he corrected him, not as a warrior or an enemy who quarrels and disputes, but as a doctor preparing drugs. Also he does not say: 'Do not restrain the transgressor', but says: 'Do not judge',*[38]

35. 2 Tm 4:2. Cf. above and below, Discourse XI.8, Discourse XIII.31.

36. 1 Tm 5:20. Cf. above and below, Discourse XI.8, Discourse XIII.31. Also used, and attributed to Basil, by Iosif in his *Missive to I.I. Tretiakov*: PIV, 203.

37. Mt 7:5.

38. Mt 7:1. Cf. above. Discourse XIII.23.

which means, 'Do not become a bitter judge',[39] except of those who are completely embittered and who do not wish to possess humility and obedience or to assume the appearance of the well-ordered, but who instead adhere in hatred and enmity to the ranks of the warrior. It is of such people that our Lord Jesus Christ says: 'But if he refuses to listen even to the church, he shall be to you as a heathen and a tax-farmer'.[40]

[27] Neither the young nor the novices shall rebuke or forbid, but shall attend only to themselves and censure themselves from every standpoint. If they see someone doing something improper and not according to the norms of reverent brothers, they shall not forbid or rebuke, but each one quietly and alone shall report to the elder with whom that other lives. If someone has no elder, then report to the superior or to one of the major elders to whom the direction of the monastery has been assigned, and not to anyone else. For the Divine Writings command young monks who live in cœnobia to act in this manner.

[28] Basil the Great says: *It is proper to tell the superior about every transgression of a brother; for an untold evil becomes an unhealed sickness. To cover up a transgression is to arrange the death of the ill man with the result that one becomes a fratricide rather than a man of brotherly love.*[41] Again he says: *If you see a brother sinning and you do not inform the person with the authority to correct him, God will demand his blood from your hand.*[42]

[29] And it is said in the Geronticon: *An elder said: 'If you see a brother doing a bad thing and you do not tell the one with the authority to correct him, you have obviously demonstrated that you hate your brother. To love a brother is to desire his profit as if it were your own, and his success as if it were your own'.*[43] This indeed is 'perfect love', and 'he who loves his brother also loves God'.[44]

39. Discourse XIII.25 to this point is adapted from *Matthew* 23:157–58; PG 57:307–9, cited in Nikon, *Pandekty* 39:288–89.

40. Mt 18:17. Cf. above and below, Discourse XIII.23,31.

41. *Longer Rules* 46; PG 31:1036AB.

42. *Longer Rules* 25; PG 31:983C. Cf. Ezk 33:7–9; and above, Discourse X.6, Discourse XI.7.

43. Cited from Nikon, *Pandekty* 10:70.

44. Cf. 1 Jn 4:21.

[30] *If one of the brothers does not accept the admonition and rebuke from the superior and the preeminent brothers, it is proper to rebuke him before all the brothers. If he remains in his insubordination, he shall be driven from the cloister.*

[31] *Indeed the divine Apostle Paul and the other Divine Writings so command. He says: 'Drive away the wicked person from among you',*[45] *for 'a little leaven ferments the whole lump'.*[46] *Again he says: 'Reprove', he states, 'and rebuke;'*[47] *also: 'Rebuke in the presence of everybody those who sin, so that others may also fear'.*[48] And in the Law it is said: 'Rebuke your neighbor with a rebuke, and you will not take on a sin for that'.[49] *And the holy Apostle Jude says: Others save with fear, pulling them out of the fire.*[50] *And the great Apostle Peter says: 'It is the will of God that pious men bridle the impure'.*[51] *And Our Lord Jesus Christ says: 'If your brother sins against you, you are to tell just him his fault; if he does not listen take one or two others along with you; if he refuses to listen to them, tell it to the church; and if he refuses to listen to the church, he shall be to you as a heathen and a tax-farmer'.*[52] And Basil the Great says: *'Cast out', so it is said, the pest from the assembly and contention shall go out'.*[53] lest he give others his scabs.[54]

[32] Our reverend and God-bearing Fathers, who followed these Divine Writings both in former times and recently, were meek and lenient when it was necessary, and brutal and merciless when it

45. 1 Cor 5:13. Also used, and attributed to Basil, by Iosif in his 'Missive to I.I. Tretiakov': PIV, 203.

46. 1 Cor 5:6; Gal 5:9. Discourse XIII.30 to this point is adapted from Basil, *Longer Rules* 47: PG 31:1036B-1037A.

47. 2 Tm 4:2. Cf. above, Discourse XI.8, Discourse XIII.25.

48. 1 Tm. 5:20. Cf. above, Discourse XI.8 Discourse XIII.25.

49. Lv 19:17. Cf. Basil, *Shorter Rules* 47; PG 31:1113A.

50. Jude 23.

51. 1 Pt 2:15.

52. Mt. 18:15–17. Cf. above, Discourse XIII.23,26; also Basil, *Shorter Rules* 47; PG 31:1113AB.

53. *Longer Rules* 47:325; PG 31:1037A. Prv 22:10. Cf. above, Discourse II.6. Also used, and attributed to Basil, by Iosif in his 'Missive to I.I. Tretiakov': PIV, 203.

54. i.e., spread his leprosy.

was proper; and not only on Holy Mount Athos and other places where there are monasteries, rather we, too, saw many and we heard of others who were holy and venerable and lived as befits monks in the monasteries in Russia. Not only pastors and directors, but also their disciples, that is, the senior and council brothers and all the monastery officials who received the direction of the monastery from them, likewise were meek and lenient when it was proper and brutal and merciless when that was proper. Not only did they themselves keep the patristic traditions, but they also constrained and chastised others and were not afraid. Nor did they cover themselves with shame before anyone, not even before the superior himself, when they saw any irregular or perverse thing done, not according to the norms of the patristic traditions. He who would understand the truth of this should read through what is written above in the *Will and Testament, Discourse X,* from the second title, which has the witness to this and the following heading: *The Response to the Censorious* and a *Brief Account of the Holy Fathers of the Monasteries of Russia.*[55]

[33] Concerning these, enough has already been said. Now let us speak about how it is not proper for the hegumen to install whomever he wants as hegumen in his place, but rather him whom the brothers, especially those who have received the direction of the monastery, select. Therefore, with the testimony of the Divine Writings, I shall not impose upon you a hegumen to take my place after my departure, but shall instead accept him whom the Lord God and his Immaculate Mother want and whom you select.[56]

[34] It is said in the holy canons, in the canons of Gregory of Agrigentum: *We command that in every monastery the hegumen or archimandrite not be installed according to the monks' ranking or seniority, but shall be someone whom all the monks of the best comprehension, that is to say, those senior in worthiness and intellect, shall select on the sole basis that he be correct in faith, chaste in life, and worthy of ruling.*[57]

55. See above, Discourse X.10–32.
56. See above, Ch. 1, notes 93–94, Ch. 2, note 57–58, and corresponding text.
57. Cf. Justinian, *Novellae* 123.33; PL 72:1035BC.

[35] From the Chapters with Emperor Justinians's Novels: *A bishop shall not always install the hegumen or archimandrite for a monastery by rank or seniority, but rather someone whom all the most intelligent and preeminent monks select, swearing by the holy Gospel and saying that they have selected him not for the sake of love or for any other thing, but knowing him to be orthodox, chaste, worthy of ruling, and able to preserve the monastic typicon and the monastery's order.*[58]

[36] And Saint Methodius the Confessor, Patriarch of Constantinople, says to the monks of the Studite Monastery: *Neither while he is alive nor after his death shall a bishop leave a bishop in his place; nor shall a hegumen install a hegumen in his place.*[59]

[37] If it is said anywhere in the *Lives* of the holy Fathers who were founders of cœnobia that before his demise someone installed a hegumen in his place, still it was not only that one, but also the accompanying brothers who selected him, especially those who received the direction of the monastery, just as the sacred canons state. And it appears nowhere in the Divine Writings that there might be a hegumen in a cœnobium without the counsel of the brothers.[60] This causes confusion, discord, and cliques.[61]

[38] Thus Basil the Great says: *This is the action of the true pastor, that he has not obtained authority by his own means, but has been selected by the others who are senior and distinguished in age and intelligence and to whom responsibility for the monastery has been confided. Let such a man be selected, and the brothers will establish authority and good order. Just as the superior is liable for guiding the brotherhood in everything, the brothers are likewise liable. This is the duty of the brothers: if any problem on the part of the superior surfaces, the council and senior brothers should remind him alone and in good order that he should not demolish our good order. And if something deserves correction, he*

58. Photius, *Nomocanon* 12.3; PG 104:845CD. Cf. Nikon, *Pandekty* 4:43^{V}. See above, Ch. 2, note 26.

59. Cited from Nikon, *Taktikon* 23:142.

60. Cf. (Pseudo-)Athanasius of Athos, *Testament* (Διατύπωσις) 12–13:277. (Meyer, 128). Manuel II Palaiologos, *Typikon* 3:1619.

61. Cf. John Tzimiskes, *Typikon*, Preface, 235–36.

shall likewise obtain profit from the brothers. And if some people are senselessly troubled about the pastor, then they, accepting his manifest proof that they have considered the matter falsely, will change their opinion of him.[62]

[39] And many of the Divine Writings state that it is not proper for a superior to install a superior in his place or to accept authority for and by himself. After he has been selected from among all the brothers, especially from among the preeminent ones, then he should in no way endeavor alone to manage the monastery's and monks' good order, for this is impossible if the rest of the brothers do not help him. Nor should all want to teach and forbid—for all this is a cause of turmoil and trouble—but just those who are so entrusted.

[40] The Divine Writings differ among themselves and are not in full agreement over the proper number of senior and council brothers who should be exerting themselves with the superior and in his absence at a given place, but sometimes say one thing and sometimes another.

[41] Basil the Great commands that there be two superiors, a greater and a lesser. The lesser shall assist the greater in all matters and when he is away or ill; and the œconomus,[63] the ecclesiarch, and the leading brothers in intellect and ability shall assist them. If something deserves correction, it shall be corrected by them. Thus we profit our brother and we correct ourselves. And if any transgressions be suspected on the part of the superior, it is proper to remind him of this. Behold that it is proper not only for the brothers, but also for the superior himself to be reminded by the preeminent council brothers.[64]

[42] Saint Theodore the Studite commands that there be ten council elders directing the monastery in addition to the superior and œconomus;[65] and Saint Athanasius commanded that in

62. *Longer Rules* 27, 43; PG 31:988BC, 1028A-1029B.

63. The text has *inokom* (as monks) instead of *ikonom* (οἰκονόμος=œconomus), as the VMCh editors pointed out (col. 581).

64. Source, if there be one, not identified.

65. Cf. Michael Monachus, *Vita . . . Theodori;* PG 99:148B-149B (VMCh 3:384).

addition to the superior and œconomus, there be ten holding responsibility for church, refectory, and monastic good order.[66] We heard this from reverend monks who were on Holy Mount Athos and in other monasteries in Constantinople[67] and Jerusalem, that even in monasteries which are not large they have ten major and preeminent brothers along with the cellarer and treasurer. All of these make twelve in number in addition to the superior,[68] and complete responsibility for the monastery is confided to them. It is these whom the Divine Writings call *the preeminent brothers in worthiness and intelligence.*[69] According to our custom, they are called 'council brothers'.

[43] These divine Fathers did not do this simply haphazardly, but in keeping with the witness of the Divine Writings. Basil the Great says: *If the superior carries out God's legislation with precision, he is nothing less than someone with the persona of our Lord.*[70] The preeminent brothers under him carefully imitated the life of the Apostles and the Lord. And as he assembled a chorus of twelve disciples, the superior has selected twelve preeminent and senior brothers, so that they carefully imitated the life of the Apostles and the Lord. In the place of the Lord Christ, they have the persona of the superior, and in place of the twelve apostles they have chosen twelve brothers preeminent in worthiness and intelligence.[71]

[44] Having thus followed these Divine Writings and the custom of the very wise, intelligent, and divinely inspired men, we counsel, exhort, and pass down as a tradition that in the Monastery of the Venerable and Glorious Dormition of the Immaculate Mother of God, things be done just as the council and preeminent brothers

66. See Petit, *Vie de S. Athanase,* 341. Cf. (Pseudo-)Athanasius, *Testament* (Διατύπωσις) 12–13:277 (Meyer, 128).

67. Iosif might have spoken with people who had been inside monasteries in Constantinople before it fell to the Ottoman Turks in 1453, but this could also be a conflation of the past and present in theological time.

68. Cf. Theodora Palaiologos, *Typikon* 7:1267.

69. Cf. Basil, *Longer Rules* 48; PG 31:1037AB.

70. Cf. *Constitutiones* 22; PG 31:1408D-1409A. See above, Discourse XI.14.

71. Cf. Symeon, *Catechism* 18.421–432, where the formal officials are compared to the Early Christian deaconate, but the informal, like-minded helpmates of the superior are compared to the Apostles.

shall choose: either, just as Saint Theodore the Studite commands, that there be ten senior brothers besides the superior and the œconomus; or let it be as it is now in the Laura of Saint Athanasius on Holy Mount Athos[72] and in the other great monasteries, with twelve council brothers.

[45] If someone says, 'There is no need for so many council brothers', he is really saying, 'There is no need for good order, reverence, and a peaceful administration in the church, refectory, or monastery, but everything shall be irregular and perverse'. Indeed, if in the early years, when men were steadfast and painstaking in monastic affairs, there were not just two or three senior and council brothers in the monastery—as Saint Theodore the Studite and Saint Athanasius bear witness, for it is said in their *Lives* and also in the *Lives* of many holy Fathers that they had under themselves very many brothers who were responsible for good order in the church, refectory, and monastery: they called some *œconomi*, others they called *ecclesiarchs,* and others *epistemonarchs*, others *directors*, and *taxiarchs, prefects, overseers,* and *rousers*, and the *assistant hegumen, assistant œconomus*, *janitors,* and *inspectors,* and they commanded them to punish with penances those who were absent from the divine chant, by means of separation or so many prostrations, just as it is now done on Holy Mount Athos[73]—then how much more proper is it now for not one or two, but all the council brothers and all the monastery officials to whom the direction of the monastery has been granted to display great zeal and struggle for good order and reverence. For the divine Chrystostom says: *If he fears only the superior, he will transgress more readily; if he fears many eyes and so many mouths, he will be more composed and frightened.*[74]

[46] And if one of this number proves wanting, leaves the

72. The Laura (literally, cave), was the original monastery of Athanasius at Mt. Athos, which by 1500 had grown to over forty monasteries.

73. See Michael Monachus, *Vita . . . Theodori,* PG 99:148B-149B.(Pseudo-) Theodore, *Iambi*; PG 99:1871A-1789C. *Rule* (Ὑποτύπωσις) 18:107 (PG 99 1709D) Petit, *Vie de S. Athanase,* 36–41. (Pseudo-)Athanasius, *Rule* (Ὑποτύπ ωσις) 8:224–25 (Meyer, 135–36).

74. See above, Discourse XIII.15.

monastery, passes away, or renounces the administration of the monastery, the senior brothers, together with the superior or in the absence of the superior, shall select another who is fit for that office.

[47] If one of those to whom the direction of the monastery is entrusted himself begins to act contrary to the traditions here written down, or if one of them is hostile in word, deed, murmuring, or contumacy, they shall assemble alone and admonish him with humility and meekness no longer to be so. If he is disobedient to them, they shall admonish him a second and third time. If he contradicts them and does not submit, then the superior, or in the absence of the superior the council brothers, shall dismiss him from the affairs of the council and choose another in his place, whomever they will, so that the number is never reduced. On this account, we shall live securely in this age, not wandering from country to country, and on this account, we shall duly obtain with all the saints the delight of indescribable blessings.

[48] If someone contradicts and does not submit, the superior shall administer to him a penance in keeping with the cœnobitic tradition. When the superior is absent, the council brothers shall administer the penance, likewise in keeping with the cœnobitic tradition, as it is stated here in Discourse XIV, which is written below.[75]

[49] If someone says: 'What is this? It is proper for priests to administer penance to transgressors and absolution to the penitent; it is not proper for lay persons to do this.' To them one shall say: 'If transgressions are unknown and secret, whether little or big, they are confessed to a priest, and we likewise obtain penance and absolution from him in secret, in keeping with the witness of the sacred canons. This concerns not secret, but open sins which pertain to the traditions written here. The brothers who have received the direction of the monastery shall administer penance together with the superior and absolution together with the superior or in the absence of the superior. For who does not know of it when someone begins to be unruly in the church, refectory, or monastery, or outside the monastery, not in keeping with the norms of the reverent

75. Cf. Theodora/Theodule Synadene, *Typikon* IV.32:1532.

brothers? Indeed lay persons and lords, fathers, and elders, who are not priests, reprimand their slaves, sons, and disciples and apply blows for such transgressions, even though they are not priests or hegumens, and they forgive the penitent.

[50] Transgressions which are committed secretly shall be confessed only to the superior, and he alone shall administer penance to the transgressors and absolution to the penitent. When the superior is absent, it shall be confessed to the priest whom the council brothers command to receive confessions. They shall not confess to other priests, and if someone so confesses, they shall not listen. If someone wants to know exactly for which of the transgressions the council brothers apply penance or absolve the penitent, he may read through Discourse XIV, which is written below.

[51] If someone says: 'Why was there not from the beginning the tradition that not only the superior, but also the major and council brothers take responsibility for good order in the church, refectory, and monastery; that together with the superior they administer penances to transgressors and absolution to the penitent; and that the preeminent and council brother rebuke and forbid transgressors with a penance and absolve the penitents'?

[52] This shall be said to him: 'In the beginning, when I came here, the brothers who accompanied me and I possessed great zeal and aptitude for struggle. We came here in order to act just as we have written in the *Will and Testament.* Then it was still the beginning, and there were neither senior nor lesser brothers. So who was here to administer penance and who was here to receive it from them? And there was still a great deal of want, of food, drink, garments, boots, and even cells fit for living. There was incessant work and all kinds of labor. We only cared that someone might simply come here to live or be tonsured, and we greatly condescended to their weaknesses.[76]

[53] The Divine Writings bear witness to this: One *should not quickly apply a heavy cross-bar to those who come to be under the yoke of Christ.*[77] As Gregory the Theologian says: *Neither can one*

76. Cf. Makarios Chumnos, *Testament* 9:1448.
77. Source not identified.

quickly straighten out a crooked sapling with one's hands, for it becomes injured and breaks and is not straightened; nor can one quickly lead a savage and uninstructed youth under a heavy yoke, if he does not first learn under a light one.[78]

[54] Now, thanks to the charity and mercy of Our Lord, God, and Saviour, Jesus Christ, and of his Immaculate Mother, the most glorified Mother of God, Mary, our common hope and protector, we have an abundance of all physical necessities, and it is proper for us to display total zeal and struggle solely over spiritual things: humility, obedience, chastity, and asceticism, and our reverence and good order in the church, refectory, and monastery.

[55] If we live negligently and lazily and are not responsible with respect to these things, then in truth we shall hear what was said by the Lord God in the holy Gospel: 'And you shall cast the wicked and slothful servant into outer darkness; there shall be weeping and gnashing of teeth'.[79] Therefore, from now on, right down to our last day and hour, let us be responsible for these with all of our soul, mind, and senses, so that in the present age we may obtain mercy from the Lord God and in the age to come, at the terrible tribunal of Christ, we shall obtain those blessings which God has prepared for those who love him, through the prayers of the most glorified Mother of God and all the saints. Amen.

78. Noted in Sreznevsky, *Materialy* 2:1614

79. Mt. 25:30. Cf. above and below, Discourse I^B.9, Extended Rule Introduction.11 (Int.11), Discourse I.9, Appendix I.6.

Tradition I of our reverend father Hegumen Iosif to the council and senior brothers and to all the monastery officials, on good order in the church and on community prayer. (XIII/I)

[1] Lo, we have heard true and precise testimony from the Divine Writings that it is proper not only for the superior, but also for all the brothers and especially the council and preeminent brothers, to have watchfulness and ardor with all their might regarding the traditions and penances written down here. Therefore the superior himself and the other brothers shall select those who are outstanding in worthiness and understanding and who desire and are able to exert themselves with the superior, together with the superior and when the superior is absent, for good order in the church, well-being in the monastery and all the necessary causes which are written down here. If they are truly and wholeheartedly concerned about this, they shall on this account obtain the heavenly kingdom as an inheritance.[1]

[2] When they see someone doing something untoward in the church, refectory, monastery, at any of the offices, or beyond the monastery, or if they happen to see anybody doing anything irregular or perverse, they shall in no way be silent, but shall reprimand with humility and meekness. If he does not listen, they shall report it to the superior, and when the superior is absent, they themselves shall reprimand and not allow this to continue. Those who are negligent in these matters shall be condemned, as has been stated before in Discourse XIII.

[3] On this account, it is proper for the council and preeminent brothers together with the superior or in the absence of the superior, to take the responsibility, so that everything in the monastery proceed gracefully and according to order and, most important, the order of the church office, and then take the responsibility for the other traditions.[2]

[4] When the superior and all the brothers assemble in the divine

1. Cf. above, Introduction (Int.12).
2. Cf. above, Discourse I^{B}.1, Discourse I.1, Discourse XII.1.

church or in the refectory for community prayer, they shall all stand or sit in their places silently and attentively. Two or one of the council and senior brothers, who have been entrusted with responsibility for the monastery, shall be properly placed near the front doors of the church, through which the brothers enter for the chant and exit, in order to supervise all who enter and exit. And if someone is not on time for the beginning of the chanting, or if someone leaves the chanting before dismissal, even just once—certainly do not leave alone anyone who often dares to leave—question and investigate him. If he does this because of a genuine need, release him without hindrance; if not, do not permit him to leave the church. Likewise investigate with firmness the cause of those who leave the chanting, and it is especially proper to regard the young monks, so they do not leave the chanting except and only when necessary, especially midnight Vigils or Matins.

[5] They shall station one brother on the right side in the corner by the wall in front, and likewise one brother shall be stationed on the left side in the corner near the front wall. And they shall observe and inspect the brothers who stand on the right side and on the left side lest there be unruliness. (It is said in the *Life* of Saint Athanasius of Athos: *Saint Athanasius stationed one brother in each chorus for the decorum of the chanters*,[3] which is to say, he stationed one of the clergy in the right choir aisle and a second in the left choir aisle.) If anyone from the choir is not on time for the beginning of the chant, leaves the chant before the dismissal, makes conversation, stands negligently without discipline, sings himself hoarse,[4] begins to sing out of turn, studies something other than his lection for Matins or the Epistle for liturgy, or does not sing, they shall reprimand him and not allow it.

[6] One brother shall be stationed in the narthex on the right side, so that he may observe and watch over those standing in the narthex and he shall not allow anyone to enter the narthex

3. Petit, *Vie de S. Athanase,* 36. Cf. (Pseudo-)Athanasius, *Rule* (Ὑποτύπωσις) 17:224 (Meyer, 135). (Pseudo-)Theodore, *Rule* (Ὑποτύπωσις) 18:107 (PG 99: 1709D).

4. Cf. *Tüpikon*, 37^V^.

or exit from the narthex. He shall inspect, just as the above-mentioned person shall. Likewise one of the council brothers shall be stationed in the narthex on the left side by the doors, reprimand those who enter or leave the narthex, inspect those standing in the narthex, and reprimand those talking and laughing. And one brother shall be stationed in the narthex by the back walls, in order to inspect, observe, and reprimand those talking and sitting unless it is necessary.[5]

[7] The doors of the narthex on the left side of the monastery shall always be bolted, except for urgent needs. The brothers shall enter and leave the church only through the front doors, and the other doors shall always be locked. When it is necessary to open them, then report this to the superior.

[8] One of the council brothers shall be stationed by the north doors in the corner on the left side, and he shall inspect the priests, deacons, members of the choir, and ordinary monks who approach the sacrificial altar, lest they approach the altar or the holy sanctuary when they are not officiating.

[9] All of those who stand by the doors, in the corners, in the narthex, and in the choir aisles, shall inspect and observe with concord and diligence, as if they were God's agents and administrators. If someone is not on time for the beginning of any chant; if someone leaves the church before the dismissal; or if someone moves from his place to another, they shall meekly, reverently, and calmly reprimand him and not allow it. If someone talks back and is disobedient, they shall administer penance to him in keeping with the witness of the Divine Writings which is in Discourse XIV.

[10] When it is time to chant the Midnight Office, and when they begin to say: 'Blessed are the undefiled',[6] then the one brother who has been so commanded shall walk around the whole church, the narthex, the sanctuary and the sacrificial altar and inspect the

5. Petit, *Vie de S. Athanase,* 36–37. Cf. (Pseudo-)Theodore, *Rule* (Ὑποτύπωσις) 18:107 (PG 99:1709D). (Pseudo-)Athanasius, *Rule* (Ὑποτύπωσις) 17:225 (Meyer, 135).

6. Ps 119:1. See above, Ch 2, The Service Typicon for an identification of the elements of the services noted here and below.

brothers place by place. If anyone is not in his place, he shall send a rouser, and if a brother is sleeping, he shall awaken that man.[7] If that man is not in his cell, then he shall report to the superior or to the council elder who has been entrusted with the responsibility for this, and he shall dispatch someone quickly to find out the cause of that brother's not coming to the church.

[11] Likewise he shall make the rounds when they begin to recite the Psalter, after the lection during the fourth ode, and after the ninth ode. Likewise he shall make the round after they begin to sing the Prayer Service[8] and the Lord's Supper,[9] at the beginning of Vespers, and at the beginning of Compline.

[12] During the chant, it is proper for the brother who has been charged with awakening the brothers in every cell to inspect those who are standing outside of the church or the refectory. When they begin the Midnight Office's 'I believe in one God', he shall walk around the church or the refectory and scrutinize those who are standing in the monastery. When they begin to chant the canon, and when they begin the ninth ode, he shall make the rounds. If he sees that any brother is standing outside the church, outside the refectory, or in the monastery during the chant, he shall forbid and reprimand, or report him to the superior or to the elder who is charged with this responsibility. He shall also make the rounds when they begin to chant the Prayer Service, when they begin to chant the Lord's Supper, and when they begin to chant the communion hymn.[10]

[13] And thus these two brothers, the one in the church or refectory, shall go about during the time of the chant and inspect, just as has been said. The second one shall go outside the church or refectory during the chant. In summertime he shall always stand

7. *Tüpikon,* 38. (Pseudo-)Theodore, *Rule* (Ὑποτύπωσις) 18:107 (PG 99: 1709D). (Pseudo-)Athanasius, *Rule* (Ὑποτύπωσις) 17:225 (Meyer, 135). Pomialovsky, *Zhitie . . . Afanasiia*, 34.

8. *moleben.*

9. *obednia.*

10. (Pseudo-)Theodore, *Rule* (Ὑποτύπωσις) 18:107 (PG 99:1709D). (Pseudo-)Athanasius, *Rule* (Ὑποτύπωσις) 17:225 (Meyer, 135). Cf. Neilos of Tamasia, *Rule* 114:1155.

outside the church by the front doors and inspect just as has been explained above.

[14] It is proper for the preeminent brothers, together with the superior or in the absence of the superior, to bear responsibility for this. When they finish chanting Matins, Liturgy, Vespers, or Compline, they shall not leave the church or the refectory, but shall stand and wait until all the other brothers exit. If some of them begin to remain behind or make conversations, they shall forbid them and drive them out, and in no way allow it.

[15] If there happens to be a layman or a guest monk with us at the community prayer, and if he is a nobleman, then it is especially proper for us not to make conversations during the prayer, so that we avoid censure and do not attract God's wrath upon ourselves. For it is the custom of laymen to censure and deride unruly monks. Let us not tempt anyone: *For he who creates temptations for laymen will not behold the light.*[11] But if it is *necessary*,[12] let us make the requisite bow, say the customary 'peace', and return to our original silence. If he begins to converse, let us meekly reprimand him, for nothing is of such profit to laymen as the good order and the reverence of monks.[13]

[16] First of all, it is proper for the superior himself and all the council brothers, the cellarer, treasurer, choirmaster and assistant cellarer to act in this way. During the chant in the church and the refectory, when brothers come to the superior with spiritual or physical matters, he shall converse with them briefly and calmly, in a whisper. Likewise it is proper for the council brothers, the cellarer, treasurer, choirmaster and assistant cellarer to speak briefly, calmly, and in a whisper during the chanting and in the refectory, or when among themselves one comes to another. If there is some need that cannot be put off, they shall go away from the chant to talk or put it off until the chanting has ended.[14]

[17] If the superior, council brothers, the cellarer, treasurer,

11. Source not identified.
12. *necessary* was omitted by a scribe.
13. Cf. above, Discourse I.30.
14. Cf. above, Discourse I.31.

choirmaster, and cellarer speak out without caution within earshot of the brothers, rather than briefly, then they also will act this way, and in the present age and in the future age we shall be condemned as indifferent and lazy.[15] The Divine Writings speak in this manner: *A monk who stands before God for individual prayer or at the community chant or sits at table and does not pray in his mind, but utters idle and unprofitable words, has withdrawn from God, and God has withdrawn from him; his prayers are not welcome, and his labors are futile.*[16]

[18] When the chant is done in the refectory, then, as in the church, the council brothers shall stand not together, but one by a door and two by a bench. Likewise the priests shall not be together, but apart: two at the big seat, but not together, two at the other big bench, and one at the bench where guests sit.[17]

[19] If it is hard for brothers to stand in the refectory for the chanting, then whomever the superior and the council brothers so command shall stand in the heated church; no one else shall go in there. And the superior and the council brothers shall station a brother in the heated church to forbid and reprimand those who talk, sit, and laugh there, and to reprimand priests who enter when they are not officiating, and also deacons, choir monks, and ordinary monks.

[20] And everybody who stands by the doors, the walls, the benches, and in the church shall take responsibility in the fear of God, just as has been said with respect to the community chant in the holy church.

[21] When they leave the community chant, the council brothers, together with the superior or in the absence of the superior, shall inspect, and if any brother remains behind in the refectory or sits down in front of the refectory, in front of the cells, or in the monastery, they shall forbid and reprimand. And it is proper to enter and leave the refectory for the chant only through the great doors.

15. Cf. above, Discourse I.6.
16. Attributed to Isaac of Scete: see above, III^{B}.3, Discourse II.5.
17. See above, Ch 2, THE MAJOR EDIFICES.

[22] It is proper that the council brothers, together with the superior or in the absence of the superior, bear this responsibility. The *Synodicon,* the daily commemoration, and the yearly memorials shall be read, and the feasts shall be arranged just as it is written in the *Synodicon.*[18] He who would be responsible for this for the sake of the Lord should read the discourse in the *Synodicon* which has this heading: 'The Account With Witness from the Divine Writings of the Salvific and Soul-profiting Books, of the *Synodicon*, and of the Daily Commemoration', concerning how it is proper for us to bear this responsibility, and what kind of profit results from this for living and dead souls.[19]

The Divine Writings in the *Will and Testament*, Discourse 1, and in Discourse XIV, First Penance, bear witness to this tradition.

18. Cf. Timothy of Evergetis, *Typikon* 36:494. Archbishop Savva, *Tipik* 36: 64–65.

19. See above, Ch 2, RELATIONS WITH THE TRANS-VOLGANS, and below, Appendix I.

Second tradition on reverence and good order in the refectory, and on food and drink. (XIII/ii)

[1] It is proper to enter the refectory to eat dinner and supper when they ring the bell. Then all the brothers, together with the superior or in the absence of the superior, shall go from the church to the refectory and say Psalm 144: 'I will exalt you, my God, my King'.[1] If someone does not know this psalm, he shall say this prayer: 'Lord Jesus Christ, Son of God, have mercy on me, a sinner'.[2]

[2] When the superior presides at the table, or when the superior is absent and the hebdomadary presides, then the cellarer, having obtained the blessing, shall serve, and the officials shall serve everyone, and the cellarer shall say: 'Bless and pray, O Lord'. And the superior or a priest shall bless the table and say: 'Christ God, bless this food and drink for your servants, for you are holy now and always and for ever and ever. Amen'.[3]

[3] And if one of the brothers is not on time for the benediction in the refectory, the cellarer shall order bread and water to be placed before him until he obtains absolution.[4]

[4] It is proper for two of the council and senior brothers to be seated higher than everybody else in order to reprimand the priests and deacons who sit and laugh. It is proper for them to sit two to a bench. The priests also shall sit not together, but apart. One, beside those who sit above everybody else, shall sit at the long seat; two shall sit at the other bench, likewise not together; one shall sit at the long seat, and one shall sit at the third bench.

[5] They all shall inspect and observe. If someone does not arrive for the benediction; if someone begins to make conversation or laugh at the table; if someone begins to eat and drink anywhere before the benediction at the brotherhood's table; if someone

1. Ps 144/145:1.

2. Entire paragraph from *Tüpikon*, 41, and *Taktikon* 1:6. Cf. above, Discourse II.1.

3. Entire paragraph from *Tüpikon*, 41.

4. See below, Discourse XIV.9. Cf. Timothy of Evergetis, *Tipikon*, 9:478. Archbishop Sava, *Tipik* 9:51.

begins to go into the refectory or out of the refectory by the pantry doors; if someone sits at another's place; if someone begins to give food away; if someone takes food and drink from in front of the brothers; if someone places something of his own before a brother; if someone begins to ask for more to eat or drink; if someone begins to substitute, not according to the monastery's custom; if someone brings some of his own food or drink to the refectory; if the foods at table are not of equal portion; if they behold anyone in the refectory with drinks which cause drunkenness; or if serving men and boys begin to stay in the refectory during dinner and supper, they shall forbid and reprimand.[5]

[6] When the brothers rise from the table with the superior, they shall all leave the refectory after the dismissal. The preeminent and council brothers, together with the superior or in the absence of the superior, shall stand and wait until all the brothers have exited and shall scrutinize and observe. If any of the brothers begins to remain in the refectory after the meal, go into the pantry, or make conversations, they shall forbid it, reprimand him, and not allow it. And they shall impose a penance upon the disobedient.[6]

[7] The cellarer, assistant cellarer, butler,[7] and all the refectory officials shall exert themselves with the superior and with the brothers, who have the direction of the monastery, over good order in the refectory. They shall have this responsibility: when the brothers begin to enter the refectory, sit before dinner or after dinner, enter the pantry, or remain after Vespers or after Compline, they shall reprimand them, forbid it, and report the disobedient to the superior or cellarer.

[8] And they shall have this responsibility: when they feed the serving men and boys after dinner or supper, if one of them begins to eat without keeping his silence, they shall forbid it, reprimand him, and send him out of the monastery in disgrace.

[9] When the brothers rise from table after dinner, they shall

5. Cf. above, Discourse II.1,7–10. Petit, *Vie de S. Athanase*, 40. Timothy of Evergetis, *Typikon* 9:479 *et al.* Archbishop Sava, *Tipik* 9:51.

6. Cf. above, Discourse II.18.

7. *chiashnik*; i.e. cupbearer.

not exit from the refectory one or two at a time; rather everybody shall stand at prayer and attention and give thanks to the Lord God who has nourished our soul and our body. They shall wait until the deacon brings the *Panaghia*[8] to the superior or to the priest. The superior shall then say: 'The blessed God, who has mercy and nourishes us from his rich gifts', etc.[9] Then all the brothers shall make a prostration before the superior, and when the superior is absent, before the priest, and thus they shall all leave the refectory with prayer and silence.[10]

[10] When they rise from the table after dinner, then the brother who has been so ordered by the superior shall stand by the great refectory doors. He shall keep watch, and if any of the brothers carries any food, drink, or vessel out of the refectory, he shall reprimand him and return it to the refectory, and he shall report the disobedient to the superior.

[11] When it is time for the brothers to drink kvass, before Vespers or at midday, they shall enter the refectory and drink in good order and quietly. For the divine Apostle Paul says: 'Whether you eat or drink, do everything to the glory of God'.[11] Therefore, just as we have said that it is proper for us to eat dinner and supper in silence and prayer, likewise it is proper to act similarly here. If any of the brothers begins to talk, laugh, make idle chatter, take kvass out of the refectory, or remain behind in the refectory, the council brothers shall forbid it and continue to reprimand him until everybody has left the refectory.

[12] The brother who has been ordered by the superior and the council brothers to inspect those who stand in the monastery shall go from his cell to the monastery when the first hour[12] strikes and walk around the whole monastery and the cells and within the monastery. If he sees any monks or lay persons in the monastery, he shall order the monks to go to their cells and send the lay people

8. See above, Ch 2, THE SERVICE TYPICON.
9. Cf. Timothy of Evergetis, *Typikon* 9:480. Archbishop Sava, *Tipik*, 52.
10. From *Tüpikon*, 9^{V}-10.
11. 1 Cor 10:31.
12. See above, Ch. 2, note 77.

away from the monastery. At the second hour he shall return to his cell.

[13] When they begin to chant the Prayer Service in the church or in the refectory, or when the brothers begin to enter the refectory to eat, then he shall stand in the monastery by the church or the refectory and forbid those monks who are standing in the monastery and order them to enter the church or the refectory. When they leave the church after the chanting or the refectory after eating and drinking, then he shall likewise forbid those who would stand in front of the refectory or church and order each to go to his own cell.

[14] During the third hour he shall remain in his cell, and at the fourth hour he shall again come out and likewise walk around the monastery. He shall do this all day until nighttime: remain in his cell for one hour, and walk around the monastery for one hour and forbid and reprimand the monks and laymen who are standing in the monastery. And he shall report the disobedient to the superior.

[15] If he sees any monks leaving the monastery, he shall inform the superior. If he sees any young boys walking in the monastery he shall not only forbid and reprimand him, but also apply blows, for it is said in the *Patericon: It is not God who brings boys into a cœnobium, but the devil, who wants to hurl us into the sin of fornication, on account of which we shall go away to the unquenchable fire.*[13]

And this covers that. The Divine Writings in the *Will and Testament*, Discourse II, and in Discourse XIV, Second Penance, bear witness to this tradition.

13. Source not identified; see above, Discourse IX.5.

Third tradition, on garments, footwear and other things. (XIII/iii)

[1] The preeminent and council brothers, who have received the direction of the monastery, are worthy to bear the responsibility, together with the superior or in the absence of the superior, for garments, footwear, and other things, so that there be nothing excessive in quantity and quality.

[2] They are also worthy to bear responsibility that none of the brothers take anything anywhere without the superior's or the cellarer's blessing: not from the church, not from the refectory, not from other places of work, and not from the cells; no vestment, no boots, no other such item; none of the iron objects, namely, pole-axes, knives, nails, and similar things; and not any of the wood-working objects, namely logs, planks, squared beams, and roofing boards for cells and other buildings.[1]

[3] If anyone finds anything anywhere, he shall report it to the superior or the cellarer and absolutely shall not conceal it.[2]

[4] Similarly, no one shall take anything from the holy church: not a book, not a candle, not any other object, without the sacristan's blessing.[3]

[5] Likewise, no one shall inscribe anything in a book without the blessing of superior or of the choirmaster. From this arise turmoil and trouble and the corruption of the Divine Writings.[4]

[6] And let it be done in this way: issue [things] to the monks as is stated in the *Will and Testament*, Discourse III. There this is discussed in detail; here we shall now speak in brief on account of those who are greedy for things, possess in excess, and know no measure.[5] Indeed Saint Ephraim says: *He who loves bright vestments is stripped of divine clothing.*[6] Therefore, if someone wants to have more than this, the superior and the brothers shall

1. Cf. above, Discourse III.32.
2. Cf. above, Discourse III.33.
3. Cf. above, Discourse III.38.
4. Cf. above, Discourse III.39.
5. Cf. above, Discourse III.26.
6. Cf. above, Discourse III.11.

not allow it, but let them have these: one new mantle and a second old one; one new cowl and a second old one; one new cassock and a second old one; three tunics, one new and two old; one new pair of boots and another dilapidated pair; several under-shoes; two winter caps and two summer caps, one new and the other old. And everything shall be simple and inexpensive.[7]

[7] It is proper for the treasurer, while issuing garments, to make an inquiry. If someone has two garments and he wants to have a third, do not give it to him. When someone takes new apparel from the storeroom he shall give back the old one, and if he does not give back the old one, then do not give him a new. If someone wishes to exchange apparel, and he really needs three skin coats, then he shall surrender a cassock or a mantle and take the skin coat. Similarly, if he desires another piece of clothing, he shall surrender something of similar value which he does not need. Everyone shall have the equivalent of two of each garment, one in good condition and one old, except in cases of debility and an office which takes place outside the monastery: then three tunics.[8]

The Divine Writings in the *Will and Testament*, Discourse III, and in Discourse XIV, Third Penance, bear witness to this tradition.

7. Cf. above, Discourse III.26.
8. Cf. above, Discourse III.28.

Tradition IV, that it is not proper to converse after Compline. (XIII/iv)

[1] The council and the preeminent brothers, who have received the direction of the monastery, shall have this responsibility, together with the superior or in the absence of the superior, that no one speak after Compline or wander from cell to cell. After Compline it is proper for each brother to depart to his own cell. If they notice or find out about anyone going from cell to cell, standing in the monastery, they shall reprimand him and not allow it.

[2] After dismissal from Compline, the inspector of the church shall circuit the monastery. If he sees anyone standing in the monastery, walking from cell to cell, or going beyond the monastery, he shall reprimand him, and if someone does not obey, he shall report him to the superior or the senior brothers.[1]

The Divine Writings in the *Will and Testament*, Discourse IV, and Discourse XIV, Penance 4, bear witness to this tradition.

1. Cf. above, Discourse IV.4.

TRADITION V, THAT IT IS NOT PROPER FOR MONKS TO GO OUTSIDE THE MONASTERY WITHOUT A BLESSING. (XIII/V)

[1] It is proper that the preeminent council brothers, who have received the direction of the monastery, bear this responsibility, together with the superior or in the absence of the superior: that no one go outside the monastery without a blessing. Monasteries which are in desolate places, situated far from cities and from villages, do not have so much need to be concerned over this. We, however, are situated in the midst of the whole world and among laymen, are always seeing villages and homesteads with our own eyes, and are always hearing their voices with our ears.[1] If all of us are not unanimously responsible about not leaving the monastery without a blessing, then in a short time we shall find ourselves negligent and unruly; we will fill the homes and feasts of laymen; and therefore in the present age we shall be a source of laughter, ridicule and abuse by laymen, and in the future age we shall be condemned to eternal torments as indifferent and lazy.

[2] On this account, it is proper that the council brothers most especially bear responsibility and watchfulness, so that no one leave the monastery without the superior's or cellarer's blessing. If someone begins to leave the cloister without a blessing for the outbuildings, the forest, or anywhere else, they shall forbid it, reprimand him, and not allow it.

[3] It is proper that the council brothers bear this responsibility. When the brothers wish to go outside the monastery to refresh themselves, it is not proper for them to go on days other than Sundays, and they shall all go together with the superior. Not one of them shall go without the superior or remain outside the monastery. If the superior is not there, then the council brother who has been entrusted with this responsibility shall go with them. Likewise, no one shall stay behind him; rather everybody shall come back to the monastery with him.

1. The text reads 'eyes' (*ochima*) instead of 'ears' (*ukhima*)—note the use of the now defunct dual number.

[4] It is proper that there always be two sentries to guard the church and monastery at night. When they have finished singing Compline, then they shall bolt the big and the little Lower Gates,[2] and subsequently no one shall pass through these gates until the night hours are over. They themselves shall go about the whole monastery, and if they see any of the brothers standing in the monastery and not in his cell, they shall reprimand him. Whoever goes into the monastery or out of the monastery shall pass through the Holy Gates, and the two sentries, having bolted the lower gates, shall go to the Holy Gates and stand there until everyone has left the monastery.

[5] They shall send away from the monastery all local people or strangers who manage to come to the monastery after supper or after Compline, or who desire to lodge at the monastery. If anyone does not obey, they shall report him to the superior or the cellarer, bolt the Holy Gates, and subsequently not allow anyone into or out of the monastery at night.

[6] If someone comes to the gates and desires to go into or outside the monastery, the sentries shall tell the cellarer or treasurer, and if they give permission, shall first inspect him to see if he is taking anything outside the monastery. Then, after bolting the Holy Gates, they shall go about the monastery and inspect the church, refectory, storerooms, icehouses, and fodder sheds.

[7] This is how they shall go back and forth to both gates until the night hours are over; then they shall depart. Indeed if in cities and laymen's homes, they fasten double bolts and secure themselves, while sentries stand guard—for all evils occur at night—then how much more proper is it that we be wholeheartedly concerned over this.

[8] It is proper that there also be two sentries during the daytime. When the. night hours are over, then the day sentries shall come. One shall stand by the Holy Gates, the other by the Lower Gates, and both big gates shall always be bolted. When something is delivered, the sentries shall open up. Once it is conveyed, they

2. See above, Discourse Ch 2, The Major Edifices, for the monastery's layout.

shall again lock up and stand by the little gates. They shall always stand watch in this manner.

[9] If monastery peasants begin to come into the monastery, they shall reprimand them. If any children bring something to sell to the monastery, order them to stand by the gates, do not permit them into the monastery. The assistant cellarer shall buy from them outside the monastery.

[10] If someone brings mead, beer, wine, or any food or fruit to the monastery, they shall observe which cell he carries it to and report this to the superior or the cellarer.[3]

[11] If monks, besides those to whom the outbuildings and mills have been assigned, begin to go outside of the monastery, or if someone goes to wash his tunic or draw water from the nearby pond, they shall inspect him. If someone simply leaves the monastery, they shall report this to the superior or the cellarer.

[12] Likewise they shall inspect what laymen or monks take away from the monastery or to the monastery, report it to the superior or cellarer, and seize and detain that man until they inform the superior or cellarer.

The Divine Writings in the *Will and Testament*, Discourse V, and in Discourse XIV, Fifth Penance, bear witness to this tradition.

[13] Let us now speak a little more about this: the monastery's bailiffs and stewards shall judge the peasants in the villages.[4] When there is an affair they cannot settle, they shall set a time before dinner on a Saturday for them to appear at the monastery. If anyone comes to the monastery for any affair, except on Saturday, he shall be immediately sent away. The monastery's peasants shall come to the monastery on Saturdays for all business, and they shall wait in an outbuilding and not come into the monastery.[5]

[14] When the peasants meet with the elders who have been assigned to administer justice in the case, they shall go to the outbuilding and listen to them carefully. Whenever the matter is

3. See below, Tradition VII.5 (XIII/vii.5).

4. Cf. above, Discourse IX.11.

5. See above, Ch. 2, THE RULE AND IOSIF'S RELATIONS WITH THE TRANS-VOLGANS, for Vassian Patrikeev's sarcastic reproach of this stipulation.

ordinary, the elders shall adjudicate and immediately dismiss it. Whenever the cases are extraordinary, the elders shall inform the hegumen or the cellarer. The hegumen shall deliberate with the cellarer and the council brothers and then send those elders back to the outbuilding. They will inform the peasants concerning the affair, and immediately dismiss them from the outbuilding, and forbid them to go into the monastery.

[15] The monastery's judges and police officers shall take their fees from the peasants, whom they have judged, at one half of what is written in the Grand Prince's *Judicial Code.*[6]

6. The 1497 *Sudebnik:* See above, Discourse Ch. 2, note 44.

TRADITION VI, ON COMMUNITY WORK AND COMMUNITY OFFICES. (XIII/VI)

[1] It is proper that the preeminent and council brothers, who have received the direction of the monastery, bear this responsibility together with the superior or in the absence of the superior, that everybody exert himself during community work, and they should also do this for community offices. If they see someone not coming to community work, coming late, leaving early, making idle chatter at work, quarreling at work, or doing anything else not in keeping with the norm of a reverent brotherhood, which is written here, the council brothers shall forbid it, reprimand him, and not allow it.

[2] When someone wishes to leave work, it is proper that he first ask the blessing of the superior or of the major elder who has been assigned with this responsibility.[1]

The Divine Writings in the *Will and Testament*, Discourse VI, and in Discourse XIV, Penance 6, bear witness to this tradition.

1. Cf. above, Discourse VI.12.

Tradition VII, That it is not proper for drinks which cause drunkenness to be in the cloister. (XIII/vii)

[1] It is proper that the preeminent, and council brothers, who have received the direction of the monastery, take this responsibility together with the superior or in the absence of the superior, that drinks which cause drunkenness not be in the cloister.

[2] The canons of the holy Fathers and the *typica* of the great monasteries may indeed command monks to drink wine only at a given time, when it is proper, and not always, and sometimes three cups, sometimes two, and sometimes one.[1] Certainly, they had wine in all the monasteries, both among the first[2] and in the present ones, but they did not drink to drunkenness. As many noble men and monks who have been in Constantinople and on Holy Mount Athos and in other places there bear witness, not only monks, but also all Orthodox Christians hate and loathe drunkenness. They all have wine, but they flee from drunkenness as from a destructive disease. Such is the custom of that land. And the custom of the land is unwritten law.[3]

[3] Another law: if we have drinks which cause drunkenness, we cannot abstain, but we drink to drunkenness. What the holy Fathers command regarding one cup, two, or three, we do not wish to hear; nor do we know the measure of their cup. This, rather is our measure: when we are so drunk, often to the point of vomiting, that we do not recognize or remember who we are, then we stop drinking. Because of such a custom and pernicious routine and sinful habit, it is not proper for us to have drinks which cause drunkenness in the cloister, lest we fall into ultimate perdition and the pit of fornication, which occurs as a result of drunkenness.[4]

1. Cf. Nikon, *Pandekty* 57:485–89. (Pseudo-)Theodore, *Rule* (Ὑποτύπωσις) 29–30:109–11 (PG 99 1713C-1616C). (Pseudo-)Athanasius, *Rule* (Ὑποτύπωσις) 22–26:226 (Meyer, 137–39). *Tüpikon*, 41^{V}.

2. This is corrected as 'the first' (*pervykh*) from the text's 'unbelievers' (*nevernykh*), as the VMCh editors pointed out.

3. Cf. below, Discourse XIV.38.

4. For these two sections, cf. above, Discourse IX^{B}.4–5.

[4] It is proper that the council brothers also take this responsibility. If they see a drunken brother in the monastery or anywhere else; if they find out that someone has drinks; or if they see in the refectory drinks which cause drunkenness, they shall absolutely not keep quiet, but reprimand and forbid.

[5] Likewise, the brothers to whom the outbuildings have been assigned shall report to the superior or the cellarer if someone conveys beer, mead, or wine[5] to an outbuilding. They shall not be silent about this even if it is a prince or boyar who has brought it. They shall entreat him that it is not permitted to bring it into the monastery, and that no one is permitted to drink in an outbuilding. If it is an abbot or a monk, then tell him amicably that he is ordered to place the mead, beer, or wine in a shed, and lock it up. When he leaves, then give it back. If he does not wish to listen to an amicable argument, then reprimand him,[6] *for a praiseworthy war is better than peace which cuts us off from God!*[7] And nothing cuts us off from God like drunkenness.

The Divine Writings in the *Will and Testament*, Discourse VII, and Discourse XIV, Penance 7, bear witness to this tradition.

5. Iosif's separate *Prescript* concerning drinks also envisions the possibility of mead, hard liquors (*vino goriachee*), beer, honey kvass, and malt beer or some other such home brew (*braga*) being conveyed to a cell or a place of work: PIV 238.

6. Iosif's *Prescript* states instead: If the Sovereign or a bishop comes, then the elder shall state with the authority of the hegumen (*igumenskim slovom*), that one must send the drink back to his train and not keep it on the grounds; and if he does not obey, then inform the hegumen: PIV, 238.

7. Nikon, *Taktikon* 16:90, attributed to Gregory of Nazianzus.

Tradition VIII, That it is not proper for women to enter the monastery. (XIII/viii)

[1] It is proper that the preeminent and council brothers, who have received the direction of the monastery, take responsibility and watchfulness, together with the superior or in the absence of the superior, that no women ever enter the monastery.

[2] If there is some need for a woman to go into the church, she shall go at night. She shall first send a report to the superior or to the cellarer. They shall send to her two or three elders who are suited for this. They shall go with her and accompany her into the church. They shall also accompany her out of the church and out of the monastery. And they shall forbid her to walk past the cells or into the refectory. If it is necessary to feed her, they shall feed her at a outbuilding, never in the cells. And they shall dismiss her immediately and not detain her in the outbuilding even a short while.[1]

The Divine Writings in the *Will and Testament*, Discourse VIII, and in Discourse XIV, Penance 8, bear witness to this tradition.

1. Cf. above, Discourse XIII.8.

Tradition IX, That it is not proper for young boys to live in the monastery or in the monastery outbuildings. (XIII/ix)

[1] It is indeed proper that the preeminent and council brothers, who have received the direction of the monastery take this responsibility, together with the superior or in the absence of the superior: it is not proper to keep young boys in the monastery or in the monastery's outbuildings. Monasteries that are in desolate places do not have so great a need to be concerned about this. If, on the other hand, we who are situated in the midst of the whole world are not concerned about this, then in a short time not only the monastery, but also our cells will be filled with boys, and on account of this negligence we shall not avoid the pit of fornication which will dispatch us into the unquenchable fire. Therefore, if the council brothers see any boys walking in the monastery, in anyone's cell, in the refectory, or at the outbuildings, they shall reprimand, forbid, and not allow it.

[2] They shall give them alms and feed them outside the monastery.[1]

The Divine Writings, in the *Will and Testament*, Discourse IX, and Discourse XIV, Penance 9, bear witness to this tradition.

[3] It is also proper for the monk-bailiff not to live in the monastery's villages; rather he shall ride over to supervise.[2]

[4] Likewise, they shall not judge peasants in the monastery, but outside the monastery or in an outbuilding.[3]

[5] No one shall buy anything from anybody in the monastery, or sell anything to anybody.[4]

[6] No one shall keep his own private serving men or horses at an outbuilding.[5]

1. Cf. above, Discourse XII.9.
2. Cf. above, Discourse IX.12.
3. Cf. above, Discourse IX.II, Discourse XIII/v.12–13.
4. Cf. above, Discourse IX.7, Tradition V.9 (XIII.v.9).
5. Cf. above, Discourse IX.9.

[7] If they see someone who has rear doors, a large casement window or a special cellar in his cell, or if someone manages to plant apple trees, cherry trees, or any other kind of fruit in the courtyard by a cell, they shall forbid and not allow it.[6]

[8] Or if they see someone walking in the monastery without his mantle or cowl, or standing in the monastery at the wrong time, or someone laughing or quarreling; if they find out that someone has taken something belonging to the monastery or to a brother without a blessing, or has found something and not told the superior or the cellarer; or if they see someone saying or doing something not in keeping with the norms of a reverent brotherhood—in the monastery, outside the monastery, or at any place of work, wherever it may occur, they shall reprimand him, forbid, and not allow it.[7]

[9] The master of the horse shall be on guard at the servants' and children's quarters. If brothers begin to come there without a blessing, he shall reprimand and report them to the superior.

[10] Likewise at the buildings where the tailors live, the chief and assistant treasurers shall be on guard, lest brothers go there. The tailors shall come to the monastery only at one time, and they shall not go past the cells. If any sewing must take place inside somebody's cell, they shall dispatch a fellow adult, not a youth.

[11] The brother who brews kvass shall be on guard, lest it be issued to cells, unless the superior or cellarer order it issued.

[12] And the brother to whom the mills are assigned shall not permit any brothers to come there to eat and drink.

[13] And the brother to whom the villages are assigned shall take this responsibility: if he sees or hears of any brother going to the villages without a blessing, he shall report to the superior, *for a little negligence intercedes to effect a great calamity*.[8]

[14] Therefore it is proper that not only the superior, but also all the brothers, and especially the council and senior brothers, be responsible with all their might for the traditions and penances which are here written down. Accordingly, the superior and the

6. Cf. above, Discourse IX.13.
7. Cf. above, Discourse IX.10.
8. Cf. above, Discourse IX.13.

council brothers, together with the superior or in the absence of the superior, if they see anybody in the church, refectory, or monastery, or at any office, or outside the monastery, doing anything irregular or perverse and not in keeping with the tradition that is here written down, they shall report the disobedient to the superior or the council elders. If they all harmoniously strive to be responsible for reverence and good order, then we shall all quickly excel in the fear of God and love of our neighbor.[9]

[15] Lo, it is obvious and confirmed for everybody, that everything written down here derives from the Divine Writings, and is also in keeping with the sickness of this present, latest generation, so that no one may have pretext to say: 'This is the last epoch, men are weak, the commandments are heavy, and it is impossible to safeguard them'.[10]

[16] Lo, it is manifest to everybody that these strictures contain no burden or constraint. Rather one must only cut off a few little and unnecessary things: riches and possessions, superfluous objects, and eating and drinking in secret, for it was to laymen that the Apostle said: 'Having food and clothing, let us be content'.[11] Those who wish to be rich fall into temptations and the snares of the Evil One.[12] How much more proper is it for monks not to desire riches, but to be content with what is necessary

[17] And where is the constraint in our arriving for the beginning of the chant and standing in good order, reverence and silence in the church? Many laymen have carried this out.

[18] What calamity is there in not leaving the monastery without a blessing? Indeed, we have seen this guarded with precision in idiorrhythmic monasteries.

[19] Where is the constraint in doing everything with a blessing or asking the superior's forgiveness when one has transgressed? For the holy Fathers say: *On account of these words, all the Adversary's stratagems collapse.*[13]

9. Cf. above, Discourse XIII.6.
10. Cf. above, Introduction (Int.12).
11. 1 Tm 6:8. Cf. above, Discourse III.16.
12. Source not identified.
13. Cf. above, Discourse II.13.

[20] Or where is the affliction in not speaking after Compline? Does the whole day not suffice for speaking?

[21] Where is the constraint in being on time for the benediction in the refectory, not speaking to anybody, not giving anything to anybody, not taking anything from anybody, or in everybody's leaving together after the meal or the chanting? This is a cause of good order and reverence, and without reverence, no fear of God, attentiveness, and humble-mindedness can exist.

[22] Those who are heedless of the traditions shall receive a penance in keeping with the sacred canons, Basil the Great, and our holy Father Theodore the Studite.

It is proper that the superior and the preeminent council brothers also read through this. [Section XIII/A]

[1] Enough has been said about how it is proper for the council brothers, who have received the direction of the monastery, to be responsible for good order in the church and the monastery and among the monks. It is also necessary now to speak of how it is proper for them to handle the direction of the monastery, together with the superior or in the absence of the superior.

[2] When the superior is in the cloister, all the brothers shall come first to the superior, then to the cellarer, and then to the treasurer regarding all spiritual and external affairs. The cellarer and treasurer shall consult with the superior, and if it is an ordinary matter these three shall settle the matter with their subordinate officials. If it is one of those matters which require consultation with others, the superior shall summon the cellarer, treasurer, and council brothers, and they shall consult and speak about everything, and everybody together shall handle the whole affair of the monastery.

[3] If the superior is not in the cloister, then for spiritual matters all the brothers shall go to the priest whom the cellarer, treasurer, and council brothers have designated. For external matters, everybody shall go to the cellarer and treasurer. If it is an ordinary matter, then the cellarer and treasurer shall handle the matter with their subordinate officials. If the matter requires consultation with the council brothers, the cellarer shall summon the treasurer and all the council brothers to his cell, and they shall consult and speak about everything, and everybody together shall handle the monastery's business.

[4] If there happens to occur an affair that is proper to report to the whole brotherhood, then the superior shall order a brother to stand at the doors after Compline or after Matins and not permit anyone into the church or out of the church (and in winter, into the refectory or out of the refectory), and he himself shall stand facing the brothers and offer this prayer: 'By the prayers of Your Immaculate Mother and our reverend and God-bearing Fathers,

Lord Jesus Christ, our God, have mercy upon us'.[1] After the brothers say 'Amen', the superior shall talk about the necessary business calmly and serenely, while the brothers are all attentive, listen with humility and the fear of God, and talk one at a time. And do not speak out at once with howls and screams, for this is a sign of unruliness and disorder. When there is agreement on the matter at hand, the superior shall face the holy icons and say in a loud voice: 'It is worthy that in truth . . .'[2] to the end, and all the brothers shall say it with him. Then the superior shall say 'Glory be to the Father, and to the Son, and to the Holy Spirit, and now and always, forever and ever. Amen. Lord have mercy, Lord have mercy, bless us, Lord. Lord Jesus Christ, Son of God, for the sake of the prayers of Your Immaculate Mother and our reverend and God-bearing Fathers and all the saints, have mercy on us and save us, for you are kind and humane'. And having turned toward the brothers, he shall dismiss and bless them all. All the brothers shall bow to the superior, and everybody shall thus exit in silence and prayer.

[5] When there is an assembly in the cell of the hegumen or of the cellarer, and the brothers have congregated, they shall go, each one, into the cell to the holy icons or to the venerable cross and make three prostrations and then one prostration before the superior. Having obtained the blessing of the superior and the brotherhood, they shall sit quietly. When everybody so enjoined has entered, the superior or cellarer shall offer this prayer: 'By the prayers of our holy Fathers, Lord Jesus Christ, Our God, have mercy upon us'. The brothers shall say 'Amen', and then rising, they shall all say: 'It is worthy . . .' and make one prostration, and then 'Glory and now . . .' . Then the superior shall say, or when the superior is absent, the cellarer, shall say this verse: 'For the sake of the prayers of Your Immaculate Mother and our reverend and God-bearing holy Fathers and all the saints, Lord Jesus Christ, our God, have mercy upon us'. After the brothers have said 'Amen', the

1. For some of the prayer formulas here, see above, Ch. 2, THE SERVICE TYPICON (penultimate paragraph).

2. For this one, see also, above, Ch. 2., ASPECTS OF ICONOGRAPHY.

superior shall speak first, or if the superior is absent, the cellarer shall speak. He shall speak calmly and gently, with fear of God and attentiveness. When someone is speaking, the others shall be silent. When that one is silent, then a second one shall speak. And thus they all shall speak one by one, reverently, pleasantly, meekly, and not with a clamor. If it proceeds in this manner, then in truth Christ will be among us, for he himself says: 'Wherever two or three are gathered in my name, I am there among them';[3] and 'I shall look', he says, 'to the man who is poor and of a contrite spirit, and who trembles at my words'.[4]

[6] Indeed we have seen this done by the great sovereigns and autocrats. When they are prosecuting a matter, they speak with good order and not with screams: first the sovereign speaks, and then all the attendants speak, one by one. If many begin to speak, they get a punishment delivered in anger by the ruler.[5]

[7] Similarly, what we saw in a certain land was wondrous, filled with complete reverence and good order, and done not by monks but by laymen. When they assemble in a tavern to drink, they sit in good order and meekly. First one speaks; then a second gets the floor from the first and speaks; and then a third gets the floor from the second and speaks. Thus they all speak gently, calmly, and in order. If anyone begins to quarrel, use filthy words or abuse someone else, they harmoniously reproach or beat him and throw him out.

[8] If laymen are responsible with respect to reverence and good order, then what answer shall we give, we who read through the Divine Writings, are versed in the *Lives* of the holy Fathers, and still are not even like laymen who have reverence and good order? For God says in the Law: 'Be reverent, children of Israel'.[6] God does not accept prayers, fasting, or mortification without reverence, good order, and humble-mindedness. Rather, he torments those who do not act in this way. Let us all, then, endeavor and struggle

3. Mt 18:10.
4. Is 66:2. Cf. above, Discourse I^{B}.19, Discourse I.14.
5. See above, Ch. 2, THE SERVICE TYPICON (concluding paragraph).
6. Cf. Ex 31:16.

with all of our might over these, so that in the present age and in the future, we can face the merciful and meek Lord Christ, to whom is the glory along with the eternal Father and the Holy Spirit, now and always and forever and ever. Amen.

On how it is proper for the council and senior brothers, together with the superior or in the absence of the superior, to administer penances to those who are heedless of the cœnobitic traditions which are here written down from the *Asecticon* of Basil the Great and from the *Typicon* of Saint Theodore the Studite.[1]

Discourse XIV

[1] It is proper that the superior and the council brothers look into this diligently. If a brother wants to take care of himself and unwillingly transgresses the traditions in some way, the superior should inquire and look into this and forgive him without a penance.

[2] If he negligently does this not once but twice and is disobedient, then he is to be administered the penance which the superior and the senior brothers, together with the superior or in the absence of the superior determine: either impose xerophagia on him, that is, eating only bread and water, for as many days as commanded; or banish him from the church or from the refectory[2]—banishment from the church means not partaking of any sacred activity and banishment from the refectory means xerophagia in the refectory or the cell for as many days as commanded; or shackle him in iron fetters; or expel him from the monastery. For it is said in the Holy Ladder: *It is better to drive someone from the monastery than to allow him to perform his own will.*[3] His own will means unruliness and disobedience, which is the origin and consummation of all evil.

[3] Let us flee from all these and walk by a straight life in the steps of our holy Fathers, with the prayers of the glorious Mother of God and all the saints. Amen.

1. The ultimate sources for the penances are the *Poenae* (Ἐπιτιμίαι) attributed to Basil the Great (B) and Theodore the Studite (ThSt): PG 31:1305–14; PG 99:1733–58. On their authenticity, see above, Ch 2, Iosif's Sources. Cf. also Neilos of Tamasia, *Rule* 121–34:1157–58. Neophytos of Cyprus, *Testmentary Rule* CB:1367–68. Theodora/Theodule Synadene, *Typikon* X.65:1542–43.

2. Cf. Pseudo-Basil, *Ascetical Discourse* 214: PG 31:880AB.

3. Climacus, Liber 14; PG 88:1200B. See above, Discourse X.42.

Penance N° 1. On good order in the church and the community prayer.

[4] If someone is not on time for the beginning of any chant, then he should beg forgiveness from the hegumen. If he does not beg forgiveness, then he shall not partake of the Holy Gifts, communion bread, or the Panaghia[4] until he is forgiven by the superior.If he did not hear the bell, then forgive him, and he shall explain in his cell what came to pass; but if he heard the bell, and carelessly did not try, he shall explain what came to pass; and also impose fifty prostrations or xerophagia for a day.[5] And if someone does not arrive on account of sickness or a monastery office, then forgive him without a penance.

[5] If someone moves from his place to another place, he shall make fifty prostrations or observe xerophagia for a day.

[6] If someone begins to leave the chanting in the church or in the refectory, he shall make one hundred prostrations or observe xerophagia for a day. If someone begins to leave the chanting before dismissal, he shall make one hundred prostrations or observe xerophagia for a day.[6]

[7] If someone converses at the chanting or laughs, he shall make one hundred prostrations or observe xerophagia for a day. And if someone does this more than once, he shall be banished for three days.

[8] If someone begins to hang back in the refectory or in the church after chanting for the sake of conversation, or if one of the choir begins to stand carelessly in the choir aisle, he shall make fifty prostrations or observe xerophagia for a day.

Penance N° 2. On reverence and good order in the refectory and on food and drink.

[9] If someone is not on time for the benediction at the refectory,[7]

4. See above, Ch. 2, The Service Typicon, and note 89.
5. ThSt 1.1–9, 2.33
6. Cf. B 42, ThSt 2.16–17. 5 B 34, Th 12.
7. Cf. Pachomius, *Precepts* 2. Timothy of Evergetis, *Typik* 9:478. Archbishop Sava, *Tipik* 9:52.

converses at the table, or laughs;[8] if someone eats before dinner;[9] if someone goes into the refectory or out of the refectory by the pantry doors, sits at another's place,[10] or takes something from in front of a brother and gives something to a brother, he shall make fifty prostrations or observe xerophagia for a day.

[10] If someone takes a vessel or food from the refectory without a blessing, or brings his own food, drink, or vessel to the refectory,[11] or if someone goes to the last table, he shall make one hundred prostrations or observe xerophagia for a day.

[11] If someone remains behind after the meal or creeps into the pantry,[12] or if someone goes into the refectory before dinner, after dinner, or after Vespers without need and a blessing, he shall make fifty prostrations and observe xerophagia for a day.

[12] If someone eats or drinks in the cell or outside his cell without a blessing, or if someone sends food or drink to the cells, he shall not partake of the Holy Gifts, the communion bread, or the Panaghia until he receives forgiveness; and after he is forgiven, he shall make one hundred prostrations. If he has been exposed, the penance is three hundred prostrations or observe xerophagia for three days.[13] If he does this often and does not desist, expel him from the cloister.

Penance N° 3. Concerning garments, footwear, and other things.

[13] If someone does not want to have the quality and quantity of garments, footwear, and other things as it is written in the *Will and Testament*, Discourse III, and if he desires to keep more than that, then do not issue him anything from the monastery storeroom, but let him have his own garments and footwear.[14]

8. B 28, ThSt 2.37.
9. Cf. ThSt 2.55.
10. ThSt 2.35.
11. B 17.
12. B 52.
13. ThSt 2.27.
14. ThSt 2.20.

[14] If someone sells, gives away, or exchanges something which has been issued to him from the monastery storeroom, he shall make one hundred prostrations or observe xerophagia for a day. If he does this often, then banish him from the church and from the refectory for a week.[15]

[15] If someone takes anything in the refectory, in the monastery, outside the monastery, or at any office without the superior's or the cellarer's blessing;[16] if someone finds something somewhere and does not report to the superior; if someone takes anything in the church—a book, a candle, or any other thing, without the sacristan's blessing; or if someone inscribes something in a book without the blessing of the superior and of the choirmaster, he shall not partake of the Holy Gifts, or any other sacred activity until he is forgiven by the superior.

[16] If someone takes something and is exposed by others; xerophagia for five days.[17] If he does this often, he shall be banished from the brotherhood or bound in iron fetters.

Penance N° 4. That it is not proper to converse after Compline.

[17] If someone converses after Compline, stands or sits in the monastery or wanders over to the cells, he shall make one hundred prostrations or observe xerophagia for a day.[18]

Penance N° 5. That it is not proper for monks to go outside the monastery without a blessing.

[18] If someone goes outside the monastery without a blessing, he shall not partake of the Holy Gifts, the communion bread, or Panaghia until he is forgiven by the superior; the penance is xerophagia for a day.[19]

15. B 25, ThSt 2.23,25,40.
16. Cf. ThSt 1.45
17. ThSt 1.22
18. B 44, ThSt 1.20, 2.5,24,28.
19. B 12,47,48. ThSt 2.19.

[19] If someone goes to the monastery's outbuildings without a blessing, or if one of the brothers starts to escort guests to the monastery or without being authorized, goes out to meet them, the penance is xerophagia for two days.

[20] If someone goes into the world, the penance is xerophagia for four days. If he does this often, he shall be expelled from the cloister.

[21] If someone begins to stand or sit in the monastery or in front of the cells without being authorized, he shall observe xerophagia for a day.

[22] If a youth goes to the cell of another youth without a blessing, he shall observe xerophagia for three days. If he does not desist, he shall be bound in iron fetters.

Penance N° 6. On community work and community offices.

[23] If the superior or the cellarer commands someone to attend to some work and he does not go, except for sickness and urgent needs; or if someone is unable to attend to community work and does not report to the superior or to the one who has called him to work; because troubles arise from this, he shall make one hundred prostrations and observe xerophagia for a day.[20]

[24] If someone jokes or makes idle chatter at work or comes after the brothers or leaves before the brothers without having received a blessing, and if he does this once,[21] he shall make one hundred prostrations or observe xerophagia for a day. And if he does this more than once, he shall be banished from the church and from the refectory for three days.[22]

Penance N° 7. That it is not proper for drinks which result in drunkenness to be in the cloister.

[25] If any brother is exposed for being drunk, he shall make one hundred prostrations or observe xerophagia for a day.[23]

20. Cf. B 18–19. ThSt 1. 18, 2.25.

21. The text reads: more than once (*ne edinoiu*): a scribal error with the additional *ne*.

22. ThSt 1.21.

23. ThSt 2.48.

[26] If they seize drinks in somebody's cell, or if someone has left the monastery to drink, he shall be banished from the church and from the refectory for forty days, and he shall be deprived of his cell in the future. If he does this often, he shall be expelled from the cloister or bound in fetters.[24]

Penance N° 8. That it is not proper for a woman to enter the monastery.

[27] If any of the brothers wants a woman to enter the monastery, he should read the witness from the Divine Writings in the *Will and Testament*, and he will recognize what perdition results from this. If he does not submit, he shall be expelled from the cloister.

[28] If a woman comes at night to pray in the church, and if any of the brothers meets or escorts her without the authorization of the superior, he shall observe xerophagia for two days.

[29] If someone takes a woman to the refectory or to a cell, he shall be banished from the church and from the refectory for one week.

Penance N° 9. That it is not proper for young boys to live in the monastery or in the monastery's outbuildings.

[30] If someone permits children in a cell and gives them alms in the monastery or in a cell, he shall observe xerophagia for four days. If he does this more than once, he shall be banished from the cloister.

[31] If someone walks in the monastery without his mantle and without his cowl, he shall make one hundred prostrations.[25]

[32] If someone heats a cell while not there,[26] he shall observe xerophagia for three days.

[33] If someone fixes up back gates or a big window, he shall observe xerophagia for three days.

[34] If someone finds out and does not report to the superior or the cellarer that a brother has left the monastery without a

24. Iosif's *Prescript* stipulates only expulsion: PIV, 238.

25. B 18, ThSt 2.4.

26. Cf. Pachomius, *Precepts* 120.

blessing or plans to do or has done another improper thing, he shall not partake of any sacred thing until he is forgiven,[27] for Basil the Great calls such a person *a fratricide*.[28] If he does this once, impose xerophagia for a week, and he shall not taste any consecrated thing.[29] If more than once, then drive him from the cloister.

[35] All the monastery officials in all offices, especially the major ones, shall observe and be responsible, so that if one of them begins to make idle chatter, jokes, or strife, or if a monk or layman who loves inactivity comes to them,[30] they shall forbid, reprimand, and report him to the superior or the council brothers.

[36] If someone has received a penance and transgresses one of the traditions again, then impose a penance upon him again. If he begins often to transgress, then impose a penance often. If someone begins to be so indecent as always to neglect the cœnobitic traditions, then impose the heaviest penances upon him or expel him from the cloister.

[37] The penances written here are only for those who are heedless of the cœnobitic traditions which are here written. For other transgressions, large or small, penances and absolution are to be administered only as the sacred canons command, so that everything may proceed according to the witness of the Divine Writings.[31]

[38] And everything which is here written, from the beginning down to the end, is in accord with the witness of the Divine Writings. I have only altered a few forms and words according to the customs of this land. For we have seen in the Writings that the unwritten custom of a land is law.[32] Note that unless it be a cause of sin, the custom of the land means an unwritten law, neither

27. ThSt 1.35

28. *Longer Rules* 46: PG 31:1036AB: see above, Discourse XIII.28.

29. Iosif's *Prescript* cites Basil in stipulating that one who does not confess his drinking be 'without blessing': PIV 238.

30. See above, Discourse VI^{B}.22, Discourse VI.15.

31. See above, Discourse XIII.47–48.

32. As in Discourse IX^{B}.9. Iosif or the redactor claims to have adduced supporting authorities earlier in the text, but in fact has not done so; see above as well, Tradition VII.2 (XIII/vii.2).

concerning faith—that one might believe a creed according to the custom of each land—nor concerning the acts which men might perform according to the custom of each land. Rather it means the unwritten law of the land and the custom because each land has a great and immeasurable difference and composition in comparison to other countries. This means that some countries are very cold, and others are very warm; some are poverty-stricken, and others are very fertile. Therefore there is no agreement regarding garments and footwear and food and drink.

[39] Basil the Great speaks similarly concerning this: *It is proper to have food and drink and clothing and foot wear in keeping with the custom of the land where one lives. These are not the cause of sin if we select only the purest foods, everywhere cut off the superfluous and unnecessary, and are satisfied with the necessary.*[33]

33. Cf. *Longer Rules* 19:276–77; PG 31:969B.

Appendix I

AN ACCOUNT WITH WITNESS FROM THE DIVINE WRITINGS ON THE SALVIFIC AND SOUL-PROFITING BOOKS, OF THE *SYNODICON* AND THE DAILY COMMEMORATION, ON HOW IT IS PROPER FOR US TO TAKE RESPONSIBILITY FOR THEM AND WHAT PROFIT RESULTS FROM THESE FOR SOULS LIVING AND DEAD.

[1] *All Scripture is divinely-inspired and soul-profiting*,[1] says Basil the Great. On this account they have been inspired by the Holy Spirit, so that men would try to find cures for body and soul, each for his own passion, from the Divine Writings. Similarly, we try to find cures for body and soul from the *Synodicon* and from the Daily Commemoration.

[2] Indeed these salvific books are the most profitable of all the Divine Writings. All the Divine Writings profit the living, give instruction in virtue, and lay down the law for the observance of the Divine Commandments. (And if someone disregards the Divine Commandments, he awaits torments after death.) These salvific and soul-profiting books also profit dead souls after death.

[3] This is because the human race is not easily led to virtue because sinful pleasures disturb us, who are indifferent to the correct life, and because the contemplation of wickedness assiduously tempts man from the time of his youth. Therefore, it was commanded to the Holy Apostles and reverend and God-bearing Fathers, our pastors and teachers, to write these salvific and soul-profiting books and to give them to the divine and holy church for the succor, relief, and comfort of the dead souls.

[4] All the Divine Writings speak of and teach what is profitable for the soul, but hardly bother with physical tranquility. On account

1. Source not identified.

of these soul-profiting and salvific books, we shall be delivered from eternal torments and shall be deemed worthy of eternal blessings in the future age. And in the present age on account of these books, there result the foundation of monasteries, the construction of divine churches, the placing in them of all the divine objects, with the all venerable icons, life-creating crosses, divine gospels, sanctified vessels, holy vestments and all the church objects that are made from gold, silver, pearls, and holy books. And from these result all the provisions for the church and physical tranquility for the priests, deacons, all the church servers and all the brothers: food and drink, garments and boots, the construction of cells, sufficiency in all necessary cell objects, and villages, vineyards, rivers, lakes, fields, and all livestock and cattle.

[5] If, then, we obtain from these salvific and soul-profiting books all the blessings in the present and future age, then it is proper for the superior and all the brothers to take responsibility with great zeal, so that on every day the divine Liturgy be celebrated in the holy church, except for those days when it is not so commanded to celebrate Liturgy. Always on Mondays and Wednesdays a requiem shall be sung and on Friday evening a Great Requiem. After Matins and after Vespers, the *Litany for the Deceased* shall be sung. The hebdomadaries and deacons and also the reader of the *Synodicon* shall take responsibility with great precision that the *Synodicon* and the Daily Commemoration be read as it is commanded and written.

[6] If we treasure this, brothers, and we thus read the divine and salvific books, then in truth our soul shall behold in itself the light of Christ and shall not darken in eternity because we shall wholeheartedly have been responsible for ourselves and our neighbors: 'He who loves his neighbor loves God'.[2] If we do not treasure them, we shall be as if we love neither God nor our neighbor, and we shall similarly be indifferent toward our soul and negligent of our salvation. And 'cursed is he who does the work of the Lord negligently'.[3] Carelessness results from laziness and wickedness, and the Lord says of the lazy and wicked servant:

2. 1 Jn 4:20–21.
3. Jer 48:10.

'Cast him into the outer darkness; there shall be lamentation and the gnashing of the teeth'.[4] We shall suffer similarly if we disdain these holy soul-profiting books through laziness and carelessness and do not read them as they are written.

[7] As no one is without sin and no one is pure from filth, we all have sinned and require help from the divine and sanctified offices, it is said, from the blood of our Lord, Jesus Christ, and from these salvific and soul-profiting books. Those who before their death are themselves sacrifices to God do not require succor from holy sacrifices and these salvific and soul-profiting books, as Gregory, Pope of Rome, says: *How can one be a sacrifice to God before death? Looking into the future, we must hate with every thought the present world as terminating and every day with tears make a sacrifice to God of a pure and undefiled conscience, of his flesh and blood. This sacrifice alone delivers the soul from eternal torments*.[5]

[8] But as we have now grown weak and we do not achieve the measure of being ourselves a sacrifice to God before death, it is difficult for anyone to pertain to the 'first lot'. What is the 'first lot'? Ourselves to be a sacrifice to God before death. But because we cannot ourselves be a sacrifice to God before death, let us introduce the second: that is, that we must have complete zeal and responsibility so that we aid ourselves and each other after death with a holy and divine sacrifice and the blood of the Master, Christ, and with these salvific and soul profiting books. Let him who would contemplate exactly what profit results from these to souls living and dead, labor in the profundity of the Divine Writings and contemplate their profit.[6]

4. Mt 25:30.
5. *Dialogues* 4:57–61 (esp. 60); PL 67:415–28 (FCh 39:266–74).
6. A long string of citations follows: *Sinodik*, 44^{v}-66.

Appendix II

Index of Biblical Citations and References

Old Testament and Apocrypha

New Testament

Mt 20:16	XIII.2
Mt 21:12	I^{B}.24
Mt 21:13	I^{B}.24, V^{B}.6
Mt 22:14	XIII.2
Mt 25:21	XI.2, XIII.3
Mt 25:26	I^{B}.9, Int.11, I.9, XIII.55
Mt 25:27	X.8
Mt 25:30	III.34, XIII.55, App I.6
Mt 25:35	VIII^{B}.26, VI.42
Mt 26:14–15, 47–49, 27:3–5	VIII^{B}.27, VI.40
Mk 8:34	V^{B}.7
Mk 10:44	VI.43
Mk 10:45	III.18
Lk 3:11	III.24
Lk 9:58	III.18
Lk 10:16	XI.2
Lk 12:20	IB^{B}.15, III.17
Lk 14:33	V^{B}.7
Lk 21:34	IX^{B}.1, VII.1
Lk 22:27	III.18
Lk 22:27–28	IV.43
Lk 22:44	Int.13
Lk 24:12	I^{B}.2, I.2
Jn 1:4	V^{B}.10
Jn 5:14	VI.38
Jn 6:30	III.20
Jn 6:38	III.18
Jn 12:26	III.24, VIII^{B}.27, VI.40, XI.2
Jn 12:49	III.20
Jn 13:4–5,14–15	III.18
Jn 13:15	VI.43
Jn 14:18	X.44
Jn 15:19	XI.2
Jn 17:24	XIII.5
Jn 20:3–4	I^{B}.2, I.2
Acts 5:1–11	II.21, III.33
Rom 13:1–2	XI.13

Bibliography

Abramovych, Dmytro, ed. *Kyevo-Pechers'kyj Pateryk* (The Pechersky Patericon). Kiev: 1930. rpt. D. Chyzhevskii. Slavische Propyläen 2. Munich: Eidos, 1954.

Acta Sanctorum (The Deeds of the Saints). 71 vols. Paris: V. Palme, 1863–1940.

Akty feodal'nogo zemlevladeniia i khoziaistva XIV-XVI vekov (Acts of Seigniorial Landholding and Economy from the 14th-16th Centuries) 3 vols. Ed. L.V. Cherepnin and A.A. Zimin. Moscow: Nauka, 1951–1961.

Akty istoricheskie, sobrannye i izdannye Arkheograficheskoiu kommissieiu (Historical Acts, Collected and Published by the Archeographic Commission). 5 vols. St Petersburg: 1841–42.

Akty sotsial'no-ekonomicheskoi istorii Severo-Vostochnoi Rusi kontsa XIV-nachala XVI v. (Acts from the Social-Economic History of North-east Rus, from the end of the 14th to the Beginning of the 16th c.) 3 vols. Moscow: Nauka, 1952–64.

Amand de Mendieta, Emmauel. *L'ascèse monastique de saint Basile. Essai historique.* Maredesous (Belgium): Éditions de Maredesous, 1948.

Ἀνδρῶν ἁγίων βίβλος. PL 73:852–1022. Trans. W.O. Chadwick ('The Sayings of the Fathers'). *Western Asceticism.* Philadephia: Westminster: 1958, 37–189.

Ankhimiuk, Iu.V. 'Slovo na "Spisanie Iosifa"–pamiatnik rannego nestiazhatel'stva' (Discourse Against "Iosif's Treatise"—A Monument from the Early Non-Possessor Movement). *Zapiski ORGBL*, 1990: 115–46.

Ante-Nicene Fathers. The Translations of the Writings of the Fathers down to A.D. 325. 10 vols. ed. Alexander Roberts and James Donaldson. Edinborough: T. and T. Clarke: 1868–94; rpt. Buffalo: Christian Literature, 1885–97; rpt. Grand Rapids: Eerdmans, 1969–73.

Antiochus Monachus *Pandectes scripturae* (Pandects of Scripture). PG 89:1420–1850 (ORT: VMCh, Dec., 1864–2172).

The Aprocrypha and Pseudepigrapha of the Old Testament in English. ed. R.H, Scott. 2 vols. Oxford: Clarendon, 1913.

Arkhangel'sky, A.S. *Nil Sorskii i Vassian Patrikeev. Ch. 1. Prepodbnyi Nil Sorskii* (Nil Sorsky and Vassian Patrikeev. Part 1. Saint Nil Sorsky). Pamiatniki drevnei pis'mennosti (Monuments of Ancient Writings) 25. St Petersburg: I. Voshchinsky: 1882; rpt. Russian Reprint Series 20. The Hague: European Printing, 1966.

———. *Tvoreniia ottsov tserkvi v drevne-russkoi pis'mennosti* (The Works of the Church Fathers in Old Russian Literary Texts) 3. Kazan: 1880.

Athanasios (Athanasius) I, Patriarch. *Rule* (1303–05). Trans. Timothy Miller first publication ever. BMFD, 1500–04.

Athanasios the Meteorite. *Canonical Rule* for the Monastery of the Transfiguration (1350–83). Trans. George Dennis. BMFD, 1459–61.

Pseudo-Athanasius of Alexandria. *Vita et gesta Sanctae beataeque magistrae Syncleticae* (Life and Deeds of the Blessed Saint, Lady Syncletica). PG 28:1487–1558.

Athanasius/Pseudo-Athanasius of Athos. Διατύπωσις τοῦ ὁσίου καὶ μακαρίου πατρὸς ἡμῶν Ἀθανάσιου(*Testament/Diatyposis* [Rule] of our Holy and Blessed Father Athanasius [after 984 or 993]). ed. Meyer, 123–130. Trans. George Dennis. BMFD, 274–280.

———. Τυπικόν ἤτοι κανονικὸν τοῦ ὁσίου καὶ θεοφόρου πατρὸς ἡμῶν Ἀθανάσιου τοῦ ἐν τῷ Ἄθῳ (*Typicon* or Canon Book of our Holy and God-Bearing Father Athanasius of Athos [974–75]). ed. Meyer, 102–22. Trans. George Dennis. BMFD, 250–270.

———. Ὑποτύπωσις καταστάσεως τοῦ ὁσίου Ἀθανάσιου (*Rule/Hypotyposis* [Outline] of the Institutes of Saint Athanasius [?963, rev. 1020]), ed. Meyer, 130–140. Trans. George Dennis. BMFD, 221–231.

Baar, A.N. van den. *A Russian Church Slavonic Kanonnik (1331–1332).* SPR 89. Paris-Hague: Mouton, 1968.

Baldin, V.I. 'Arkhitektura Troitskogo sobora Troitse-Sergievoi Lavry' (The Architecture of the Trinity Sobor of the Troitse-Sergiev Laura). AN 6 (1956), 21–50.

Baldin, V.I. and Iu.N. Gerasimov, 'Dukhovskaia Tserkov' Troitse Sergieva Monastyria' (The Troitse-Sergiev Monastery, Dukhov Church). AN 19 (1972), 53–65.

Barskov, Ia.L. *Pamiatniki pervykh let russkogo staroobriadstva* (Monuments from the First Years of the Russian Old Believers). St Petersburg: 1912.

Barsukov, N.P. *Istochniki russkoi agiografii* (Sources of Russian Hagiography). St Petersburg: M.M. Stasiulevich, 1882; rpt. Leipzig: Zentralantiquariat, 1970.

Basil of Caesarea (Basil The Great). *The Ascetic Works of Saint Basil.* Trans. and introd., W.K.L. Clarke. London, etc.: MacMillan, 1925.

———. *Longer Rules (Regulae fusius tractatae).* Wagner, 223–338 (PG 31:889–1052).

———. *Shorter Rules (Regulae brevius tractatae).* Clarke, 229–351 (PG 31:1051–1306).

———. *St Basil. Ascetical Works.* Trans. Sister Mary Monica Wagner. FC 9.

Pseudo-Basil of Caesarea. *An Ascetical Discourse and Exhortation on the Renunciation of the World and Spiritual Perfection.* (Sermo asceticus et exhortatio de renunciations saeculi, et de perfectioni spirituali). FC 9:15–31 (PG 31:625–48).

———. *(Another) Ascetical Discourse*: *Ascetical Discourse* (Sermo asceticus). Clarke, 141–44 (Wagner, 207–15). (PG 31: 869–82).

———. *Constitutiones asceticae* (Ascetical Constitutions). PG 31: 1315–1428.

———. *Introduction to Longer Rules*. Wagner, 223–31. (PG 31: 889–902).

———. *Poenae* (Penances). PG 31:1305–14.

Bauer, Walter F. *A Greek-English Dictionary of the New Testament and Other Early Christian Literature*. Trans. William F. Arndt and F. Wilbur Gingrich. Chicago and London: Univ. of Chicago. 1971

Beck, Hans-Georg. *Kirche und theologische Literatur im Byzantinischen Reich.* Munich: C.H. Beck, 1959.

Begunov, Iu.K. ' "Slovo inoe"—novonaidennoe proizvedenie russkoi publitsistiki XVI v. o bor'be Ivana III s zemelevladeniem tserkvi" ('Another Discourse'—A Recently Discovered Work of Russian Public Controversy from the Sixteenth Century concerning Ivan III's Struggle with Church Landholding). TODRL 20 (1964), 351–64.

Beliaev, N.M. *Ikon Bozhei Materi Umileniia, iz sobraniia Soldatenkovykh* (The Icon of the Compunction of the Mother of God, from the Soldatenkov Collection). Prague: Kondakov Institute, 1932.

Beliakova, E.V. 'Ustav pustyna Nila Sorskogo' (The Rule of Nil Sorsky's Hermitage). *Literatura drevnei Rusi. Istochnikovedenie*. pp. 96–106.

Belokurov, S.A. ed. *Zhitie prep. Iosifa Volokolamskogo sostavlennoe neizvestnym* (The Anonymous Life of St Iosif Volotsky). ChOIDR 1903, 2, 1–46.

Belovdova, T.N. 'Rannaia redaktsiia Zhitii prepodobnogo Dmitriia Prilutskogo, vologdskogo chudotvortsa' (The Early Redaction of the Life of Dmitrii Prilutsky, the Volodga Wonder-Worker). TODRL 45 (1992), 249–58.

Bernstein, Alan E., The Formation of Hell. *Death and Retribution in the Ancient and Early Christian Worlds*. Ithaca/London: Cornell, 1993.

Bezglova, I.F. ' "Dostoino est" Opekalovskogo rospeva' (The 'It is worthy' of the Opekalovsky Score), TODRL 36 (1981), 308–19.

Bezobrazov, M. 'Zametka o "Dioptre" ' (Note on *Dioptra*). ZhMNP 11–12, 1893, 27–47.

Billington, James H. *The Icon and the Axe: An Interpretive History of Russian Culture*. New York: Knopf, 1966; Vintage, 1970.

Birkfellner, Gerhard. *Das römische Paterikon. Studien zur serbischen, bulgarischen, und russischen Überliefungen der Dialoge Gregors des Grossen mit seiner Textedition.* 2 vols. Vienna: Akad. Wiss., 1979.

Borisov, N.E. *Tserkovnye deiateli srednevekovi Rusi XII-XVII vv*. (Medieval Rus Churchmen, 12th-17th Centuries). Moscow: University, 1988.

Borzakovsky, V.S. *Istoriia Tverskago kniazhestva* (A History of the Principality of Tver). St Petersburg: I.G. Martynov, 1876. rpt. Hague: Mouton, 1969.

Brumfield, William Craft. *A History of Russian Architecture.* Cambridge, Eng.: University, 1993.

Bryer, A.A.M. 'The Late Byzantine Monastery in Town and Countryside'. *Studies in Church History* 16 (1979), 219–41.

Budge, E.A. Wallis, trans. and ed. *The Histories and Sayings of the Monks and Ascetics of the Egyptian Desert by Palladius, Hieronymus and Others. The Syriac Texts according to the Recension of 'Anan-Isho of Beth 'Abhe*. 2 vols. London/Leipzig: W. Durgulin, 1904.

Budovnits, I.U. *Monastyri na Rusi i bor'ba s nim krestian v XIV-XVI vekakh* (Monasteries in Rus and the Peasantry's Struggle against them in the 14th-16th Centuries) Moscow: Nauka, 1966.

———. *Russkaia publitsistika XVI veka* (Russian Public Controversy in the 16th Century). Moscow-Leningrad: ANSSSR, 1947.

Buganov, V.I., ed. *Razriadnaia kniga, 1475–1598 gg.* (The Muster Book for 1475–1598). Moscow: Nauka, 1966.

Bulanin, D.M. ' "Paranesis" Efrema Sirina'. *Slovar' knizhnikov*. 1:296–99.

Bulgakov, N.A. *Prepodobnyi Iosif Volotskii* (St Iosif Volotsky) St Petersburg: 1865.

Bushkovitch, Paul. *Religion and Society in Rusia, The Sixteenth and Seventeenth Centuries*. New York: Oxford, 1992.

Butler, Dom Cuthbert, SJ. *The Lausaic History of Palladius. A Critical Discussion with Notes on Early Egyptian Monasticism.* Texts and Studies 6. Cambridge, England: University, 1898.

Bychkova, M.E. *Sostav klassa feodalov Rossii v XVI v. Istoriko-geneologicheskoe issledovanie* (The Composition of Russia's Class of Feudal Lords in the 16th Century. Historical-Geneological Study). Moscow: Nauka, 1986.

Byzantine Monastic Foundation Documents. A Complete Translation of the Surviving Founder's Typika *and Testaments*. Ed. John Thomas and Angela Constantinides Hero, asst. by Giles Constable. Washington, D.C.: Dumbarton Oaks, 1999 (http:/doaks.org/typ000.html, to be printed).

Cameron, Averil, *Christianity and the Rhetoric of Empire*. Satner Classical Studies 55. Berkeley et al.: University of California, 1991.

Casey, R. P. 'Early Russian Monasticism'. *Orientalia Christiana periodica* 19 (1953), 372–423.

Cheremeteff, Maria. *The Transformation of the Russian Sanctuary Barrier and the Role of Theophanes the Greek*. Ph.D. Diss. Chicago: 1987.

Chteniia v Imperatorskom Obschchestve istorii i drevnostei rossiiskikh (Lectures at the Imperial Society for Russian History and Antiquities).

Moscow: Moscow University, 1846–.

Cherniavsky, Michael. 'The Old Believers and the New Religion'. *Slavic Review* 25 (1966), 1–39.

Chernov, S.Z. *Volok Lamskii v XIV – pervoi poloviny XVI v. Struktury zemlevladeniia i formirovanie voenno-sluzhiloi korporatsii* (Volokolamsk in the 14th-First Half of the 16th c. Structures of Landholding and the Formation of the Military Service Corporation). *Akty Moskovskoi Rusi. Mikroregional'nye issledovaniia* (Acts of Muscovite Rus. Micro-Regional Studies). Vol 1. Moscow: Institute of Archeology, 1998.

Chertoritskaia, T.V., 'Cheti sborniki v sostave Veliki Minei chet'ykh' (Codices of Readings within the Great Menology of Readings). TODRL 46 (1993), 98–108.

Chyzhevskii (Tschizevskij), Dmytro. *History of Russian Literature from the Eleventh Century to the End of the Baroque*. SPR 12. The Hague: Mouton, 1960.

Clark, Francis, *The Pseudo-Gregorian Dialogues*, 2 vols., Leiden: E.J. Brill, 1987.

Pseudo-Clement, Pope of Rome. *The Clementine Homilies.* Ante-Nicene Fathers 8:223–346 (PG 2:57–468).

Collins, Daniel E., 'Early Russian Topoi of Deathbed and Testament'. *Medieval Russian Culture*, vol. 2. ed. Michael S. Flier and Daniel Rowland. Berkeley, Los Angeles, London: University of California, 1994, 134–59.

Cotelier, J.B., ed. *Sanctorum senum apophthegmata* (The Sayings of the Holy Elders). *Ecclesiae graecae monumenta* (Monuments of the Greek Church) 1. Paris, 1677, 340–712.

Councils: see Percival.

Crummey, Robert O. *The Formation of Muscovy*. London: Longman, 1987.

———. *The Old Believers and the World of Anti-Christ. The Vyg Community and the Russian State, 1694–1855.* Madison: University of Wisconsin, 1970.

Cyril of Scythopolis, *Kyrillos von Skythopolis*. Ed. Eduard Schwartz. Texte und Untersuchungen zur Geschichte der altchristlichen Literatur 4.2. Leipzig: Hinrichs, 1939.

———. *Zhitie sv. Savy Osviashchennogo sv. Kirillom Skifopol'skim v drevnerusskim perevode po rukopisi Imperatorskogo Obshchestva li-*

ubitelei drevnei pis'mennosti s prisoedineniem grecheskogo podlinnika i vvedeniem (The Life of Sabbas the Sanctified Composed by Cyril of Scythopolis, in the Old Russian Translation, according to a manuscript of the Imperial Society of Devotees of Ancient Literature, with the Addition of the Greek Original and an Introduction). ed. I. Pomialovsky. St Petersburg: OIDR, 1890 (Old Russian version also in VMCh, Dec., 444–551).

Danilova, Irina. *Freski Ferapontogo monastyria/The Frescoes of St Pherapont Monastery*. Moscow: Iskusstvo, 1971.

Davies, Norman. *God's Playground. A History of Poland*. 2 vols., New York: Columbia, 1982.

Demkova, N.S., and S.A. Iakunina. 'Kormchaia XV v. iz sobraniia Permskogo pedagogicheskogo instituta' (A Canon Law Book of the 15th Century from the Repository of the Perm Pedagogical Institute) TODRL 43 (1990), 330–37.

Dergacheva, N.V. 'K literaturnoi istorii drevnerusskogo Sinodika XV-XII vv.' (The Literary history of the Old Rus' Synodicon). *Literatura drevnei Rusi. Istochnikovedenie*. pp. 63–76.

———. 'Rodoslovie Dionisiia Ikonnika' (The Geneology of the Dionisii the Iconographer). *Pamiatniki kul'tury. Novye otkrytiia*. Moscow: 1988, 210–25

———. 'Tipologiia sinodikov v russkoi pis'mennosti XV-XVII vv. (A Typology of Synodica in Russian Literary Texts of the 15th-17th Centuries'. *Metodicheskie rekomendatsii po opisianiiu slaviano-russkikh rukopisnykh knig* (Methodological Recommendations for the Description of Slavic-Russian Manuscript Books) 3.2 (1988), 246–70.

Dewey, H.W. 'The 1497 Sudebnik'. *American Slavonic and East European Review* 15 (1956), 325–38.

Dictionnaire de spiritualité ascetique et mystique, doctrine et histoire. 16 vols. to date. eds. Marcel Viller, SJ, et al. Paris: G. Beauchesne, 1932–95.

Dmitrieva, R.P. 'Agiograficheskaia shkola mitropolita Makariia (na materiale nekotorykh zhitii)' (The Hagiographic School of Metroplitan Makarii—Based on Several Lives). TODRL 48 (1993), 208–13.

———. 'Svetskaia literatura v sostave monasatyrskikh bibliotekakh XV i XVI vv.' (Kirillo-Belozerskogo, Volokolamskogo monastyrei i Troitse-Sergievoi lavry) (Secular Literature in Monastery Library

Holdings of the 15th and 16th Centuries. [The Kirillov-Belozersk and Volokolamsk Monasteries and the Trinity St Sergius Laura]). TODRL 28 (1974), 202–30.

———. 'Volokolamskie cheti sborniki XVI v' (16th-century Volokolamsk Codices of Readings). TODRL 28 (1974), 202–30.

Dmitrievskij, A.A. 'Bogosluzhenie v russkoi tserkvi v pervye piati vekov' (The Divine Service in the Russian Church during First Five Centuries). *Pravoslavnyi sobesednik* (Orthodox Interlocutor) 1882, 2: 138–60, 3: 212–90; 9: 346–73; 10: 147–67; 12: 372–94; 1883, 7–8: 345–74; 10: 198–229; 12: 420–85.

———. *Bogosluzhenie v russkoi tserkvi v XVI veke* (The Divine Service in the Russian Church in the 16th Century). Kazan: University, 1882.

———. *Opisanie liturgicheskikh rukopisei khraniashchikhsia v bibliotekakh Provoslavnogo Vostoka* (Description of the Liturgical Manuscripts Preserved in the Libraries of the Orthodox East). 2 vols., Kiev: University, 1895–1901.

Dmytryshyn, Basil, *Medieval Russia. A Source Book, 850–1700.* 3rd ed. Fort Worth *et alibi*: Holt, Rinehart and Winston, 1991.

Dobrotoliubie ili slovesa i glavizny sviashchennogo trezveniia, sobrannyia ot pisanii sviatykh i bogodukhnovennykh ottsov (The *Philokalia*, or Discourses and Chapters of Sanctified Sobriety, Collected from the Holy and Divinely-Inspired Fathers). Ed. and trans. Archimandrite Paisii Velichkovsky. 4 pts. in 2 vols. Moscow: Sinod, 1857.

Doens, Irénéé. 'Nicon de la Montagne Noire'. *Byzantion* 24.1 (1954), 131–40.

Dopolneniia k Aktam istoricheskim (Supplement to Historical Acts). 12 vols. St Petersburg: Archeographic Commission, 1846–72.

Dorotheus of Gaza. *Discourses and Sayings.* Ed. and trans. Eric P. Wheeler. Cistercian Studies 33. Kalamazoo, 1977.

———. *Oeuvres spirituelles.* Ed. and trans. L. Regnault and J. de Preville. Sources chrétiennes 92. Paris: Cerf: 1963–65. (Greek edition, French translation.)

———. *Vita S. Dosithei.* Acta SS Februarii 3:382–84.

Dosifei Toporkov. *Nadgrobnoe slovo prepodobnomu Iosifu Volokolamskomu.* (Funeral Oration to St Iosif Volotsky). Kurganovsky, pp. 125–38.

Druzhinin, V.G. 'Neskol'ko neizvestnykh literaturnykh pamiatnikov iz sbornikov XVI-go veka' (Several Unknown Literary Monuments from the Collections of the Sixteenth Century). *Letopis' zaniatii Arkheograficheskoi kommissii* (Annal of the Studies of the Archeographic Commission) 21 (1909), 1–113.

DuCange, Charles du Fresne. *Glossarium ad scriptores mediae et infimae graecitatis* (Glossary for the Writers of Medieval Greek). 2 vols. rpt. Vratislav: Koebner, 1891.

———. *Glossarium mediae et infimae latinitatis* (Glossary of Medieval Latin). 10 vols. Niort: L Favre, 1883–87; rpt. Paris: Librarie des sciences et des arts, 1937–38.

Dujčev, I. 'The *Paterikon* of Volokolamsk and the Heresies'. *Canadian-American Slavic Studies.* 13 (1979), 121–25.

Dukhovnye i dogovomye gramoty velikikh i udel'nykh kniazei XIV-XVI vv. (Testaments and Treatises of the Grand and Appanage Princes of the 14th-16th C.). eds. L.V. Cherepnin and S.V. Bakhrushnin. Moscow: ANSSSR, 1950.

The Edificatory Prose of Kievan Rus'. ed. William R. Veder and Anatolij A. Turlov. HLEULET 6: 1994.

Entsiklopedicheskii slovar' (Encyclopedic Lexicon). 41 vols. in 82. St Petersburg: F.A. Brokgauz (Brockhaus) and I. A. Efron, 1890–1904; 4 suppl. vols., 1906–07.

Ephraim the Syrian. *Sancti patris nostri Ephraem Syri Opera omnia quae exstant Graece, Syriace, Latine ad mss. Codices Vaticanos* (All the Extant Works in Greek, Syriac, and Latin of Our Holy Father Ephraim the Syrian, in the Vatican Codices). 3 vols. ed. J.-S. Assemani. Rome: Vatican, 1732–46.

———. Τὰ τού ὁσίου πατρος Ἐφραίμ τοῦ Σύρου πρὸς τῆν Ἑλλάδα μεταβληθέντα (The Works of our Holy Father Ephraim the Syrian Translated into Greek). Ed. E. Thwaites. Oxford: 1709.

———. *Tvoreniia Sviatogo Efrema Sirina* (The Works of St Ephraim the Syrian). 8 vols. in 4. Moscow. 1875–1907.

Epifanii Premudrii (Epiphanius the Wise). *Zhitie i zhizn' prepodobnogo ottsa nashego igumena Sergiia* (The Life and Lifestyle of our Holy Father Hegumen Sergii). ed. N. S. Tikhonravov. rpt. Müller. pt. 1.

Evans, Helen, and William D. Wixom, eds., *The Glory of Byzantium. Art ad Culture of the Middle Byzantine Era, A.D. 843–1261*. New York: Metropolitan Museum of Art, 1997.

Fathers of the Church, the. A New Translation. New York: 1947, Washington, 1959.

Fedotov, George. *The Russian Religious Mind.* 2 vols. Cambridge, Mass: Harvard University Press: 1946–66.

———. *A Treasury of Russian Spirituality.* London: Sheed and Ward, 1950, 1952.

Fennell, J.L.I. *Ivan the Great of Moscow.* London: Macmillan, 1961; New York: St Martin's, 1962.

———. *A History of the Russian Church to 1448.* London/New York: Longman. 1995.

Florovsky, Georges. 'The Problem of Old Russian Culture'. *Slavic Review* 21.1 (1962), 1–15.

———. *Puti russkogo bogosloviia* (Ways of Russian Theology). Paris: YMCA Press, 1937. Trans. Robert Nichols. 2 vols. (Vols. 5–6 of The Collected Works of Georges Florovsky, 14 vols. 1972–89) Belmont: Nordland, Büchervertriebsanstalt, 1979–87.

Franklin, Simon, and Jonathan Shepard, *The Emergence of Rus, 750–1200*. London/New York: Longman, 1996.

Freshfeld, E.M. A *Manual of Eastern Roman Law. The 'Procheiros Nomos'*. Cambridge, England: University Press, 1928.

Galatariotou, Catia. 'Byzantine Ktetorika Typika. A Comparative Study'. *Revue des études byzantines* 45 (1987), 77–138.

Gavriushkin, N.K., 'Mitropolit Daniil - Redaktor "Dialektiki"' (Metropolitan Daniil - The Editor of John Damascene's *Dialectics*). TODRL 41 (1988), 357–63.

Goetz, L.K. *Das Kiever Hohlenklöster als Kulturzentrum des vormongolischen Russlands,* Passau: M. Walderbauische, 1904.

Gol'dberg, A.L., 'Tri "poslaniia" Filofeia. Opyt tekstologicheskogo analiza' (Three 'Epistles' of Filofei. An Attempt at a Textological Analysis). TODRL 37 (1976), 139–49.

Goldfrank, David. 'Burn, Baby, Burn. Popular Culture and Heresy in Late Medieval Russia'. *Journal of Popular Culture* 31/4 (1998) 17–32.

———. 'Iosif Volotskii'. MERSH 14 (1979), 229–32.

———. 'Judaizers'. MERSH 15 (1980), 143–46.

———. 'Nil Sorskii'. MERSH 25 (1981), 11–14.

———. 'Old and New Perspectives on Iosif Volotsky's Monastic Rules'. *Slavic Review* 24 (1975), 279–301.

———. 'Theocratic Imperatives, the Transcendent, the Worldly, and Political Justice in Russia's Early Inquisitions'. *Religious and Secular Forces in Late Tsarist Russia.* (In Honor of Donald W. Treadgold). ed. Charles E. Timberlake. Seattle: University of Washington 1992, pp. 30–47.

———. 'Who Put the Snake on the Icon and the Tollbooths on the Snake?'. *Kamen' Kraeug"l'n"*, 180–99.

Goleizovsky, N.K. ' "Poslanie ikonopistsu" i otgoloski isikhazma v russkoi zhivopisi na rubezhe XV-XVI vv. ("The Epistle to the Icon Painter" and Echoes of Hesychasm in Russian Painting at the Juncture of the 15th and 16th Centuries). VV 26 (1965), 219–38.

Golubinsky, E.E. *Arkheologicheskii atlas ko vtorom polovine 1 toma Istorii Russkoi tserkvi* (Archeological Atlas to the Second Half of the First Volume of the History of the Russian Church). Moscow: OIDR, 1906; rpt. SPR 117/5. The Hague: Mouton, 1969.

———. *Istoriia kanonizatsiii sviatykh v russkoi tserkvi* (History of the Canonization of Saints in the Russian Church). Moscow: OIDR, 1913.

———, *Istoriia Russkoi tserkvi* (History of the Russian Church). 2 vols. in 4. Moscow: OIDR, 1900–19. rpt. SPR 117/1–4. The Hague: Mouton, 1969.

Gonneau, Pierre. *La maison de Sainte Trinité: un grand monastère russe du Moyen-Age tardif (1345–1533)* Paris 1992

———, 'The Trinity-Sergius Brotherhood in State and Society'. MRKIS/ CIM, 116–145

———, 'Les troublions au monastère (*bezchinniki monastyrskie*): indiscipline et partage du pouvoir à la Trinité Sainte-Serge au XVe siècle'. *Revue des études slaves* 63 (1991), 195–206.

Gormin, Vladimi, Liudmila Yarosh *et al. Novgorod. Art Treasures and Architectural Monuments, 11th-18th Centuries.* Leningrad: Aurora, 1984.

Gorsky, A., and K. Nevostruev. *Opisanie slavianskikh rukopisei Moskovskoi sinodal'noi biblioteki* (Description of the Slavonic Manuscripts of the Moscow Synod Library). 5 vols. Moscow: Sinod, 1855–1917; rpt. Monumenta linguae slaviae dialecti veteris. Fontes et dissertationes (Monuments of Old Slavonic. Sources and Studies) 2. Wiesbaden: Harrassowitz, 1964.

Gove, Antonina Filonov. *The Slavic Akathistos Hymn*. Munich: Otto Sanger, 1988.

Grabar, Igor. *Istoriia russkogo iskusstva* (History of Russian Art). 6 vols. Moscow: I. Knebel, 1910–14.

Granstrem, E.E. 'Ioann Zlatoust v drevnei russkoi i iuzhnoslavianskoi pis'mennosti (XI-XIV vv.)' (John Chrysostom in Old Russian and South Slavic Writings 11th-14th Centuries.). TODRL 29 (1974), 186–93.

Gregory I (the Great), Pope/Pseudo-Gregory. *Dialogues*. Trans. O.J. Zimmerman, OSB. FC 39. (PL 77:149–432, for 1, 3–4; PL 66:125–204 for 2. The Life of St Benedict).

Gregory Nazianzus, the Theologian. *Funeral Oration on the Great Basil, Bishop of Caesarea in Cappodocia*. NPF-2 7:394–422 (Oratio 43; PG 36:493–606).

Gregory Pakourianos. *Typikon* for the Monastery of the Mother of God *Petritzonitissa* in Bačkovo (1083). Trans. Robert Jordan. BMFD, 519–63.

Gregory of Sinai. *Praecepta ad hesychastas* (Doctrines for Hesychasts). PG 150:1335–1346.

Halecki, Oscar, *From Florence to Brest (1439–1596)*. Rome: Sacrum Poloniae Millennium, 1958; 2nd ed. Hamden, Conn.: Archon, 1968.

Halkin, François, SJ. ed. *Bibliotheca hagiographica graeca* (Bibliography of Greek Hagiography). 3rd ed., Subsidia hagiographica 8a. Brussels: Société des Bollandistes, 1957.

———, ed. *Sancti Pachomii vitae graecae* (The Greek Lives of Saint Pachomius). Subsidia hagiographica 19. Brussels: Société des Bollandistes, 1932.

———, ed. *Vita Sancti Pachomii* (The Life of Saint Pachomius). Trans. A.N. Athanassakis; intro. B.A. Pearson; Greek and English texts: Missoula, Mont.: Scholars' Press, 1975.

Haney, Jack V., *From Italy to Muscovy: The Life and Works of Maxim the Greek*. Humanistische Bibliothek, Reihe 1: Abhandlungen, Bd. 19. Munich: Wilhelm Fink, 1973.

Hannick, Chr., 'Die griechische Überlieferung der Dialog des Papstes Gregorius und ihre Verbrietung bei den Slaven im Mittelalter'. *Slovo* 24 (1974), 41–57.

Hapgood, Isabel, ed. and trans. *Service Book of the Holy Orthodox-*

Catholic and Apostolic Church. Rev. ed. New York: Association, 1922.

Harvard Library of Early Ukrainian Literature. English Translations. Cambridge, Mass: Harvard Ukrainian Research Institute, 1989–.

Hasenfratz, Hans Peter, *Die toten Lebdenden. Eine religiosenphänomenolog-ische Studie zum sozialen Tod in archaische Geselleschaften.* Leiden: E.J. Brill, 1983.

Hausherr, Irinée, SJ. 'La méthode d'oraison hesychaste'. *OC* 9.36: Rome: 1927, 109–210.

———. 'Les grands courants de la spiritualité orientale'. *Orientalia Christiana Periodica* 1 (1935), 114–38.

Hellie, Richard, trans. and ed. *The Sudebniks of 1497, 1550, 1589, and 1606.* 2 pts. The Laws of Russia. I.2. (forthcoming).

———, ed. *The Laws of Russia. Series I. Medieval Russia.* Salt Lake City: Charles Schlacks, 1992—

Hemmerdinger-Iliadou. 'L'Ephrem Grec et la littérature slave'. *Actes du XIIe Congres international des études byzantines.* 2 vols. Belgrade, 1964, 2:343–46.

Heppell, Muriel. *The* Paterik *of the Kievan Caves Monastery.* HLEULET 1: 1989.

———. 'Slavonic Translations of Early Byzantine Ascetical Literature'. *Journal of Ecclesiastical History* 5.1 (April, 1954), 86–100.

Hippolytus/Pseudo-Hippolytus of Rome. *Slovo sviatogo Ippolita ob antikhriste v slavianskom perevode po spisku XII veka* (The Discourse of Saint Hippolytus concerning the Antichrist in Slavic Translation, according to a 12th-century Copy). ed. K. Nevostruev. Moscow: 1868.

Hösch, Edgar. *Orthodoxie und Häresie in Altrussland.* Studien zur Geistesgeschichte des östlichen Europa 7. Wiesbaden: Harrassowitz, 1975.

Hollingsworth Paul, trans and ed. *The Hagiography of Kievan Rus'.* HLEULET 2: 1992.

Holzwath, I., *Der 'Prosvetitel" des Joseph von Volokolamsk.* Inaug. Diss. Berlin: 1944.

Hurwitz, Ellen, *Andrej Bogoljubskij. The Man and the Myth.* Studia historica et philologica 12. Sectio Slavica 4. Florence: Licosa, 1980.

Huttenback, Henry. 'The Judaizing Heresy and the Origins of Muscovite Antisemitism'. *Studies in Medieval Culture* 4.3 (1974), 496–506.

Iablonskii, V. *Pakhomii Serb i ego agiograficheskiia pisaniia* (Pakhomii the Serb and his Hagiographical Writings). St Petersburg: 1908. rpt.

Munich: Eidos, 1963.

Ikonnikov, V.S. *Maksim Grek i ego vremia: Istoricheskoe issledovanie* (Maksim the Greek and His Era: an Historical Study). 2nd ed., Kiev: University, 1915.

Iosif, *Poslaniia Iosifa Volotskogo* (The Letters of Iosif Volotsky). eds. A.A. Zimin and Ia. S. Lur'e. Moscow and Leningrad: Nauka, 1959.

———. *Prosvetitel' ili oblichenie eresi zhidovstvuiushchikh* (The Enlightener or Exposure of the Heresy of the Judaizers). 4th ed., Kazan: University, 1903; rpt. Westmead: Gregg, 1972.

Iosif, Ieromonakh. *Opis' rukopisei, perenesennykh iz biblioteki Iosifova monastyria v biblioteku Moskovskoi dukhovnoi akademii* (Inventory of the Manuscripts Transferred from the Iosifov Monastery Library to the Library of the Moscow Theological Seminary). Moscow: 1882; also in ChOIDR 1881, 3.

Irina Doukaina Komnene (Comnena), Empress. *Typikon* for the Convent of the Mother of God *Kecharitomene* in Constantinople (1110–16). Trans. Robert Jordan. BMFD, 664–719.

Isaac of Syria (Isaac of Nineveh). *Mystic Treatises by Isaac of Nineveh*. Trans. and introd. A.J. Wensinck. Amsterdam, 1923.

———. *Tvoreniia izhe vo sviatykh ottsa nashego avvy Isaaka Sirianina* (The Works of our Holy Father, Abba Isaac the Syrian). 3rd ed. Sergiev Posad: 1911.

Issledovaniia po istochnikovedeniiu istorii SSSR dooktiabr'skogo perioda (Studies in Source Analysis for the History of the USSR, Pre-October Period).

Istoriia russkogo iskusstva (History of Russian Art). Ed. Academy of Sciences of the USSR. Institute of the History of the Arts. 13 vols. Moscow: ANSSSR, 1953–64.

'Issledovatel'skie materialy dlia "Slovar' knizhnikov i knizhnosti ranei Rusi": Pisateli i knizhniki XI-XVII vv.' (Research Material for the "Lexicon of Bookmen and Literature of Old Rus": Writers and Bookmen of the 11th-17th Centuries). TODRL 40 (1985), 31–189.

Istrin, V., *Otkrovenie Mefodiia Patarskogo i apokroficheskie videniia Daniila v vizantiiskoi i slaviano-russkoi literaturakh* (The Revelation of Methodius of Patara and the Apochryphal Visions of Daniel in Byzantine and Slavonic-Russian Literatures). Moscow: University, 1897; also in ChOIDR 1897, 2.

Ivina, L.I. *Krupnaia votchina severo-vostochnoi Rusi kontsa XIV pervoi polovinу XVI v.* (A Large Domain of Northeast Rus from the End of the Fourteenth to the First Half of the Sixteenth Century). Leningrad: Nauka, 1979.

'The Izbornik of 1076'. *The Edificatory Prose of Kievan Rus'*, pp. 3–120.

Jagić, Vratroslav, 'Tipik hilandarski i niegov grčki izbor.' *Spomenik.* Srpska Kral'evska Akademija. XXXI.31 (1898), 1–66.

Joachim, Metropolitan of Zichna, *Typikon* for the Monastery of St John the Forerunner on Mount Menoikeion (1332). Trans. Timothy Miller. BMFD, 1590–1612.

John Cassian, *Institutes of the Cœnobia.* NPF-2 11:201–90 (PL 49: 34–476); newer edition: *De Institutis Cenobiorum Libri XII.* Ed. J.C. Guy. Source Chrétiennes, 109 (1965, with a French translation).

John Chrysostom. *Adversus Judaeos Orationes* (Discourses against the Jews) 1–8. PG 48:843–942 (ORT 1, 4–8: *Margarit*: 846–962).

———. *A Commentary on the Gospel of St Matthew.* NPF-1 10. PG 57–58.

———. *De incomprehensibili . . . orationes* (Discourses on the Inconceivable). PG 48:701–48 (ORT: *Margarit*: 777–846).

———. *Homilies on Ephesians.* NPF-I 13:49–172. PG 62:9–176.

———. *Homilies on the Gospel According to St John.* NPF-I 14:1–334. PG 59:23–482.

———. *Homilies on Philippians.* NPF-1 12:181–255. PG 62:177–298.

———. *Homilies on Second Corinthians.* NPF-I 12:271–420. PG 59:23–482.

———. *In laudem eorum, qui comparunt in ecclesia . . . et in ilud, vidi dominum*, Hom. 1 (On those who congregate in the church . . . and on 'I have seen the Lord', Hom. 1). PG 56:97110 (ORT: Margarit: 969–82).

———. *Liber de virginitate* (Treatise on Monasticism). PG 48: 533–96.

———. *Margarit* (The Pearl: ORT of *Margaritos,* a Greek collection of Chrysostom's sermons and discourses). VMCh, Sept., 773–1193.

———. *Quod regulares feminae viris cohabitare non debent* (Woman under vows must not live with men). PG 47:513–32.

John Climacus. *Liber ad Pastorem* (A Treatise for the Pastor). PG 88:1165–1210.

———. *St John Climacus: The Ladder of Divine Ascent.* Trans. Archimandrite Lazarus Moore; intro. M. Heppel. London: Faber & Faber; New York: Harper, 1959 (PG 88:631–1164). New trans., C. Luiheid and N. Russell, *The Ladder of Divine Ascent*, New York: Paulist, 1982

John of Damascus. *An Exact Exposition of the Orthodox Faith. Writings.* Trans. Frederic H. Chase, Jr. FC 37. New York: 958, 165–405 (PG 94:789–1228).

John II Komnenos. *Typikon* for Pantokrator Monastery in Constantinople (1136). BMFD 737–74.

John of Pantelleria: *Typikon* for the Monastery of St John the Forerunner (? ca. late 8th c.). Trans. Gianfranco Fiacccadori. BMFD 62–65 (ORT: Mansvetov, *Tserkovnyi ustav*, 441–45).

John of Phoberos. *Typikon* for the Monastery of St John (1113/ 1144). Trans. Robert Jordan. BMFD, 880–949.

John, Patriarch of Jerusalem, *Vita S. Joannis Damasceni* (Life of St John of Damascus). Acta SS Maii 2, 110–118.

John the Scholastic (Ioannes Scholasticus). *Positae post canones synodorum constitutionis capitula. Collectio 87 capitulorum* (Constitutions Enacted after the Canons of the Councils. The Collection in 87 Chapters). J.N. Pitra, Cardinal, ed. *Iuris ecclesiastics graecorum historia et monumenta* (Monuments and History of Greek Ecclesiastical Law). vol. 2, Rome: 1868, 385–405 (ORT: Sreznevsky. *Obozrenie*, Appendix, 67–103).

John Tzimiskes, Emperor. *Typikon* (971–72). Trans. George Dennis. BMFD, 235–44.

Jordan, Robert. 'The Monastery of Theotokos Evergetis, its Children and Grandchildren'. *Theotokos Evergetis*. ed. Mullet and Kirby, 215–45.

Justinian (I), Emperor. *The Digest of Roman Laws. Theft, Rapine, Damage, and Insult.* Trans. C.F. Kolbert. Middlesex, England: Penguin, 1979.

———. *Novellae ad religionem pertinentes* (New Laws pertaining to Religion). PL 72:921–1054.

Kadlubovsky, A. *Ocherki po istorii drevnerusskoi literatury zhitii sviatykh* (Essays on the History of Old Russian Hagiographical Literature). Warsaw: 1902. ed. *Russkii filologicheskii vestnik* (The Russian Philological Messenger) 1–2, 1901.

Kagan, M.D, N.V. Ponyrko, M.V. Rozhdestvenskaia. 'Opisanie sbornikov XV v. knigopistsa Efrosina' (Description of the Codices of the Fifteenth-Century Scribe Efrosin). TODRL 35 (1980), 3–300.

Kaiser, Daniel. *The Growth of Law in Medieval Russia.* Princeton: University, 1980.

———, trans. and ed. *The Laws of Rus. Tenth to Fifteenth Centuries.* The Laws of Russia. I.1. (1992).

Kalugin, F. *Zinovii, inok Otenskii, i ego bogoslovsko-polemicheskie i tserkovno-uchitel'nye proizvedeniia* (The Otensky Monk Zinovii and his Theological-Polemical and Ecclesio-Didactic Works). St Petersburg: A Katansky, 1894.

Kamen' Kraeug"l'n" The Cornerstone. *Rhetoric of the Medieval Slavic World.* Essays Presented to Edward L. Kennan on his Sixtieth Birthday by his Colleagues and Students. Ed. N.S. Kollmann, D. Ostrowski, A. Pliguzov, D. Rowland. *Harvard Ukrainian Studies* 19 (1995/1997).

Kazakova, N.A. 'K Izucheniiu vkladnykh knig' (The Study of Donation Books). *Rukopisnoe nasledie Drevnei Rusi* (The Manuscript Heritage of Old Rus). ed. A. M. Panchenko. Leningrad: Nauka, 1972, 260–66.

———. 'Knigopisnaia deiatel'nost' i obshchestvenno-politicheskie vzgliady Guriia Tushina' (The Book-Copying Activities and Socio-Political Views of Gurii Tushin). TODRL 17 (1961), 170–200.

———. *Ocherki po istorii russkoi obshchestvennoi mysli. Pervaia tret' XVI v.* (Essays on the History of Russian Social Thought. The First Third of the 16th Century.) Leningrad: 1970.

———. *Vassian Patrikeev i ego sochineniia* (Vassian Patrikeev and his Works). Moscow-Leningrad: Akademiia Nauk, 1960.

———, and Ia. S. Lur'e, *Antifeodal'nye ereticheskie dvizheniia na Rusi XIV-nachalla XVI v.* (Anti-feudal Heretical Movements in Rus', 14th-Beginning of the 16th c.). Moscow-Leningrad: Akademiia Nauk, 1955.

Kazhdan, Alexander P. 'Vizantiiskii monastyr' XI-XII vv. kak sotsial'naia gruppa' (The llth-12th Century Byzantine Monastery as a Social Group). VV 31 (1971), 48–70.

Khoroshev, A.S. *Politicheskaia istoriia russkoi kanonizatsii (XI-XVI vv.)* (The Poliitcal History of Russian Canonization 11th-16th Centuries). Moscow: University, 1986

Khrushchov, I. *Issledovanie o sochineniiakh Iosifa Sanina, prep. Igumena Volotskogo* (A Study of the Works of St Iosif Sanin, Hegumen of Volok). St Petersburg: IAN, 1868.

Kirill of Turov, 'Collected Prose'. *Sermons and Rhetoric of Kievan Rus'*, 55–158.

Kivelson, Valerie, *Autocracy in the Provinces. The Muscovite Gentry and Political Culture in the Seventeenth Century.* Stanford: University, 1996.

Klibanov, I. *Reformatsionnye dvizheniia v Rossii v XIV-pervoi polovine XVI vv.* (Reformation Movements in Russia in the 14th to the First Half of the 16th Centuries). Moscow: ANSSSR, 1960.

Kliuchevsky, V.O. *Drevnerusskie zhitiia sviatykh kak istoricheskii istochnik* (Old Russian Saints' Lives as an Historical Source). Moscow: K. Soldatnikov, 1871. rpt. Moscow: Nauka, 1988.

———. 'Pskovskie spory' (Pskovian Quarrels). *Sochineniia* (Works) 7. Moscow: Gos. izd. pol. lit., 33–105.

Kloss, B.M. 'Biblioteka moskovskikh mitropolitov v XVI v.' (The Library of the Moscow Metropolitans in the 16th Century). *Problemy paleografii i kodikologii v SSSR* (Problems of Paleography and Manuscript Study in the USSR). ed. A.D. Liubinskaia. Moscow: 1974: 114–25.

———. 'Iosifo-Volokolamskii monastyr' i letopisanie konsta XV-pervoi poloviny XVI v.' (The Iosifov-Volokolamskii Monastery and Chronicle Writing of the End 15th-Mid-16th Centuries.). *Vspomogatel'nye istoricheskie ditsipliny* (The Auxiliary Historical Disciplines). 6 (1974), 107–25.

———. 'Neizvestnoe poslanie losifa Volotskogo' (An Unknown Epistle of Iosif). TODRL 28 (1974). 350–52.

———. *Nikonovskii svod i russkie letopisi XVI-XVII vekov* (The Nikon Chronicle Compilation and Russian Chronicles of the 16th and 17th Centuries). Moscow: Nauka, 1980.

———. 'Nil Sorskii i Nil Polev-"spisateli knig"' (Nil Sorsky and Nil Polev—"Book Copyists"). *Drevnerusskoe iskusstvo: Rukopisnaia kniga* (Old Rus Art. The Manuscript Book). St Petersburg (1974), 150–67.

Kniga glagolaemaia Starchestvo (The Book called the *Geronticon*). M.E. Saltykov-Shchedrin State Public Library, Leningrad. Kirillov-Beloozerskii Collection. Codex No. 721/1198. 3^{v}-163 (Microfilm).

Kniga kliuchei i Dolgovaia kniga Iosifo-Volokolamskogo monastyria XVI v. (The Steward's Book and the Book of Debts of the Iosifov-

Volokolamsk Monastery of the 16th Century). eds. M.N. Tikhomirov and A.A. Zimin. Moscow-Leningrad: ANSSSR, 1948.

Kniga zhitii sviatykh. Cheti-minei Sv. Dimitriia Rostovskogo. (The Book of Saints' Lives. The Menology of Readings St Dmitrii of Rostov). 12 vols. Moscow: Sinod, 1837 (orig. 1689).

Kobrin, V.B. 'Poslanie Iosifa Volotskogo Arkhimandritu Evfimiiu' (Iosif Volotsky's Epistle to Archimandrite Evfimii). ZORGBL 28 (1966), 229–39.

Kochin, G.E. *Materialy dlia terminologicheskogo slovariia drevnei Rossii.* (Materials for a Terminological Dictionary of Old Russia). Moscow-Leningrad: ANSSSR, 1937; rpt. Slavica Reprint 27. Vaduz, Leichtenstein: European Printing Establishment, 1969.

Kollmann, Jack E., Jr.. *The Moscow Stoglav ("Hundred Chapters") Council of 1551.* 2 vols. Diss. Univ. of Michigan: 1978.

Kologrivof, Ivan. *Essai sur la sainteté en Russie.* Bruges: Ch. Beyaert, 1953.

Kormovaia kniga Iosifo-Volokolamskogo monastyria = Das Speisungsbuch von Volokolamsk. Eine Quelle zur Sozialgeschichte russischer Klöster im 16. Jahrhundert. Trans and ed. Ludwig Steindorff *et al.* Bausteine zur slavische Philologie und Kulturgeschichte. Neue Folge. Editionen 12. Cologne/Wiemar/Vienna: Böhlau, 1998.

Kornilii Komel'sky. 'Kornilii Komel'skii, II. Ustav ili pravila' (Kornilii Komel'sky, II. Typicon or Rules). ed. Bishop Amvrosii. *Istoriia Rossisskoi ierarkhii* (History of the Russian Hierarchy) vol. 4. Moscow: Sinod, 1812.

Kozhanchikov, D., ed. *Stoglav* (The Hundred Chapters). St Petersburg: IAN, 1863; rpt. Slavica Reprint 33. Düsseldorf: Vaduz, 1969.

Krushel'nitskaia, E.V., 'Zaveshchanie-ustav Gerasima Boldinskogo' (The Testament-Rule of Gerasim Boldinsky). TODRL 48 (1983), 264–70.

Krutova, M.S. ' "Zlataia tsep' " kak tip sbornika' ("The Golden Chain" as a Type of Miscellany). *Literatura drevnai Rusi. Istochnikovedenie*, 39–62.

Kukushkina, M.V. 'Biblioteka Solovetskogo monastyria v XVI v.' (The Solovetsky Monastery Library in the 16th Century). *Arkhegraficheskii ezhegodnik za 1970 g.* (The Archeographic Annual for 1970). 1971, 357–72.

Kuntsevich, G.Z. *Chelobitnia inokov Tsariu Ivanu Vasil'evichu* (The Monks' Petition to Tsar Ivan Vasilevich). Petrograd: 1916.

Kurganovsky, Gerontii, Archimandrite. *Volokolamskii-Iosifov muzhskii monastyr' i ego sovremennoe sostoianie* (The Iosifov-Volokolamsk Monastery and its Present Condition). St Petersburg, 1903.

Kuzmina, V.D. 'Drevnerusskie pis'mennye istochniki ob Andree Rubleve' (Old Russian Literary Sources concerning Andrei Rublev). *Andrei Rublev i ego epokha* (Andrei Rublev and his Epoch). ed. M.P. Alpatov. Moscow: 1971, 103–24.

Ladder: See John Climacus. *The Ladder of Divine Ascent.*

Lampe, G.W.H., ed. *A Patristic Greek Dictionary*. London Oxford: Clarendon, 1961–68.

Langer, Lawrence N. 'The Black Death in Russia: its Effects upon Urban Labor', *Russian History* 2 (1975), 53–67.

Laurina, V.K. 'Vnov' raskrytaia ikona "Soshestvie vo ad" iz Ferapontova monastyria i moskovskaia literatura kontsa XV veka' (A Newly Discovered Icon of the Harrowing of Hell from Ferapontov Monastery and Moscovite Literature of the End of the Fifteenth Century). TODRL 22 (1966), 165–84

Leclercq, Jean OSB and Michael Casey OCSO, intro. and trans. 'Cistercians and Cluniacs: St Bernard's Apologia to Abbot William'. *Bernard of Clairvaux: Treatises* I. Cistercian Fathers I. Spencer, Mass: 1970, 3–69.

Le Goff, Jacques. *The Birth of Purgatory*. Trans. Arthur Goldhammer. Chicago: University, 1984.

Lelekova, Olga V. *Ikonostas 1497 g. Uspenskogo sobora Kirillova-Belozerskogo monastyria. Issledovanie i restavratsiia* (The Iconostasis of 1497 of Kirillov-Belozersk Monastery. Study and Restoration). Moscow: Institute of Restoration, 1988.

Leonid, Archimandrit. 'Monastyrskie stolovye obikhodniki' (Monastic Table Customaries). ChOIDR, 1880, 3, 1–113.

Levochkin, I.V. 'Izbornik Sviatoslava i russkie sborniki XV-XVII vv.' (Sviatosvlav's Miscellany and Russian Miscellanies of the 15th-17th Centuries). TODRL 40 (1985), 373–78.

Likhachev, D.S., R.P. Dmitrieva, T.V. Dianova, L.M. Kostiukhina, I.V. Pozdeeva, T.A. Kruglova, M.M. Lereman, M.D. Kagan. *Knizhnye tsentry drevnei Rusi. Iosifo-Volokolamskii monastyr'* (Book Centers of Old Rus. The Iosifo-Volokolamskii Monastery). Leningrad: Nauka, 1991.

Lilienfeld, Fairy von. *Nil Sorsky und Seine Schriften. Die Krise der Tradition im Russland Ivans III.* Berlin: Evangelische Verlaganstalt, 1963.

Lisitsyn, M., *Pervonachal'nyi slaviano-russkii Tipikon. Istorikoarkheologicheskoe issledovanie* (The Original Slavic-Russian Typicon. A Historical-Archeaological Study). St Petersburg, 1911.

Literatura drevnei Rusi. Istochnikovedenie (The Literature of Old Rus'. Source Studies). ed. D.S. Likhachev and N.V. Panyrko. Leningrad: Nauka, 1988.

Lur'e, Ia. S. *Ideologicheskaia bor'ba v russkoi publitsistike kontsa XV-nachala XVI veka* (The Ideological Struggle in Russian Public Controversy in the End of the 15th-Beginning of the 16th Century). Moscow-Leningrad: Nauka, 1960.

———. 'Iosif Volotskii kak publitsist i obshchestvennyi deiatel'' (Iosif Volotsky as a Publicist and Public Figure). PIV, 10–97.

———, ed. *Istoki russkoi belletristiki. Vozniknovenie zhanrov siuzhetnogo povestvovaniia v drevnerusskoi literature.* (Sources of Russion Fiction: The Rise of Genres of Topical Narration in Old Russian Literature). Leningrad: 1970.

———. 'Kratkaia redaktsiia "Ustava" Iosifa Volotskogo. Pamiatnik ideologii rannego iosiflianstva' (The Brief Redaction of Iosif Volotsky's Rule. A Monument of Early Iosifite Ideology). TODRL 12 (1956), 116–38.

———. *Obshcherusskie letopisi XIV-XV vv.* (Common-Russian Chronicles of the 14th-15th Centuries). Leningrad: 1976.

———. '"Sobranie na likhoimstev" – neizdannyi pamiatnik russkoi publitsistiki kontsa XV v.' (Collection against the Greedy—An Unpublished Monument of Russian Public Controversy from the end of the 15th c.). TODRL 21 (1965), 132–46.

———. 'Unresolved Issues in the History of the Ideological Movements of the Late Fifteenth Century', *Medieval Russian Culture* (Vol. 1), ed., Henrik Birnbaum and Michael S. Flier, *California Slavic Studies* 12 (1984), 150–71.

———. 'Ustav Kornilii Komel'skogo v sbornike pervoi polovine XVI v.' (The Rule of Kornilii Komel'sky in a Codex from the First Half of the

16th c.) A.M. Panchenko, ed. *Rukopisnoe nasledie Drevnei Rusi* (The Manuscript Heritage of Old Rus). Leningrad: Nauka, 1972, 253–59.

———, and A.A. Zimin. *Poslaniia Iosifa Volotskogo* (The Epistles of Iosif Volotsky). Moscow-Leningrad: Nauka 1959.

Makarii, Metropolitan of Moscow and All Russia. *Velikiia Minei chetii, sobrannye vserossiiskim Mitropolitom Makariem* (The Great Menology of Readings, Collected by Makarii, Metropolitan of All Russia). 22 vols. St Petersburg: Arkheograficheskaia kommissiia, 1868–1917.

Makarii, Metropolitan of Moscow. *Istoriia Russkoi tserkvi* (History of the Russian Church). lst-3rd eds. 12 vols. St Petersburg: I. Iu. Bokram, 1877–89; rpt. Slavica 13–14. Düsseldorf: Brucken-Europe, 1968–69.

Makarios Chumnos. *Testament* for the *Nea Mone* of the Mother of God in Thessalonike (shortly before 1374). Trans. Alice-Mary Talbot. BMFD, 1446–53.

Malinin, V.N. *Starets Eleazarova monastyria Filofei i ego poslaniia* (The Eleazarov Monastery Elder Filofei and his Epistles). Kiev: Pechersky Lavra, 1901

Maloney, George A., SJ. *Russian Hesychasm: The Spirituality of Nil Sorskij.* SPR 269. Hague-Paris: Mouton, 1973.

Mansi, Johannes Dominicus. *Sacrorum conciliorum. Nova et amplissima collectio* (The Holy Councils. A New and Complete Collection). 53 vols. in 58. Paris-Leipzig: H. Welter, 1901–27 (partial English trans. of vols. 1–13: NPF-2 14).

Mansvetov, I. *Tserkovnyi ustav (tipik). Ego obrazovanie i sud'ba v grecheskoi i russkoi tserkvi* (The Church Typicon. Its Formation and Fate in the Greek and Russian Churches). Moscow: I. Lissner and Iu. Roman, 1885.

Manuel II Palaiologos, Emperor. *Typikon* for the Monasteries of Mount Athos (1406). Trans. George Dennis. BMFD, 1617–22.

Mary, Mother, and Archimandrite Kallistos Ware. *A Festal Menaion.* London: Faber and Faber, 1969.

Matthew I, Patriarch of Constantinople. *Testament* for the Monastery of Charsianeites Dedicated to the Mother of God *Nea Peribleptos* (1407). Trans. Mary-Alice Talbot. BMFD, 1633–62.

Mark the Hermit (Marcus Eremita), 'Opuscula' (Little Works). PG, 65:905–1140.

Meester, Placide de, *De monachico statu iuxta disciplinam byzantinam*

(On the Monastic Order and the Byzantine Rules). Vatican City: 1942.

Meyendorff, Jean. *Byzantine Theology: Historical Trends and Doctrinal Themes*. New York: Fordham, 1974.

———. Grégoire Palamas, *Defense des Saints Hésychastes*. Spicilegium sacrum lovaniense 30–31. Vol. 1, 1959; vol. 2, 2nd ed., 1973.

———. 'Partisans et ennemies des biens ecclésiastiques au sein du monachisme russe aux XVe et XVIe siècles'. *Irénikon* 29 (1956), 28–46.

———. *St Gregory Palamas and Orthodox Spirituality* (Orig. *St Grégoire Palamas et la mystique orthodoxe*. Paris: Seuil, 1959). Trans. Adele Fiske. Crestwood, NY: St Vladimir Seminary, 1974.

Meyer, Philipp. *Die Haupturkunden für die Geschichte der Athosklöster.* Leipzig: Heinrich, 1894.

Meyers, Gregory. 'Slavonic Witnesses of Evergetic Liturgy and Music: The Order of the Washing of the Feet on Great and Holy Thursday'. *Works of Worship . . . Everegtis*, ed. Mullet and Kirby, 367–85.

Michael Monachus. *Vita et conversatio s.p.n. et confessoris Theodori Praepositi studitorum* (The Life and Conduct of our Holy Father and Confessor, Hegumen Theodore Studite). PG99:114–234 (ORT: VMCh, Nov., 355–440).

Michael VIII Palaiologos. *Typikon* for the Monastery of St Demetrios of the Palaiologoi-Kellibara in Constantinople. Trans. George Dennis. BMFD, 1241–1282.

———, *Typikon* for the Monastery of the Archangel Michael on Mount Auzentios near Chalcedon. Trans. George Dennis. BMFD, 1215–34.

Michels, Georg. 'The First Old Believers in Tradition and Historical Reality'. *Jahrbücher für Geschichte Osteuropas* 41.4 (1993), 481–508.

———. 'Self-Immolation During the Russian Church Schism'. *The Carl Beck Papers in Russian and East European Studies.*

———. 'The Violent Old Belief, an Examination of Religious Dissent on the Karelian Frontier'. *Russian History/Histoire russe* 19.1–4 (1992), 203–29.

Migne, Jacques-Paul, ed. *Patrologiae cursus completus, series graeca* (The Complete Patrology. Greek Series) 161 vols. in 166. Paris: Migne, 1857–66.

———. *Patrologiae cursus completus, series latina.* (The Complete

Patrology. Latin Series). 221 vols. in 222. Paris: Migne, 1844–80.

Mikhel'son, T.N. 'Zhivopisnyi tsikl Ferapontova monastyria' (The Iconographic Program of Feraponotov Monastry). TODRL 22 (1966), 144–64.

Miklosich, Franz Ritter von. *Lexicon palaeoslovenico-graeco-latinum emendatum auctum*. (Enlarged and Corrected Lexicon of Old Slavonic to Greek and Latin). Vienna: G. Braumueller, 1862–65; rpt. Aalen: Scientia Verlag, 1963.

Miller, David B. 'Donors to the Trinity-Sergius Monastery as a Community of Venerators: Origins, 1360s-1462', MRKIS/CIM 450–74.

———, 'Legends of the Icon of Our Lady of Vladimir: a Study of the Development of Muscovite National Consciousness'. *Speculum* 43.4 (1968), 657–70.

Modern Encyclopedia of Russian and Soviet History 55 vols. to date: Gulfbreeze, Florida: Academic International, 1976–93.

Mohyla, Peter. *Eukhologion al'bo molitvoslov, ili trebnik* (Euchologion, that is Prayer-Book or Missal). Kiev: 1646.

Morozova, L.E., 'Kolichestvennye metody i vopros on avtorstve "Otveta na poslanie Iosifia Volotskogo I.I. Tret'iakovu" ' (Quantitative Methods and the Question of the Author of "The Response to Iosif Volotsky's Epistle to I.I. Tret'iakov"). *Problemy izucheniia narrativnykh istochnikov po istorii russkogo srednevkov'ia* (Issues in the Study of Narrative Sources for the History of Russia's Middle Ages). Moscow: Institute of History, 1982, 5–24.

———. 'Vopros ob avtore "Poslaniia vel'mozha Ioannu o smerti kniazia", pripisaemogo Iosifa Volotskomu' (The Question of the Author of "The Epistle to the Magnate Ioann on the Death of a Prince," Attributed to Iosif Volotsky', *Problemy istorii SSSR* (Issues in the History of the USSR). 1979, 8, 37–57.

Moshin, L.G., *et al.*, *Russkie monastyri/Russian Monasteries*. Moscow: Ocharovannyi strannik (The Enchanted Pilgrim), 1995.

Moskovskaia Rus' (1359–1584): kul'tura i istoricheskoe samosoznanie = Culture and Identity in Muscovy, 1359–1584. Ed. Gail Lennhoff and Janet Martin. Moscow: ITZ-Garant, 1997.

Müller, Ludolf. *Die Legenden des Heiligen Sergij von Radonež*. rpt. of N.S. Tikhonravov, *Drevnija zhitiia prepodobnogo Sergiia Radonezhskogo* (The Old Lives of Saint Sergii of Radonezh). 2 pts. Moscow,

1892. Separate introduction and bibiliography. Slavische Propylaien 17. Munich: Wilhelm-Fink, 1967.

Mullet, Margaret, and Anthony Kirby, ed. *The Theotokos Evergetis and Eleventh-Century Byzantine Monasticism.* Belfast Byzantine Texts and Translations 6.1. Belfast: Queens University of Belfast, 1994.

———. *Works of Worship at the Theotokos Evergetis, 1050–1200.* Belfast Byzantine Texts and Translations 6.2. Belfast: Queens University of Belfast, 1997.

Nasrallah, J. 'Un auteur antiochien du XIe siècle: Nicon de la Montaigne Noire (vers 1025-début du XIIe s.),' Proche-Orient chrétien 19 (1969), 150–61.

Neilos, Bishop of Tamasia. *Rule* for the Monastery of the Mother of God in *Machairas* in Cyprus (1210). Trans. Anastasius Bandy. BMFD, 1126–67.

Neilos Damilas. *Testament* and *Typikon* for the Convent of the Mother of God *Pantanassa* at Baionaia on Crete (c. 1400). Trans. Alice-Mary Talbot. BMFD, 1467–81.

Nektarii. *Istoricheskoe opisanie Iosifova Volokolamskogo vtoroklassnogo monastyriia* (Historical Description of the Iosifov-Volokolamsk, Second Ranking Monastery). Moscow, 1887

Neophytos of Cyprus. *Testamentary Rule* for the Hermitage of the Holy Cross near Ktima (1214). Trans. Catia Galatariotou. BMFD, 1348–70.

Nevostruev, K.N. 'Rassmotrenie knigi I. Khrushchova, "Issledovanie o sochineniiakh Iosaifa Sanina, prep. Igumena Volotskogo" ' (A Review of the Book *A Study of the Works of St Iosif Sanin, Hegumen of Volok*). *Otchet o XII prisuzhdenii nagrad grafa Uvaraova* (Report from the 12th Award in Honor of Count Uvarov), St Petersburg: 1870, 84–186.

New Catholic Encyclopedia. 15 vols. New York: McGraw-Hill, 1967.

Nestor of Kiev-Pechersky. 'Lesson on the Life of Boris and Gleb'. *The Hagiography of Kievan Rus'*, 3–32.

———. 'The Life of Our Venerable Father Feodosii.' *The Hagiography of Kievan Rus*, 33–95.

Nicétas Stéthatos. *Le Paradis spirituel et autres textes annexes.* ed. Marie Chalendard. Paris: Cerf, 1945 (PG 120:852–1069).

Nikon of the Black Mountain (Nikon ho Mauroeites; Nicon Monachus, of Raithos Monastery on the Black Mountain near Antioch). *Pandekty . . . Nikona Chernogortsa.* (The Pandects of . . . Nikon of the

Black Mountain—Church Slavic trans.). Spaso-Prilutskii pod Vologdoi: 1670; rpt. Pochaev, 1795 (Table of contents in PG 106:1359–82).

———. *Taktikon . . . Nikon Chernogortsa.* (The Taktikon . . . of Nikon of the Black Mountain—Church Slavic trans.). Pochaev: 1795 (original Greek, to Discourse 4: *Taktikon Nikona Chernogortsa,* ed. V.N. Beneschevich. 1. Petrograd: 1917.). Trans. of Discourses 1–2, Robert Allison. BMFD, 377–439.

Nikol'sky, N. K. 'Obshchinnaia i keleinaia zhizn' v Kirillo-Belozerskom monastyre v XV, XVI, i nachale XVII vekov' (Communal and Cell Life in the Kirillov-Beloozersk Monastery in the 15th, 16th, and the Beginning of the 17th Centuries). *Khristianskoe chtenie* (Christian Readings). St Petersburg, 1907.

Nil Sorsky. *Nila Sorskogo, Predanie i Ustav* (Nil Sorsky's Tradition and Typicon). ed. M.C. Borovkova-Maikova. Pamiatniki drevnei pis'mennosti i iskusstva (Monuments of Ancient Writings and Art) 179. St Petersburg: 1912.

———. *Nil Sorskij und Seine Schriften.* See Lilienfeld.

———. *Saint Nil Sorsky (1433–1508). La Vie. Les écrits. Le skite d'un starets de Trans-Volga.* Trans. and ed., Sr. Sophia M. Jacamon, OSB. Spiritualité et vie monastique 32. Bégrolles-en-Mauges: Abbaye de Bellefontaine, 1980.

NPF-1, NPF-2. See *A Select Library of Nicene and Post-Nicene Fathers.*

Opisanie rukopisei Solovetskogo monastyria nakhodiashchikhsia v biblioteke Kazanskoi dukhovnoi akademii (Description of the Manuscripts found in the Library of the Kazan Theological Seminary). 3 vols. Kazan: 1881–89.

Orientalia Christiana analecta. Rome: Pont. Inst. orient. stud., 1923–.

Ostrowski, Donald. 'Church Polemics and Monastic Land Acquisition in Sixteenth-Century Muscovy'. *Slavonic and East European Review* 64 (1986), 355–79.

———, 'Loving Silence and Avoiding Pleasant Conversations. Thc Political Views of Nil Sorskii'. *Kamen' Kraeug"l'n"*, 476–96.

———. 'Toward Establishing the Canon of Nil Sorsky's Works'. *Oxford Slavonic Papers.* 31 (1998), 35–50.

The Oxford Dictionary of Byzantium. ed. A.P. Kazhdan. 3 vols. New York and Oxford: Oxford University, 1991.

Paisii Iaroslavov. 'Skazanie izvestno o Kammenom monastrye' (The True

History of Kammeny Monastery). *Pravoslavnyi sobesednik* (Orthodox Interlocutor) 1 (1861), 199–214.

Pachomius the Great. 'Instructions'. Viellieux. *Pachomian Koinona* 2:13–41.

———. 'Precepts'. Viellieux. *Pachomian Koinona* 3:144–67.

Pakhomii Logofet (Pachomius the Logothete). *Pakhomij Logofet. Werke in Auswahl.* rpt. of the edition by V. Iablonskii. intro. D. Tschizewskij (Chyzhevskii). Slavische Propyläen 117. Munich: Eidos, 1963.

———. *Zhitie i zhizn' prepodobnogo i bogonosnogo ottsa nashego Sergiia* (The Life and Conduct of our Sainted and God-bearing Father Sergii). Ed. N.S. Tikhonravov; rpt. Müller, pt. 2.

———. *Zhitie mitropolita vseia Rusi sviatogo Aleksiia, sostavlennoe Pakhomiem Logofetom* (The Life of Metropolitan of all Rus Aleksii, composed by Pakhomii Logofet). (Obshchestva liubitelei drevnei pis'mennosti i iskusstva izdaniia [Society of Devotees of Old Literature and Art Editions] 4). St Petersburg: 1877–78.

Palladius, BP. of Helenopolis and of Aspona. *Palladius: the Lausaic History*. Trans. Robert T. Meyer. Ancient Christian Writers 34. Westminister, Md.: Newman Press, 1965 (PG 47:5–82).

Palladius und Rufinus: Ein Beitrag zur Quellenkunde des ältesten Mönchtums. Texte und Untersuchungen von Erwin Preuschen. Giessen: J. Ricker, 1897.

Pamiatniki kul'tury. Novye otkrytiia (Monuments of Culture. New Discoveries).

Pandekty: See Nikon of the Black Mountain. *Pandekty*.

Pargoire, Jules, 'Constantinople: Le monastère de Évergétis'. *Echos d'Orient* 9 (1906), 366–73; 10 (1907), 155–67, 259–63.

Pascal, Pierre. *Avvakum et les debuts du Raskol*. Bibliothèque de l'Institut français en Leningrad 18. Paris: Librairie ancienne Honoré Champion, 1938.

Paterik skitskii (The Scete Patericon), in Old Russian. VMCh, Dec., 2511–2830.

Pavlichenkov, B. 'Ansambl' Iosifova-Volokolamskogo monastyria' (The Iosifov-Volokolamsk Monastery Ensemble). AN 10 (1958), 127–52.

Pavlov, A.S. *Istoricheskii ocherk sekuliarizatsii tserkovnykh zemel' v Rossii* (A Historical Study of the Secularization of Church Lands in Russia). Odessa: 1871.

Percival, Henry R., ed. *The Seven Ecumenical Councils of the Undivided Church. Their Canons and Dogmatic Decrees, together with the Canons of all Local Synods which have received Ecumenical Acceptance.* NPF-2 14 (Orig., Mansi, 1–14).

Petit, Louis, ed. *Vie de S. Athanase l'Athonite. Analecta Bollandiana* 25 (1906), 5–89. Text in Greek.

Petras, David. *The Typikon of Patriarch Alexios the Studite. Novgorod-St Sophia 1136.* Cleveland: Starr, 1991.

Philipp Solitarius. Ἡ Διόπτρα. (The Mirror). Ὁ Ἄθος. Ἁγιορειτικὸν περιδικόν. (Athos. The Journal of the Holy Mountain) 1.1 (1919), 1–262 (Latin trans. of different redaction: PG 127:703–878).

Photius, Patriarch. *Syntagma canonum.* (Syntagma of Canons: the Nomocanon of Fourteen Titles). PG 104:441–976.

Pitirim, Archbishop, 'O Volokolamskom paterike' (The Volokolamsk Patericon). *Bogoslovskie trudy* (Theological Works) 10 (Moscow, 1974), 175–222.

Pliguzov, A.I. ' "Kniga na eretikov" Iosifa Volotskogo' (Iosif Volotsky's "Book Against the Heretics"). *Istoriia i paleografiia* (History and Paleography) 1–2 (1993), 93–138.

———. 'Letopischik Iosifa Sanina' (The Little Annal of Iosif Sanin). *Letopisi i khroniki. Sbornik statei 1984* (Annals and Chronicles 1984). ed. V.I. Buganov. Moscow: Nauka, 1984, 174–86.

———. 'O khronologii poslanii Iosifa Volotskogo' (The Chronology of Iosif Volotsky's Epistles). *Russkii feodal'nyi arkhiv* (Russian Feudal Archive) 5 (1992), 1043–61.

———. 'Polemika o novgorodskikh eretikov i "Otvet Kirllovskikh startsev" ' (The Polemic over the Novgorod Heretics and "The Response of the Kirillov Elders"). Ἰουδαϊκή Ἀρχιολογία: in Honor of Professor Moshe Altbauer. ed. Wolf Moskovich et al. Jews and Slavs 3. Jerusalem: 1955, 135–55.

———. ' "Prenie s Iosifom" ' ("The Dispute with Iosif"), IISSSR 1989, 49–72.

———. 'Tekstologicheskaia istoriia "Sobraniia nekoego startsa" ' (The Textological History of the "Compilation of a Certain Elder"). *Istochniki po kul'ture i klassovoi bor'be feoldal'nogo perioda* (Sources for the Culture and Class Struggle of the Feudal Period). ed. N.N.Pokrovskii and E.K. Romodanovskaia. Novosibirsk: Nauka, 1982, 5–16.

———. ' "Traktat o neprikosnovennosti tserkovnykh i monastyrskikh imushchestv" ' ("The Treatise on the Inviobility of Monastic Properties"). *Metody izucheniia istochnikov po istorii russkoi obshchestvennoi mysli perioda feodalizma* (Methods of Studying the Sources for the History of Russian Social Thought of the Feudal Period). ed. L.E. Morozova, V.M. Sergeev, O.R. Kvirkvelliia. Moscow: 1989, 50–62.

———. 'Vstuplenie Vassiana Patrikeeva v polemiku o monastyrskikh zemliakh i tvorcheskaia istoriia "Sobraniia nekoego startsa" ' (Vassian Patrikeev's Joining the Polemic over Monastic Lands and the Literary History of "The Compilation of a Certain Elder"). IIISSSR 1987, 4–48.

———. 'Vtoraia redaktsiia mineinogo Zhitiia Iosifa Volotskogo' (The Second Redaction of the Menaion Life of Iosof Volotsky). IIISSSR 1985, 29–55.

Podskalsky, Gerhard. *Christentum und theologische Literatur in der Kiever-Rus' (988–1237)*, Munich: Beck, 1982.

Pokrovskaia, V. F. 'Opisanie monastyrskoi trapezy (po rukopisi kontsa XVI v.)'. (A Description of a Monastery Refectory [According to a Manuscript from the End of the 16th c.]). TODRL 33 (1979), 293–95.

Polnoe sobranie russkikh letopisei, (Complete Collection of Russian Chronicles). Vols. 1–24, St Petersburg-Petrograd-Leningrad: Archeographic Commission, 1841–1921; 2nd ed. 5 vols. Leningrad, 1925–29; reprints and new editions and volumes, Moscow: 1959–.

Pomialovsky, I.V. *Zhitie Evfimiia Velikogo* (The Life of Euthymius the Great). *Palestinskii paterik* (The Palestine Patericon). vyp. 2. St Petersburg: 1893. Text in Greek.

———. ed. *Zhitie prepodobnogo Afanasiia Afonskogo, po rukopisi Moskovskoi sünodal'noi biblioteki* (The Life of Saint Athanasius the Athonite, according to a Moscow Synod Library Manuscript). St Petersburg: IAN, 1895. Text in Greek.

Porfirii. Bishop of Chigirin. *Opisanie grecheskikh rukopisei monastyria sviatoi Ekateriny na Sinae* (Description of the Greek Manuscripts of the St Catherine Monastery on Sinai). 2 vols. ed. V. N. Beneshevich. St Petersburg: IAN, 1911–17.

'Povest' o Nile-Sorskom Skite' (The Tale of Nil Sorsky's Scete). In G.M. Prokhorov, *Pamiatniki literatury vizantiiskogo-russkogo obhschestvennogo dvizheniia*, 455–70.

Preobrazhenskii, V.S. *Slaviano-russkii Skitskii Paterik. Opyt istoriko-bibliograficheskogo issledovaniia* (The Slavic-Russian Scete Patericon. Historical-Bibliographical Investigation). Kiev: 1909.

Prokhorov, G.M. 'Avtografy Nila Sorskogo' (Nil Sorsky's Autographs). *Pamiatniki kul'tury. Novye otkrytiia. 1974 g*. Moscow, 1975, 37–54.

———. 'Keleinaia isikhastskaia literatura (Ioann Lestvichnik, Avva Dorofei, Isaak Sirin, Simeon Novyi Bogoslov, Grigorii Sinait) v biblioteke Troitse-Sergievoi lavry s XIV po XVII v.' (Hesychastic Cell Literature [John Climacus, Abba Dorotheus, Isaac of Syria, Symeon the New Theologian, Gregory of Sinai] in the Troitse-Sergiev Lavra Library, 14th-17th c.). TODRL 28 (1974), 317–24.

———. 'Knigi Kirilla Belozerskogo' (The Books of Kirill of Beloozero), TODRL 27 (1981), 50–70.

———. *Pamiatniki literatury vizantiisko-russkogo obshchestvennogo dvizheniia epokha Kulikovskogo bitvy* (Monuments of the Literature of Byzantine-Russian Social Movements from the Epoch of the Battle of Kulikovo). Dissertation. Leningrad: Institute of Russian Literature, 1978.

———. 'Poslaniia Nila Sorskogo' (The Letters of Nil Sorsky). TODRL 29 (1974) 125–43.

———. 'Prenie Grigoriia Palamy s "khiony i turki" i problema "zhidovskaia mudrvuiushchikh"' (Gregory Palamas's Debate with "the Chions and the Turks")' TODRL 27 (1972), 329–69.

Prosvetitel': See Iosif Volotsky. *Prosvetitel'*.

Pypin, A.N. *Istoriia russkoi literatury* (History of Russian Literature). St Petersburg: M.A. Stanislavich, 1898.

Quasten, Johannes, *Patrology*. 3 vols. Westminister, Md.: Newman, 1950–60.

Raeff, Marc, 'An Early Theorist of Absolutism: Joseph of Volokolamsk'. *American Slavic and East European Review* 8.1 (April, 1949), 77–89.

Reddaway, W.F., et al., eds. *The Cambridge History of Poland*. 2 vols. Cambridge, England: University Press, 1950, 1941.

Reinhart, Johann Michel. 'Die "Dialoge" Gregors des Grossen in der kirchenslavischen Literatur'. *Österreichische Osthefte* 27 (1985), 231–49.

Rozov, N.N., *Kniga v Rossii v XV veke* (The Fifteenth-Century Russian Book), Leningrad: Nauka, 1984

Rybakov, B.A. *Remeslo na Rusi* (Artisanry in Old Rus). Moscow: ANSSSR, 1948.

———. 'Voinstvuiushchie tserkovniki XVI v.' (Militant Churchmen of the 16th c.). *Antirelogioznik* (Anti-religion journal) 3, 4 (1934), 21–31.

Sava, Archbishop of Serbia. 'Tipik hilandarski' (The Hilender/ Chilandar *Typicon*). Ed. Bishop Dimitrij. *Spomenik*. Srpska Kral'evska Akademija. XXXI.29 (1898), 37–69.

Savva Cherny, *Zhitie i prebyvanie v'krattse prepodobnogo ottsa nashego igumena Iosifa, grada Volokolamskogo* (The Life and Sojourn of our Father, Saint Iosif the Hegumen, from Volokolamsk). VMCh, Sept., 453–99.

Sedel'nikov, A.D., 'Vasilij Kalika. L'histoire et la légende'. *Revue des études slaves* 7 (1927), 227–40.

Sedova, R.A., 'Sluzhba mitropolitu Petru' (The Service for Metropolitan Peter). TODRL 45 (1992), 23–48.

A Select Library of the Nicene and Post-Nicene Fathers of the Christian Church. 1st series. 14 vols. ed. Philip Schaff. 2nd series. 14 vols. ed. Schaff and Henry Wace. New York: Christian Literature, 1886–90, 1890–1900; rpt. Grand Rapids: Eerdmans, and New York: Scribners, 1952–56, 1974–78.

Semenchenko, G.V., 'Zaveshchaniia tserkovnykh ierarkhov XV v. kak istoricheskii istochniki' (The Testaments of 15th-Century Prelates as a Historical Source). *Istochnikovedenie otechestvenoi istorii 1984* (Source Studies of Native History 1984). Moscow: 1986, 154–62.

Serebriansky, N. *Ocherki po istorii monastyrskoi zhizni v Pskovskoi zemle* (Essays on the History of Monastic Life in the Pskov Territory). Moscow: 1908.

Sermons and Rhetoric of Kievan Rus'. ed. Simon Franklin. HLEULET 5: 1991.

Sidorova, T. 'Realisticheskie cherty v arkhitekturnykh izobrazheniiakh drevnerusskikh miniatur' (Realistic traits in Old Russian Miniature Depictions) AN 10 (1958), 73–100.

Sinitsyna, N.V. *Tretii Rim. Istoki i evoliutsiia russkoi srednevekovoi kontseptsii* (The Third Rome. Sources and Evolution of a Medieval Russian Conception). Moscow: 1998.

———, 'Poslanie Maksima Greka Vasiliiu III ob ustroistve afonskikh monastyrei (1518–1519 gg.)' (Maksim Grek's Letter to Vasilii III on the Organization of the Athos Monasteries 1518–1519). VV 26 (1965), 110–36.

Sinodik Volokolamskogo monastyria. (The *Synodicon* of the Volokolamsk Monastery) Institute of Russian Literature, Leningrad. Separate Acquisitions of 1953. No. 27 (Microfilm).

Skaballanovich, Mikhail. *Tolkovyi Tipikon: Ob'iasnitel'noe izlozhenie Tipikona s istoricheskim vvedeniem* (The Explicated *Typicon*. An Exposition of the Typicon with Commentary and an Historical Introduction). 3 vols. Kiev: N.T. Korchak-Novitsky, 1910–15.

Slovar' knizhnikov i knizhnosti drevnei Rusi (Lexicon of Bookmen and Letters of Old Rus). ed. D.S. Likhachev. 3 vols in 5. Leningrad: Nauka, 1987–1993.

Sluzhebnik (Service Book). ed. Holy Synod. Moscow: 1913.

Smirnov, S. *Drevnerusskii dukhovnik* (The Old Russian Father Confessor). Moscow: Sinod, 1914.

Smirnova, E.S., *Moskovskaia ikona xiv-xvii vekov* (The Muscovite Icon, 14th-17th Centuries). Leningrad: Aurora, 1988.

Smolitsch, Igor. *Russisches Mönchtum. Entstehung, Entwicklung und Wesen, 988–1917*. Das östliche Christentum. Neue Folge 10–11. Wurzburg: Augustinus, 1953.

Sobranie akafistov (Collection of *Akathistoi*). Moscow: Sinod, 1903.

Sokolof, D., Archpriest, trans. and ed. *A Manual of the Orthodox Church's Divine Service*. Jordanville, NY: Trinity Monastery, 1962.

Solovii, Meletius OSBM. *The Byzantine Divine Liturgy: History and Commentary*. Trans. D.E. Wysochansky, OSBM. Washington, D.C.: Catholic University, 1970.

Sophocles, E.A. *Greek Lexicon of the Roman and Byzantine Periods (from B.C. 146 to A.D. 1100)*. 2 vols. New York: Scribners, 1887; rpt. Frederick Ungar, 1957.

Špidlík, Thomas, SJ. *Joseph de Volokolamsk. Un chapitre de la spiritualité russe:* OCA 146, 1956.

'Stolovoi obikhodnik Troitse-Sergieva monastyria. I (1467–1474); II (1533–1547)' (The Table Customary of the Trinity-St Sergius Monastery). ed. Archim. Leonid. *Istoricheskoe opisanie Sviato-Troitsiia Sergievy lavry* (A Historical Description of Holy Trinity St Sergius Laura). A.V. Gorsky, ed. Moscow, 1890. 2:16–22, 22–44.

Sreznevsky, I.I. *Materialy dlia slovaria drevnerusskogo iazyka po pis'mennym pamiatnikam* (Materials for a Dictionary of Old Russian, according to Written Monuments). 3 vols. St Petersburg: 1893; rpt. Graz: Akademische, 1955.

———. *Obozrenie drevnikh russkikh spiskov Kormchei knigi* (Survey of the Old Russian Copies of the Canon Law Book). St Petersburg: 1897.

Starchestvo: See *Kniga glagolaemaia Starchestvo.*

Steindorff, Ludwig. 'Commemorations and Administrative Techniques in Muscovite Monasteries'. *Russian History/Histoire russe* 22.4 (1995), 433–54.

———. *Memoria in Altrussland. Untersuchungen zu den formen christlicher Totensorge*. Quellen und Studien zur Geschichte der östlichen Europa 38. Stuttgart: F. Steiner, 1994.

———. 'Princess Maria Golenina. Perpetuating Identity through Care for the Deceased'. CIM/MRKIS, 557–77.

———et al. *Das Speisungsbuch von Volokolamsk.* See *Kormovaia kniga Iosifo-Volokolamskogo monastyria.*

Stoglav: See Kozhanchikov, ed. *Stoglav.*

Stroev. P.M. *Spiski ierarkhov i nastoiatelei monastyri rossiiskiia tserkvi* (Lists of the Hierarchs and Monastery Superiors of the Russian Church). St Petersburg: V.S. Balashev, 1877.

Symeon Metaphrastses, *Opera* (Works). PG 114–116.

Symeon the New Theologian (Neotheologus, Novus Theologus, Junior). *Catéchèses.* intro. Basile Krivochéine. Trans. Joseph Paramelle. Sources chrétiennes 96, 104, 113. Paris: Cerf: 1963–65. (Greek edition, French translation.)

———, *The Discourses*. Preface Basil Krivochéine. Intro. George Maloney. Trans. C.J. di Catanzaro. New York/Ramsey/Toronto: Paulist, 1980. (Engish edition of *Catéchèses.*)

———, *O ezhe kako podobaet prebyvati inokom* (How Monks Should Conduct Themselves). Russian National Library (M. Saltykov-Shchedrin State Public Library), St Petersburg. Solovetskii Collection, Codex No. 271/793, 1–23^{v} (Microfilm). (Catechism 26, amplified with sections from Catechism 5).

Szeftel, Marc. 'Joseph Volotsky's Political Ideas in a New Historical Perspective'. *Jahrbücher für Geschichte Osteuropas* n. f. 13. 1 (April, 1965), 19–29.

Taft, Robert. 'The *Synaxarion* of Evergetis in the History of Byzantine

Liturgy'. *Theotokos Evergetis*. ed. Mullet and Kirby, 274–93.

Taktikon: See Nikon of the Black Mountain, *Taktikon*.

Taube, Moishe. 'The Kievan Jew Zacharia and the Astronomical Works of the Judaizers'. *Jews and Slavs* 3. Ed. W. Moskovich *et al.* Jerusalem: 1995, 168–98.

———, 'The "Poem on the Soul" in the *Laodicean Epistle* and the Literature of the Judaizers'. *Kamen' Kraeug"l'n"*, 671–85.

Theodora Palaiologina. *Typikon* for the Convent of Lips in Constantinople (1294–1301). Trans. Alice-Mary Talbot. BMFD, 1265–86.

Theodora/Theodule Synadene. *Typikon* for the Convent of the Mother of God *Bebaia Elpis* in Constantinople (1327–35). Trans. Alice-Mary Talbot. BMFD, 1522–78.

Theodore, Bishop of Petra. Βίος καὶ πολιτεία τοῦ ἁγίου πατρός ἡμῷν αββᾶ Θεοδοσίου. (The Life and Community of our Holy Father Theodosius). ed. Hermann Usener. *Der Heilige Theodosius. Schriften des Theodosios und Kyrillos*. Leipzig: B.G. Teubner, 1890, 1–101 (ORT: VMCh, Jan., 564–630).

Theodore/Pseudo-Theodore Studite. Ὑποτύπωσις καταστάσεως τῆς μονῆσ τοῦ Στουδίου (*Rule/Hypotyposis* [Outline] of the Institutes of the Studion Monastery [after 842]). Dmitrievskii, *Opisanie liturgicheskikh rukopisei* I.1:224–38 (first recension). PG 99: 1703–20 (second recension). Trans. Timothy Miller, BMFD, 97–119 (both recensions).

———. *Iambi de variis argumentis* (Iambic Versis on Various Themes). PG 99: 1799–1812.

———. *Poenae monasteriales* (Monastic Penances). PG 99:1733–58.

———. *Testamentum* (Testament [?826]). PG 99:1813–24. Trans. Timothy Miller, BMFD, 75–83 (here considered authentically Theodore's).

Theologie de la vie monastique. Études de la Tradition patristique. ed. Faculté de Théologie S.J. de Lyon-Fourvière. Paris: Aubier, 1961.

Thomas Aquinas, *Summa theologica*. 3 vols. Trans. Fathers of the English Dominican Province. New York: Benziger Brothers, 1947.

Thomas, John. 'Documentary Evidence from the Byzatine Monastic *Typika* for the History of the Evergetine Reform Movement'. *Theotokos Evergetis*. ed. Mullet and Kirby, 246–73.

Thomiada, Magistra. *Acta S. Febroniae Virg. Mart.* (The Deeds of the Martyred Virgin St Febronia). Acta Sanctorum. juni 7,12–31 (ORT from VMCh: KZhS, June 16–30, 85–102).

Thomson, Francis J. 'The Nature of the Reception of Christian Byzantine Culture in Russian in the Tenth to Thirteenth Centuries and its Implications for Russian Culture'. *Slavica Gandensa* 5 (1978), 107–39.

———. 'Saint Anthony of Kiev - The Facts and the Fiction. The Legend of the Blessing of Athos upon Early Russian Monasticism'. *Byzantinoslavica* 56 (1995), 637–78.

Tikhomirov, M.N. 'Monastyr'-Votchinnik XVI v'. (A Monastery-Seigneur of the 16th Century). *Istoricheskie zapiski* (Historical Notes) 3 (1938), 130–68.

Tikhoniuk, I.A. 'Zagadka arkhimadrita Evfimiia. K istokam konflikta Iosifa Volotskogo i mitropolita Zosimy' (The Enigma of Archimandrite Evfimii). *Problemy otechestestvennoi istorii i kul'tury perioda feodalizma. Chteniia pamiati V.B. Kobrina. Tezisy dokladov i soobshchenii* (Issues in the History and Culture of our Country from the Period of Feudalism. Readings in Memory of V.B. Kobrin. Theses from Lectures and Reports). Moscow, 1992 172–76.

Timothy of Evergetis. *Typikon* (1054–70, rev. 1098–1118). Trans. Robert Jordan. BMFD, 472–506.

Titov, A.A. *Opisanie slaviano-russkikh rukopisei, nakhodiashchikhsia v sobranii A. A. Titova* (Description of the Slavonic-Russian Manuscripts found in the Collection of A.A. Titov). 2 vols. Moscow: 1900.

———. *Rukopisi slavianskie i russkie prinadlezhashchie I.A. Vakrameevu* (Slavonic and Russian Manuscripts Belonging to I.A. Vakrameev). 5 vols. Moscow: E. Lissner, 1888–1906.

———. *Vkladnye i zapisnye knigi Iosifova Volokolamskogo monastyria XVI veka i uprazdnennye monastyri i pustyni Iaroslavskoi Eparkhii* (The Donation and Record Books of the Iosifo-Volokolamsk Monastery from the Sixteenth Century and the Closed Monasteries and Hermitages of the Iaroslav Eparchy). *Rukopisi slavianskie i russkie prinadlezhashchie I.A. Vakrameevu* 5: Moscow: 1906.

Trudy otdela drevnerusskoi literatury (Works of the Section of Old Russian Literature). Academy of Sciences, USSR. Institute of Literature. Leningrad/St Petersburg. 1934–.

Toropov, S., and K. Shchepetov, *Iosifov-Volokolamskii Monastyr'* (The Iosifov-Volokolamsk Monastery). Moscow: 1946.

Treadgold, Donald, W. *The West in Russia and China: Religious* and *Secular Thought in Modern Times.* (2 vols.). 1. *Russia, 1472–1917.*

Cambridge: University, 1973.

Tüpikon siest' Oustav (The *Typicon* or *Ustav*). Moscow: 1906 [on imprint as 'Year 7414' since Creation], 1956 [according to the Dumbarton Oaks Catalogue] [a slightly modernized version of the 'Jerusalem Typicon'].

Tvorogov, O.V., 'Drevnerusskie chet'i sborniki XII-XIV vv.' (Old Rus' Miscellany Books of the 12th-14th Centuries). TODRL 41 (1988), 197–214; 44 (1990), 196–225; 47 (1993), 35–53.

———. 'Opisanie i klassifikatsiia spiskov sbornikov "Zlatoust" ' (Description and Classification of the Manuscript Copies of the "Chrysostom" Compilation). TODRL 39 (1985), 278–84.

Udal'stova, A.M., 'Trapeznaia Makar'evskogo monastyria v Kaliazina' (The Refectory of the Makariev Monastery in Kaliazin). AN 34 (1986), 230–37.

Vaillant, A. 'Le Saint Ephrem Slave'. *Byzantinoslavica* 19 (1958), 279–86..

Vasmer, Max (Masks Fasmer). *Russisches etymologisches Wörterbuch.* 3 vols. Heidelberg: Carl Winter, 1953–58: Russian edition: *Etimologicheskii slovar' russkogo iazyka.* 4 vols. Moscow: Progress, 1964.

Veilleux, Armand, *Pachomian Koinona.* 3 vols. Cistercian Studies 45–47. Kalamazoo, 1981–82.

Vernadsky, George. 'The Heresy of the Judaizers and the Policies of Ivan III'. *Speculum* 8 (1933), 436–59.

———. *Kievan Russia.* New Haven: Yale, 1947.

———. *The Mongols and Russia.* New Haven: Yale, 1953.

———. *Russia at the Dawn of the Modern Age.* New Haven: Yale, 1959.

Vilinskii, *Zhitie s. Vasiliia Novogo v russkoi literature* (The Life of St Basil the Younger in Russian Literature). 2 parts. Zapiski Imperatorskogo Novorossiiskogo universiteta. Istoriko-filologicheskoi fakul'tet (Notes of the Imperial University of New Russia. History-Philology Faculty) 7,6. Odessa: 1913, 1911.

Vizantiiskii vremennik (Byzantine Periodical). New Series. Moscow: 1947–.

Vodoff, Wladimir. 'Compte rendue' of Goldfrank, *The Monastic Rule of Iosif Volotsky* (first edition). *Revue d'histoire des religions* 203.2 (1986), 20–05.

———. 'La terminologie du christianisme russe' *Revue d'histoire des religions* 198 (1981), 187–95.

'Volokolamskii paterik' (The Volokolamsk Patericon). *Seminarii po drevnerusskoi literatury Moskovskikh vyshikh zhenskikh kursov* (The Moscow Women's Advanced Curriculum Seminars in Old Russian Literature) 5, 1915. (See also Pitirim).

Voronov, N., and I. Sakharova. 'Novye materialy ob ansemble Iosifova-Volokolamskogo monastyria' (New Materials concerning the Ensemble of Iosifov-Volokolamsk Monastery). AN 6 (1956), 107–31.

Wagner: See Basil of Caesarea. *Writings*.

Ward, Benedicta, SLG, *The Sayings of the Desert Fathers. The Alphabetical Collection.* Cistercian Studies 59. Kalamazoo: Cistercian/London: Mowbray, 1975 *(Apophthegmata patrum.* PG 65:71–440).

Weber, Max. *Economy and Society.* eds. Guenther Roth and Claus Wittrich. 3 vols. New York: Bedminster, 1968.

Wieczynski, Joseph L. 'Hermetism and Cabalism in the Heresy of the Judaizers'. *Renaissance Quarterly* 28.1 (1975), 17–28.

Wijk, Nicolaas van. *The Old Church Slavonic Translation of the* Ἀνδρῶν ἁγίων βίβλος. *eds. D. Armstrong, R. Pope, and C.H. Schonveld. The Hague: Mouton, 1975*

———. *'Podrobnyi obzor tserkovno-slavianskogo perevoda Bol'shogo Limonariia' (A Detailed Survey of the Church Slavonic Translation of the Great Limonarius). Byzantinoslavica* 6 (1935–1936), 38–83.

———. "La traduction slave de l' Ἀνδρῶν ἁγίων βίβλος et son prototype grec, *Byzantion* 13 (1938), 233–44.

Yiannias, John J. 'The Elevation of the Panaghia'. *Dumbarton Oaks Papers* 26 (1972), 227–36.

Zagrebin, V.M., and V.V. Kolosov. 'Pandekty Nikona Chernogortsa v pergamennom spiske XV v.' (The Pandects of Nikon Chernogorets in a 15th-Century Parchment Codex). *Pamiatniki kul'tury. Novye otkrytiia 1974.* Moscow, 1975, 35–36.

Zapiski Otdela rukopisi Gosudarstvennoi biblioteki SSSR imeni V.I. Lenina (Notes of the Manuscript Division of the V.I. Lenin State Public Library of the USSR). Moscow, 1938–.

Zen'kovsky, Serge. *Russkoe staroobriadchestvo. Dukhovnye dvizheniia semnadtsatogo veka* (Russian Old Ritualism. Spiritual Movements of the Seventeenth Century). Forum Slavicum 21. Munich: Wilhelm Fink: 1970.

———. 'Nil Polev', ZhMNP 1881, 8, 189–96.

Zhmakin, V.I. *Mitropolit Daniil i ego sochineniia* (Metropolitan Daniil and his Works). Moscow:1881; also in ChOIDR 1881, 1–2.

Zhurnal Ministerstva narodnogo prosveshcheniia (The Journal of the Ministry of Public Education). Moscow: 1843–1917.

Zimin, A.A. *I.S. Peresvetov e ego sovremenniki* (I.S. Peresvetov and his Contemporaries). Moscow: ANSSSR, 1958.

———. 'Iz istorii sobraniia rukopisnykh knig Iosifo-Volokolamskoi monastyria' (The History of the Iosifov-Volokolamsk Collection of Manuscript Books). ZORGBL 38 (1977), 15–27.

———. 'Kratkie letopistsy XV-XVI vv.' (Brief Little Annals of the 15th-16th c.). *Istoricheskii arkhiv* (Historical Archive) 5 (1950), 2–39.

———. *Krupnaia feodal'naia votchina i sotsial'no-politicheskaia bor'ba v Rossii (konets XV-XVI v.)* (The Large Seigniorial Estate and the Social-Political Struggle in Russia [End 15th-16th c.]). Moscow: Nauka, 1977.

———. *Rossiia na poroge novogo vremeni* (Russia at the Threshhold of a New Era). Moscow: Mysl', 1972.

———. *Tysiachnaia kniga 1550 g. i Dvorovaia tetrad' 50-kh godov XVI v.* (The Book of the Thousand from 1550 and the Palatine Registry of the 1550s). Moscow-Leningrad, ASSSR, 1950.

Zinovii Otensky, *Istiny Pokazanie* (A Demonstration of the Truth). ed. Kazan Theological Seminary: 1863.

Žužek, Ivan, SJ. *Kormčaja kniga. Studies on the Chief Code of Russian Canon Law.* OCA 168, 1964.

Index

CISTERCIAN TEXTS

Bernard of Clairvaux

- Apologia to Abbot William
- Five Books on Consideration: Advice to a Pope
- Homilies in Praise of the Blessed Virgin Mary
- Letters of Bernard of Clairvaux / by B.S. James
- Life and Death of Saint Malachy the Irishman
- Love without Measure: Extracts from the Writings of St Bernard / by Paul Dimier
- On Grace and Free Choice
- On Loving God / Analysis by Emero Stiegman
- Parables and Sentences
- Sermons for the Summer Season
- Sermons on Conversion
- Sermons on the Song of Songs I–IV
- The Steps of Humility and Pride

William of Saint Thierry

- The Enigma of Faith
- Exposition on the Epistle to the Romans
- Exposition on the Song of Songs
- The Golden Epistle
- The Mirror of Faith
- The Nature and Dignity of Love
- On Contemplating God: Prayer & Meditations

Aelred of Rievaulx

- Dialogue on the Soul
- Liturgical Sermons, I
- The Mirror of Charity
- Spiritual Friendship
- Treatises I: On Jesus at the Age of Twelve, Rule for a Recluse, The Pastoral Prayer
- Walter Daniel: The Life of Aelred of Rievaulx

John of Ford

- Sermons on the Final Verses of the Songs of Songs I–VII

Gilbert of Hoyland

- Sermons on the Songs of Songs I–III
- Treatises, Sermons and Epistles

Other Early Cistercian Writers

- Adam of Perseigne, Letters of
- Alan of Lille: The Art of Preaching
- Amadeus of Lausanne: Homilies in Praise of Blessed Mary
- Baldwin of Ford: Spiritual Tractates I–II
- Geoffrey of Auxerre: On the Apocalypse
- Gertrud the Great: Spiritual Exercises
- Gertrud the Great: The Herald of God's Loving-Kindness (Books 1, 2)
- Gertrud the Great: The Herald of God's Loving-Kindness (Book 3)
- Guerric of Igny: Liturgical Sermons Vol. I & 2
- Helinand of Froidmont: Verses on Death
- Idung of Prüfening: Cistercians and Cluniacs: The Case for Cîteaux
- Isaac of Stella: Sermons on the Christian Year, I–[II]
- The Life of Beatrice of Nazareth
- The School of Love. An Anthology of Early Cistercian Texts
- Serlo of Wilton & Serlo of Savigny: Seven Unpublished Works
- Stephen of Lexington: Letters from Ireland
- Stephen of Sawley: Treatises

MONASTIC TEXTS

Eastern Monastic Tradition

- Besa: The Life of Shenoute
- Cyril of Scythopolis: Lives of the Monks of Palestine
- Dorotheos of Gaza: Discourses and Sayings
- Evagrius Ponticus: Praktikos and Chapters on Prayer
- Handmaids of the Lord: Lives of Holy Women in Late Antiquity & the Early Middle Ages / by Joan Petersen
- Harlots of the Desert / by Benedicta Ward
- John Moschos: The Spiritual Meadow
- Lives of the Desert Fathers
- Lives of Simeon Stylites / by Robert Doran
- Mena of Nikiou: Isaac of Alexandra & St Macrobius
- The Monastic Rule of Iosif Volotsky (Revised Edition) / by David Goldfrank
- Pachomian Koinonia I–III (Armand Veilleux)
- Paphnutius: Histories/Monks of Upper Egypt
- The Sayings of the Desert Fathers / by Benedicta Ward
- The Spiritually Beneficial Tales of Paul, Bishop of Monembasia / by John Wortley
- Symeon the New Theologian: TheTheological and Practical Treatises & The Three Theological Discourses / by Paul McGuckin
- Theodoret of Cyrrhus: A History of the Monks of Syria
- The Syriac Fathers on Prayer and the Spiritual Life / by Sebastian Brock

Western Monastic Tradition

- Anselm of Canterbury: Letters I–III / by Walter Fröhlich
- Bede: Commentary...Acts of the Apostles
- Bede: Commentary...Seven Catholic Epistles

- Bede: Homilies on the Gospels I–II
- Bede: Excerpts from the Works of St Augustine on the Letters of the Blessed Apostle Paul
- The Celtic Monk / by U. Ó Maidín
- Life of the Jura Fathers
- Peter of Celle: Selected Works
- Letters of Rancé I–II
- Rule of the Master
- Rule of Saint Augustine

Christian Spirituality

- The Cloud of Witnesses: The Development of Christian Doctrine / by David N. Bell
- The Call of Wild Geese / by Matthew Kelty
- The Cistercian Way / by André Louf
- The Contemplative Path
- Drinking From the Hidden Fountain / by Thomas Spidlík
- Eros and Allegory: Medieval Exegesis of the Song of Songs / by Denys Turner
- Fathers Talking / by Aelred Squire
- Friendship and Community / by Brian McGuire
- Gregory the Great: Forty Gospel Homilies
- High King of Heaven / by Benedicta Word
- The Hermitage Within / by a Monk
- Life of St Mary Magdalene and of Her Sister St Martha / by David Mycoff
- A Life Pleasing to God / by Augustine Holmes
- The Luminous Eye / by Sebastian Brock
- Many Mansions / by David N. Bell
- Mercy in Weakness / by André Louf
- The Name of Jesus / by Irénée Hausherr
- No Moment Too Small / by Norvene Vest
- Penthos: The Doctrine of Compunction in the Christian East / by Irénée Hausherr
- Praying the Word / by Enzo Bianchi
- Rancé and the Trappist Legacy / by A. J. Krailsheimer
- Russian Mystics / by Sergius Bolshakoff
- Sermons in a Monastery / by Matthew Kelty
- Silent Herald of Unity: The Life of Maria Gabrielle Sagheddu / by Martha Driscoll
- Spiritual Direction in the Early Christian East / by Irénée Hausherr
- The Spirituality of the Christian East / by Thomas Spidlík
- The Spirituality of the Medieval West / by André Vauchez
- The Spiritual World of Isaac the Syrian / by Hilarion Alfeyev
- Tuning In To Grace / by André Louf
- Wholly Animals: A Book of Beastly Tales / by David N. Bell

MONASTIC STUDIES

- Community and Abbot in the Rule of St Benedict I–II / by Adalbert de Vogüé
- The Finances of the Cistercian Order in the Fourteenth Century / by Peter King
- Fountains Abbey and Its Benefactors / by Joan Wardrop
- The Hermit Monks of Grandmont / by Carole A. Hutchison
- In the Unity of the Holy Spirit / by Sighard Kleiner
- A Life Pleasing to God: Saint Basil's Monastic Rules / By Augustine Holmes
- The Joy of Learning & the Love of God: Essays in Honor of Jean Leclercq
- Monastic Odyssey / by Marie Kervingant
- Monastic Practices / by Charles Cummings
- The Occupation of Celtic Sites in Ireland / by Geraldine Carville
- Reading St Benedict / by Adalbert de Vogüé
- Rule of St Benedict: A Doctrinal and Spiritual Commentary / by Adalbert de Vogüé
- The Rule of St Benedict / by Br. Pinocchio
- The Spiritual World of Isaac the Syrian / by Hilarion Alfeyev
- St Hugh of Lincoln / by David H. Farmer
- The Venerable Bede / by Benedicta Ward
- Western Monasticism / by Peter King
- What Nuns Read / by David N. Bell
- With Greater Liberty: A Short History of Christian Monasticism & Religious Orders / by Karl Frank

CISTERCIAN STUDIES

- Aelred of Rievaulx: A Study / by Aelred Squire
- Athirst for God: Spiritual Desire in Bernard of Clairvaux's Sermons on the Song of Songs / by Michael Casey
- Beatrice of Nazareth in Her Context / by Roger De Ganck
- Bernard of Clairvaux: Man, Monk, Mystic / by Michael Casey [tapes and readings]
- Bernardus Magister...Nonacentenary
- Catalogue of Manuscripts in the Obrecht Collection of the Institute of Cistercian Studies / by Anna Kirkwood
- Christ the Way: The Christology of Guerric of Igny / by John Morson
- The Cistercians in Denmark / by Brian McGuire
- The Cistercians in Scandinavia / by James France
- A Difficult Saint / by Brian McGuire

- A Gathering of Friends: Learning & Spirituality in John of Ford / by Costello and Holdsworth
- Image and Likeness: Augustinian Spirituality of William of St Thierry / by David Bell
- Index of Authors & Works in Cistercian Libraries in Great Britain I / by David Bell
- Index of Cistercian Authors and Works in Medieval Library Catalogues in Great Britian / by David Bell
- The Mystical Theology of St Bernard / by Étienne Gilson
- The New Monastery: Texts & Studies on the Earliest Cistercians
- Nicolas Cotheret's Annals of Cîteaux / by Louis J. Lekai
- Pater Bernhardus: Martin Luther and Saint Bernard / by Franz Posset
- Pathway of Peace / by Charles Dumont
- A Second Look at Saint Bernard / by Jean Leclercq
- The Spiritual Teachings of St Bernard of Clairvaux / by John R. Sommerfeldt
- Studies in Medieval Cistercian History
- Studiosorum Speculum / by Louis J. Lekai
- Three Founders of Cîteaux / by Jean-Baptiste Van Damme
- Towards Unification with God (Beatrice of Nazareth in Her Context, 2)
- William, Abbot of St Thierry
- Women and St Bernard of Clairvaux / by Jean Leclercq

MEDIEVAL RELIGIOUS WOMEN

edited by Lillian Thomas Shank and John A. Nichols:

- Distant Echoes
- Hidden Springs: Cistercian Monastic Women (2 volumes)
- Peace Weavers

CARTHUSIAN TRADITION

- The Call of Silent Love / by A Carthusian
- The Freedom of Obedience / by A Carthusian
- From Advent to Pentecost / by A Carthusian
- Guigo II: The Ladder of Monks & Twelve Meditations / by E. Colledge & J. Walsh
- Halfway to Heaven / by R.B. Lockhart
- Interior Prayer / by A Carthusian
- Meditations of Guigo II / by A. Gordon Mursall
- The Prayer of Love and Silence / by A Carthusian
- Poor, Therefore Rich / by A Carthusian
- They Speak by Silences / by A Carthusian
- The Way of Silent Love (A Carthusian Miscellany)
- Where Silence is Praise / by A Carthusian
- The Wound of Love (A Carthusian Miscellany)

CISTERCIAN ART, ARCHITECTURE & MUSIC

- Cistercian Abbeys of Britain
- Cistercians in Medieval Art / by James France
- Studies in Medieval Art and Architecture / edited by Meredith Parsons Lillich *(Volumes II–V are now available)*
- Stones Laid Before the Lord / by Anselme Dimier
- Treasures Old and New: Nine Centuries of Cistercian Music (compact disc and cassette)

THOMAS MERTON

- The Climate of Monastic Prayer / by T. Merton
- Legacy of Thomas Merton / by P. Hart
- Message of Thomas Merton / by P. Hart
- Monastic Journey of Thomas Merton / by P. Hart
- Thomas Merton/Monk / by P. Hart
- Thomas Merton on St Bernard
- Toward an Integrated Humanity / edited by M. Basil Pennington

CISTERCIAN LITURGICAL DOCUMENTS SERIES

- Cistercian Liturgical Documents Series / edited by Chrysogonus Waddell, OCSO
- Hymn Collection of the…Paraclete
- *Institutiones nostrae:* The Paraclete Statutes
- Molesme Summer-Season Breviary (4 volumes)
- Old French Ordinary & Breviary of the Abbey of the Paraclete (2 volumes)
- Twelfth-century Cistercian Hymnal (2 volumes)
- The Twelfth-century Cistercian Psalter
- Two Early Cistercian *Libelli Missarum*

STUDIA PATRISTICA

- Studia Patristica XVIII, Volumes 1, 2 and 3

CISTERCIAN PUBLICATIONS

HOW TO CONTACT US

Editorial Offices & Customer Service

- **Cistercian Publications**
  WMU Station 1201 Oliver Street
  Kalamazoo, Michigan 49008 USA

  Telephone 616 387 8920
  Fax 616 387 8390
  e-mail cistpub@wmich.edu

Canada

- **Novalis**
  49 Front Street East, Second Floor
  Toronto, Ontario M5E 1B3

  Telephone 1 800 204 4140
  Fax 416 363 9409

U.K.

- **Cistercian Publications UK**
  Mount Saint Bernard Abbey
  Coalville, Leicester LE67 5UL

- **UK Customer Service & Book Orders**
  Cistercian Publications
  97 Loughborough Road
  Thringstone, Coalville
  Leicester LE67 8LQ

  Telephone 01530 45 27 24
  Fax 01530 45 02 10
  e-mail MsbcistP@aol.com

Website & Warehouse

- **www.spencerabbey.org/cistpub**

- **Book Returns (prior permission)**
  Cistercian Publications
  Saint Joseph's Abbey
  167 North Spencer Road
  Spencer MA 01562-1233 USA

  Telephone 508 885 8730
  Fax 508 885 4687
  e-mail cistpub@spencerabbey.org

Trade Accounts & Credit Applications

- **Cistercian Publications / Accounting**
  6219 West Kistler Road
  Ludington, MI 49431 USA

  Fax 231 843 8919

Cistercian Publications is a non-profit corporation. Its publishing program is restricted to monastic texts in translation and books on the monastic tradition.

A complete catalogue of texts in translation and studies on early, medieval, and modern monasticism is available, free of charge, from any of the addresses above.